Teaching in a World of Violent Extremism

Teaching in a World of Violent Extremism

Eleazar S. Fernandez

PICKWICK *Publications* · Eugene, Oregon

TEACHING IN A WORLD OF VIOLENT EXTREMISM

Pickwick Publications
An Imprint of Wipf and Stock Publishers
199 W. 8th Ave., Suite 3
Eugene, OR 97401

www.wipfandstock.com

PAPERBACK ISBN: 978-1-5326-9803-3
HARDCOVER ISBN: 978-1-5326-9804-0
EBOOK ISBN: 978-1-5326-9805-7

Cataloguing-in-Publication data:

Names: Fernandez, Eleazar S., editor.

Title: Teaching in a world of violent extremism / edited by Eleazar S. Fernandez.

Description: Eugene, OR: Pickwick Publications, 2021. | Includes bibliographi-
cal references.

Identifiers: ISBN 978-1-5326-9803-3 (paperback). | ISBN 978-1-5326-9804-0
(hardcover). | ISBN 978-1-5326-9805-7 (ebook).

Subjects: LCSH: Pedagogy. | Teaching. | Violence—Religious aspects. | Ethics.

Classification: BL65 T25 2021 (print) | BL65 (ebook)

05/14/21

Contents

Acknowledgments | vii
List of Contributors | ix

Introduction | 1

1. The Smoldering Embers of Violent Extremism and the Raging Fire of Terrorism | 15
   —ELEAZAR S. FERNANDEZ

2. Pedagogy and Curriculum to Prevent and Counter Violent Extremism: Human Rights, Justice, Peace, and Democracy | 48
   —REY TY

3. What and How Shall We Teach in a World of Violent Extremisms | 84
   —BOYUNG LEE

4. Undoing Violence with the Brain in Mind | 100
   —RODOLFO R. NOLASCO JR.

5. Theological Ethics in a World of Violent Extremism | 116
   —ELLEN OTT MARSHALL

6. Religious Extremism in the History of Early Christianity | 136
   —J. SAMUEL SUBRAMANIAN

7. Teaching Revelation and Questions of Violent Extremism | 156

—TAT-SIONG BENNY LIEW

8. Fundamentalism as Toxic Spirituality: Exploring the Psycho-spiritual Structure and Dynamics of Violent Extremism | 178

—DANIEL S. SCHIPANI

9. Spiritual Practice and Formation in a World of Violent Extremism | 208

—RUBEN L. F. HABITO

10. Local Peacebuilding in Response to Violent Extremism | 235

—WENDY KROEKER

11. Threshold Concepts in Teaching Islam: An Exploration of Pedagogical Content Knowledge for Jihad and War | 260

—MUALLA SELÇUK

12. Christian Theology in an Age of Violent Religious Fundamentalisms: From Intrareligious Dialogue to Interreligious Engagement | 287

—SATHIANATHAN CLARKE

Acknowledgments

From its moment of conception to the day of its birthing, a project of this kind has had a long iteration. I do not exactly know the day of its beginning, but the gestation period has been quite long. Maybe the seed of this project was planted in my childhood years, even before I knew about the term "violent extremism," but the most immediate triggering event that jolted and catapulted this matter to my consciousness was what is now referred to as the event of September 11, 2001, and the haunting image of two hijacked planes blowing up the once-proud Twin Towers that crumbled to dust. In this iteration, this project would not have seen the light of day without individuals who have given their commitment, time, and skills. More than technical expertise, this is a labor of love and choice for those who have contributed to make this project possible. I know that they have busy lives, but they have chosen to participate in the project because they believe in it.

Obviously, there would not be an edited volume without essay contributors. It is but fitting that I express my appreciation for the essay contributors: Sathianathan Clarke, Ruben L. F. Habito, Wendy Kroeker, Boyung Lee, Tat-siong Benny Liew, Ellen Ott Marshall, Rodolfo R. Nolasco Jr, Daniel S. Schipani, Mualla Selçuk, J. Samuel Subramanian, and Rey Ty.

Important projects happen because of the labors of people behind the scene. I am thankful for Max Brumberg-Kraus and Deb Jance for editing and proofreading help.

Completing this project in a time of global pandemic when we do not know exactly when it will be over only added to the challenge of getting this project done. When the threat of coronavirus is a constant companion and uncertainty is in the air, I am glad that my wife, Jo, has helped me sustain my energy and zest for life as the morning glory from her flower garden greets me with its morning smile, while the ranunculus lures me away from the ridiculous to restore my focus. And, before I forget, when my heart is aching as the nation is in turmoil in the wake of the killing of George Floyd, the bleeding heart, another flower in our garden, nudges me gently to move from a place of "breaking apart" to the place of "breaking open" so that I can contribute to the work of healing even while bleeding. Thank you, Jo, for the spaciousness of your heart to welcome this, another project, in our home and in our lives.

August 10, 2020

Remembering my mother's birthday while the morning glory, petunia, dahlia, hibiscus, and cosmos are in bloom.

Contributors

Sathianathan Clarke is the Bishop Sundo Kim Chair in World Christianity and Professor Theology, Culture, and Mission at Wesley Theological Seminary, Washington, DC. Some of his works are: *Competing Fundamentalisms: Violent Extremism in Christianity, Islam, and Hinduism* (Westminster John Knox, 2017), *The Oxford Handbook of Anglican Studies* (co-editor, Oxford University Press, 2015), *Dalit Theology in the 21st Century: Discordant Voices, Discerning Pathways* (Oxford 2010), *Religious Conversion in India: Modes, Motivations, and Meanings* (co-editor, Oxford University Press, 2003), and *Dalits and Christianity: Subaltern Religion and Liberation Theology in India* (Oxford University Press, 1998).

Eleazar S. Fernandez is Professor of Constructive Theology at United Theological Seminary of the Twin Cities in New Brighton, Minnesota. Among his writings are *Teaching for a Multifaith World* (editor, Pickwick, 2017), *Teaching for a Culturally Diverse and Racially Just World* (editor, Cascade, 2014), *New Overtures: Asian North American Theology in the 21st Century* (Sopher, 2012), *Burning Center, Porous Borders: The Church in a Globalized World* (Wipf and Stock, 2011), *Reimagining the Human: Theological Anthropology in Response to Systemic Evil* (Chalice, 2004), *Realizing the America of our Hearts: Theological Voices of Asian Americans* (co-editor, Chalice , 2003), *A Dream Unfinished: Theological Reflections on America from the Margins* (co-editor, Wipf and Stock, 2007), *Hacia Una Teologia de la Lucha* (Verbo Divino, 2002), and *Toward a Theology of Struggle* (Orbis, 1994). Prof. Fernandez is also President of Union Theological Seminary, Philippines.

Ruben L. F. Habito is Professor of World Religions and Spirituality and Director of Spiritual Formation at Perkins School of Theology, Southern Methodist University, Dallas, Texas. Among his works are: *Zen and the*

Spiritual Exercises: Paths of Awakening and Transformation (Orbis, 2013), *The Gospel Among Religions: Christian Ministry, Theology and Spirituality in a Multireligious World* (co-editor, Orbis, 2010), *Vida Zen, Vida Divina: un Dialogo entre Budismo Zen y Cristianismo* (Mexico D.F.: Editorial Pax, 2008), *Healing Breath: Zen for Buddhists and Christians in a Wounded World.* 3rd ed. (Wisdom Publications, 2006), *Experiencing Buddhism: Ways of Wisdom and Compassion* (Orbis, 2005).

Wendy Kroeker is Assistant Professor of Peace and Conflict Transformation Studies as well as Academic Director, Canadian School of Peacebuilding, at Canadian Mennonite University, Winnipeg, Canada. Prof. Kroeker specializes in community conflict transformation processes as an instructor in CMU's peace and conflict transformation studies department and in locations around the globe. In addition to her research on peace education, post-conflict peacebuilding and transformative peace processes, her writings include: *Multi-Dimensional Peacebuilding: Local Actors in the Philippines* (Lexington 2020), "The peacebuilding spaces of local actors" (Routledge 2020), "Emancipatory peace building and conflict transformation: Mindanao as a case study" (Routledge, forthcoming), and "Constant Motion: Multi-Dimensional Peacebuilding for Peace Processes" (Palgrave, forthcoming).

Boyung Lee is Senior Vice President of Academic Affairs, Dean of the Faculty, and Professor of Practical Theology, Iliff School of Theology, Denver, Colorado. Among her published works are, *Transforming Congregations through Community: Faith Formation from the Seminary to the Church* (Westminster John Knox, 2013), Equipping Teachers of Sexual Ethics in Faith Communities (in *Teaching Sexuality and Religion in Higher Education.* Routledge, 2020). Subversive Leadership of Asian and Asian American Women (in *Asian and Asian American Women in Theology and Religion: Embodying Knowledge*, Palgrave Macmillan, 2020), Teaching Spirituality with Qualitative Research Methods (in *Qualitative Research in Theological Education: Pedagogy in Practice*, SCM Press, 2018).

Tat-siong Benny Liew is Class of 1956 Professor in New Testament Studies at the College of the Holy Cross, Worcester, Massachusetts. Among his works are: *Colonialism and the Bible: Contemporary Reflections from the Global South* (co-editor, Lexington Books, 2018), *Present and Future of Biblical Studies* (editor, Brill Academic Publishers, 2018), *Psychoanalytic Mediations between Marxist and Postcolonial Readings of the Bible* (co-editor, SBL Press, 2016), *Reading Ideologies: Essays on the Bible and*

Interpretation in Honor of Mary Ann Tolbert (editor, Sheffield Phoenix Ltd, 2011), *They Were All Together in One Place? Toward a Minority Biblical Criticism* (co-editor, Society of Biblical Literature, 2009), *What Is Asian American Biblical Hermeneutics: Reading the New Testament* (University of Hawaii Press, 2007), and *Politics of Parousia: Reading Mark (Inter)Contextually* (Brill, 1999).

Ellen Ott Marshall is Associate Professor of Christian Ethics and Conflict Transformation at Candler School of Theology, Emory University, Atlanta, Georgia. Prior to joining the Candler faculty in 2009, Dr. Ott Marshall worked with the refugee resettlement programs of the Church World Service and the United Methodist Committee on Relief (UMCOR). Among her published works are: *Introduction to Christian Ethics: Conflict, Faith, and Human Life* (Westminster John Knox, 2018), *Conflict Transformation and Religion: Essays on Faith, Power, and Relationship* (editor, Palgrave MacMillan, 2016), *Christians in the Public Square: Faith that Transform Politics* (Abingdon, 2008), *Though the Fig Tree Does Not Blossom: Toward a Responsible Theology of Christian Hope* (Abingdon, 2006), *Choosing Peace through Daily Practices* (editor, The Pilgrim, 2005).

Rodolfo R. Nolasco Jr. is Professor of Pastoral Theology at Garrett-Evangelical Seminary, Chicago, Illinois, since 2018. He earned his Doctor of Theology degree in Pastoral Psychology from Boston University. Among his writing projects are: *The Contemplative Counselor: A Way of Being* (Fortress, 2011). *Compassionate Presence: A Radical Response to Human Suffering* (Wipf and Stock 2016), *God's Beloved Queer: Identity, Spirituality, Practice* (Wipf and Stock 2019), *Heart Ablaze: Awakening the Queer Spirit* (Church Publishing Inc., Forthcoming) and *Depression, Dark Night of the Soul and Joy* (Cascade, Forthcoming).

Daniel S. Schipani is Emeritus Professor of Pastoral Care and Counseling at Anabaptist Mennonite Biblical Seminary at Elkhart, Indiana, and Affiliate Professor of Spiritual Care at McCormick Theological Seminary, at Chicago. He received his PhD from Princeton Theological Seminary, Princeton, New Jersey. His published works include: *Where Are We? Pastoral Environments and Care for Migrants—Intercultural and Interreligious Perspectives* (co-editor, 2018), *Multifaith Views in Spiritual Care* (editor, 2013), *Interfaith Spiritual Care: Understandings and Practices* (co-editor, Pandora, 2009), *Spiritual Caregiving in the Hospital: Windows to Chaplaincy Ministry* (co-editor, Pandora, 2011), *Mennonite Perspectives on Pastoral*

Counseling (editor, 2007), and *Through the Eyes of Another: Intercultural Reading of the Bible* (co-editor 2004).

Mualla Selçuk is a professor at Ankara University in the Department of Philosophy and Religious Sciences-field of Religious Education. Her research interests focus on Teaching Islam in diverse societies and contemporary ways of teaching Islam. She has worked on many projects in interreligious and intercultural context including an Islamic Worldview and the Dictionary of Encounter projects. She also served at different administrative positions including being the first woman member of the Religious High Council for the Presidency of Religious Affairs Turkey, the dean of the Divinity Faculty that trains national and international Muslim teachers and leaders, and the first Muslim President of Religious Education Association (REA). Her recent book is on the *Concept of Human Being in Christianity and Islam* (2019) as co -editor and an author with Martin Thurner.

J. Samuel Subramanian is Associate Professor of New Testament Theology at United Theological Seminary of the Twin Cities. He serves as the Director of the United Methodist Center at United. Among his published writings are, *The Synoptic Gospels and the Psalms as Prophecy* (T & T Clark, 2008), *Resourcing New Testament Studies: Literary, Historical, and Theological Essays in Honor of David L. Dungan* (co-editor, T & T Clark, 2011), *The Four Gospels: An Introduction for Teaching and Preaching* (Foundery Books, 2020).

Rey Ty is a scholar, consultant, and widely-sought lecturer on topics that include interfaith peacebuilding, human rights, gender, refugees, migrant labor, statelessness, climate crisis, and other social issues. He is an adjunct professor at the Department of Peace Studies, Institute of Religion, Culture, and Peace of Payap University in Thailand. He teaches PhD level courses in research methodology as well as cultural, religious, and gender dimensions of peacebuilding and sits in the dissertation committees of doctoral candidates. He has taught in various universities in the United States of America and in the Philippines. Many of his writings are published in peer-reviewed journals and popular non-academic materials on his field of specialization. Dr. Ty received his Master's degree in Asian Studies (Political Science) from the University of California at Berkeley. Pursuing additional studies, he received his second Master's degree in Political Science and doctorate degree from Northern Illinois University with a focus on human rights and peace education.

Introduction

In the past few years, I edited two books that addressed important and timely issues of our times. These two edited volumes were well received and found useful by a wide audience, even beyond theological circles. These two books are: *Teaching for a Culturally Diverse and Racially Just World* (2013) and *Teaching for a Multifaith World* (2017).

The first book, *Teaching for a Culturally Diverse and Racially Just World*, came at a time of great social unrest and protest as a result of the killing of Trayvon Martin and the acquittal of George Zimmerman (Florida) and followed by the killing of Michael Brown (Ferguson, Missouri) and Eric Garner (New York City) by police officers. Various groups have found the book relevant and prophetic. Colleges, seminaries, and faculty members have used the book as a resource. Wabash Center sponsored a session for this book at the American Academy of Religion annual gathering (2014).

The second, *Teaching for a Multifaith World*, addressed the challenge of dwelling together in a life-giving way in a world that has become more religiously diverse. Again, this book was timely as religions are often at the thick of major conflicts in the world. This book was also given a session time at the American Academy of Religion annual gathering. I am glad that colleagues have found the book relevant and useful.

Observing what is going on around us and alarmed at its rise or proliferation, I see the need for another book, which would be the third in a series: *Teaching in a World of Violent Extremism*. It is not that violent extremism is a new phenomenon. No, it is not; it is ancient. Recently, however, we have witnessed its rise to the point that it has been at the forefront of our attention and has become a defining issue of our time, especially when it culminates in acts of terrorism. It has become an issue that cannot be brushed aside not simply because of the increasing number of casualties, but because it has defined who we are as a people and as a global society.

I am aware of the difficulty in defining "violent extremism" because it is a politically loaded term, like the term "terrorism." The term "violent extremist" has been hurled loosely against those who hold opposite views to one's own. Because of its nebulous character and our difficulty in defining the term, there is a temptation to say, following the now infamous words of Justice Potter Stewart, "I know it when I see it."[1] This inability to define the term has serious consequences: it leads to our inability to respond appropriately and effectively to the challenge. It is my hope that as we pursue this project, we will be able to refine our definition and expand its heuristic usefulness.

There are, however, markers that can be used to make judgments as to why and when an individual or group has become extremist. As a working definition, we can adopt J. M. Berger's account of extremism as a "belief that an in-group's success or survival *can never be separated* from *the need for the hostile action against an out-group*. The hostile action must be part of the in-group's definition of success."[2] It is important to bear in mind that the hostile action against an out-group is "definitional," "non-negotiable," and "unconditional" in contrast to being "conditional" and "situational."

A few examples may be useful here. To attack a group or nation in order to protect the life of an in-group is conditional; this is not extremism. On the other hand, to insist that the out-group must be exterminated after it has surrendered because it's impossible to exist in the presence of the out-group is another matter. This moves into the realm of the unconditional; hence, into the realm of extremism. White groups may attack black neighborhoods in response of the killing of a white kid. This would still fall within the conditional. But when the attacked is couched with the understanding that black communities have to be removed and be segregated because their presence would prevent white communities from becoming successful, we are moving into the realm of the unconditional—the extremist position.[3] War is not necessarily extremist, but a genocidal war is another matter. Genocidal war is extremist.

It should be noted that not all extremists are violent; not all violence is extremism. There are extremists who would rather escape from this world. Violence is pervasive, but most violence is not extremism. Not all terrorist is extremist; not all extremist is terrorist. Violent extremism is not identical with terrorism. Terrorism is a tactic; violent extremism is a belief system.[4]

---

1. Cited in Berger, *Extremism*, 1; emphasis added.
2. Berger, *Extremism*, 44.
3. Berger, *Extremism*, 45–46.
4. Berger, *Extremism*, 30.

Violent extremism is a belief system that justifies, encourages, condones, and supports terrorism.[5] On the other hand, terrorism is a tactic and, following Lisa Schirch, it employs violence to achieve an ideological goal, which is directed primarily at the civilian population. Terrorism, from Latin word *terreo* (to fill with panic, alarm, and great fear), is meant to terrorize or spread great fear among the populace. Terrorism is primarily an attack against society and human security.[6]

I have given basic definition of the word violent extremism (belief system) as distinguished from terrorism (tactic), but I still see the need to go beyond simple definition in order to establish clearer parameters or markers on what constitutes violent extremism, especially as we engage in naming and classifying some expressions of extremism and violence in our society. The sharper the conceptual framework or instrument, the more useful it is for our goal of undoing violent extremism.

If violent extremism is a belief system, what are its basic tenets? A sharp or precise answer to this question will yield helpful account of violent extremism.

Informed by Berger's definition of violent extremism, I find Schirch's account of the four characteristics of violent extremist beliefs useful because it provides specificity: (1) violence is necessary because it is tactically superior and/or redemptive; (2) brutal violence against unarmed civilians is justified to achieve purification of society and/or because civilians are responsible for their governments; (3) violent extremism follows an authoritarian narrative that is intolerant, patriarchal, and anti-participatory democracy; and (4) violent extremists embrace ideological goals related to their identity and grievances.[7]

With these four characteristics of violent extremist beliefs before us, let us test them in relation to some known expressions of violence and extremism. Schirch offers a few test examples to prove the usefulness of her categories.

In June 2016 in Orlando, Florida, Oman Mateen, an Afghan refugee with a history of mental illness entered a gay nightclub and killed fifty people. Was this an act of terrorism, especially that, from the dominant U.S. Islamophobic imaginary, Mateen is a Muslim, or because of loose gun laws which an ill person had easy access? But a tape-recorded message was found on which the gunman pledged allegiance to ISIS and expressed his political goal of preventing U.S. violence in Syria and Iraq against

5. Schirch, *The Ecology of Violent Extremism*, 5.
6. Schirch, *The Ecology of Violent Extremism*, 6–7.
7. Schirch, *The Ecology of Violent Extremism*, 16–17.

Muslims. Although Mateen acted on his own, he subscribed to extremist ideology: clear political goals, superiority narratives, and a brute violence that targets civilians was necessary. On these bases the action of Mateen falls under the category of violent extremism.

Also, in August 2017 white nationalists marched in Charlottesville, Virginia, to protest the plan to remove the statue of Confederate general Robert E. Lee from the city park. One white nationalist rammed his car into the counter protestors, killing one woman and injuring others. The white nationalist propaganda asserted white supremacy, carried grievance against racial/ethnic minorities, and explicit directions to use violence to achieve their political goals. The white nationalist group fits well under the category of violent extremism.

How about the Black Lives Matter (BLM) movement? The Federal Bureau of Investigation (FBI) has monitored Black Lives Matter (BLM) movement for what it refers to as "black supremacist extremist" or "black identity extremists." BLM leaders resist such label and accusation and reaffirm their commitment to human rights and rejection of the use of violence. BLM does not fall into the category of violent extremism because it does not justify killing, and it does not articulate a superiority narrative.

School shootings that are carried out by white young men with mental illness do not fall into the category of violent extremism. Even though they inflict mass casualties with gruesome spectacles, they do not have coherent ideology or political goals. It is not carried out under the narrative of racial-ethnic superiority. Hence, they do not fall under the category of violent extremism.

With greater clarity on what we mean by violent extremism, let me now focus our attention on the growing and raging fire of violent extremism. When we think about this, what easily comes to mind are the famous ones that are labeled acts of terrorism. But there are those that often fall outside the radar screen of many, such as the Neo-Nazis in Europe and the white nationalist-supremacist-alt right group in the U.S. We are also witnessing the rise of violent extremism in other parts of the world, such as India, Pakistan, Afghanistan, Myanmar, Sri Lanka, Somalia, Nigeria, Iraq, and more. Some of these extremisms are placed under the umbrella of violent fundamentalism. It is no wonder that there are those who speak of the "clash of fundamentalisms" or the "clash of barbarisms."[8]

Why do we have this heightening of extremism, many of which are violent, and a growing number have resorted to terrorism?

8. Ali, *The Clash of Fundamentalisms*; Achcar, *The Clash of Barbarisms*. Cf. Huntington, *The Clash of Civilizations*.

There are certainly various drivers or factors that contribute to the rise of violent extremism. Instead of one cause, there's a constellation of drivers or factors leading to its emergence and growth. Multiple lenses must be employed to take account of violent extremism. Only an interdisciplinary approach can offer a reliable account of the subject.

A reading of the context, especially the interconnection of the immediate local and the wider world, is critical in taking account of the rise of contemporary expressions of violent extremism. My purpose in naming this is not to establish a direct correlation between a context and violent extremism, which could lead to terrorism, but to highlight the critical role that context plays.[9] There is no one-size-fits-all explanation; there is no single linear arrow that leads from one point to the next. Without dismissing the benefits that globalization has brought to the formation of global village, in many ways it also has produced asymmetrical power relations and unequal access to resources, and has generated tensions, grievances, conflicts, as well as uncertainties of various sorts.

It appears that human understanding and behavior are greatly shaped at the most foundational level by fear and security. True, a crisis may provide an opportunity to welcome new and better possibilities, but as people experience or perceive major threats, the likelihood of hearts constricting and moral imagination shrinking is high.

A study by Robert Putnam, author of *American Grace*, is very revealing.[10] Perhaps contrary to common expectations, the increasing ethnic and religious diversity has triggered social isolation and, in more diverse communities, people trust their neighbors less. They retreat to their private spaces or put up walls of fear and division.

As the threat, real or perceived, heightens, acts of self-securing also heighten and the door to the slippery slope of false securities becomes wide open. We can see symptoms of this fear and self-securing in the acquisition and proliferation of high-powered weapons and in walls of division or exclusion that are rising, both physical and socio-psychological. We can see ominous symptoms when markers of identity and belonging are redrawn and are religiously policed. Ominous symptoms are present when the demarcation line between in-group and out-group thickens and strict policing is enforced to protect the purity of the in-group from the contaminant—the out-group, and when betrayal of this purity map is deemed a serious and unforgivable sin. The constricting mindset thickens and worsens when it turns into "us-versus-them," and that the "them" (out-group) is scapegoated as the cause for

9. Schirch, *The Ecology of Violent Extremism*, 21–52.

10. Putnam and Campbell, *American Grace*, 291.

the crisis. When the out-group or the scapegoated is seen as an embodiment of the demonic and the world is seen as a battlefield between good and evil, violence against the scapegoated is just a hairline away. Labeled as such, when violence is unleashed against the scapegoated and the demonized, their suffering would deserve little or no empathy at all.

While there is no direct correlation between extremism and violence, as other extremists would rather withdraw into seclusion, when the right mixture of extremist markers and context come into play, extremism can easily slide into the slippery slope of violent extremism.

Politicians or religio-political leaders who know how to stoke fears and rub salt in wounds as well as spew extremist solutions for our social maladies have, of late, been elected into positions of national leadership, or have retained their political position. This is happening in various parts of the world. It is easy to lash out against these political demagogues as the cause but, at a deeper level, they are symptoms of a deeper problem, a great social unraveling. Seeing no viable alternatives, many victims of predatory global capitalism have become vulnerable to extremist ideas and movements.

How shall we undo extremism, especially the militant and violent ones? Beyond undoing extremism, how shall we train individuals who are radically passionate for what they believe in while maintaining critical openness?

Observing what is happening, I have realized that history does not move in linear manner according to modern trajectory: from ignorance to enlightenment; from tribalism to cosmopolitanism; from dogmatism to open-mindedness; and from fear of diversity to celebration of diversity.

This defies common sense, but research consistently proves it to be true. Presenting facts that contradict deeply held beliefs is more likely to reinforce those beliefs than compel people to change them. We may show a chart that reveals income inequality to people who have built their lives on the promise of upward mobility, and it is less likely to change their minds than to cause them to call us socialists or communists.[11]

This tells us that an education that seeks to undo extremism must move beyond modernist educational presuppositions: correct information does not necessarily lead to a change in perception, much less to a change in behavior. Complicating the situation is the reliability of the information in the age of "fake news." This suggests that there is something deeper—beyond facts and rationality—that shapes people's reception, interpretation, and action. If this is the case, we need to find this out in order to be effective in our educational work of undoing extremism. What is this?

11. Palmer, *Healing the Heart of Democracy*, 51.

I suggest that an education that proactively seeks to undo extremism must examine seriously the context, geopolitics, history, and drivers that give birth, trigger, and nourish extremisms of various kinds. A structural and historical account must be done to expose the interlocking structures and practices that produce violent extremisms. We cannot ignore this. Otherwise, our educational efforts would simply be addressing the symptoms of a deeper problem.

Moreover, I suggest that we address the issue of security and fear if we are to address extremism. Security and fear are at the heart of extremism. We need to ask people what they are worried about, or what they are afraid of. What are the threats, both real and imagined, that they are struggling against? What is it that is threatening their sense of security? What is it that is undermining or threatening what they value or care about?

What has lured many individuals to extremist movements? What are they seeking out and what are the extremist groups offering?

My research has led me to this constellation of ideas: crisis and grievance, identity and belonging, sense of purpose, and narrative. People who are joining extremist movements are experiencing or perceiving a crisis and a threat, and they are seeking identity, belonging, sense of purpose, and participation in a cause with a narrative much larger than themselves. One of modernity's failures is that it has focused on believing at the expense of belonging, which is tied to the quest for identity. People join groups or movements primarily due to their need for belonging and participation in something greater than themselves and, in this belonging and participation, they discover and articulate what they believe.

Thus, teaching to undo extremism, especially its violent kind, must address the subject of crisis, fear, and security as well as the sense of identity, belonging, sense of purpose, and participation in a larger story or narrative. The undoing of extremism requires a positive step in the direction of developing an alternative narrative that provides a new script for one's life.

How shall we educate individuals and communities in a world of violent extremism? How are we to prepare religious leaders who are capable of leading congregations and communities in undoing violent extremism? What curriculum design, educational programs, and pedagogies shall we pursue and employ to develop competent civic leaders and ministers in a world of violent extremism? More particularly, how shall we organize educational programs and develop pedagogies if we are to address the issue of fear and security as well as develop healthy identity and cultivate the sense belonging in a just and caring community? What and how shall we teach if we are to empower individuals/communities to develop healthy and liberating narratives, narratives that can counter narrow and sometimes violent extremism? What academic programs shall we launch and promote to undo violent extremism and lead individuals and communities in the direction of passionate civic engagement and openness to differences? How do we create resilient communities?

Description and Overview

This book project has twelve (12) chapters with an Introduction. In the Introduction the editor presents the rationale of the book and gives a brief account of each chapter.

Chapter 1, by Eleazar S. Fernandez, "The Smoldering Embers of Violent Extremism and the Raging Fire of Terrorism," gives us a few examples of violent extremisms in various parts of the world. Fernandez identifies the common ideological framework undergirding violent extremisms and names some of the common metaphors that are often used in taking account of the rise of violent extremisms and terrorisms, such the swamp and cancer metaphors. He proceeds to take account of the converging drivers of violent extremism, such community grievances, identity and belonging, ideology, globalization and its discontents, and counterterrorism. Fernandez wraps up his essay by making the point that the best way to study the growth of violent extremism is not to think in terms of causes and effects, whether single or multiple, but of convergence and confluence of various factors and drivers and their interactive dynamics. He believes that an ecological metaphor or a living systems framework is more helpful in dealing with the emergence, growth, and spread of violent extremism.

Chapters 2 and 3 address the subject of curriculum and pedagogy. Rey Ty's essay, "Pedagogy and Curriculum to Prevent and Counter Violent Extremism: Human Rights, Justice, Peace, and Democracy" (chapter 2), states at the very outset the direction he is taking in the form of four questions: What pedagogical practices shall we employ in the work of ending violent extremism? What shall be the elements of the curriculum? What shall we teach in a world of violent extremism? And, what case study demonstrates the successful use of education to undo violent extremism? After defining some contested terms (e.g., terrorism, extremism, violence, radicalism, etc.) and making a distinction between countering violent extremism (CVE) and preventing violent extremism (PVE), Ty makes it clear that it is not his aim to counter violent extremism and terrorism (hard approach); rather, his commitment is in preventing violent extremism (soft approach) primarily through education and other sustainable means. For Ty, the content of a curriculum that seeks to undo violent extremism must include logos, pathos, ethos, and agape, and must appeal to the whole person. Be it formal, non-formal, and informal education, the core curriculum must include teaching and learning about rights, justice, peace, and democracy.

For her part Boyung Lee, "What and How Shall We Teach in a World of Violent Extremisms" (chapter 3), addresses the topic of curriculum and pedagogy by taking a brief assessment of the three schools of thought on curriculum: traditionalists, conceptual-empiricists, and reconceptualists. Focusing only on the content (traditionalist) is problematic: it assumes an apolitical or value-free view of the curricular content. The conceptual-empiricist school attempts to improve the traditionalist school by making the delivery of the educational content appropriate to the age levels of students, but still the content remains unquestioned, which supports the maintenance of the dominant way of thinking. Lee advocates for the reconceptualist school because it offers greater promise in the work of undoing violent extremism, especially that its main concern is to develop critical and inquiring minds and it gives importance on the life experiences of students as a crucial starting point in educational work. Moreover, because the curriculum is not neutral or ideology free, it is never taken for granted but subjected to continuing interrogation so as to demystify modes of thinking and dwelling that perpetuate domination and violent extremism.

The rest of the chapters (chapters 4, 5, 6, 7, 8, 9, 10, 11, and 12) address the subject of violent extremism and how to undo it from the perspective of various disciplines. Taking us to the realm of the human brain and how it functions in relation to the development of strong beliefs and emotions, such as violent extremism, is Rodolfo R. Nolasco Jr.'s essay, "Undoing Violence with the Brain in Mind" (chapter 4). Following a common assumption in psychology, Nolasco says that we are first and foremost intuitive bodies with rational tails, which means that we use reason to justify our intuitions and emotions. Working below our conscious and rational justifications is a complex network of neurally-based cognitive and affective systems. Overtime, a constellation of beliefs and behaviors as well as emotions associated with them develop and become deeply etched. Religion, for Nolasco, provides a home for a worldview and moral grammar that generates strong passions of what is considered right and wrong which, when it goes wrong, can lead to violent extremist ideas and actions. Being a force that binds, religion can contribute to the formation of in-group and outgroup. When the perfect mixture of inner and outer factors find convergence, with the in-group possessing all the marks of goodness and the out-group the marks of evil, worse things are to be expected. The in-group may project a scapegoat which, when it has the power, can carry out its life-negating intentions. Nolasco calls us to take account of this phenomenon seriously and pursue the way of Jesus, which runs counter to the exclusivist-life-negating ways of violent extremism.

Chapter 5, "Theological Ethics in a World of Violent Extremism," by Ellen Ott Marshall, builds on the two known approaches to teaching violent extremism (case study approach and an approach that focuses on authentic traditions vis-à-vis the anomalies) and proposes a third approach. Marshall calls this third approach "internal critical engagement," an approach that offers correctives to the weaknesses of the first two. Internal engagement confronts head-on the presence of violent extremist tendencies in one's religious traditions. Beyond exposing and disarming extremist tendencies at the core of one's religious traditions, Marshall articulates some dispositions and practices that include constructive confrontation and creative transformation.

Taking us to the discipline of history, particularly that of early Christianity, is J. Samuel Subramanian's essay, "Religious Extremism in the History of Early Christianity" (chapter 6). Subramanian takes account of the developments of extremist thinking and practices in the history of Christianity, especially from the early beginnings of Christianity, under four categories, namely, church government, canonization of the New Testament, christological controversies, and women in ministry. His exploration has yielded some insights on the beginnings of extremism. We can see the trend from small communities of faithful followers of Jesus that organized themselves around charisms or gifts to organizations with more rigid hierarchies and structures, a closely guarded canon of scriptures, highly developed christological creed, and male leadership that marginalized the role of women. Those who did not conform to the orthodox formula were declared heretics and burned at the stake. Teaching to help undo violent extremism must, for Subramanian, make students grapple with this historical development. Knowing this history may shed light and make us alert on how religious extremism continues to manifest in the life of the church.

Going deeper into the Christian tradition is Tat-siong Benny Liew's essay, "Teaching Revelation and Questions of Violent Extremism" (chapter 7). Liew's essay addresses violent extremism from a biblical perspective, particularly by interpreting the Book of Revelation. Liew focused his exegetical skills on the Book of Revelation as an example of a text in which words and images of conflict and extreme violence are present. After doing hermeneutical work, he addresses the issue of teaching a text that is loaded with violence in ways that do not reinforce violent extremism. Liew finds the constructivist approach helpful in the work of undoing violent extremism because it enables the students to exercise their critical faculties and to make their own judgments. Instead of offering the definitive and singular interpretation to the waiting students, which is the kind of approach that yields to extremist interpretation, he encourages multiple interpretations. Moreover, he calls students' attention as to the kind of authority we give to the Bible. Students may see violent extremist materials in the biblical text, but it is another matter for them to say that we have to commit violent extremism because the Bible teaches it.

Shifting to the field of ministry, we have an essay by Daniel S. Schipani, "Fundamentalism as Toxic Spirituality: Exploring the Psycho-spiritual Structure and Dynamics of Violent Extremism" (chapter 8). Schipani addresses fundamentalism from multiple perspectives, naming it as a form of toxic spirituality that harms the human spirit, which tends to find expressions in diverse forms of violent extremist actions. To help undo violent extremism, we must address the root of this toxic spirituality involving educational and spiritual care practice. Before we can proceed with the task of undoing and pursuing spiritual care, we have to, as Schipani has suggested, identify the main elements of the fundamentalist mindset and expose its toxicity. We cannot take this lightly because fundamentalism, which impairs the health of the human spirit, can cause irreparable damage and death. Equipped with a view of a holistic human health, spiritual care providers are able to assess better the spiritual situation of the person and help him or her assess available resources in the direction of healthy integration.

Continuing and connecting with the topic of spirituality and care of one's spiritual life is an essay by Ruben L. F. Habito, "Spiritual Practice and Formation in a World of Violent Extremism" (chapter 9). In his essay Habito takes us into what he considers is at the root in the formation of violent extremism, which is the "us" and "them" or tribalistic mentality. Using a Buddhist lens, Habito contends that tribalism is an illusion: we are all intrinsically and intricately interconnected. Living as if we are not interconnected leads to tribalism, which begets various forms of malaise and, in the context of this project, violent extremism. Beyond naming our malaise, he invites us to imagine a new world in which peace and harmony reigns. This is possible, however, only when an awakened self is being born, a self that has turned away from sin (Christian tradition) or has overturned craving into contentment, greed into generosity, ill will into good will, and delusion into wisdom. Awakened to a new understanding that we are interconnected and doing spiritual practices to nurture the life-giving power in ourselves, we are on the way to unshackling ourselves from the grip of violent extremism.

Chapter 10, "Local Peacebuilding in Response to Violent Extremism," by Wendy Kroeker, pursues the work of equipping our local communities in the work of peacebuilding in response to violent extremism. She starts with examining the contested and complex nature of some terms because what may be considered part of the solution may also be part of the problem, such as the work of countering violent extremism and terrorism, which could be part of the drivers of extremism. There are multiple drivers of extremism, some of which fall under grievances. But there are structural or systemic factors as well. If the drivers are complex, this is also true of the possible solutions, which constitutes the rest of Kroeker's essay. She uses a peace framework for addressing violent extremisms. If we want to build peaceful communities, we must invest in creating healthy and resilient communities. In the context of extreme violence, Kroeker calls for a comprehensive and holistic approach that involves multiple stakeholders and attentive consideration of the context and history of the community.

Expanding our horizons, especially the response of other faiths in relation to violent extremism, is an essay by Mualla Selçuk, "Threshold Concepts in Teaching Islam: An Exploration of Pedagogical Content Knowledge for Jihad and War" (chapter 11). Selçuk makes a case for the critical importance of threshold concepts because they provide gateways to new ways of seeing things and interpreting subjects. Jihad and war are examples, for Selçuk, of threshold concepts, which includes three major characteristics or functions: transformative, integrative, and troublesome. With its three functions, threshold concepts are useful in providing fresh insights for teaching and learning Islam, especially in religious education where a monolithic approach is prevalent and students often get stuck in absolute truth at the expense of other views. With the notion of threshold concept and a learning model developed by the author (Conceptual Clarity Model), the core question pursued by the essay is how to teach jihad and war that prevents narrow and, sometimes, violent extremism, while helping students maintain loyalty to their faith and at the same time remaining open and respectful of other faith commitments.

The final chapter (chapter 12) by Sathianathan Clarke, "Christian Theology in an Age of Violent Religious Fundamentalisms: From Intrareligious Dialogue to Interreligious Engagement" takes us to the world of interfaith engagement. The title of the essay itself already reveals its intention and direction: it is suggesting that we move from intrareligious dialogue toward interreligious engagement. While acknowledging the contribution of intrareligious or interfaith dialogue, especially in understanding the substance and spiritual depths of various religious traditions, these conversations that normally happen in serene religious and academic places, are not sufficient if we are to address the conflicts, sometimes violent, that citizens encounter when they share in social and material spaces that are charged with religious fervor. As a foundational forward step, Christian interreligious engagement must make a public confession and renunciation of its supremacist assumptions. Moreover, beyond seeking common ground (love of God and neighbor) as informed by our common Word, Clarke calls our engagement to take the daring step of bonding together for the more difficult "uncommon work" in order to affirm our "common worth."

Moving Forward: Contributing our Share

Violent extremism is a complex challenge and undoing it is not going to be an easy one. Undoing it at an early stage requires right timing and appropriate resources. When it slides into the slippery slope of terrorism, the task of undoing becomes all the more complex. There is no "silver bullet" solution or a precision instrument to launch a "surgical strike" that would only affect the violent extremists. There is no single solution or approach to it because, like a web, it is connected to other aspects of society. An ecological metaphor is appropriate in describing this web of relation. Addressing this matter requires a systems-based and interdisciplinary approach.

I am aware of the immensity and complexity of the challenge and how limited our response is. If, like an ecosystem, everything is interrelated, one response must be seen in relation to the whole. Undoing violent extremism through the teaching of religion is but one among others, because religion is only one aspect of our social life. Unfairly, religion often gets the blame for the atrocities done in the name of violent extremism. Religion is an easy target. Still, religion plays a significant part. Because it plays a significant part in the lives of individuals and communities, we must do something to align it as a power for the common good, especially in preventing and undoing violent extremism. I agree with Ban Ki-Moon's comment, former secretary-general of the United Nations, that religious actors and institutions have been underutilized. He thus calls for a mechanism to further engage religious actors and institutions in dealing with violent extremism and terrorism.[12]

Yes, religious actors and institutions have been underutilized while unfairly blamed. Countering terrorism is not, however, the immediate concern of religious leaders in general and of this project in particular. That work belongs to counterterrorism. We should be acutely aware of this distinction. Our concern is violent extremism (belief system) and the ways in which we can undo it creatively and effectively and with a clear understanding that it is one among many, especially in the purview of peacebuilding.[13] It is in

12. https://berkleycenter.georgetown.edu/features/religion-governments-and-preventing-violent-extremism-what-have-we-learned.

13. Schirch, *The Ecology of Violent Extremism*, 59.

this spirit and context that we have launched this project with the hope of contributing our share into this larger and complex challenge.

Bibliography

Achar, Gilbert. *The Clash of Barbarisms: The Making of the New World Disorder*. New York: Routledge, 2016.

Ali, Tariq. *The Clash of Fundamentalisms: Crusades, Jihads and Modernity*. London: Verso, 2002.

Berger, J. M. *Extremism*. Cambridge: MIT Press, 2018.

Fernandez, Eleazar, ed. *Teaching for a Multifaith World*. Eugene, OR: Pickwick, 2017.

———. *Teaching for a Culturally Diverse and Racially Just World*. Eugene, OR: Cascade, 2013.

Huntington, Samuel. *The Clash of Civilizations and the Remaking of World Order*. New York: Simon & Schuster, 1996.

Palmer, Parker. *Healing the Heart of Democracy: The Courage to Create a Politics Worthy of the Human Spirit*. San Francisco: Jossey-Bass, 2011.

Putnam, Robert, and David Campbell. *American Grace: How Religion Divides and Unites Us*. New York: Simon & Schuster, 2010.

Schirch, Lisa, ed. *The Ecology of Violent Extremism: Perspectives on Peacebuilding and Human Security*. New York: Rowman & Littlefield, 2018.

1

The Smoldering Embers of Violent Extremism and the Raging Fire of Terrorism

—Eleazar S. Fernandez

S moldering embers of violent extremism have turned into raging fires of terrorism. This fire of terrorism is raging in multiple directions, wreaking havoc, instilling fear, sowing paranoia, and heightening calls for countermeasures around the world that have only intensified the cycle of violence. This is not just the general violence that we are so familiar with, but it is a form of violence that is undergirded by or intertwined with violent extremist beliefs. Violent extremism is not of course a new phenomenon. It has been with us since ancient times. But, regardless of where one was or if she or he was already born on this date, the terrorist attack of the Twin Towers of the World Trade Center in New York City on September 11, 2001 has become a historic high mark in the history and discourse of violent extremism and terrorism. The image of the Twin Towers being blown up by two aircrafts and the fumes of smoke that emanate from the skyscrapers as they crumble to dust remains deeply etched in public memory. The September 11, 2001 terrorist attack has brought the phenomenon of violent extremism and terrorism to the people's attention on a global scale.

Several acts of terrorism followed in the wake of the September 11 tragedy in various places around the world. Using information from the Global Terrorism Database (GTD), which is the most comprehensive databases on global terrorism, it shows that there has been a rise in terror attacks since September 11, 2001. From 1,906 terror attacks in 2001, by 2008, terror attacks rose to 4,805. The year 2014 had the most terror attacks (16,903) in a single year. However, there had been a decline between 2014 and 2017 as the number fell from 16,903 in 2014 to 14,964 in 2015, to 13,592 in 2016, and 10,897 in 2017.[1] Whatever these figures indicate, terrorism is happening, and the ground has become all the more fertile for terrorism to sprout.

Catastrophic as these acts of terrorism have been, when we review the number of deaths due to terrorism, we can say that it is still far less compared to the number of deaths due to heart disease and stroke, road accidents, and opioid overdose. Most of the deaths are concentrated in a few countries such as Syria, Nigeria, Iraq, and Pakistan. Yet, terrorism is dreadfully disturbing not simply because of the number of casualties, but because it is sowing seeds of terror. Media images of bombings, beheadings, burnings, and mutilated bodies are gruesome, and they evoke terror, panic, anxiety, and depression. Because of its unpredictability, it is difficult to anticipate where and when it is going to happen. It could happen at a mall or at a worship place; it could happen while one is shopping or drinking coffee in Berlin, London, Paris, or New York. Because it is aimed at what is called "soft target"—the civilian population—everyone feels vulnerable.

Before we proceed further, it is important to note that while many acts of terror can be considered outgrowths of violent extremism, not all of them are expressions of violent extremist belief systems. I would like to remind us again, as I indicated in the Introduction, that we should make a distinction between violent extremism and terrorism. Terrorism is a tactic while violent extremism is a belief system that may justify acts of terror. As a tactic, terrorism includes recruitment and planning. Violent extremism is potentially catastrophic, but, unless it is accompanied by recruitment and planning, it remains in the realm of belief system. An act may be identified as terrorism in relation to the magnitude of the atrocities and the terror it has wrought on the civilian population, but if it is not undergirded by a violent extremist belief system, it cannot be considered as terrorism that comes out of violent extremism. In short, not all terrorisms are expressions or outgrowths of violent extremism.

I must remind the readers further that the main subject matter of this project is violent extremism, not terrorism. Any mention of terrorism in this study is relevant only insofar as an act of terrorism may be a visible expression of violent extremism. Because terrorism is visible on the surface, it provides a great entry point in studying violent extremism, which is much harder to detect, especially at its incipient stage.

Even with this limited focus on violent extremisms that have led to acts of terror, still, acts of terror coming from the cauldron of violent extremism

---

1. https://www.indiatoday.in/world/story/9-11-terror-attack-anniversary-global -terrorism-1597985-2019-09-11.

are the major acts of terrorism around the world. This is the terrorism of the more well-known violent extremism of Al-Qaeda (also spelled al-Qaida and al-Qaʾida), which was founded by Osama bin Laden and Abdullah Yusuf Azzam in 1988 and responsible for the bombing of U.S. Embassies in Nairobi, Kenya, and Dar es Salaam in Tanzania (1998), the September 11, 2001 Twin Towers attack, and the bombings in Bali (Indonesia) in 2002, to name a few.[2] There is also the terrorism of ISIL (The Islamic State of Iraq and the Levant) or of the ISIS (Islamic State of Iraq and Syria), which has some affiliates in other countries, which is known for its beheadings, massacre, and destruction of cultural heritage sites.

Other violent extremist and terrorist groups, which may have or had connections with Al-Qaeda and ISIS/L, also operate in Africa. Two of the well-known violent extremist terrorist groups are Al-Shabaab and Boko Haram.

Al-Shabaab is a jihadist violent extremist terrorist group based in East Africa, particularly Somalia, which originally had ties with Al-Qaeda before it splintered into various groups due to internal conflicts and also a series of defeats. Al-Shabaab is responsible for the deadly Westgate shopping mall attack in Nairobi, Kenya, on September 21, 2013, which resulted in 71 deaths (62 civilians, five Kenyan soldiers, and four attackers) and about 200 people wounded in the mass shooting.[3] Another deadly incident is what is now referred to as the Mogadishu (Somalia) bombings of October 14, 2017, in which 587 people died and 316 were injured.[4]

Another violent extremist-terrorist group, considered deadlier than ISIS in the number of killings it has carried out, is the Islamic State in West Africa or Islamic State's West Africa Province (abbreviated as ISWA or ISWAP), formerly known as Jamāʾat Ahl as-Sunnah lid-Daʿwah waʾl-Jihād, which is commonly known as Boko Haram (founded in 2002). It is a jihadist terrorist organization based in northeastern Nigeria and also active in Chad, Niger, and northern Cameroon. Since 2009 Boko Haram is responsible for killing tens of thousands and displacing about a couple of million from their homes, based on the information provided by the Global

2. https://www.cnn.com/2013/10/06/world/africa/africa-embassy-bombings-fast-facts/index.html.

3. https://web.archive.org/web/20130922155502/http://www.washingtonpost.com/world/africa/gunmen-use-grenades-open-fire-at-nairobis-most-upscale-mall/2013/09/21/a9403b3a-22a8-11e3-ad1a-1a919f2ed890_story_1.html. Also, https://fas.org/sgp/crs/row/R43245.pdf.

4. https://hiiraan.com/news4/2018/Mar/157047/committee_587_dead_in_oct_14_terror_attack.aspx.

Terrorism Index (GTI).[5] Al-Qaeda and ISIS affiliates are also engaged in terroristic acts in Asia. They are at work in Afghanistan, Pakistan, Sri Lanka, India, and the Philippines. In recent years Afghanistan has overtaken Iraq as the deadliest country for terrorism. According to GTI, one quarter of worldwide terrorism-related deaths in 2017 happened in Afghanistan.[6] In 2018, although the total deaths from terrorism fell globally, Afghanistan shouldered 46 percent of the 15,952 deaths.[7] On August 18, 2019, a suicide bomb attack killed at least sixty-three people at a wedding party in Kabul and injured 182 more. A local affiliate of ISIS claimed responsibility for the attack.[8] The neighboring Pakistan has also suffered several violent extremist terrorist attacks, some of which were carried out by ISIS or Al Qaeda affiliates, such as Jamaat-ul-Ahar.[9] The terrorism of Al-Qaeda and ISIS through their affiliates has not spared Indonesia and the Philippines. From May 23 to October 23, 2017, jihadist terrorist groups (Maute, Abu Sayyaf Salafi jihadist, Bangsamoro Islamic Freedom Fighters) with ties to ISIS staged a siege of Marawi City. The Philippine armed forces launched an offensive that lasted for five months. At the end of the battle, Marawi City was in ruins and suffered major war casualties, including thousands of residents who were displaced.[10]

Thus far we have only identified and taken account of the terroristic acts of violent extremist groups like Al-Qaeda and ISIS and their affiliates that are identified with Islamic groups. This account would be incomplete and unfair if we limit our account to Islamist inspired terrorism. There are other violent extremist groups that we should not fail to mention, which are identified or associated with other religious faiths. Continuing our focus on Asia, I would like to highlight the rise and violent extremist acts of Indian fundamentalist groups that are associated with Hinduism and fundamentalist groups in Myanmar (Burma) and Sri Lanka that are associated with Buddhism. This is not to say that religion, this time Hinduism and Buddhism, is the driver. It

5. https://edition.cnn.com/2015/11/17/world/global-terror-report/;   http://economicsandpeace.org/wp-content/uploads/2015/11/Global-Terrorism-Index-2015.pdf.

6. https://www.nbcnews.com/news/world/afghanistan-becomes-world-s-deadliest-country-terrorism-overtaking-iraq-n942086.

7. https://www.businessinsider.com/the-taliban-is-now-the-worlds-deadliest-terror-group-2019-11.

8. https://www.vox.com/world/2019/8/18/20811041/kabul-deadliest-attack-year-afghanistan-us-taliban-peace-deal.

9. https://www.un.org/securitycouncil/sanctions/1267/aq_sanctions_list/summaries/entity/jamaat-ul-ahrar-%28jua%29.

10. https://www.aljazeera.com/news/2017/09/philippines-army-rebel-groups-join-forces-marawi-170906112401721.html; https://www.businessinsider.com/isis-losing-in-iraq-syria-9-places-where-its-still-a-threat-2017-11#philippines-7.

often escapes our attention how these two faiths (Hinduism and Buddhism) can be identified with violent extremism and terrorism when they are commonly associated with pluralism and openness, in contrast to Abrahamic faiths (Judaism, Christianity, and Islam), which have strong associations of a long and bloody history of violent extremist acts.

There is an alarming rise of religio-political fundamentalism in India that is associated with Hinduism that we should be concerned about, especially that it has gained popular support and has pursued its violent extremist acts with the seeming approval of the highest governmental offices of the country. This is particularly true with the political triumph of the Bharatiya Janata Party (BJP), home of the religious right and political subset of the Hindu fundamentalist group Rashtriya Swayamsevak Sangh (RSS), and the assumption of Narenda Modi as India's Prime Minister, who has been identified with RSS. The RSS, a vanguard of Hindu nationalism, has pursued its fundamentalist-violent extremist views systematically by implementing programs on education—including the rewriting of history textbooks—health, and community development and by infiltrating various institutions—such as the judiciary and the police—to promote the Hindu nationalist ideology.[11]

Not satisfied with systematic promotion of its nationalist-fundamentalist agenda, RSS has instigated or supported violent mobs to attack other minority groups and targeted killings of individuals who are liberal or left leaning and those who are critical of the Indian-Hindu fundamentalist agenda. Hindu fundamentalist violence took on a new feverish pitch and strident cadence with the brutal burning of fifty-nine Hindu pilgrims on February 27, 2002. Popularly known as the Gujarat violence of 2002, Muslims became the target of Hindu attacks. One should not fail to notice the "well-thought out, methodical, and state-complicit nature of the violence," as some have pointed out.[12] The Sangh *parivar* (the umbrella organization of all militant Hindu organizations) was well prepared to carry out the brutal and sadistic attacks. By the end of the two-month riot (March 2002), the estimated casualties ranged between a thousand dead (official report) and two thousand (unofficial report), nearly 150,000 Muslims were driven from their homes, and five hundred mosques and shrines were destroyed.[13]

Hindu fundamentalist attacks against the Muslim minority have continued to the present, which include the Malegaon bombings of 2006 (40 fatalities and 125 injuries, most of whom were Muslim pilgrims), and the

---

11. https://www.mcgilldaily.com/2017/09/the-rise-of-hindu-fundamentalism/.

12. Clarke, *Competing Fundamentalisms*, 123.

13. Clarke, *Competing Fundamentalisms*, 123.

killing of a 16 year old boy, Hafiz Junaid, on June 22, 2017, in the presence of about two hundred Hindu onlookers, which came after several incidents of assaults against Muslims over cow slaughtering and eating beef.[14] During an investigation, no one testified that he or she had witnessed the attack. In a society terrorized by Hindu fundamentalist groups, it is heart-rending to know, says Yasir Piracha, that an entire crowd of Hindus had "chosen not to see" the sadistic event done to a Muslim boy. India, continues Piracha, has entered an era in which vigilante Hindus can hunt Muslims for sport and "do not need to worry about witnesses: there will never be any."[15]

Not only a Muslim but also a Christian minority in an overwhelmingly Hindu country has been the target of violent attacks by Hindu extremist groups and mobs. About the scale of the Gujarat riot that was directed against Muslims, the attack against Christians happened in the District of Kandhamal, Odisha (old name is Orissa) in 2008. With the killing of Swami Lakshmanananda Saraswati in the background, Christians became the target of Hindu riots directed by Hindu fundamentalist groups in the region. In the aftermath of the riot, it was reported that at least fifty-nine persons lost their lives and about 18,500 Christians were displaced.[16] More than 4,300 houses of Dalits and Adivasi Christians were destroyed and about eighty houses of worship, mostly by arson.[17] Christians continue to remain vulnerable to attacks by fundamentalists with the rise of Hindu fundamentalism. Even Hindus are not completely free from attacks when some members of their family become Christians.

Similar to the Hindu majority in India, in Buddhist majority countries, especially of the Theravada kind, Buddhist fundamentalist-extremism is in ascendancy, sometimes resulting in violent acts. This is happening in Myanmar, Sri Lanka, and Thailand. Militant Buddhist monks of the Ma-BaTha and the 969 Movement are inciting violence against the Rohingya Muslims in Myanmar, the Bodu Bala Sena (BBS) against Muslims in Sri

---

14. https://www.hindustantimes.com/india-news/man-stabbed-to-death-2-injured-on-mathura-train-after-fight-with-passengers-for-allegedly-carrying-beef/story-BiJyILYlUloErWASvKQ51M.html.

15. Piracha, "The Rise of Hindu Fundamentalism." See https://www.mcgilldaily.com/2017/09/the-rise-of-hindu-fundamentalism/.

16. Clarke, *Competing Fundamentalisms*, 124. Also, Hari Kumar and Heather Timmons, "Violence in India is Fueled by Religious and Economic Divide," *New York Times*, September 3, 2008. https://www.nytimes.com/2008/09/04/world/asia/04christians.html ?pagewanted=all&_r=0&mtrref=en.wikipedia.org&gwh=5F9B5EFFDF00C0C9FA406 82CE0FF8FE6&gwt=pay&assetType=REGIWALL.

17. Clarke, *Competing Fundamentalisms*, 124. Also, from the journal *Gyanodaya*, "The Recent Attacks on Christians in Kandhamal and Its Impacts," in *The Recent Attacks on Christians in Orissa: A Theological Response*, 6.

Lanka, and Thai monks against Muslims in Southern Thailand.[18] Barely a year after its founding (2012), BBS carried about 241 attacks against Muslims and sixty-one attacks against Christians in a report compiled by Sri Lanka Muslim Congress (SLMC).[19]

Violent extremist groups are also rising in Myanmar with a strong religious influence and inspiration from Buddhism. In contrast to pictures we normally see of crimson-robed monks meditating or praying, these monks are carrying swords and preaching vituperative sermons with strong Islamophobic overtones, inspiring Buddhists to attack Muslims. Although the attacks have been directed against Muslims, Christian minorities are no less worried. As it has been argued, these attacks against Muslims may have historical reasons, but the intensity and frequency of the attacks have reached new heights. Referring to Muslims, "You can be full of kindness and love, but you cannot sleep next to a mad dog," says Ashin Wirathu.[20] As a result of this rise in violent extremism, Buddhist lynch mobs have killed more than two-hundred Muslims and displaced more than 150,000 people, mostly Rohingya Muslims, from their homes.[21]

After an account of violent extremist groups and their terroristic acts in other parts of the world, let us take a cursory look at Europe and then United States of America. Violent extremism and terrorism are also rising and festering in Europe. With the influx of newcomers and the growing resistance of host countries to welcome them, we have a large group of people who feel discriminated and alienated from European society. Muslims, in particular, constitute about forty-four million of the population, with many, especially the younger ones, straddling between being Europeans and Muslims.[22] In the context of a rising Islamophobia, it is not a surprise that they have experienced discrimination and have found closer affinity with those of similar sentiments, and religion has become an important home for their identities. Given this situation, many have become more vulnerable to Islamist-extremist influence. In 2016, although only one source of terrorism, jihadist attacks were a key source of casualties and deaths (causing 374 out of 379 casualties or 99 percent and 135 out

18. https://www.huffpost.com/entry/buddhist-fundamentalism_b_57a8a806e4b0c cb02372ec46.

19. http://www.srilankaguardian.org/2014/04/sri-lanka-tweaking-muslims.html.

20. https://www.nytimes.com/2013/06/21/world/asia/extremism-rises-among-myanmar-buddhists-wary-of-muslim-minority.html.

21. https://www.nytimes.com/2013/06/21/world/asia/extremism-rises-among-myanmar-buddhists-wary-of-muslim-minority.html.

22. https://www.cfr.org/conference-calls/rise-violent-extremism-europe.

of 142 fatalities or 95 percent). They also accounted for 718 out of 1002 terrorism-related arrests or 72 percent.[23]

These jihadist-extremist attacks did not continue without counter-extremist attacks, especially by those who feel threatened by these terroristic acts and by the growth of Muslims and the influx of new immigrants from mostly Muslim-dominated countries. Thus, Europe has suffered from the rise of violent assaults by ethno-nationalist and rightwing extremists, targeting refugees and ethnic minorities.[24] We still remember the July 22, 2011 act of terror in Norway by a Norwegian right-wing extremist that claimed seventy-seven lives.[25]

Now let us focus on the U.S. right wing violent extremist groups that are also rising and gaining ascendancy in the U.S., often claiming Christian inspiration, and becoming more vocal and brazen with the election of Donald Trump as president. There is a long list of violent extremist groups in the U.S., which includes the Ku Klux Klan, white nationalists, neo-Nazis, racist skinheads, anti-government militias, and the alt-right, which has a wider following, to name a few. Today, the most prominent of the right-wing subcultures is the alt-right. The Southern Poverty Law Center (SPLC) reported that over one hundred people were killed or injured by perpetrators allegedly influenced by the alt-right movement, which has access to the mainstream population and the ability to reach young recruits.[26]

A more recent and widely publicized violent extremist act happened on August 13, 2017, at a "Unite the Right" rally in Charlottesville, Virginia. At that event, one white nationalist by the name of James Alex Fields slammed his car into a crowd of anti-extremist protesters, killing Heather Heyer and injuring nineteen others. It drove home the point that these white nationalists are not just "douchebags playing neo-Nazi on the internet" but extremist groups capable of unleashing serious violence.[27] It should be noted that Heyer's death was not an isolated case. The Southern Poverty Law Center estimates that Heyer was the thirty-seventh person murdered by individuals inspired by alt-right ideology in the past four years. Since Heather's death,

---

23. https://www.csis.org/analysis/trends-extremist-violence-and-terrorism-europe-through-end-2016.

24. https://www.csis.org/analysis/trends-extremist-violence-and-terrorism-europe-through-end-2016.

25. https://www.worldatlas.com/articles/the-deadliest-terror-attacks-in-europe.html.

26. https://haenfler.sites.grinnell.edu/subcultural-theory-and-theorists/right-wing-subcultures/.

27. https://www.salon.com/2018/02/09/surge-in-alt-right-violence-at-least-43-murders-in-the-last-four-years/.

six people have been killed by alt-right extremists. This brings a total to forty-three deaths and sixty-seven injuries.[28]

Violent Extremist Ideology

In spite their differences, there is a common feature among the various groups we have identified: they are undergirded by violent extremist beliefs and ideologies. On a closer scrutiny, they show the basic tenets of violent extremism: (1) violence is necessary because it is tactically superior and/ or redemptive; (2) brutal violence against unarmed civilians is justified to achieve purification of society and/or because civilians are responsible for their governments; (3) an authoritarian narrative that is intolerant, patri-archal, and anti-participatory or anti-democratic; and (4) ideological goals related to identity and grievances.[29]

Al-Qaeda, ISIS, and Al Shabaab share some ideological beliefs. They have shared grievances, such as that the West is waging war against Islam and westoxification of Islam is happening. From their point of view, state governments—including that of Muslim majority countries—have become corrupt and leaders have been corrupted. These leaders cannot be trusted to change the situation. True Muslims must unite and resist the Western crusaders and their imperialist agenda and uproot corruption. Islam must be purified from westoxification and other forms of impurities. We should notice that when ISIL took control of territory in Iraq and Syria, it engaged in a campaign of "cultural cleansing": it destroyed Assyrian artifacts in the Mosul museum, the collections of Greco-Roman ruins in Palmyra, and Shi-ite and Christian places of worship.[30]

From a Muslim violent extremist perspective, because the captivity of the Muslim world is extreme, there is no other recourse but a jihadist war. A jihadist war must be waged not only against the "far enemy" (West) but also the "near enemy," which includes those Muslims who are conniv-ing with Western powers. There must be no compromise to the defilers and apostates. Terror must be unleashed for purification to happen and civilians are not exempt as targets because they are responsible for their

---

28. https://www.salon.com/2018/02/09/surge-in-alt-right-violence-at-least-43-murders-in-the-last-four-years/.

29. Schirch, *The Ecology of Violent Extremism*, 16–17.

30. https://www.britannica.com/topic/Islamic-State-in-Iraq-and-the-Levant/Expansion-and-declaration-of-a-caliphate.

governments. Ultimate devotion to the cause is expected, which may lead to victory or martyrdom.[31]

Although Indian-nationalist extremists and Burmese-fundamentalist extremists are two different groups and operate in two different places, they exhibit some similar features of violent extremism. Whether real or imagined, both groups are expressing deep-seated grievances and are "perceiving threats" to their existence and identity. Both see the presence of Muslims with alarm and as a major threat to their ethnic-religious identity. Seeing the rise of Muslims as a threat, Indian fundamentalist-extremists construct their narrative and identity in light of that threat. They are zealously advocating for the restoration of the Hindu worldview (Hindutva), which they perceive has been under threat from secularist leaders and citizens. They support politicians and political campaigns that favor the fundamentalist agenda. Anyone undermining or perceived as accommodating to secular-liberal worldview is considered a threat, and must be stopped.

In Sri Lanka as well as in Myanmar, Sinhalese-Buddhist-nationalist-fundamentalism and Burmese-Buddhist-nationalist-fundamentalism are also rising respectively. Sinhalese-Buddhist fundamentalists assert the ideological line of the inseparable link between the island of Sri Lanka, the Sinhalese people, and Buddhism. In effect they argue that Sri Lanka is a Buddhist nation for the Sinhalese people who have the especial role as curators or guardians of Buddhism. Sri Lanka is a "gift from Buddha to the Sinhalese."[32] This Sri-Lankan identity, from the point of view of the Sinhalese-Buddhist fundamentalists, has been threatened by Muslim and Christian minorities, and by those who claim that Sri-Lanka is a multi-cultural, multi-religious country. In light of this perceived threat to the ethnic-religious identity of the state, the BBS has been able to channel Sinhalese-Buddhist chauvinist passions and incite attacks against Muslims and Christians.[33]

Burmese-Buddhist-fundamentalists have also perceived threats from minorities in Myanmar, especially against Muslims. In their eyes, "The biggest threat. . . comes from their Muslim neighbors, who they view with atavistic suspicion: they say Muslims steal Buddhist women, outbreed the Buddhist majority and plot terror attacks."[34] Certainly, there are local encounters with Muslims that are immediate in the experience of Buddhists in Myanmar that would feed into these perceived threats. We

31. https://www.hudson.org/research/9777-al-qaeda-s-ideology.

32. https://srilankabrief.org/2013/05/on-buddhist-fundamentalism/; https://www.sunypress.edu/p-2802-buddhist-fundamentalism-and-min.aspx.

33. http://www.srilankaguardian.org/2014/04/sri-lanka-tweaking-muslims.html.

34. https://www.theguardian.com/cities/2017/may/08/buddhist-extremists-anti-muslim-mandalay-ma-ba-tha.

cannot, however, dismiss, especially with the war on terror, how Burmese-Buddhist nationalists have consumed Islamophobia, fed to them by the Western media. Islam has received bad publicity with Muslim violent extremists invoking Islam and Allah, even when these violent extremists are not really steeped in their understanding of and commitment to the Islamic faith. In the minds of many, Islam is a violent and dangerous religion. The rise of xenophobic populism in the West, which has high Islamophobic elements, has played well in to the hands of Buddhist nationalists, lending justification to their narratives.

"Jihadi Muslims," says Eindaw Bar Tha, a Buddhist monk, "want to overwhelm the country, so we have to protect it."[35] Since the state government, which should be responsible for protecting the country and its majority Buddhist citizens, has not protected or has not been effective in protecting the rights of the Buddhist majority, Buddhist nationalists/fundamentalists must take upon themselves the task of protecting themselves and their faith, which could lead to violent acts. This perceived grievance is providing fuel for redemptive violence. When carried out with the resources and support available, this could lead to terroristic acts against the objects of grievance. In the case of Myanmar and Sri Lanka, it is directed primarily against the Muslim minority population. Christians, however, are also worried of their situation.

The alt-right, like other violent extremist groups, has its list of grievances as well that is fueling deep resentments. Alt-right propaganda highlights and nourishes these grievances of disillusioned and indignant whites, mostly young men who dominate its ranks. As in other extremist groups, the alt-right is reactionary in nature: it is reacting to what it has perceived as an assault on what the United States of America should be and be about. At the center of this list of grievances is the perceived displacement or marginalization of whites from the center of U.S. society, especially disempowered white men. As one alt-right writer said, "And all of modern society seems to offer literally nothing to young White men. It's as if society doesn't want them to tune in, show up and have a stake in the future of that institution."[36]

Along with the alt-right's list of grievances is its list of reasons or causes for its marginalization, which includes immigration of peoples, especially from the Global South, federal government's liberal and affirmative action policies, Jewish conspiracy, and left-wing groups, including liberation movements and LGBTQI, etc. Given what it identifies as threats and grievances,

35. https://www.theguardian.com/cities/2017/may/08/buddhist-extremists-anti-muslim-mandalay-ma-ba-tha.

36. https://www.splcenter.org/20180205/alt-right-killing-people.

it is not a surprise that ideologically it is white supremacist, anti-immigrant, anti-Semitic, Islamophobic, homophobic, and anti-feminist, and it supports white separatism and severe immigration restrictions.

Although they collide in many aspects, the alt-Right and other white nationalist groups as well as jihadists share common fears and grievances, dreams, core values, and strategies. They are feeling marginalization and disempowerment brought about by some forces, such as the presence of out-groups, global network of powers, corrupt state-governments, and liberal-secular movements that are advocating or open to multicultural-ism, gender justice, and homosexuality. These forces are to be blamed for what the violent extremist group's identify as the cause of their misery: loss of social and economic status, inability to find partners (e.g., disillusioned young white nationalist men), and sense of control of their imagined future. Beyond economics, im/migration is considered a threat because it redefines the identity of the nation. A white supremacist, for example, cannot imag-ine a multi-ethnic-multi-racial state in which non-whites share power with whites. Similarly, a Muslim-jihadist cannot imagine living in a secular state or non-Islamic state. Although white supremacists are Islamophobic and Muslim-jihadists are anti-West, they share something in common: they are both segregationists. They are both intolerant, or, to put it strongly, they have a hatred of the "other." Now, what is considered lost ground has to be reclaimed or recovered. If the government and other institutions cannot be trusted or are impotent to protect what the violent extremists believe is rightfully theirs, then the extremist groups must assume responsibility to secure the lost ground and advance the cause. Redemptive violence is neces-sary in order to gain lost grounds or restore former glory.

Framework for Understanding the Rise of Violent Extremism: The Ecology Metaphor

Metaphors are relevant in helping us understand and address complex ideas or issues. A metaphor provides a lens or framework in imagining the re-lationship of various parts within a wider and integrated perspective. One such metaphor that is useful in dealing with the issue of violent extremism is ecology. It calls our attention to the interweaving or interconnection of ev-erything. Ecological metaphor communicates the point that violent extrem-ism is not something separate from the rest of society. What happens in one area affects another; intervention in one area will have an effect in another. Because everything is interrelated or intertwined, a systems-based approach is important in understanding and intervening in violent extremism. We cannot approach the issue in isolation from other issues. It takes us in the direction of interdisciplinary work. No single field has the explanatory power to illumine all aspects; no single approach can address the issue comprehensively and effectively. No single solution is possible.

Beyond saying that there is no single solution to violent extremism, an ecological or systems-based approach reminds us that the solutions we propose or offer must be evaluated in a holistic manner. The positive side of interconnection is that what we do in one aspect will have an impact in another, which means that when done right, our actions will have positive consequences in others. On the other hand, when we fail to see the effects of a solution in relation to the wellbeing of the whole system, the intended solution may cause more harm rather than bring healing to the system. There have been several cases when solutions, because proponents have failed to see the intricate interweaving of the system, have led to more problems.

It would help us understand better if we bring to our attention two common ecological metaphors that have been commonly used in counter-terrorism discourse: the swamp metaphor and the cancer metaphor.

The swamp is a popular metaphor often used in counter-terrorism works. Heads of state, military generals, and counter-terrorism experts often talk about "draining the swamp" in their programs to combat terrorism. Before we move in haste, let us imagine a swamp. A swamp or wetland is an important part of the earth's ecosystem; it plays an important role in maintaining ecological balance. Swamps or wetlands act as giant sponges and reservoirs from heavy rain and flashfloods, thus moderating their destructive effects. They also protect seaboards from storm surges and soil erosion, especially swamps with healthy mangroves. Swamps also serve as filters for wastes coming from factories and homes. Swamps and wetlands are the natural habitat of various species of plants and animals.

But there is that sinister and dreaded side of swamps that has settled in the minds of many. It can be the habitat of those dreaded creatures, like alligators and snakes. It can also be the breeding grounds of mosquitoes and pests that are carriers of harmful pathogens that can cause diseases. And, because many wetlands have become wastelands or dumpsites, they are associated with foul and toxic odors. Once wetlands are associated with wasteland, abuse of wetlands gets perpetuated.

With this social imaginary of swamps and wetlands, it is not a surprise why "draining the swamp" has become a popular metaphor for those who are working to counter terrorism. "Draining the swamp" is a metaphor for destroying the habitat where terrorists live or get their support. It is a metaphor for bombing villages and cities that are infested by terrorists. In this swamp society the terrorists are comparable to the alligators and snakes that must be flushed out and killed. When the base or habitat of the terrorists is destroyed, the terrorists are left with no means of support. Thus, they will not flourish.

This kind of interpretation is problematic, and it exacerbates the challenge. Wrongly, it assumes that alligators, snakes, scorpions, mosquitoes and others are the problems, when in fact they are part of the ecosystem. "Draining the swamp" would not only kill alligators, snakes, scorpions, and mosquitoes, but also other forms of life in the habitat. Bombing villages to flush out terrorists has not been effective in preventing violent extremism and terrorism. On the contrary, the destruction of villages has undermined the resilience of the villagers and they have become more susceptible or vulnerable to violent extremism. We cannot save a village by bombing a village.

Still the swamp as an ecological metaphor is helpful, if used properly. The swamp itself is not the problem or the alligators and snakes. They are all part of the larger ecosystem. What is foreign to the swamp's ecosystem is the bomb or the chemicals that are dumped into the swamp, perhaps with the good intention of flushing out toxins in the swamp. But this is dangerous and could backfire, especially since we do not know how living creatures in the swamp would respond to the intrusion of new chemicals. The intrusion of chemicals into the swamp may be responsible for the rise of cancer among humans and animals in and near the swamp.

This leads us to the second metaphor that is widely popular with government officials, social activists, and now among those who are at the forefront of the war on terror: the cancer metaphor. When applied to the war on terror, it is obvious that the terrorists are considered the cancerous cells that must be removed by "surgical strikes," and this must be done decisively and with urgency before the cancerous cells could spread at a level that would overwhelm the social body. Another common approach in dealing with cancerous cells is by chemotherapy, the purpose of which is to kill the cancerous cells to prevent it from spreading. In relation to terrorism, the terrorists have to be stopped before they can spread and do more damage.

It is important to have a clear understanding how cancer cells develop and how violent extremist terrorists develop if the cancer metaphor is to be useful and effective. When cells grow in size or speed beyond the normal and start to invade other areas, we can say that they have reached a cancerous level. Like normal cells that undergo mutation, individuals can undergo mutation leading to violent extremism and terrorism when the right combination of factors is present. This difference, however, must be noted: while cancer cells can never revert back into healthy cells, individuals can experience healing and be restored into healthy individuals. In this regard, the cancer metaphor gives the impression that the individual is beyond restoration to become a healthy member of society.

Similar to the metaphor of "draining the swamp" which also brings unintended consequences that are disastrous, the common cures for cancer have also consequences that can be destructive. Chemotherapy, for example, kills not only the bad cells but also the good cells. When the good cells are killed in the process of killing the bad cells, the individual is left without natural defenses to fight against common diseases. When the immune system is compromised, the individual is vulnerable to diseases. Sometimes it is difficult to tell if the person has died of cancer or of the effects of chemotherapy. When applied to society, the immuno-compromised communities are more vulnerable to violent extremist ideas and radicalization.

This tells us that responses to violent extremism and terrorism, like responses to cancer, must be assessed ecologically or holistically, if the intended response is not to exacerbate the problem but to contribute to greater well-being. By maintaining a healthy village (healthy swamp or healthy body), we can address soundly and effectively the challenge of violent extremism and terrorism, which is a product of an unhealthy relationship within the social body. The challenge is to find healthy alternatives to cancer treatment (physical body) or approaches to restoring the vitality of the swamp. In the case of cancer, it may involve some healing therapies that restore the vitality and resilience of the body.

We are familiar with approaches that exacerbate rather than provide solutions to existing problems or challenges. Many treatments target one physical problem, but may have side effects or collateral damages, which the patient does not know or is not informed. Prolonged intake of some medications to cure heart disease or diabetes may damage the liver, kidney, and pancreas. Others may deplete the calcium-magnesium in the body, which causes severe muscle cramps. That is why a holistic approach is needed, because the human body is one living organism. A medical practitioner should know how his or her prescription would affect the whole human body, not just on the diseases that he or she is trying to address.

We can go to the realm of development projects and find examples of noble intentions producing the opposite. Instead of alleviating poverty, they have become obstacles to development. Experts often introduce something new or foreign to a locality. Let us take the case of the golden apple snail (*Pomacea Canaliculata*) or "golden kuhol" in the Philippines. It was introduced between 1982 and 1984 to supplement sources of food protein for low-income Filipinos.[37] But it had other unintended or unforeseen

37. https://www.tandfonline.com/doi/abs/10.1300/J064v18n02_07.

consequences. The promised potential turned into a menace for farmers. Growing rapidly, they fed voraciously on any succulent greens, including the newly transplanted rice seedlings and other crops. The snails' rapid growth and distribution threatened rice production and that of other crops and food security. What was considered a blessing became a curse; what was considered a friend became an enemy.

Converging Drivers of Violent Extremism

There is not a one-directional trajectory of causes and effects when we talk of the growth of violent extremism. A better explanation, I believe, is the convergence and interweaving and inter-influencing of factors and drivers of violent extremism. Let me identify a few of these converging factors and drivers.

Community Grievances

Community grievances, which I have mentioned earlier, are among the main drivers of violent extremism and terrorism. In any account of violent extremism, a list of grievances has come out as drivers of extremist violent acts. These grievances cover three major aspects: economic, political, and social aspects.

Economic inequality is one of the drivers of violent extremism and terrorism. Again, I am using drivers rather than causes because there are no direct correlations between socio-economic inequality and deprivation and violent extremism and terrorism. Many of those who are economically deprived are not violent extremists and have not resorted to terrorism. Also, violent extremists and terrorists are not limited to the economically deprived. Some of those who participate in violent extremist acts are well educated and affluent. Still, socio-economic inequality is a factor or a driver, and it has emerged as one of the grievances of violent extremists and terrorists.

Without a doubt, the global market has produced immense wealth. Global daily financial transactions have totaled in the trillions. Technological advancements have led to increased production and distribution of goods and services. Notwithstanding all these achievements, many are without basic necessities, and many are dying of hunger.

Death has been the plight of many amidst the rhetoric that economic globalization provides salvation. Many are dying slowly due to sickness and starvation, while others are left with no other options but to die quickly. The poverty and the death of the many only prove the sinister side of the much-trumpeted rising tide of economic globalization. It is not a rising tide that is going to lift all boats on an ocean of poverty. No less than the Central Intelligence Agency's (CIA) 2000 report made the projection that the "rising tide of the global economy will create many economic winners, but it will not lift all boats."[38] Contrary to the belief that "a rising tide raises all boats," the reality has been that "a rising tide raises all yachts."[39] Worse, the poor do not even have boats, and they are drowning in the tsunami of corporate profits.

When economic disparity and massive poverty become the order of the global household, we can expect negative consequences: poor health, short life span and high mortality rate, high illiteracy rate, stagnant communities, increased criminality, and rampant depression. Poverty begets disease and disease begets poverty. Those who cannot afford to buy nutritious food and have no access to safe drinking water, sanitary living condition, basic health care, and good education are more likely to get sick. When they are sick, they cannot support their families; thus, the cycle of poverty and disease continues. In considering a society as a whole, we find that the greater the economic disparity among its people, the worse the overall health of the people in that society. Poor communities lack good educational opportunities for advancement; hence, the likelihood of being buried in their miserable situation is high. Furthermore, social inequity, economic disparity, and massive poverty lead to socio-political instability and a host of social maladies. Socio-political instability leads to extremism of various sorts and violence. With lives ruined and dreams turned to dust, people are left vulnerable to gang recruitment and other violent extremist organizations.

Political grievances go along with economic grievances as drivers of violent extremism and terrorism. In fact, political grievances are more prevalent than economic grievances in the rhetoric and recruitment materials of violent extremist groups. Corruption, political violence, repression, militarization, and human rights abuses all contribute to fertilizing the soil for violent extremism to sprout and grow. The United States Agency for International Development (USAID) has named seven political grievances that correlate with violent extremism, namely: (1) denial of basic political rights and civil liberties; (2) gross violation of human rights; (3) corruption and impunity of the elites; (4) safe havens, poorly governed or ungoverned areas; (5) violent local conflicts that can be exploited; (6) state

38. Cited in Delgado, *Shaking the Gates of Hell*, 77.
39. Borg, *The Heart of Christianity*, 141.

sponsorship of violent extremist groups; (7) weak or nonexistent opposi-
tions (USAID 2009)."[40]

In many of these politically volatile situations, Western governments,
particularly the United States, have supported or have been identified with
authoritarian and repressive regimes in various parts of the world. From the
point of view of the politically disenfranchised, Western governments and
their local lackeys have become allies in the oppression and marginalization
of the masses. It is no wonder that state governments (near enemy) and Western governments (far enemy) have received the ire of the disenfranchised and
have become targets of violent extremisms and terrorisms.

Social grievances are also drivers of violent extremism, especially social
exclusion, discrimination, and victimization. Social exclusion and discrimination are especially common experiences among diaspora communities
from their host countries. We have several cases of this in Europe, especially
with the influx of more refugees. When walls of exclusion and discrimination
rise, the excluded and discriminated are forced to find people who are in the
same situation who can identify with their predicament. In this situation, they
are more vulnerable to the influence of violent extremist ideas.

The feeling of humiliation is also a common social grievance among
those who drift into violent extremism and sometimes resort to terrorism.
The occupation and control of predominantly Muslim lands by the U.S.
in Iraq and Afghanistan, Chechnya by Russia, and Palestine by Israel is
interpreted by the Muslim world as a form of humiliation. In addition
to this political humiliation is cultural humiliation. The imposition and
proliferation of Western values and morality in Muslim dominant countries is experienced as a great humiliation because it calls into question the
foundation of Islamic values and morality.[41]

Identity and Belonging

Identity is a relational concept. Identity exists and develops in relationship
with others. It is a constant dance with others. Identity develops always in
relation to its surroundings, particularly in relationship with people and
social events. There is no space outside of this relationship in which we
become who we are. Social relations constitute the main ingredients for
identity formation. Our relationship defines who we are.

40. Schirch, *The Ecology of Violent Extremism*, 37.

41. For a more detailed account of the various kinds of humiliation, please refer to
the essay of Krosrokhavar, "The Psychology of the Global Jihadists," in *The Fundamentalist Mindset*, 139–55.

Identity evolves through the process of differentiation. Several factors contribute to the process of differentiation. The development of national consciousness, for example, may be triggered and hastened by outside political forces, such as conquest and colonization by foreign powers. The once loosely defined and scattered multi-ethnic groups may feel the need to bond together in response to the invaders. As time evolves, a national consciousness or a nation-state may be given birth.

Human communities see and construct difference in the process of identity formation. The constructions of "we" and "they" and "us" and "them" are all part of identity formation. There may be difference/es, but difference is not the problem. The main problem is our attitude toward difference and how we deal with difference. To be different from another is not the same as being against. The good news is that we can be different but not necessarily against each other. Audre Lorde puts it succinctly: the main problem "is rather our refusal to recognize those differences, and to examine the distortions which result from our misnaming them and their effects upon human behavior and expectation."[42]

Sadly, the dominant identity formation in our society is that of being "over against the other." It seems easy to fall into this destructive pattern; it is basically finding an identity that is set in opposition to another. Even more, it elevates one's primary identity marker over another. In the context of unequal power relations, it can be individually and corporately imposed on others. When one's identity is equated with the cultural norm, systemic violence starts. Various forms of fundamentalism, whether religious or secular, can be interpreted as an expression of an identity posed "over against the other."

We can see ominous symptoms when markers of identity and belonging are redrawn and are religiously policed. Ominous symptoms are present when the demarcation line between in-group and out-group thickens and strict policing is enforced to protect the purity of the in-group from the contaminant—the out-group, and when betrayal of this purity map is deemed a serious and unforgivable sin. The constricting mindset thickens and worsens when it turns into "us-versus-them," and that the "them" (out-group) is scapegoated as the cause for the crisis. When the out-group or the scapegoated is seen as an embodiment of the demonic and the world is seen as a battlefield between good and evil, violence against the scapegoated is just a hairline away. Labeled as such, when violence is unleashed against the scapegoated and the demonized, their suffering would deserve little or no empathy at all.

42. Lorde, *Sister Outsider*, 115.

There are several components around which identity and belonging are formed. It may be around ethnicity-nationality, language, race, gender, sexuality, religion, and shared experiences, including victimization, humiliation, and fear. "Identity politics," says Scott M. Thomas, "draws its strength from bonds of culture, religion, history, and memory, and not entirely from material or functional sources."[43] One of these strands may play a prominent role over another depending on the context and stage in one's life. White nationalists fear that the changing demographic as a result of immigration will change the white identity of the United States of America. Muslim extremists fear that Jews and Christians are in the business of destroying Islam. German neo-Nazis fear that Muslim immigrants are going to destroy their culture and way of life.

Ethno-nationalism is a major factor in identity formation that contributes to the many drivers of violent extremism. I mentioned this phenomenon in the rise of Indian nationalism (Hindutva) and ethno-religio-nationalism in Myanmar and Sri Lanka. Ethno-nationalism is also present among minoritized ethnic groups that are struggling for political independence, but are constantly crushed and frustrated by the dominant groups, such as Palestinians in Israel-Palestine, the Tamils in Sri-Lanka, Uighur Muslims in the Peoples Republic of China, and Chechen in Russia.

An idea that I have found useful in understanding the drivers of violent extremism and terrorism is one proposed by Deepa M. Ollapally, which is consistent with my view that the drivers must be seen in convergent dynamic interaction.[44] Focusing on South Asia, Ollapally contends that the trajectory of violent extremism must consider a three-way identity struggle: ethno-religious, secular, and geopolitical identities.[45] This does not discount other drivers, such as relative economic deprivation, elite manipulation, and state repression and lack of political institutional access. Rather, it is meant to fill some gaps of the commonly identified drivers.

The ethno-religious dimension has been identified as one of the fault lines in violent extremist conflicts. Although distinct, both ethnic and religious dimensions often converge in a conflictive situation. That is why it makes sense to merge both: ethno-religious. It is not accurate to say that ethnic formation is the main driver of violent extremism because people of various ethnic groups have a long history of dwelling peacefully. It is common to find those who say that religion is the main driver, especially with the

---

43. Thomas, *The Global Resurgence of Religion and the Transformation of International Relations*, 122.

44. Ollapally, *The Politics of Extremism in South Asia*.

45. Ollapally, *The Politics of Extremism in South Asia*, 2–3.

proliferation of jihadist terrorisms and the rise of Islamophobia. Likewise, religion cannot be considered as the main driver because people of different religious affiliations have a long history of dwelling peacefully. There must be other dimensions at play that draw these two (ethnicity and religion) into the mix that provide the occasion for the rise of violent extremism. Why do some turn to extremism and others choose a moderate path?

The notion of the "secular" must be brought into the mix.[46] A weak secularism, more particularly "political secularism," contributes to extremist outcomes when it merges with ethno-religious extremism. Strong political secularism provides that "principled distance" in which the interest of the dominant religious group is not equated with the interest of the state, and the voices of other ethnic-religious groups are not silenced, but allowed enough participation in the political life.

There is one more that is often overlooked or less explored which, for Ollapally, plays a crucial role: "geopolitical identity." This is particularly true in the South Asian context. Conflicts between states and their power plays and the involvement of powerful nation-states all contribute to the drivers of violent extremism. With ethnic, religious, and linguistic identities spilling across state borders, and neighboring nation-states asserting sovereignties being drawn into the conflict, we can see how geopolitical identity intertwines with violent extremism.[47]

What triggers or tilts the balance to extremism needs to be seen, contends Ollapally, against the "broader congruence or competition between secular, ethnoreligious, and geopolitical identity formations. It is the outcome of this struggle (or convergence for that matter) that all too often tips the balance toward moderation or extremism."[48]

Ideology

Some of the drivers of violent extremism can be classified under ideology. These ideological drivers may include political, economic, social, and religious ideologies. Violent extremism is driven by ideologies of different kinds. For white nationalists, this political ideology is white supremacy. With white supremacy as the ideological line, it is not a surprise that it stands in opposition to immigration (except from white countries), multiculturalism, and diversity. Its overriding concern is to maintain the purity of the white

---

46 Ollapally, *The Politics of Extremism in South Asia*, 15.

47. Ollapally, *The Politics of Extremism in South Asia*, 3–4.

48. Ollapally, *The Politics of Extremism in South Asia*, 14.

race. For the Hindu-nationalist it is the revival of Hindutva; for the Sinhalese-fundamentalist, it is Sri-Lanka for the Sinhalese.

Religion, among others, occupies a prominent place in violent extremism discourse and is considered a major driver. There are those who consider religion as the major culprit, such as Christopher Hitchens, who thinks that "religion poisons everything. As well as a menace to civilization, it has become a threat to human survival."[49] Even Hans Küng who theologizes from a Christian perspective assumes a negative view of religion when he says that the "most fanatical and cruelest political struggles are those that have been colored, inspired, and legitimized by religion."[50] Religion plays an important role but, like others, is not the simple singular cause of violent extremism and terrorism. There are more religious people who are not violent extremists and many are liberal and pacifists. Being religious does not make one a violent extremist. Conversely, it does not necessarily follow that being non-religious or secular makes one a non-violent extremist. There are people who do not identify with any religion but are violent extremists. Be it religion or ethnicity or political disenfranchisement, there is no single and linear cause and effect relation when it comes to the development of violent extremism. Yes, religion is critical contributor to the rise of violent extremism, but it is only one among other drivers and violent extremism forms only when the right convergence of context, drivers, and circumstances happen at the right time. Religion, contrary to the Western secular mindset that has given birth to religion as an academic discipline, cannot be separated from the totality of life. If I continue to speak of "religious conflicts," it is primarily to highlight the crucial role of religion in many global conflicts and not to isolate it from the complex web of social relations. It may be a critical triggering factor in some conflicts, but it is hardly the sole factor. "Rarely is religion the principal cause of conflict," argues David Smock, "even when the opposing groups, such as Protestants and Catholics in Northern Ireland, are differentiated by religious identities. But religion is nevertheless a contributing factor to conflict in places as widely scattered as Northern Ireland, the Middle East, the Balkans, Sudan, Indonesia, and Kashmir.[51]

Though violent conflicts with religious motivation are not new, globalization provides a new context and a new framework for understanding the many and most recent expressions of religious conflicts. Not only has globalization accelerated the encounters of various religious believers, it has generated tensions, reactions, and violent conflicts in which religion has

49. Underwood, "Religion and Terrorism," in *The Root of All Evil*, 1.
50. Küng, cited in Smock, *Interfaith Dialogue and Peacebuilding*, 3.
51. Smock, *Interfaith Dialogue and Peacebuilding*, 3.

played a crucial role as well. It is significant to note that as homogenizing and predatory globalization spreads, movements of various motivations—ethnic, religious, nationalistic, cultural—are rising also.[52]

The erosion of religiously-based traditional worldview by modernist, secularist, market-driven worldview and values, the collusion of Western-educated Global South leaders with foreign powers, and the massive violation of people's rights have given birth to cynicism and other forms of antiglobalist sentiments. These are often supported by religious motivations, the most desperate and disastrous expression of which is terrorism—a terrorism intertwined with (and often responding to) the terrorism of the global market and imperial project of some countries of the global north.[53] Within the past decade or so, religion has been associated with the vociferous rhetoric of patriotic and xenophobic political leaders and parties, ethnic cleansing, tribal wars, imperialistic-militaristic American exceptionalism, militant fundamentalism, and the devastating and vicious acts of terrorism and counter-terrorism.

Religious fundamentalism and militant extremism are not new, and they are not the monopoly of one religion. Religious fundamentalism, which does not necessarily lead to militant extremism, is a reaction to . perceived threats: its basic impulse is reactive. In essence, it is a reaction to what is perceived by adherents of a particular religious faith as a threat to their cherished worldview and values or core convictions. In the context of the United States, the term fundamentalism is used to describe conservative Protestant Christians who have rejected the modernist-liberal trend of biblical hermeneutics and theological interpretation as well as the progressive agenda of many mainline Christian denominations. In recent years, however, the term fundamentalism has acquired a fatal twist: it has become closely linked to or is often identified with violent extremism and terrorism.

Let us take a closer look at this fundamentalism to understand it better and respond accordingly. Fundamentalism has common markers even if fundamentalist groups respond differently to circumstances. Richard Antoun identifies some of these markers: a quest for purity in a world perceived as impure; the affirmation of the necessity of certainty in the face of perceived uncertainties; making the sacred scriptures speak directly to present-day issues; sharp engagement with the reigning establishment; taking religion into all facets of life; selective modernization

---

52. Lochhead, *Shifting Realities*, 100.

53. See Berquist, *Strike Terror No More*; Griffith, *The War on Terrorism*; Juergensmeyer, *Terror in the Mind of God*; Duchrow and Hinkelammert, *Property for People*, particularly 109–39; Chomsky, *Pirates and Emperors*.

and acculturation; and understanding the world as the locus of struggle between good and evil.[54]

Gabriel Almond, R. Scott Appleby, and Emmanuel Sivan offer a more in-depth and comprehensive account of fundamentalism's markers. They identify nine characteristics of fundamentalism—five ideological and four organizational. The five ideological markers are reactivity to the marginalization of religion, selectivity, moral Manichaeaism, absolutism and inerrancy, millennialism and messianism. The four organizational markers are elect (chosen membership), sharp boundaries, authoritarian organization, and behavioral requirements.[55]

While I am not going to offer an in-depth examination of these markers, naming them does give us a general sense of the nature of fundamentalism. Looking at this list of markers, it appears that no single marker can stand by itself. We find many of them present in various communities and organizations. Selective appropriations of tradition and sacred texts as well as engagement with modernity are present in various movements we do not normally label as fundamentalist. Further, an additive understanding of all these markers does not constitute fundamentalism. These markers do not constitute a simple checklist. What we call fundamentalism is constituted by the dynamic interaction of various markers, with some markers constituting the organizing center and others providing the energy. Fundamentalism is a functional system. Almond, Appleby, and Sivan name millennialism and messianism as powerful catalysts; selectivity as the way a community pares down the essentials in the face of the threats; and boundary as the way a community defines identity vis-à-vis the outsiders. The overall impulse of fundamentalism, however, is reactivity or reaction to perceived threats.[56]

The most dominant and pervasive form of fundamentalism is primarily a reaction to the perceived threats of modernity, particularly its secularizing thrust and its perceived attendant evils (individualism, sexual permissiveness, high rates of divorce, out-of-wedlock births, alcoholism, drugs, pornography, etc.). Whoever or whatever is the perceived bearer of secularization or responsible for diluting the purity of the faith is considered an enemy. A religious establishment may be identified as an enemy by fundamentalists if that religious establishment is perceived as "liberal." Fundamentalism may be intertwined with cultural and ethno-nationalist components in which case its reaction could be directed against another ethnic group. Another target of fundamentalists' reaction is the secularizing state, particularly when a

54. Antoun, *Understanding Fundamentalism*, 164.

55. Almond et al., *Strong Religion*, 92–98.

56. Almond et al., *Strong Religion*, 99.

state supports such agendas as secular education, divorce, legalized abortion, gay marriages, and empowerment of women. Fundamentalist reaction to the state intensifies when the leaders are perceived as corrupt and as corruptors of the minds of the people. Various forms of fundamentalism, contend Almond, Appleby, and Sivan, "share this family resemblance: across the board they identify three antagonists—the tepid or corrupt religious establishment, the secular state, and secularized civil society—as objects of sustained opposition by true believers."[57]

With fundamentalist groups seeing the world as a battlefield between good and evil, the surrounding environment as a threat to their purity, and various groups as enemies that must be stopped at whatever cost, fundamentalism can easily slide into the slippery slope of violent extremism. By no means is fundamentalism equivalent to violent extremism. There is no direct correlation between fundamentalism and violent extremism. Some fundamentalist groups would rather withdraw into seclusion. But when the right mixture of fundamentalist markers and context come into play, fundamentalism can find expression in violent extremism. Examples abound of fundamentalism providing the ideological motivation for violent extremism. Terrorism, which itself assumes many forms and tactics (such as suicide attack, proxy bombing, piracy, kidnapping, assassination, aircraft hijacking, narco-terrorism, nuclear terrorism, bioterrorism, agro-terrorism, etc.), is one such vehicle of violent fundamentalist extremism.

The resurgence of religion, after years of trying to banish it from the face of the earth, demonstrates the significance of religion in human society, either for good or for ill. Religion plays a positive role, which is why human communities continue to thirst for it. Even those who say they are spiritual but not religious are not, in my understanding, denying religion itself or religious sensibilities. It is not a wholesale rejection of religious sensibilities; rather, it is a response to a context in which organized religion has been identified, if not actively involved, in harming humanity and creation.

The history of religion is, of course, mixed; hence, we cannot be a Pollyanna about its promise. Nonetheless, religion has something positive to offer that modernist-secularism does not; it has something to contribute to the peace and healing of our world that narrow and self-serving nationalism and wars have destroyed; and it has something to contribute to our quest for greater well-being which predatory globalization can destroy and has destroyed. Recognizing this crucial and positive role that religion can play, Richard Falk has this to say: "The prospects of creating some form of human global governance in the 21st century seem likely to depend on whether the

---

57. Almond et al., *Strong Religion*, 101.

religious resurgence is able to provide the basis for a more socially and politically responsible form of globalization than what currently exists."[58]

Paul Knitter has identified two vital, if not determinative, contributions that religions can offer to the building of our global civil society: vision and energy.[59] Primarily through symbols and narratives, religions offer their followers a vision of hope—a vision of a different world and a hope that the world they are currently in can be changed. This vision of a different world, along with the hope that another world is possible, is nourished and vitalized by the energy that religions instill in believers as they act on their conviction. And, when success is not visible on the immediate horizon or nonexistent, committed believers pursue and persevere even when stakes are high, such as threat to one's life, because of the empowering energy that religions provide to their followers.

Crucial, indeed, is the role of religion in society and, much more so, in times of global fragmentation. When the forces of predatory globalization crush communities, impoverish the populace, trample human dignity, push many into diaspora, distort priorities and values, commodify lives, destroy the ecosystem, leave families fragmented and alienated, drive the multitude into cynicism and despair, and consume the lives even of the winners, religion provides transcendent orientation and "antisystemic" force.[60] To be sure, religion can be easily co-opted by traditional and emerging political forces, such as what Mark Juergensmeyer calls "guerrilla antiglobalism," but the crucial point is to channel the vision and energies of the various religious communities for the creation of the global common good.[61] This means that the "antisystemic" force of religion must be directed toward the creation of the common good and an ethics of global responsibility. All religious communities are called to the enormous and complex task of articulating and channeling the "antisystemic" force of religions so that it may become a midwife for the birthing of a new and better tomorrow. Obviously, this cannot be done by one religion.

Globalization and its Discontents

There is a large body of writings that tries to relate predatory globalization to the rise of violent extremism. Again, this is not to be viewed in a simple

---

58. Falk, cited in Raiser, *For a Culture of Life,* 38.

59. Knitter, *One Earth,* 71.

60. Beyer, cited by Schreiter, *The New Catholicity,* 16.

61. Juergensmeyer, "Religious Antiglobalism," 144–45.

one-way traffic, cause-effect relation, but predatory globalization is providing the context or soil that is fertile for violent extremism to grow.

Globalization has been defined in many ways, depending on the concerns and perspective of a particular scholar. There is, however, a general agreement that it is about the increasing interconnections of our common life at the global level, which is also to say that our interconnections extend to specific localities. We are globalized to the point that the global is lived locally and the local is lived globally. The global is not simply "out there" but also "in here," wherever our location is. The slogan "think globally and act locally" is not as simple as it sounds, because the lines crisscross. Even the terms "Third World" and "First World" are complex, for much of the Third World lives in the First World, and the First World in the Third World. Many scholars today would rather use the term "Global South" and "Global north."

Even as there are global trends and connections, the global is being played out also in the local in different ways, or, to put it in another way, the global is received by various localities in different ways.[62] As the globalization of the local is happening, so is the localization of the global. It is not surprising that a hybrid term has emerged: "glocalization" (*dochakuka* in Japanese).[63] Important in studying globalization are not only the global dynamics, but also the local impacts of globalization. What are the impacts of the global interactions in our own localities or neighborhoods? How does the global dynamics manifest in specific localities? Conversely, how is the local influencing and affecting the global, that is, the interconnections of the locals?

Globalization is multidimensional, covering such aspects, to appropriate Arjun Appadurai's categories for mapping the complex and disjunctive order of the new global cultural economy, as technoscapes, financescapes, mediascapes, ideoscapes, and ethnoscapes.[64] I would like to add mediascapes as the universal consequences of the HIV/ AIDS (human immunodeficiency virus/acquired immunodeficiency syndrome), SARS (severe acute respiratory syndrome), swine flu (H1N1), and the most recent and deadly one, COVID-19. Another dimension that needs to be included is ecoscapes as we are being confronted with a serious ecological

---

62. See Hoedemaker, *Secularization and Mission*, especially p. 23 in which he talks about the globalization of what is basically a Western problem and its reception in different cultures.

63. See Robertson, "Globalization," 64. Also, Arthur, *The Globalization of Communications*, 11.

64. Appadurai, "Disjuncture," 295–310. Also cited by Richmond, *Global Apartheid*, 32–33. Also, see Robertson, "Globalization," 53–68. Robertson argues for the multidimensional aspect of globalization.

crisis. Finally, not to be forgotten is religioscapes, especially since encounters among believers of various religions are becoming more common in localities that were once relatively homogenous.

I cannot expound all these dimensions of globalization here, but all these dimensions play an important part in providing a context that fertilizes the soil for the growth of violent extremism, although it also provides a context for the possibility of a global village for its citizens to thrive. In some ways I have already mentioned some of them, such as economics, finance, ideology, and religion. What I would like to mention, although only in a cursory manner, is the role of technology and media in the formation and spread of violent extremism.

Technology and media play an important role in the spread of images and ideas and, often, instantaneously. We are experiencing the power of technologies to "extend" as well as to "compress." As technologies extend our reach, so they also "compress both our sense of time and our sense of space."[65] While not all localities are hooked up to the most advanced communication technologies, many local centers are now within reach by technological advancements. Tied to the rapid advancement in technology is the world of media. Through advancements in media technology, news and entertainment are spread throughout the world instantly. Those with sophisticated communications technologies can watch events that are happening in other parts of the world instantaneously in their living rooms.

The constant flow of information all over the world is a mixed blessing. We are suffering from what Pierre Babin refers to as the "*pollution of information*."[66] The biggest challenge is to sort out the profound from the trivial or the sublime from the ridiculous, which are, of course, shaped by our values and priorities. It is critical that we be more discerning as we are bombarded with competing information and images. To be discerning, however, is not enough: one must be creative and resourceful as well. Antihegemonic movements of various sorts, including violent extremists and terrorists, are not far behind in using new telecommunications technologies. Technology and media have played an important role in the spread of violent extremism and in the recruitment of terrorists. The idea that "[g]lobal jihadism is the product of a globalized world, particularly its media," makes sense.[67] The media has given the jihadist the opportunity to achieve "symbolic recognition" in the absence of "real recognition."

65. Schreiter, *The New Catholicity*, 11.

66. Babin, cited in Arthur, *The Globalization of Communications*, 24; emphasis original.

67. Khosrokhavar, "The Psychology of the Global Jihadists," in *The Fundamentalist Mindset*, 147.

When the image of the Twin Towers being blown up by two hijacked air-crafts was aired in major media outlets for months, it gave the actors the chance to achieve the fame that they had not received from the West, from their fellow Muslim believers, and the whole world. The exhibitionism of September 11, 2001 on the world scale television for months was a huge self-image booster for the long-humiliated victims who turned into trium-phant conquerors capable of terrorizing the West.

While we can celebrate some of its achievements, globalization has also become a juggernaut: homogenizing culture, crushing and marginal-izing many, undermining traditional beliefs and community life, destruct-ing the ecosystem, and spreading various forms of diseases. For those marginalized and crushed, globalization is not moving to the desired "global village" but "global pillage." Instead of the dreamed global village, many have experienced globalization as a nightmare. Global pillage or global fragmentation is the underside to the official version of globaliza-tion. This is a view from those who have been victimized by globaliza-tion. The concern and perspective of the Global South and marginalized communities start with this unfortunate reality of a globalized world that is fragmented economically, politically, and socially, which has serious repercussions in the field of religion.[68]

Among those who have been crushed or marginalized by globalization, we can speak of the spread of a global culture of despair, cynicism, power-lessness, and fatalism. Feeling betrayed by the promises of globalization, many have succumbed to false hope. A global culture of powerlessness and fatalism can be observed. The sense of powerlessness of many has reached the level of fatalism. The sense of powerlessness, fatalism, and cynicism may find other expressions such as "badass" behavior and violence.

It would be inaccurate, however, to confine one's presentation of the global culture only in terms of homogenization or the globalized culture of escape or surrender to the inevitable. Globalization has generated "an-tiglobalist" movements of various sorts, ethnification, primitivism, and counter-hegemonic movements, which I distinguish from "antiglobalism." "Antiglobalism" may take, says Robert Schreiter, the form of either funda-mentalism or revanchism. Whatever form it takes, its logic is retreat from the onslaught of globalization altogether.[69] It is significant to note that as the homogenizing globalization spreads, movements of various motivations—ethnic, religious, nationalistic, cultural—are also rising. The threat of mono-culturalism brought by the homogenizing globalization has encountered the

68. Wilfred, "The Language of Human Rights," 212–13.
69. Schreiter, *The New Catholicity*, 21–25.

assertion of multiculturalism and multi-ethnic identities. "Universalism, both secular and religious," says David Lockhead, "has encountered the rise of a stubborn particularism in the guise of resurgent nationalism."[70] As new boundaries are being redefined and artificially imposed divisions of the Cold War politics vanish, ethnic conflicts and culture wars have intensified. In this situation in which people attempt to redraw boundaries that once seemed safe, new forms of "heresies" are likely to be identified.[71]

It may not be fully accurate that this phenomenon be totally attributed to predatory and homogenizing globalization. Nonetheless, one major reaction to the rapacious activities of predatory globalization that has drawn the attention of the world and has shaped geopolitics is the rise of fundamentalism and its linkage with international terrorism.

As a shorthand term that represents not just the economy but also the spread of Western project and modernity, globalization has surfaced in many fundamentalist militants' rhetoric as a threat that must be stopped by all means and at all cost. Often undergirded by religious motivations, the militants see their acts of terrorism as a religious duty directed against those who represent, or against any representation of, ungodliness, decadence, and unbridled political and economic greed. Fundamentalist militants feel that the traditional values that they hold dear have been eroded by the global capitalist market or by Hollywood entertainment industries. After years of seeing their dreams betrayed and cherished cultural-religious values undermined, many have "lost faith" in the Western-secular-democratic project and are turning to religion for vision and empowerment.

Counterterrorism

By its very name, it is intended to respond to, eliminate, or end terrorism, but it may be working contrary to its intended outcome. It could be that, as Schirch suggested, "State-based responses to terrorism become part of the ecology of causes driving violent extremism."[72] Several research projects have found a correlation or link between counterterrorism and an increase in terrorism. What has been purported as surgical strike is far from the truth, for many of these surgical strikes have much collateral damages. Drone warfare, for example, has killed more civilians than terrorists, which then becomes an occasion for recruiting more terrorists. The collateral damage of the war on terror extends beyond the direct victims of drone or surgical strikes. Funding

70. Lochhead, *Shifting Realities*, 100.
71. Kutz, *Gods in the Global Village*, 213–14.
72. Schirch, *The Ecology of Violent Extremism*, 15.

for education, health, and other services to support the needy and build resilient communities has been cut or sacrificed in favor of funding the war on terror, often without much transparency and public accountability. Moreover, as the war on terror intensifies, state governments that have joined this war have also drifted toward authoritarianism. And, in the name of security, the public has been willing to sacrifice civil liberties. Here is a solution to a problem that has larger repercussions to human security, which contributes to the problem it is trying to solve.

Framework, Drivers, and Convergences: Concluding Comments

From this study, it shows that the best way to study the growth of violent extremism is not to think of cause and effect, whether single or multiple causes. It is not even of multiple and multi-directional causes and effects. Much more helpful is to think of convergence and confluence of various factors and drivers and their interactive dynamics. An ecological metaphor or living systems, as suggested earlier, is more helpful in dealing with the emergence, growth, and spread of violent extremism.

With the complexity and the multiple factors that are involved in understanding violent extremism, there is no single field of discipline that can fully explain or address the issue of violent extremism, much more to help undo it. Addressing violent extremism requires the cooperation of various fields of discipline and various groups, including governmental agencies, private, and civil society, both at the local and international level. Beyond dealing with symptoms of violent extremism, we must deal with deep structural factors that breed violent extremism, which means addressing the drivers. It tells us that a stable, economically productive, sustainable, healthy, equitable, peaceful, resilient, and participatory society is our strongest defense against the growth of violent extremism and terrorism.

Bibliography

Achar, Gilbert. *The Clash of Barbarisms: The Making of the New World Disorder*. New York: Routledge, 2016.

Ahmed, Akbar S. *Islam Today: A Short Introduction to the Muslim World*. New York: Tauris, 1999.

Ali, Tariq. *The Clash of Fundamentalisms: Crusades, Jihads and Modernity*. London: Verso, 2002.

Almond, Gabriel, et al. *Strong Religion: The Rise of Fundamentalisms around the World*. Chicago: The University of Chicago Press, 2003.

Antoun, Richard. *Understanding Fundamentalism: Christian, Islamic, and Jewish Movements.* 2nd ed. New York: Rowman & Littlefield, 2008.

Appadurai, Arjun. "Disjuncture and difference in the global Cultural Economy." In *Global Culture: Nationalism, Globalization and Modernity,* edited by M. Featherstone, 295–310. London: Sage, 1990.

Berquist, Jon, ed. *Strike Terror No More: Theology, Ethics, and the New War.* St. Louis: Chalice, 2002.

Borg, Marcus. *The Heart of Christianity: Rediscovering a Life of Faith.* New York: HarperSanFrancisco, 2003.

Chomsky, Noam. *Pirates and Emperors, Old and New: International Terrorism in the Real World.* Cambridge: South End, 2002.

Clarke, Sathianathan. *Competing Fundamentalisms: Violent Extremism in Christianity, Islam, and Hinduism.* Louisville: Westminster John Knox, 2017.

Delgado, Sharon. *Shaking the Gates of Hell: Faith-Led Resistance to Corporate Globalization.* Minneapolis: Fortress, 2007.

Duchrow, Ulrich, and Franz Hinkelammert. *Property for People, Not for Profit: Alternatives to the Global Tyranny of Capital.* Geneva: WCC Publications, 2004.

Fernandez, Eleazar, ed. *Teaching for a Multifaith World.* Eugene, OR: Pickwick, 2017.

———. *Teaching for a Culturally Diverse and Racially Just World.* Eugene, OR: Cascade, 2013.

Griffith, Lee. *The War on Terrorism and the Terror of God.* Grand Rapids: Eerdmans, 2002.

Hoedemaker, Bert. *Secularization and Mission: A Theological Essay.* Harrisburg, PA: Trinity, 1998.

Huntington, Samuel. *The Clash of Civilizations and the Remaking of World Order.* New York: Simon & Schuster, 1996.

Juergensmeyer, Mark. *Terror in the Mind of God: The Global Rise of Religious Violence.* Updated ed. Berkeley: University of California Press, 2000.

———. "Religious Antiglobalism." In *Religion in Global Civil Society,* edited by Mark Juergensmeyer, 135–48. New York: Oxford University Press, 2005.

Knitter, Paul. *One Earth, Many Religions: Multifaith Dialogue and Global Responsibility.* Maryknoll, NY: Orbis, 1995.

Küng, Hans. *Global Responsibility: In Search of a New World Ethic.* New York: Crossroad, 1991.

Kutz, Lester. *Gods in the Global Village: The World's Religions in Sociological Perspective.* Thousand Oaks, CA: Pine Forge, 1995.

Lochhead, David. *Shifting Realities: Information Technology and the Church.* Geneva: WCC Publications, 1997.

Lorde, Audre. *Sister Outsider: Essays and Speeches.* Freedom, CA: The Crossing, 1984.

Ollapally, Deepa, M. *The Politics of Extremism in South Asia.* New York: Cambridge University Press, 2008.

Palmer, Parker. *Healing the Heart of Democracy: The Courage to Create a Politics Worthy of the Human Spirit.* San Francisco: Jossey-Bass, 2011.

Patna Regional Theological Center, ed. *The Recent Attacks on Christians in Orissa: A Theological Response.* Patna: Prabhat Prakashan, 2009.

Peters, Ted. *Sin: Radical Evil in Soul and Society.* Grand Rapids: Eerdmans, 1994.

Putnam, Robert, and David Campbell. *American Grace: How Religion Divides and Unites Us.* New York: Simon & Schuster, 2010.

Raiser, Konrad. *Ecumenism in Transition: A Paradigm Shift in the Ecumenical Movement.* Geneva: WCC Publications, 1991.

Richmond, Anthony H. *Global Apartheid: Refugees, Racism, and the New World Order.* New York: Oxford University Press, 1994.

Robertson, Roland. "Globalization and the Future of 'Traditional Religion.'" In *God and Globalization: Religion and the Powers of the Common Life,* Vol. 1, edited by Max Stackhouse with Peter Paris, 53–68. Harrisburg, PA: Trinity, 2000.

Schirch, Lisa, ed. *The Ecology of Violent Extremism: Perspectives on Peacebuilding and Human Security.* New York: Rowman & Littlefield, 2018.

Schreiter, Robert. *The New Catholicity: Theology between the Global and the Local.* Maryknoll, NY: Orbis, 1997.

Smock, David. *Interfaith Dialogue and Peacebuilding.* United States Institute of Peace, 2002.

Strozier, Charles, B., et al, eds. *The Fundamentalist Mindset: Psychological Perspectives on Religion, Violence, and History.* New York: Oxford University Press, 2010.

Thomas, Scott M. *The Global Resurgence of Religion and the Transformation of International Relations: The Structural Struggle for the Soul of the Twenty-First Century.* New York: Palgrave, 2005.

Underwood, Lori, ed. *The Root of All Evil: Religious Perspectives on Terrorism.* New York: Lang, 2013.

Wilfred, Felix. "The Language of Human Rights: An Ethical Esperanto." In *Frontiers in Asian Theology: Emerging Trends,* edited by R. S. Sugirtharajah. Maryknoll, NY: Orbis, 1994.

2

Pedagogy and Curriculum to Prevent and Counter Violent Extremism

Human Rights, Justice, Peace, and Democracy

—REY TY

Introduction

Problem Statement

Violent extremism occurs in many parts of the world, including Asia. Violent extremism has spread from Bangladesh to India, Myanmar, Pakistan, the Philippines, West Papua in Indonesia, and elsewhere.[1] In Bangladesh, extremists target and kill Buddhists, Christians, and Hindus who espouse secularism.[2] In Myanmar, violent extremists attacked the Rohingya who, as a result, fled to the neighboring Bangladesh as refugees.[3] In Pakistan, terrorists and suicide bombers attack Christian neighborhoods and non-mainstream Ahmadi Muslim communities.[4] In the Philippines, the security and paramilitary forces engage in extrajudicial execution to exterminate drug pushers, drug users, and people who voice their opposition to government policies, among whom are journalists and

---

1. Ty, *Statement of Concern Over Religiously Motivated Violence.* Executive Committee of the Christian Conference of Asia.

2. Ty, *Pastoral Solidarity Visit to Bangladesh.* Christian Conference Asia.

3. Ty, "The Rohingya Refugee Crisis," 16.

4. Ty, *Report of the Pastoral Solidarity Team Visit to Pakistan.* Christian Conference of Asia.

church people. In West Papua, security forces unceremoniously gun down peaceful indigenous Papuan protesters.[5]

Underlying causes of violent extremism include many factors, among which are inequality, poverty and oppression, as well as miseducation, fake news, and socialization that spawn negative otherness, discrimination, hatred, and racism. This chapter unearths more causes of violent extremism in the findings section. Societies can counter violent extremism using the hard approach or the soft approach. The reactive or hard approach, as in the case of Indonesia, involves sending people to the so-called deradicalization centers and taking over of some mosques.[6] The proactive or soft approach involves using education as a tool to promote peace and to counter violent extremism. The rise of the far-right movements intensifies xenophobia, which poses challenges to education.[7] This chapter deals with the soft approach of the use of education to defeat violent extremism.

Questions

This chapter addresses the subject of curriculum and pedagogy, raising the following research queries:

1. What pedagogical practices shall we employ in the work of ending violent extremisms?

2. What shall be the elements of the curriculum?

3. What shall we teach in a world of violent extremism?

4. What case study demonstrates the successful use of education to undo violent extremism?

Purpose

To probe and respond to the queries in the current context of violent extremism, the purpose of this chapter is to explain the pedagogy appropriate to quash violent extremism, to discuss the elements of the curriculum, and to identify the content in teaching and learning to promote mutual understanding.

5. Ty, *Pastoral Solidarity Visit to West Papua*. Christian Conference of Asia.

6. Jones, *Countering violent extremism in Indonesia*.

7. Kitayama, *The rise of the far right in Japan and challenges posed for education*.

Theory of Violent Extremism

Preventing violent extremism (PVE) refers to soft approaches that deal with VE proactively before it happens, whereas countering violent extremism (CVE) denotes hard approaches that deal with VE reactively after it occurs. PVE is akin to development work and addresses the root causes of VE, while CVE is analogous to counterterrorism.[8] Violent extremist organizations (VEO) of all political, religious, and cultural shades exist around the world.

There are precursors to the concepts of CVE and PVE. CVE was a sanitized term that replaced the criticized counterterrorism approaches, which depended on suppressive and intelligence-gathering tactics.[9] In fact, to see the close affinity between terrorism and violent extremism, counter-terrorism think tanks house many pieces of literature about violent extremism.[10] Ban Ki-moon, then the United Nations Secretary-General, first presented the term PVE to the General Assembly (2015) in the U.N. Plan of Action to Prevent Violent Extremism, identifying the push and pull factors as the root causes of violent extremism. PVE takes place at three levels: (1) primary prevention, aiming at everyone in the whole population; (2) secondary prevention, targeting at defined risk groups who are prone to perpetrate acts of crime; and, (3) tertiary prevention, pursuing individuals and groups who exhibit problematic behavior. CVE and PVE lie in a continuum from tactical repressive measures to strategic trust-building efforts.[11] See Figure 2.1 below.

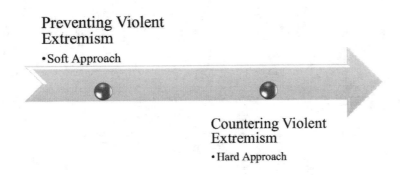

Preventing Violent Extremism
• Soft Approach

Countering Violent Extremism
• Hard Approach

Figure 2.1: Continuum of Eradicating Violent Extremism

8. Sommers, *Youth and the field of countering violent extremism.*
9. Austin and Giessmann, *Transformative approaches to violent extremism.*
10. Nasser-Eddine, et al., *Countering violent extremism.*
11. RAN, *Lessons from Crime Prevention in Preventing Violent Extremism by Police.*

There are three phases in violent extremism: (1) the sensitivity phase, (2) the group membership phase, and (3) the action phase.[12] The sensitivity phase involves a person's identification with factors that engender violent extremism, which are in three general levels: the macro structural level, meso cultural and group level, and micro individual level,[13] which include the push and pull factors. More specific factors are: (1) individual, (2) social, (3) political, (4) religious, (5) ideological, (6) cultural, (7) identity driven, (8) deprivation or traumatic experiences, (9) group dynamics, (10) role of recruiters to the cause of violent extremism, and (11) the impact of social media.[14] Drivers for the rise of violent extremism include centrifugal or push and centripetal or pull factors.[15] The push factors are the structural conditions, while the pull factors are the personal motivations. Some major systemic push factors include the lack of economic and social upward mobility; discrimination; marginalization; lack of good governance; erosion of the rule of law; human rights abuses; longstanding unresolved hostilities; and radicalization while under detention. Among the psychological pull factors are individual biography and stimuli; shared grievances and victimization as a result of hierarchy, oppression, or foreign interference; distorted beliefs, ideologies, as well as cultural and ethnic dissimilarities; leadership and social networks. The General Assembly (2006) of the United Nations adds intolerance and extremism as the root causes of the rise of acts of violence.[16] Studies show that in many neighborhoods and villages, community elders exclude young people who are therefore easy preys of VEOs for recruitment.[17] In addition, when state repression surges, VEO activities increase as well.[18] See Figure 2 below.

12. Doosje, et al., "Terrorism, radicalization, and de-radicalization," 79–84.

13. Köhler, *Understanding De-radicalization: Methods, Tools, and Programs for Countering Violent Extremism.*

14. Ranstorp, *The root causes of violent extremism.*

15. General Assembly, *Plan of Action to Prevent Violent Extremism: Report of the Secretary-General.*
Report A/70/674.

16. General Assembly, *The UN Global Counter-Terrorism Strategy.* (A/RES/60/288).

17. Sommers, *Thwarting Violent Extremism: A New Approach.*

18. Sommers, *Thwarting Violent Extremism: A New Approach.*

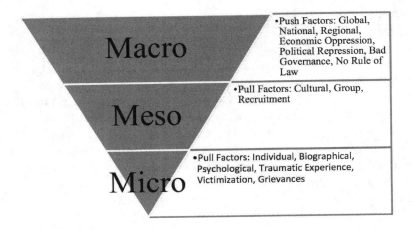

**Figure 2.2: Push and Pull Factors at the Micro, Meso,
and Macro Levels for Violent Extremism**

Literature Review of the Concept "Violent Extremism"

The term violent extremism is broader than the term terrorism. Yet, both terms are problematic, as they defy having universally fixed definitions and lack conceptual precision. U.S. President George W. Bush (September 16, 2001) used the terms "war on terrorism"[19] and a few days later Bush (September 20, 2001) used the term "war on terror" in his speech to Congress.[20] The term terrorism fell into disrepute; hence, the United Nations prefers to use the term violent extremism in its stead. Different governments, such as Australia, Canada, Norway, Sweden, the United Kingdom, and the United States, as well as intergovernmental organizations, such as the Organization for Economic Cooperation and Development (OECD) and the United Nations Educational, Scientific, and Cultural Organization (UNESCO) have their own formal definitions of violent extremism. Some definitions stress that beliefs alone is a sufficient indicator of violent extremism, while others indicate that violent extremism is a function of both beliefs and acts, as discussed below.

The Parliament of Australia (2015) defined the term violent extremism as people's views and activities that either support or utilize violence to

19. Bush, Remarks by the President upon arrival. The South Lawn: White House.
20. Bush, *Address to a Joint Session of Congress and the American People.*

accomplish ideological, religious or political objectives, including terrorist acts as well as other types of communal violence, which are politically driven.[21] Public Safety Canada (2009) refers to violent extremism as politically, religiously, or ideologically motivated offense, clarifying that these views are only problematic and are a menace to national security when these ideas turn into violent acts.[22] The Norwegian Ministry of Justice and Public Safety (2014) indicates that violent extremism identifies violent extremism as activities of individuals or groups, which have no qualms about the employment of violence in furtherance of their ideological, religious, or political aims.[23] The Government Offices of Sweden identifies violent extremism as the belief according to which one accepts, supports, or uses the use of violence.[24] HM Government of U.K. (2015; 2011) states that extremism is the verbal or active rejection of basic values, such as individual liberty, tolerance of different religions, mutual respect, democracy, and rule of law, as well as calls for the death of British armed forces everywhere in the world.[25] The U.S. Agency for International Development (USAID) indicates that violent extremism involves the advocacy, engagement in, preparation, or support for violence, which is ideologically driven or justified in order to advance economic, social, or political goals.[26] The Federal Bureau of Investigation (FBI) adds that violent extremism includes the encouragement, condoning, justification, or support for acts of violence in order to attain social, economic, ideological, political, or religious aims.[27]

As far as intergovernmental organizations are concerned, the Organization for Economic Cooperation and Development (OECD) defines violent extremism as the promotion of ideas that provoke and enflame violence to advance certain opinions and incite animosity that set in motion violence between and among communities.[28] UNESCO (2017) explains that violent

21. Parliament of Australia, *Australian Government Measures to Counter Violent Extremism: A Quick Guide.*

22. Public Safety Canada, "Assessing the Risk of Violent Extremists," 1–2.

23. Norwegian Ministry of Justice and Public Safety, *Action Plan Against Radicalization and Violent Extremism.*

24. Government Offices of Sweden, "Sweden Action Plan to Safeguard Democracy Against Violence Promoting Extremism," in *Government Communication* 2011/12:44.

25. HM Government (UK), Counter-extremism strategy. London: Counter-Extremism Directorate, Home Office, 2015; HM Government (UK), Prevent strategy. Norwich: The Stationery Office, 2011.

26. USAID, The Development Response to Violent Extremism and Insurgency: Putting Principles into Practice. *USAID Policy.*

27. USAID, The Development Response to Violent Extremism and Insurgency: Putting Principles into Practice. *USAID Policy.*

28. Organization for Economic Cooperation and Development Assistance

extremism encompasses the belief and actions of people who support or utilize the use of violence to attain political, religious, or ideological goals.[29]

In the course of my lived experiences in coordinating interreligious
and peace programs and reading mainstream news and journal articles,
I am engaged in a phenomenological investigation and description of the
meaning of the terms and phenomena of terrorism, violent extremism, and
radicalization, all of which are vague political concepts, for which reason I
oppose their usage. First, rather than terrorism, I would rather use the terms
violations of the rule of law, criminal laws, international human rights laws,
international humanitarian laws, and the laws of war, as there are clear indicators in all these legal instruments. Second, I am likewise worried with the
use of the term violence, as oftentimes we only focus on physical harm that
one commits against another but forget structural violence, which includes
economic oppression and exploitation.[30] Third, I reject the popular use of the
term "radicalization" and "extremism" in the mainstream news media, which
have deeply penetrated and populated the scholarly literature in a wrong way.
The term radical in political science parlance refers to the left-wing ideology,
which is a well-known concept in the academic literature. Left-wingers are
radical as they seek to dig into the root (etymology: Latin *radix*) causes of social problems and seek to engage in progressive social change, not to return
to the old ways through otherness, marginalization, and coercive means, as
with the present-day use of the term radicalization. Correctly used, the term
radical refers to and falls on the extreme left, while reactionary falls on the
extreme right. However, the term radical now wrongly refers to extreme-
right wing ideology, which defies simple logic. I have the same squabble
with the term extremism, as extremism should be applicable to both the left
and the right, but the popular usage now wrongly refers only to the extreme
right-wing reactionary ideology.

Though often starting with the proviso according to which any religious,
cultural, or ethnic group can be engaged in violent extremism, many organizations wrongly pin down Muslims only as perpetrators of violent extremism.
Two institutions have it right and have done an outstanding job to identify reactionary and ultra-right wing groups now falling under the rubric of "violent
extremism," though I still have reservations for the use of this terminology.
They are the Southern Poverty Law Center (SPLC) and the Radicalization
Awareness Network (RAN) Center of Excellence. SPLC maps out ultra-right

---

Committee, *DAC High Level Meeting, Communiqué of 19 February 2016.*

29. UNESCO, *Preventing Violent Extremism through Education: A Guide for Policy Makers.*

30. Galtung, "Violence, Peace and Peace Research."

wing and reactionary White nationalist and other groups that promote hate and engage in hate crimes. RAN conducts research on far-right extremism (RAN, 2020) and Islamist extremism.[31] However, we must be aware that funders, including governments, of researchers and think tanks directly or indirectly dictate the discourse, norms, and ideology that underpin reports and other research outputs regarding violent extremism.[32]

Nevertheless, condensing from the different definitions above, I now concede and use the term extremism to denote extreme-right reactionary ideology, which is farther to the right of the conservative ideology that resorts to the use of physical force to achieve certain goals. Why only extreme-right wing and not extreme-left wing? That is because the long-standing, well-established, and well-defined term to refer to left-wing political violence is social and political revolution. Hence, I make it a point to clarify that violent extremism is not to be confused with revolution, as the agenda are polar opposites, though some popular literature and news items systematically commit this semantic and conceptual error.

Intolerance and hatred of one group of people over other ethnic, national, cultural, religious, or political communities at times leads to the persecution and acts of physical violence that target the latter.[33] Violent extremism (VE) refers to the extreme right-wing reactionary ideology that resorts to acts of physical violence with a view to resolve differences and conflicts to restore or maintain hegemonic control over society, economy, politics, culture, and religion, harking back to the bygone golden era of "pure race" or "pure religion." Violent extremism can be political, religious, or race-related and operate locally, nationally, or internationally. Violent extremism identifies enemies who are the targets of hatred and attacks.[34] The Southern Poverty Law Center, for instance, regularly updates a hate map across the U.S. A violent extremist can be atheist, Buddhist, Christian, Hindu, Jewish, or Muslim.[35]

Methodology

This chapter dialectically uses the qualitative ethnographic, phenomenological, and discourse analysis research design to search for meanings from

31. Ranstorp, *Lessons from Crime Prevention in Preventing Violent Extremism.*

32. Christodoulou, "Boosting Resilience" and "Safeguarding Youngsters at Risk."

33. Teaching Tolerance Project, *The Shadow of Hate: A history of Intolerance in America.*

34. Ahmed and Bashirov, "Religious fundamentalism and violent extremism."

35. Southern Poverty Law Center, *Hate groups across the U.S.*

my lived experiences with participants in programs that I have coordinated in the U.S. and Thailand. Through ethnography, I have been engaged in participant observation in several interreligious and peace programs. With the use of discourse analysis, I am able to analyze the different meanings and interpretations of violent extremism as well as expose the relationship between knowledge and power.[36] Phenomenology is the science of experience. It refers to the study of phenomena, things, concepts, ideas, and events as they appear in a person's lived experiences and relations with others in the world, the purpose of which is to explain the essence, structure, and meaning of phenomena, in this case, my perspectives of the phenomena related to violent extremism.[37] My personal experiences in working with participants from different parts of the world in different educational settings whose aim was to quash violent extremism provide rich data that are the fodder for the findings in this chapter. I use several sources of data for triangulation involving multiple case studies. Research methods for data collection include participant observation, interviews, and document analysis that lead to the inductive grounded theory. This chapter presented both the emic views of students and participants as well as my etic views as an outsider, all of whom are co-producers of knowledge.

My database includes case studies involving conflict areas. In the U.S., I have coordinated youth leadership programs for Muslim, Christian, indigenous and minority adult and youth leaders from the Philippines where there are revolutions taking place; bi-communal Greek Orthodox and Muslim youth programs from both sides of divided Cyprus; and, women's leadership programs for Sri Lankans when the civil war was raging. In Thailand, I have coordinated several programs on peace building, conflict resolution, and human rights, involving participants from Australia, Aotearoa New Zealand, East Asia, South Asia, Southeast Asia, and West Asia. In addition, I have also led field visits to conflict areas, such as Bangladesh, India, Myanmar, Pakistan, refugee camps in the Myanmar-Thai border, and West Papua in Indonesia. Additionally, in my official capacity as Peacebuilding Coordinator, I have visited Bahrain, Lebanon, and the United Arab Emirates, interviewing prominent governmental and civil society leaders. See Figure 2.3 below.

36. Foucault, *The Archaeology of Knowledge.*
37. Heidegger, *Being and Time*; Husserl, *Ideas.*

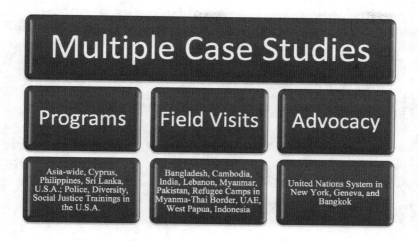

Figure 2.3: Ethnographic Participant Observation in Multiple Case Studies

Findings

Pedagogy

This section answers the first research question: What pedagogical practices shall we employ in the work of defeating violent extremisms? The term pedagogy has two meanings. Etymologically, it has two Greek words: *paidos* and *agogos*, which mean child and leader, respectively, which means the teaching profession or the science of education. In the strictest sense, pedagogy refers to the education of children. However, in the wider sense, as in the case of how Freire used the word, pedagogy refers to education in general.[38] The education of adults is andragogy.[39]

The youngest Nobel peace laureate thus far Malala Yousafzai said: "With gun you can kill terrorists; with education you can kill terrorism."[40] Clearly, the United Nations Educational, Scientific, and Cultural Organization[41] (UNESCO, 2017) and the United Nations General Assembly[42] (2015 December 17) emphasize that education plays important role to prevent

38. Freire, *Pedagogy of the Oppressed*.

39. Knowles, *The Modern Practice of Adult Education: From Pedagogy to Andragogy*.

40. Yousafzai, *Violent extremism and communications*, 42.

41. UNESCO, *Preventing violent extremism through education: A guide for policy makers*.

42. General Assembly, December 17, 2015.

violent extremism and it can take place in different settings. It can be in formal education, non-formal education, and informal education. **Formal education** refers to teaching and learning in school settings, from pre-school to tertiary level education where students get some officially recognized certification of attendance and satisfactory completion of courses, such as diplomas. **Non-formal education** refers to short-term courses that academic institutions, places of worship, not-for-profit organizations, or business enterprises organize, at times offering a certificate at the end of the program. **Informal education** refers to learning in family, daily-life, social movements, and other settings outside the school. See Figure 2.4 below.

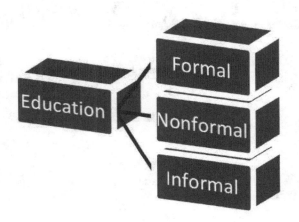

Figure 2.4: Types of Education

In terms of the time during which education takes place, it can be either proactive or reactive. Educational intervention to defeat violent extremism must take place at the earliest time possible at home, in the school, in the community, and places of worship. As a saying goes, old dogs have difficulties learning new tricks. However, educating people not to espouse or condone violent extremism after it occurs is still necessary. Pro-active education takes place before acts of violent extremism happens, while reactive education occurs after they transpire. Children at a very young age enter into values formation in order to learn inclusive values while adults need to engage in values transformation to unlearn prejudices that lead to violent extremism. When acts of violent extremism take place, they are teachable moments that the family, schools, workplaces, places of worship, organizations, governments, mass media, and social media can use to teach and promote inclusive cooperation and oppose exclusiveness and bigotry. See Figure 2.5 below.

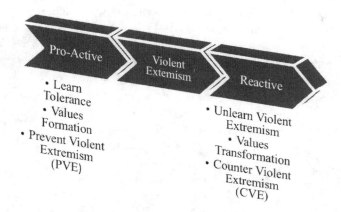

Figure 2.5: Time Element in Education to Eradicate Violent Extremism

Children and adults learn differently. In traditional educational systems, children are engaged in formative learning during which they learn top down from formal sources of authority and socialization, whereas adults are engaged in transformative learning during which they see distortions in their own views, emotions, and values. However, non-traditional or alternative children's education, such as Montessori, is more experiential, rather than teacher-led, pedantic, and authoritative.[43]

Adults learn best when the following conditions exist.[44] First, education must be problem-centered, not content-oriented. In this case, education must focus on identifying and solving the problem of violent extremism. Second, experience is the basis upon which adults learn. Following this line of thinking, education must center on sharing personal experiences related to violent extremism. Third, adult learners need to know the reasons for which they are learning something. Thus, adult learners need to know that the objective of the educational program is to abolish violent extremism. Fourth, as adults are internally—not externally—motivated, they are ready to learn what is relevant to their life or work. Hence, the learning content must not be abstract but relate to real-life issues of violent extremism. Being self-directed, adults must be responsible for deciding to study as well as engage in planning and evaluating their instruction. Clearly, adult learners do

43. Rousseau, *Emile or on Education.*
44. Knowles, *The Modern Practice of Adult Education: From Pedagogy to Andragogy.*

not want instructors to tell them top-down what they need to learn. Rather, adult learners must be involved in conceptualizing the content and process of learning how to suppress violent extremism.

Institutions of socialization include, among others, family, school, places of worship, and workplace where people learn new ideas, skill sets, and values. Socialization refers to the process by which people learn and internalize certain values and attitudes that they will accept as their own, which in their mind are normal, natural, and correct. Children learn new concepts, abilities, and principles early on in life, which could promote tolerance on the one hand or violent extremism on the other hand. Hence, ending violent extremism has to start when children are in the formative stages.

There are different stages in learning: dualism, multiplicity, relativism, and commitment.[45] Individuals move from being immature learners to mature thinkers. Problems arise when individuals or groups of persons have immature dualist thinking in which they believe there is only one correct way of seeing or doing things. They are the ones who potentially would erupt into acts of violent extremism, as they only see one way of being, becoming, and doing things. They only rely on their parents, teachers, or religious leaders for the one and only correct answer to their queries. In the worst-case scenario, alienated young adults fall victim to the brainwashing of their recruiters who exploit their suffering to join the cause of violent extremism. As they progress in time, they see a multiplicity of social realities outside of their usual surroundings and classroom lectures. They still stick to their own viewpoints but open their eyes to the world at large beyond the confines of their homes and schools. As they further develop, they begin to understand that ideas and principles depend on specific contexts and perceptions. In this way, they start to engage in more nuanced and critical thinking. They become mature thinkers when they contemplate and reason beyond what books and authoritative figures say, critically creating and committed to their own principles and philosophies. Mature thinkers learn to be comfortable with differences and diversity. See Figure 2.6 below.

---

45. Perry, *Forms of Ethical and Intellectual Development in the College Years.*

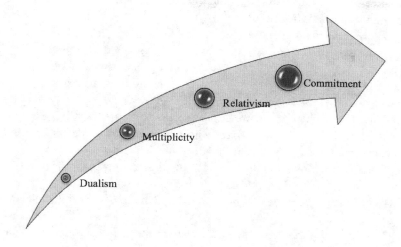

**Figure 2.6: Intellectual and Ethical Development
from Immature to Mature Thinkers**

Adults use a disorienting dilemma, during which things happen that do not fit their pre-conceived notions, as an opportunity to unlearn their assumptions and learn new things, hence engaging in a personal transformation of their perspectives about themselves and society, belief systems, and behavior.[46] For this reason, adults will do well to get out of their comfort zone and experience disorienting dilemmas where values clash, which provide intense awareness and opportunities of change as well as teachable moments as well as possibilities for transformative learning. For example, oftentimes, people of the same color, ethnic, religious, national, or cultural backgrounds sit together at lunch. Instead of doing that, they can get out of their bubbles to see, meet, mingle with, interact, listen to, enter into dialogue with, debate, or engage in some common activities with people of different colors, religions, national origins, economic status, or castes during which they will experience a disorienting dilemma. In this way, they can learn about the situation, say, of African Americans, women, refugees, migrant workers, rural folks, poor people, or others from different castes. The context in which learning takes place as well as ethical and social concerns offers constraints to adult learners.[47] There are both opportunities and

46. Mezirow, *Transformative Dimensions of Adult Learning.*
47. Merriam and Baumgartner, *Learning in Adulthood.*

challenges that shape adult learning in relation to social justice, corporate globalization, and inclusion.[48]

Three elements are important in the education to quell violent extremism: the content, the process, and the relationship with the status quo. First, the succeeding sections discuss the curriculum and the content. Second, the educational process varies. In schools, teaching and learning are usually top-down where the teacher imparts knowledge to students. However, despite this hierarchical structure in schools, teachers can enter into Freirean horizontal dialogue (Freire, 2017) with the pupils, thereby changing the power dynamics. Teachers can provide a safe zone to facilitate discussions by posing questions about the heritage, language, culture, national origin of pupils, as well as hopes and fears. When the pupils answer these questions, they become the source of knowledge about their own realities. Posing questions, therefore, empowers the pupils. The power relations in the classroom transform from top-down to bottom up through horizontal dialogue among the members of the peer group of the pupils. As far as adults are concerned, for learning to be effective, they must be engaged in a bottom-up educational process, which takes into consideration their actual experiences and perceptions in relation to violent extremism. Third, education must not merely be the reproduction of the existing knowledge and values, which might even be at the core of the causes of violent extremism. Thus, the purpose of education to undo violent extremism is the social change: the transformation of the knowledge, skills, and attitudes of individuals, groups, and society toward things as they are in social reality.

Curriculum

This section answers the second research question: How shall we organize the content of the curriculum? Curriculum refers to the subjects, content, lessons, and courses that schools, colleges, universities, and academic institutions offer. The content of the curriculum that do away with violent extremism must encompass (1) knowledge, (2) skills, and (3) attitudes (KSA) in formal, non-formal, and informal educational settings. In formal education, teaching and learning not to espouse but to reject violent extremism is possible through integration into existing courses, by having a few lessons interspersed in the existing curriculum. In non-formal education, an entire noncredit program focuses on the reasons and the ways by which individuals, groups, and communities reject and oppose violent extremism. In informal education, the print, broadcast and social media disseminate

---

48. Ross-Gordon, et al., *Foundations of Adult and Continuing Education.*

the message through such means as comic strips, cartoons, posters, memes, TV spots, as well as inserted dialogues or messages in pop music, movies, and the like. In Japan, for example, a school uses the stories of Anne Frank[49], a superhero, and a Bosnian student to learn about identity issues, living together, and fighting extremism.[50] Such educational efforts must involve rational thinking (head), feelings and emotions (heart), observation and field visits (feet), as well as actions for change (hands). We must engage learners in rational thinking as well as in their feelings, emotions, and passion.[51] See Figure 2.7 below.

Figure 2.7: Appeal to the Whole Human Being

Thus, the content of education to eliminate violent extremism must include logic (logos), feelings (pathos), ethics (ethos), and more importantly all-encompassing love (agape). See Figure 2.8 below.

49. Frank, *Anne Frank: Diary of a Young Girl.*
50. Kitayama, et al., "Reimagining Japan and Fighting Extremism."
51. Nussbaum, *Upheavals of Thought.*

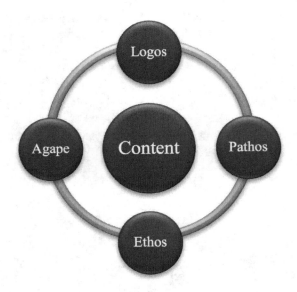

Figure 2.8: Content of Formal Education

At home and in schools, children proactively learn about empathy, open-mindedness, and tolerance.[52] The United Nations Educational, Social, and Cultural Organization (UNESCO) defines tolerance as "harmony in difference" and "respect, acceptance, and appreciation of the rich diversity" of the different cultures in the world, our expressions, and different ways of being human.[53] The Security Council of the United Nations calls for the promotion of religious and political tolerance, economic development, inclusiveness, social cohesion, halting and resolving conflicts, as well as reintegration and rehabilitation as a way out of violent extremism.[54]

In addition, children learn to be compassionate, recognize bullying behavior, learn emotional and social intelligence, and engage in respectful relationships, and connect with each another across cultural, ethnic, linguistic, religious, and racial diversity.[55] Moreover, they have to learn to develop their cultural intelligence, by which we mean learning about, understanding, and appreciate different cultures, ethnicities, and

---

52. Bullard, *Teaching Tolerance*.

53. UNESCO, *Declaration of Principles on Tolerance*.

54. Security Council, *Threats to international Peace and Security Caused by Terrorist Acts*.

55. Sanders and Cardoso, *You, Me and Empathy*.

diversity.[56] Furthermore, they learn to be anti-biased, inclusive, and respectful of all, support social justice, and participate actively together for the common goals of harmony, unity, justice, and peace.[57] Equipped with this knowledge and these values, they learn to challenge prejudice and become change agents at their young age.[58]

People have different learning styles: some are visual learners; others are auditory, reading and writing, or kinesthetic (VARK).[59] Hence, educational endeavors must appeal to all types of learners. For instance, visual learners need to see photos, films, tables, or charts about violent extremism and steps to undo them, while auditory learners need to listen to lectures, discussions, audiobooks, or music. Learners who do best by reading and writing need to read books, electronic books, online posts, and blogs, as well as take down lecture notes. Kinesthetic learners need to engage in hands-on activities, such as partake in exposure trips, field visits, and immersion in various communities to experience first-hand inclusive or open communities as well as exclusive or closed communities.

Schools are a battleground of ideas: on the one hand, they reflect the power relations in society but on the other hand, they are also places in which students, teachers, and the administration can actively teach and learn to undo unequal power relations in social class, religion, and color.[60] We need to be aware that curriculum embeds an ideology, which could be either conformist or liberating. Consequently, we need to include an emancipatory ideology that embraces inclusion and social harmony, especially in an extreme-right wing political atmosphere.[61] Schools can challenge the power relations in society.[62] In changing minds, we need to reshape education that is exclusionary oppressive to one that is inclusive and liberating, especially in this age during which extreme right-wing ideology and fascism are on the rise.[63] In the face of the rise of fascism today, reimagining education is necessary. As knowledge, power, and education are connected, educators must be committed to critical education that promotes empathy, justice, and peace.[64] Teachers have to facilitate learners to bring about profound social change

56. Seitzinger and Ty, *Cultural Intelligence.*
57. *Teaching Tolerance,* https://www.tolerance.org/about.
58. *Teaching Tolerance,* https://www.tolerance.org/about.
59. Fleming, *Teaching and learning Styles: VARK strategies.*
60. Apple, *Education and Power.*
61. Apple, *Ideology and Curriculum.*
62. Apple, *Can Education Change Society?*
63. Apple, *Official Knowledge.*
64. Apple, *Knowledge, Power, and Education.*

and build a just world.[65] Instead of relying on individual teachers to scramble for ways to address extremism, there need to be collective visions and strategies to address colonial legacy and systemic inequality as well as challenge and combat racism at its roots.

For these reasons, the core curriculum in formal, non-formal, and informal education to combat violent extremism must include teaching and learning about rights, justice, peace, and democracy. While these concepts carry different meanings, some of their features overlap with one another. An exemplary point of departure is the Universal Declaration of Human Rights (United Nations, 1948), which discusses non-discrimination and equality as well as economic, social, cultural, civil, and political rights as well as duty to the community. The concept of peace of the University of Peace (2011) of the United Nations encompasses dismantling the culture of war; human rights; intercultural solidarity; inner peace; as well as justice and compassion.[66] Democracy in its minimalist definition refers only to political rights of the Universal Declaration of Human Rights, meaning running for public office, voting, and elected as public official.[67] Justice, for its part, is summarized as fairness and treating others as one wishes to be treated.[68] Embedded in the Universal Declaration of Human Rights are justice, peace, and democracy. See Table 2.1 below.

Table 2.1: Alignment of Human Rights, Peace, Democracy, and Justice © 2020 Rey Ty

Universal Declaration of Human Rights[69]	Peace (U.N.)	Democracy	Justice
Inherent dignity, equal and inalienable rights: basis of freedom, **justice, & peace**	← preamble; (2) "justice and compassion"		← preamble

65. Brookfield and Holst, *Radicalizing Learning*.

66. University of Peace, *Peace Education*.

67. Huntington, *The Third Wave*; Przeworski, *Crises of Democracy*.

68. Confucius, *Analects*; Rawls, *A Theory of Justice*; Sen, *The idea of Justice*.

69. Non-derogable rights, which are rights that cannot be limited or suspended under all circumstances, are in boldface, namely Articles 6, 7, 8 (paragraphs 1 and 2), 11, 15, 16 and 18 of the International Covenant on Civil and Political Rights; marked in underscore and boldface here in UDHR.

Universal Declaration of Human Rights[69]	Peace (U.N.)	Democracy	Justice
HR violations result in barbarity	(1) Dismantling a culture of war		
Rule of law to avoid rebellion against tyranny and oppress			Golden Rule: Treat others as you would like to be treated.
Promote social progress and better standards of life in larger freedom			
1. Free and equal in dignity and rights; reason and conscience; brotherhood	(3) Human rights and responsibilities; (6) personal peace		Confucius (Analects 12:2)
2. No distinction of any kind, such as race, color, sex, language, religion, political or other opinion, national or social origin, property, birth or other status	(4) Intercultural solidarity		Bible (Leviticus 19:18; Matthew 7:12; Luke 6:31)
3. CIVIL RIGHTS:[70] Right to **life**, liberty, and security of person			
4. **No slavery or servitude; prohibit slavery and slave trade**			John Rawls (1999)
5. **No torture or cruel, inhuman or degrading treatment or punishment**			
6. **Recognition everywhere as a person before the law**			Amartya Sen (2011)
7. Equal before the law; without discrimination to equal protection of the law			
8. Effective remedy by the competent national tribunals			
9. No arbitrary arrest, detention or exile			

70. The term "civil liberties" in the U.S. is equivalent to the term "civil rights" of the United Nations. In the U.S., "civil rights" refer to the equal rights of minorities.

Universal Declaration of Human Rights[69]	Peace (U.N.)	Democracy	Justice
10. Full equality to a fair and public hearing by an independent and impartial tribunal			
11. Presumption of innocence; **no retroactivity of the law**			
12. No arbitrary interference with privacy, family, or home or correspondence nor attacks upon honor and reputation			
13. Freedom of movement and residence within a country; right to leave any country and return to one's country			
14. Seek asylum from persecution; not for non-political crimes or acts			
15. Right to a nationality; no arbitrary deprivation of nationality nor denial to change nationality			
16. Right to marriage for legal age; equal rights to marriage and dissolution; free and full consent			
17. Own property alone and in association with others; no arbitrary deprivation of property			
18. Right to freedom of **thought, conscience, and religion**; change religion or belief			
19. Freedom of opinion and expression			
20. Freedom of peaceful assembly and association; no compulsion to join an association			

Universal Declaration of Human Rights[69]	Peace (U.N.)	Democracy	Justice
21. POLITICAL RIGHTS: Take part in government of one's country directly or through freely chosen representative; equal access to public service; will of the people as the basis of government authority through periodic and genuine elections which shall be by universal and equal suffrage and shall be held by secret vote or by equivalent free voting procedure		1) Elections: a) vote for representatives; b) run as a candidate to be elected; c) serve as a representative	
22. Social security: economic, social, and cultural rights			
23. ECONOMIC RIGHTS: Right to work, free choice of employment, just and favorable conditions of work; protection against unemployment; equal pay for equal work; just and favorable remuneration to ensure existence worthy of human dignity and supplemented if necessary by social protection			
24. Right to rest and leisure, including limitation of working hours and periodic holidays with pay			
25. SOCIAL RIGHTS: Standard of living adequate for health and well-being for oneself and family, including food, clothing, housing, and medical care and social service, and security during unemployment, sickness, disability, widowhood, old age, or lack of livelihood beyond one's control; motherhood and childhood entitled to special care and assistance; children born out of wedlock enjoy same social protection			

Universal Declaration of Human Rights[69]	Peace (U.N.)	Democracy	Justice
26. CULTURAL RIGHTS: Right to education; free in elementary stage; compulsory; education for the full development of the human personality and to respect human rights and fundamental freedoms; promote understanding, tolerance, and friendship of all; parents have a prior right to choose children's education			
27. Freely participate in cultural life of the community; enjoy the arts and share in scientific advancement and its benefits; right to the protection of the moral and material interests resulting from any scientific, literary or artistic production of which he is the author.			
28. Social and international order that realizes the rights and freedoms here	(4) Intercultural solidarity		
29. Duties to the community in which alone the free and full development of personality is possible; limitations determined by law to respect the rights and freedoms of others and meeting the just requirements of morality, public order and the general welfare in a democratic society.	(3) Human rights and responsibilities		
30. Nothing here implies for any state, group, or person any right to destroy any of these rights and freedoms			
31. (Ksentini Report, U.N. 1994). Linkage between human rights and the environment.	(5) "Environmental care"		

Teaching values, which are universal, such as human rights, is a powerful tool to offset the attraction of violent extremism. Member countries of the United Nations unanimously adopted the Universal Declaration of Human Rights (UDHR) with eight countries abstaining (CCNMTL, 2020; UNAC, 2020) and two not voting.[71] The eight countries that abstained and the two that did not cast their votes either do not exist now as such or are not opposed to human rights: Byelorussia, Czechoslovakia, Poland, Saudi Arabia, South Africa, Soviet Union, Ukraine, and Yugoslavia. Almost all countries with Muslim majority were signatories to the UDHR. Human Rights Watch (1997) contentiously argues that since Saudi Arabia is a member state of the United Nations, it is bound to customary international law, including human rights.[72]

Thus, schools can impart universal human rights as norms that all human beings share.[73] For this reason, in civic education, citizenship education, and cosmopolitan education, schools must use human rights as foundations upon which teachers and students engage in classroom teaching and learning.[74] Students need to understand the context in which they live. Most countries have people of different cultural and ethnic backgrounds who speak different languages, for which reason schools must challenge the nationalistic version of citizenship education and need to integrate mutual respect, rights and responsibilities, multiculturalism, and diversity in teaching and learning.[75]

The content and pedagogy of teaching and learning must adopt a holistic approach that integrates lived experiences, social analysis, and reflections about suffering, joy, and transformation with a view to foster justice and peace.[76] Education must provide a safe zone where people learn about each other, their lived experiences, and the effects of the economy, politics, and culture on their lives.[77]

Informally, people can teach and learn about human rights, justice, peace, and democracy in different ways. For example, having friends from different ethnic, cultural, religious, or linguistic communities is a good starting point. In addition, educators can integrate the message of human rights and corollary concepts into children's television programming, drawing

71. Müller-Neuhof, "Menschenrechte."
72. Human Rights Watch, "International human rights standards."
73. Starkey, "Human Rights, Cosmopolitanism and Utopias."
74. Osler and Starkey, "Extending the Theory."
75. Osler and Starkey, "Extending the Theory."
76. Enns, "Editorial."
77. Enns, "Editorial."

books, basic comics, and children's storybooks in words and narratives appropriate to their age group. In addition, at times when acts of violent extremism occurs, these events must be used as teachable moments, during which people learn about the acts, the causes, the effects, and the actions needed to end violent extremism.

What Do We Teach in a World of Violent Extremism?

This section answers the third research question: What shall we teach in a world of violent extremisms? The General Assembly (2017) indicates that tolerance and interfaith, intercultural, and inter-civilizational understanding are the most vital factors to eliminate violent extremism.[78] To achieve these goals, people need to go outside their comfort zones and engage in intercultural and interreligious dialogue. In this way, formal, non-formal, and informal educational contexts can have curriculum contents of human rights, justice, peace, and democracy under the rubrics of civics, citizenship education, interfaith and interreligious dialogue, multicultural education, human rights education, education for democracy, education for justice, and peace education. Formally, student can take part in domestic field visits or study abroad programs. Non-formally, adult learners can take part in evening or weekend courses that incorporate learning about social classes, ethnicity, culture, gender, and other identities. Informally, adults get exposure to or engage in an immersion program in a different community or go abroad to learn about social realities.

Furthermore, the General Assembly (2016) strongly calls for the end of foreign occupation, oppression, and poverty as well as the promotion of economic growth, sustainable development, the rule of law, human rights, intercultural understanding, and the respect of different cultures and religions as guarantees to end violent extremism.[79] Furthermore, the Security Council (2015) of the United Nations asserts that young people and women must be included and represented in decision making at all levels in order to prevent as well as resolve conflicts. Inter-generationally, adults can train the youth and women about methods in the peaceful settlement of conflict, which include among others negotiation, enquiry, mediation, conciliation, arbitration, judicial settlement, good offices, regional arrangements, and other methods.[80]

---

78. General Assembly (GA), *Measures to eliminate international terrorism.*
79. General Assembly, *The United Nations global counter-terrorism strategy review.*
80. *Charter of the United Nations.*

As the Secretary General of the United Nations reported, the General Assembly (2015) has a concrete Plan of Action to prevent violent extremism.[81] The plan includes the promotion of human rights, multiculturalism, engaging communities, empowering the youth, gender equality, women empowerment, education, skills development, and employment facilitation, strategic communications, the internet, and social media. In short, active citizenship through different means such as interreligious dialogue, transformative community service learning, and participatory action research are necessary for a vibrant democratic way of life to thrive. Direct communication among people of different backgrounds is a powerful preventive tool to prevent people who are dissatisfied for whatever reason from committing acts of violent extremism, especially when interlocutors provide alternative solutions.[82]

In its Resolution A/RES/70/109 published in December 17, 2015, the United Nations General Assembly gave clear guidelines and instructions on December 10, 2015 on the ways in which education can help shape a world against violence and violent extremism.[83] Governments need to make all efforts using comprehensive approaches to prevent and counter intolerance, violent extremism, and sectarian violence by addressing structural, social, and individual conditions that promote such exclusiveness and sectarian and extremist violence. The learning content must include the promotion of dialogue, mutual understanding, tolerance, human rights, cooperation, civic education, life skills, democratic principles and practices in formal, non-formal, and informal education at all levels.

A Case Study of the Successful Use of Education to Mitigate Violent Extremism

I would like to end this chapter by presenting the case study of Dr. Alzad Sattar who uses formal, non-formal, and informal education to stop violent extremism at all fronts. Sattar is 70 percent Sama, 20 percent Tausug, and 10 percent Yakan, all of which are different ethnicities, which are Muslim in the Philippines. He grew up in a Tausug community, for which reason he speaks Tausug fluently. When I was working as the training coordinator of the International Training Office of the Division of International Affairs at Northern Illinois University (NIU), Sattar attended a one month-long non-formal interfaith peace program in 2007, as an adult leader, which had

81. General Assembly, *Plan of action to prevent violent extremism.*

82. Zgryziewicz, *Violent Extremism and Communications.*

83. General Assembly. December 17, 2015.

Muslim, Indigenous, Christian, and Atheist participants from the conflict-ridden southern Philippine island of Mindanao and the Sulu archipelago. At that time, he was concurrently the Dean of Student Affairs and Adviser of United Muslim Students Association at Basilan State College in Isabela City, Basilan Province, Philippines.

When he attended the program, I observed that he was very religious. He well represented the image of a devout Muslim, always seeking to connect with Muslim Americans and sharing with us his knowledge about Islam. For one month during the entire program, he stayed with a Unitarian Universalist couple who worked at NIU. They had a great impact on Sattar, as I noted that his homestay was a nodal point in his life, for the reason that he opened up his mind to people who were not Muslims. His homestay provided an informal educational opportunity for both Sattar and the American couple to learn from each other. After attending the program, Sattar created the Peace and Development Center at Basilan State College, which was a concrete manifestation of the positive outcome of his participation in a non-formal interfaith and peace educational program of which I was the training coordinator.

Before attending the non-formal educational interfaith and peace program at NIU, Sattar already received his two bachelor's degrees in political science (1996) and education (1998) as well as a master's degree in Islamic studies (2005), all of which were in the Philippines. After attending the interfaith and peace program at NIU, he proceeded to study and complete an M.A. in Coexistence and Conflict Resolution at Brandeis University, U.S.A.[84] By 2019, he obtained his doctorate in Educational Administration from Basilan State College.[85]

From 1996 to 2007, Sattar taught in a madrasah or Islamic school during weekends. Clearly, teaching in a madrasah provided an opportunity on Saturdays and Sundays for Sattar to advance his advocacy for interfaith peace. Connected with Basilan State College from 1996 to the present as of this writing in 2020, Sattar rose to the rank of associate professor by 2016, teaching political science and Islamic studies. He also held administrative positions at the college where he taught, including Assistant Vice President for Academic Support Services, Dean of Academic Programs, Dean of Institute of Islamic Studies (IIS), Dean of Students Affairs, Presidential Executive Assistant, and Director for Peace and Development Center.

Clearly, his personal experience with an interfaith peace program left an indelible mark on his life, so much so that his academic growth moved

84. Sattar, *The Contribution of Interfaith.*
85. Sattar, *Madrasah Education Program (MEP).*

from a purely Islamic-focused study for his bachelor's degree to a master's degree research on the positive interactions of Muslims and Christians in the southern Philippines. For his formal education at the graduate level, he specifically focused his studies on interfaith relations for his M.A. degree and on using the madaris to quell violent extremism for his doctorate.[86] Madaris is the plural form of madrasah or Islamic school. Using the research methods of participant observation, interviews, and focused group discussions, his master's thesis investigated the contributions of interfaith organizations to peaceful coexistence and their role in the peace process between the government and the Moro Islamic Liberation Front (MILF), which was an armed revolutionary group.[87] Sattar was engaged in informal education while conducting research on interfaith relations, as he interviewed MILF combatants and organizational leaders of different religions. Clearly, interfaith dialogue and cooperation are a venue for effective informal education that promote interfaith cooperation and quell violent extremism.

His intellectual growth deepened, as he extended his new knowledge, skills, and values to think of ways by which the madaris can be an instrument of peace. Using mixed methods, his doctoral dissertation investigated the contributions of madaris education to counter violent extremism in the Autonomous Region in Muslim Mindanao (ARMM).[88] As a community organizer, Sattar was involved in informal education by creating the Inter-Faith Council of Leaders in Basilan in 2010. The purpose is to promote harmony, good relationship, peaceful coexistence, and siblinghood among Muslims, Christians, and people of other faiths in the province. For his non-formal education involvements, Sattar regularly gives presentations on interfaith dialogue in Islamic perspective, culture of dialogue, and countering violent extremism.

For seven years, Sattar was the Undersecretary for Madaris Education of the Department of Education of the Philippines, from 2012 to 2019. He put in place reforms at the Bureau of Madaris Education, strengthening the program by introducing innovative programs that respond to the needs of the changing times. As a result, madaris education program is going beyond teaching Islam only. As undersecretary, he was able to connect the madrasah education program to peace education through the development of curriculum and textbooks. The curriculum includes the life history of the Prophet Muhammad, his coexistence with Jews in Medina, and his treatment of

86. Sattar, *The Contribution of Interfaith Organizations to Coexistence.*

87. Sattar, *The Contribution of Interfaith Organizations to Coexistence.*

88. Sattar, *Madrasah Education Program (MEP): Contributions to Counter Violent Extremism in the Autonomous Region in Muslim Mindanao (ARMM).*

Christian visitors for whom he offered to pray at his mosque Masjid an-Nabawi in Medina. The curriculum also includes the Medina Charter, which enshrines the proof that Prophet Muhammad lived in peaceful coexistence with the Jews. Sattar could have focused on teaching about Islam only when he prepared the curriculum for the formal education in madrasi. However, with his accumulated knowledge, skills, and attitudes (KSA) regarding interfaith dialogue and cooperation, Sattar decided to add and integrate the appreciation of interfaith dialogue and cooperation in his teaching about Islam in the formal education setting in madrasi. Madrasah includes schools at all levels, from pre-school up to post-graduate levels. Sattar only drafted the curriculum up to high school level as that is the scope of the Ministry of Education. While madaris could be public or private, now madaris in the Philippines are all private, although they receive some assistance from the government through subsidy.

As of this writing, he is now a member of Parliament of the 80-member Bangsamoro Transition Authority (BARMM) with a term from February 22, 2019 to June 30, 2022. His focus now is to institutionalize madrasah education in BARMM through legislation, of which he is the main author, of a bill currently under second reading.[89] Madrasah education is a component of the provisions of the Bangsamoro Organic Law (BOL), which needs an enabling law for its operationalization.

To find out whether his efforts to mainstream countering violent extremism through the Islamic schools is successful, Sattar co-authored with Arriola, conducting a mixed methods research that investigated the perceptions of 313 out of a total of 930 Asiatidz (Islamic teachers) who were teaching in both the Integrated or Pilot Madrasah (IPM) and the Traditional Weekend Madrash (TWM).[90] Their findings revealed that the Madrasah Education Program contributes to undoing violent extremism. In his lifelong trajectory, from being a devout Muslim, Sattar continued to be a devout Muslim. On top of that, after attending an interfaith peace-building program that opened his horizon to non-Muslims, specifically Christians and indigenous people, Sattar commenced to embarked on not only working for interfaith cooperation but also mainstreaming interfaith understanding in both the integrated and weekend Madrasah educational system, which his research confirms to contribute toward the elimination of violent extremism. Sattar has made great strides to quell violent extremism through formal education through the Madrasah system, non-formal

89. Sattar and Dandamun-Latiph, *An Act Creating the Office of the Bangsamoro Director-General.*

90. Sattar and Arriola, "Contributions of Madrasah."

education through seminars and public lectures, and informal education through the passing of legislative bills.

Summary and Conclusion

This chapter illustrated different forms of education, how different forms of education can eradicate violent extremism and pave the way to dialogue, mutual understanding, and goodwill. It also presented a case study that illustrated the use of education to eradicate violent extremism. See Figure 2.9 below.

Figure 2.9: The Role of Education in Eradicating Violent Extremism

In our educational endeavors to quell violent extremism, three elements are important. They include (1) pedagogy, (2) curriculum, and (3) content of teaching and learning. See Figure 2.10 below.

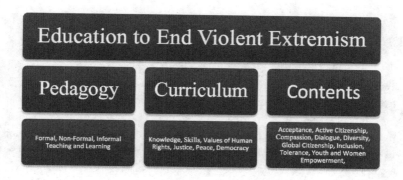

Figure 2.10: Elements of Education to Eliminate Violent Extremism

Occurrences of acts of violent extremism are manifestations of historically and socially embedded structural problems, such as colonialism, patriarchy, social inequality, hierarchism, colorism, religious chauvinism, fascism,
casteism, racism, exclusion, and miseducation. Pedagogical practices, curriculum, and content of teaching and learning shall lead to an outcome where
intolerance and violent extremism decrease at the minimum and eradicated
at best, while empathy and peace improve. See Figure 2.11 below.

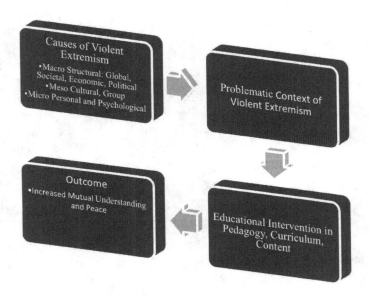

**Figure 2.11: Ty's Grounded Theory of the Pedagogy and
Curriculum to End Violent Extremism**

In general, children deductively learn new abstract knowledge, skills,
and attitudes in formal education settings, while adults learn best inductively
from concrete real-life experience. In addition, both children and adults are
products of socialization in the family, schools, and places of worship where
they learn to favor or reject violent extremism. In this regard, we must explore
using all educational entry points—formal, non-formal, and informal—to put
a stop to violent extremism. Parents, religious leaders, and teachers have a
major role to play in educating children, while adults learn from their life
situations. In general, lesson plans and curriculum for children in formal
education integrate the teaching of human rights and other related concepts
to undo violent extremism, while teaching the same content to adults in both

non-formal and informal education settings can be separate courses with very specific focuses based on their lived experiences.

The curriculum must impart knowledge, skills, and attitudes that promote tolerance, compassion, empathy, open-mindedness, and inclusiveness. Teaching and learning must involve human rights, interreligious understanding, and the rule of law. While children learn in schools, both children and adults need to get out of their comfort zones, interact with people of different backgrounds, enter into dialogue with people of other communities, and engage in service learning as active citizens. A comprehensive methodology involving proactive and reactive approaches is imperative for the successful end to violent extremism. The outcome of this pedagogy, curriculum, and lessons is a decrease in intolerance, hatred, and violent extremism on the one hand and increase in tolerance, compassion, mutual understanding, and peace on the other.

Children and adults must learn tolerance and unlearn discrimination. For formal education, the top-down approach in deductively teaching mutual understanding is the name of the game for the most part. For non-formal education, adults learn best inductively about inclusion and unlearn hatred through bottom-up approaches based on their lived experiences. Parents, neighbors, peers, and religious leaders provide rich opportunities to learn about inclusiveness in informal education. While neighborliness is necessary, it is not sufficient. Learners need to go outside their comfort zones, see, and hear first-hand about the conditions and feelings of people of different backgrounds through direct interaction as well as working together. Learning to undo violent extremism, therefore, must include reason, passion, observation, and action.

Bibliography

Ahmed, Zahid Shahab, and Bashirov, Galib. "Religious Fundamentalism and Violent Extremism." In *The Difficult Task of Peace: Crisis, Fragility and Conflict in an Uncertain World*, edited by F. Rojas-Aravena, 245–260. Hampshire, UK: Palgrave Macmillan, 2020.

Apple, Michael W. *Ideology and Curriculum*. Abingdon-on-Thames, UK: Routledge, 2018.

———. *Official knowledge: Democratic Education in a Conservative Age*. Abingdon-on-Thames, UK: Routledge, 2014.

———. *Can Education Change Society?* Abingdon-on-Thames, UK: Routledge, 2012a.

———. *Knowledge, Power, and Education*. Abingdon-on-Thames, UK: Routledge, 2012b.

———. *Education and Power*. Abingdon-on-Thames, UK: Routledge, 2011.

Austin, Beatrix, and Hans J. Giessmann, eds. *Transformative Approaches to Violent Extremism*. Berghof Handbook Dialogue Series No. 13. Berlin: Berghof Foundation, 2018.

Bible. Nashville: Thomas Nelson, 2017.

Brookfield, Stephen D., and John D. Holst. *Radicalizing learning: Adult education for a just world*. New York: Jossey-Bass, 2010.

Bullard, Sara. *Teaching Tolerance: Raising Open-Minded, Empathetic Children*. Minot, ND: Main Street Books, 1997.

Bush, George W. *Address to a joint session of Congress and the American people*. Washington, D.C.: United States Capitol, September 20, 2001.

————. Remarks by the President upon arrival. The South Lawn: White House, September 16, 2001.

Charter of the United Nations. New York: United Nations, 1945.

Christodoulou, Eleni. "'Boosting Resilience' and 'Safeguarding Youngsters at Risk': Critically Examining European Commission's Educational Responses to Radicalization and Violent Extremism." *London Review of Education* 18(1) (2020) 18–24.

CCNMTL. Drafting History. New York: Columbia University Center for New Media Teaching and Learning (CCNMTL), 2020. https://ccnmtl.columbia.edu/projects/mmt/udhr/udhr_general/drafting_history_10.html

Confucius. *Analects*. London: Penguin Classics, 1998.

Doosje, Bertjan, et al. "Terrorism, Radicalization, and De-radicalization." *Current Opinion in Psychology* 11 (2016) 79–84.

Enns, Fernando. Editorial. *The Ecumenical Review* 72(1) (2020). https://onlinelibrary.wiley.com/doi/full/10.1111/erev.12494

Fleming, Neil D. *Teaching and Learning Styles: VARK Strategies*. Christchurch, New Zealand: Fleming, 2001.

Foucault, Michel. *The Archaeology of Knowledge*. London: Routledge, 2002.

Frank, Anne. *Anne Frank: Diary of a Young Girl*. New York: Bantam, 1993.

Freire, Paolo. *Pedagogy of the Oppressed*. London: Penguin Classics, 2017.

Galtung, Johan. "Violence, Peace and Peace Research." *Journal of Peace Research*, 6(3) (1969) 167–191.

General Assembly (GA). *Measures to Eliminate International Terrorism*. (A/72/467). New York: United Nations (December 7, 2017).

General Assembly. *The United Nations Global Counter-Terrorism Strategy Review. Resolution 70/291*. (A/RES/70/291). New York: United Nations, July 19, 2016.

General Assembly. *Plan of Action to Prevent Violent Extremism: Report of the Secretary-General. Report A/70/674*. New York: United Nations, December 24, 2015.

General Assembly. *A World against Violence and Violent Extremism. Resolution 70/109*. (A/RES/70/109). New York: United Nations, December 17, 2015.

General Assembly. The UN Global Counter-Terrorism Strategy. (A/RES/60/288). New York: United Nations, September 20, 2006.

Government Offices of Sweden. Sweden Action Plan to Safeguard Democracy against Violence Promoting Extremism. Government Communication 2011/12:44. https://www.government.se/49b75d/contentassets/b94f163a3c594 1aebaeb78174ea27a29/action-plan-to-safeguard-democracy-against-violence-promoting-extremism-skr.-20111244

Heidegger, Martin. *Being and Time*. New York: HarperPerennial, 2008.

HM Government (UK). *Counter-Extremism Strategy*. London: Counter-Extremism Directorate, Home Office, 2015.

HM Government (UK). *Prevent Strategy*. Norwich: The Stationery Office, 2011.

Human Rights Watch. International Human Rights Standards. New York: Human Rights Watch, 1997. https://www.hrw.org/reports/1997/saudi/Saudi-07.htm#:~:text=SAUDI%20ARABIA&text=Despite%20its%20assertions%20to%20the,norms%20of%20customary%20international%20law.

Huntington, Samuel. *The Third Wave: Democratization in the Late 20th Century*. Tulsa: University of Oklahoma Press, 2012.

Husserl, Edmund. *Ideas: General Introduction to Pure Phenomenology*. New York: Collier, 1962.

Jones, Sidney. *Countering Violent Extremism in Indonesia*. IPAC Report No. 11. Jakarta: Institute for Policy Analysis of Conflict, 2014.

Kitayama, Yuka. "The Rise of the Far Right in Japan and Challenges Posed for Education." *London Review of Education* 16 (2) (2018) 250–67.

Kitayama, Yuka, et al. "Reimagining Japan and Fighting Extremism with the Help of a Superhero: A Teacher's Tale." In *Race Equality Teaching*, 21–27. London: University College London IOE Press, 2017.

Knowles, Malcolm. *The Modern Practice of Adult Education: From Pedagogy to Andragogy*. Wilton, CT: Association Press, 1980.

Köhler, Daniel. *Understanding De-Radicalization: Methods, Tools, and Programs for Countering Violent Extremism*. London: Routledge, 2017.

Merriam, Sharan. B., and Lisa M. Baumgartner. *Learning in Adulthood: A Comprehensive Guide*. New York: Jossey-Bass, 2020.

Mezirow, Jack. *Transformative Dimensions of Adult Learning*. New York: Jossey-Bass, 1991.

Müller-Neuhof, Jost. "Menschenrechte: Die mächtigste Idee der Welt." *Der Tagesspiegel* (in German). "Human rights: the most powerful idea in the world." *The Daily Mirror* (December 10, 2008). https://www.tagesspiegel.de/politik/menschenrechte-die-maechtigste-idee-der-welt/1392182.html.

Nasser-Eddine, Minerva, et al. *Countering Violent Extremism (CVE) Literature Review*. Edinburgh, Australia: Counter Terrorism and Security Technology Center, Defense Science and Technology Organization, 2001.

Norwegian Ministry of Justice and Public Safety. *Action Plan against Radicalization and Violent Extremism*, December 8, 2014. https://www.regjeringen.no/en/dokumenter/Action-plan-against-Radicalisation-and-Violent-Extremism/id762413/.

Nussbaum, Martha C. *Upheavals of Thought: The Intelligence of Emotions*. Cambridge: Cambridge University Press, 2003.

Organization for Economic Cooperation and Development Assistance Committee. *DAC High Level Meeting, Communiqué of 19 February 2016*. https://www.oecd.org/dac/DAC-HLM-Communique-2016.pdf

Osler, Audrey, and Hugh Starkey. "Extending the Theory and Practice of Education for Cosmopolitan Citizenship." *Educational Review* 70:1 (2018) 31–40.

Parliament of Australia. Australian Government Measures to Counter Violent Extremism: A Quick Guide, February 2015. https://www.aph.gov.au/About_Parliament/Parliamentary_Departments/Parliamentary_Library/pubs/rp/rp1415/Quick_Guides/Extremism

Perry, William. *Forms of Ethical and Intellectual Development in the College Years: A Scheme*. New York: Jossey-Bass, 1998.

Przeworski, Adam. *Crises of Democracy*. Cambridge: Cambridge University Press, 2019.

Public Safety Canada. Assessing the risk of violent extremists. *Research summary*, 14(4) (September 2009) 1–2. https://www.publicsafety.gc.ca/cnt/rsrcs/pblctns/ssng-xtrms/index-en.aspx

RAN. *Lessons from Crime Prevention in Preventing Violent Extremism by Police.* Amsterdam: The Radicalization Awareness Network (RAN) Centre of Excellence, January 15, 2020.

Ranstorp, Magnus. *Islamist extremism*. Amsterdam: The Radicalization Awareness Network (RAN) Centre of Excellence, 2019.

———. *The Root Causes of Violent Extremism*. RAN Issue Paper (04/01/2016). Amsterdam: The Radicalization Awareness Network (RAN) Centre of Excellence, 2016.

Rawls, John. *A Theory of Justice*. Cambridge, MA: Belknap Press, 1999.

Ross-Gordon, Jovita M., et al. *Foundations of Adult and Continuing Education*. New York: Jossey-Bass, 2016.

Rousseau, Jean Jacques. *Emile or on Education*. New York: Basic Books, 1979

Sanders, Jayneen, and Sofia Cardoso. *You, Me and Empathy: Teaching Children about Empathy, Feelings, Kindness, Compassion, Tolerance and Recognizing Bullying Behaviors*. Camperdown, NSW, Australia: Educate2Empower Publishing, 2017.

Sattar, Alzad T. Madrasah education program (MEP): Contributions to counter violent extremism in the Autonomous Region in Muslim Mindanao (ARMM). Isabela City, Basilan, Philippines: Basilan State College, 2019.

———. The contribution of interfaith organizations to coexistence and their possible role in the peace process between the government of the Republic of the Philippines (GRP) and the Moro Islamic Liberation Front (MILF) in Mindanao, Philippines. Waltham, MA: Brandeis University, 2011.

———, and Arriola, Benjier H. "Contributions of Madrasah Education Program to Counter Violent Extremism." *American Journal of Educational Research* 8(7) (2020) 450–56.

———, and Dandamun-Latiph, M. C. An Act Creating the Office of the Bangsamoro Director-General for Madaris Education in the Ministry of Education and to Strengthen and Institutionalize Madaris Education and Appropriating Funds Therefor and for Other Purposes. Cotabato City, Philippines: Bangsamoro Autonomous Region in Muslim Mindanao, 2019.

Security Council. *Maintenance of International Peace and Security*. *Resolution 2250*. (S/RES/2250). New York: United Nations, December 9, 2015.

Security Council. *Threats to international peace and security caused by terrorist acts*. *Resolution 2178*. (S/RES/2178). New York: United Nations. September 24, 2014.

Seitzinger, Anne, and Rey Ty. *Cultural Intelligence*. DeKalb, IL: Northern Illinois University Division of International Programs, July 17, 2012.

Sen, Amartya. *The Idea of Justice*. Cambridge, MA: Belknap, 2011.

Sommers, Marc. Thwarting Violent Extremism: A New Approach. Washington, DC: Alliance for Peacebuilding, 2020. https://allianceforpeacebuilding.org/thwarting-violent-extremism-a-new-approach/.

———. *Youth and the Field of Countering Violent Extremism*. Washington, DC: Promundo-US, 2019.

Southern Poverty Law Center (2020). Hate groups across the U.S., 2020. Retrieved on June 15, 2020 from https://www.splcenter.org/hate-map

Starkey, Hugh. "Human Rights, Cosmopolitanism and Utopias: Implications for Citizenship Education." *Cambridge Journal of Education* 42:1 (2012) 21–35.

Sterkenburg, Nikki. *A Practical Introduction to Far-Right Extremism*. Amsterdam: The Radicalization Awareness Network (RAN) Centre of Excellence, 2019.

Teaching Tolerance. (2020). https://www.tolerance.org/about

Teaching Tolerance Project. *The Shadow of Hate: A History of Intolerance in America*. Montgomery, AL: Southern Poverty Law Center 2006.

Ty, R. "The Rohingya Refugee Crisis: Contexts, Problems, and Solutions." In *Sur International Journal on Human Rights* 16(29) (2019) 49–62.

———. *Pastoral Solidarity Visit to Bangladesh*. Chiang Mai: CCA, 2017a.

———. *Report of the Pastoral Solidarity Team Visit to Pakistan*. Chiang Mai: CCA, 2017b.

———. *Pastoral Solidarity Visit to West Papua*. Chiang Mai: CCA. 2017c.

———. *Statement of Concern over Religiously Motivated violence*. Medan, Indonesia: Executive Committee of the Christian Conference of Asia, 2016.

UNAC. Questions and Answers about the Universal Declaration of Human Rights. Ottawa: United Nations Association in Canada (UNAC), 2020. https://web.archive.org/web/20120912162219/http://www.unac.org/rights/question.html

UNESCO. *Preventing Violent Extremism through Education: A Guide for Policy Makers*. Paris: United Nations Educational, Social, and Cultural Organization (UNESCO), 2017. https://unesdoc.unesco.org/ark:/48223/pf0000247764_eng

UNESCO. *Declaration of Principles on Tolerance*. Paris: United Nations Educational, Social, and Cultural Organization, 1995.

Universal Declaration of Human Rights. New York: United Nations, 1948.

University of Peace. *Peace Education: Theory and Practice*. Costa Rica: University of Peace, 2011.

USAID. The Development Response to Violent Extremism and Insurgency: Putting Principles into Practice, *USAID Policy*. September 2011. https://www.usaid.gov/sites/default/files/documents/1870/VEI_Policy_Final.pdf

Zgryziewicz, R. *Violent Extremism and Communications*. Riga, Latvia: NATO Strategic Communications Centre of Excellence, 2018.

3

What and How Shall We Teach in a World of Violent Extremisms

—BOYUNG LEE

A few years ago, I led a mandatory immersive learning course for a fellowship program I directed at my previous institution to Colombia for two weeks. Fifteen fellows and I traveled to different places in the country as human rights accompaniers, partnered with the FOR Peace Presence in Colombia. The majority of the participants had hardly traveled outside of the United States before. All of them had backgrounds in various social justice movements and personally experienced various forms of oppression throughout their lives. As a faculty director, despite the tremendously rewarding sense of satisfaction I got from working with such trailblazers, I struggled with some of them who challenged the immersion itself. They wondered why they were in another country when there were countless oppressed people, including themselves, in the U.S. whose human rights were not respected. Despite their commitments to anti-oppression work, they could not recognize: (1) their privilege in a global context as U.S. citizens; (2) their unintended and unknown participation in the oppression of the people in the Global South; (3) critical needs for global solidarity to end oppression. In other words, ideological beliefs and foundations of their social justice work were very U.S.-centric, which might hinder them from contributing to the ending of global oppression as they hoped and thought. Although they were critical of American exceptionalism embedded in the U.S. educational system and ideologies, they were still the products of the system. However, being in Colombia for two weeks, where we witnessed countless human rights violations done by familiar U.S. entities, challenged us to begin a life-long learning journey: we must unlearn our own ideological assumptions and perspectives that could harm people in other communities and relearn social justice work based on global solidarity.

Using our U.S. passport privilege or residency, our partners in Colombia asked us to be international watchers and presence for the poverty-stricken people whose fundamental rights to live and work had been under constant threat. Most of them were Afro-Colombian farmers who experienced multiple displacements from the land they had been living in since the forced slavery from Africa in the sixteenth century. We repeatedly encountered forced displacement by their government and U.S.-backed transnational companies and horrendous life situations as a result of their resistance: loss of land and access to water, poverty, undiagnosed illness, trauma and PTSD from witnessing the assassination of their loved ones, no educational opportunities for their children, etc.[1] In fact, in each place we visited, we saw their unimaginable living conditions mostly in a wilderness near the equator. We heard heartbreaking stories while being surveilled by paramilitary groups serving for powerful foreign companies. Many young people expressed complete despair and hopelessness of their lives, while some showed their strong desire for revenge and fury toward the United States. They believed that the U.S. government had supported corrupt Colombian politicians and business leaders to protect the economic interests of the U.S. and to maintain its military strongpoints in Latin America. Our Colombian friends also argued that their government ignored human rights violations committed by paramilitary groups serving for translational corporations like Chiquita Bananas, Del Monte, Coca Cola, and Drummond Company Inc. while making astronomical profits.[2] Some of these young Colombians, according to our partners, would join extremist groups out of despair, desire for revenge, and/or need to make their ends meet.

What we witnessed and heard from the Colombians greatly resonates with critical points made in the first two chapters of this book that violent extremism often emerges out of "a complex environment of vulnerable individuals, community grievances, national ideological campaigns, and global factors."[3] Moreover, in this age of globalization, vulnerable life

1. According to the United Nations High Commissioner for Refugees (UNHCR), there are about 7.7 million internally displaced people in Colombia as of 2018 mainly due to conflicts between paramilitaries and gang war fares, https://www.unhcr.org/en-us/colombia.html.

2. The 2015 report of the Amnesty International says that the numerous transnational corporations have been involved in displacement and conflicts in Colombia, sometimes collaborating with paramilitary groups who kill and threaten human rights defenders and resisting displaced people, https://www.amnesty.org/download/Documents/AMR2326152015ENGLISH.PDF.

3. Schirch, *The Ecology of Violent Extremism*, 5–6.

situations of individuals are entwined with community grievances, which are often caused by neoliberal global capitalism, as we witnessed in Colombia. Neoliberalists promote a free-market based world through liberalization, privatization, deregulation, and depoliticization.[4] Social services, including public education and health care, do not have to be accessible, dependable, and efficient for everyone but only for those who can afford to buy them in the marketplace.[5] Values like competition are embedded in the free market-driven educational system which is a primary promotional tool for neoliberalism.[6] People learn through both explicit and implicit curricula at school that they need to have more and better buying power to be full citizens. Otherwise, they become a burden to society. In such an educational system, empathy, global solidarity, care for the poor, and the like are not considered being worthy.[7] Individual and communal grievances of the people without buying power, and thus being labeled as failures, can create a potential breeding condition for violent extremist beliefs. Therefore, any consideration of education and extreme violence of our time, whether it is in the Global North or South, must critically analyze ideologies embedded in the educational system that may promote interests of the dominant few at the expense of the majority. Particularly, an in-depth analysis of the curriculum—whether or not the power imbalance, dehumanization, nationalism, colonialism, and other hierarchical worldviews are justified—is necessary as they likely create conditions for personal and communal grievances. In the following sections, utilizing different curriculum theories, I will explore what and how of teaching theological and religious education in an age of violent extremism.

Curriculum—An Ideological Matter?

What does it mean to teach toward undoing violent extremism? What should we educators do to help our students not only know about violent extremism but also become change agents for a different world? The question of what to teach is a foundational subject in curriculum discussion. The conventional definition of curriculum is a fixed course of study which comes from its Latin root, *currere*, to run.[8] However, in curriculum studies, hardly any educators base their work on this simple definition as the curriculum is

4. Litonjua, "Third World/Global South," 112.
5. McGregor, "Neoliberalism and Health Care," 87.
6. David Harvey, *A Brief History of Neoliberalism*, 65.
7. Thompson and Austin, "The Impact of Revisionist," 39–53.
8. Merriam-Webster Dictionary, online, "curriculum."

a much more complicated matter than a course of study. Depending on one's ideologies and perspectives, the definition and emphasis of the curriculum can be hugely varied. William Pinar, a noted curriculum theorist, categorizes different thoughts of the curriculum into three large schools: Traditionalists, Conceptual-empiricists, and Reconceptualists.[9] Although his seminal work is more than four decades old, it is still a widely used category with different variations. For example, Allan Glatthorn and colleagues who present four different curriculum categories in their 2019 book, *Curriculum Leadership: Strategies for Development and Implementation,*[10] rename Pinar's three types and add another category: Content-oriented (Traditionalists); Process-oriented (Conceptual-empiricists), Value-oriented (Reconceptualists), and Structure-oriented, one that pays attention to different components within the curriculum. As the first three categories come from different ideologies that lead scholars to approach teaching with different purposes and foci, reviewing these three, I believe, provides important insights on what and how to teach or not to teach to undo violent extremism.

Traditionalists in Pinar's categorization or Content-oriented approach, according to Glatthorn, et al., refer to those who take the most conventional approach to teaching.[11] They significantly pay attention to the efficient means of transmitting a fixed body of knowledge, values, and skills that a particular society values as cultural heritage and the necessity for the smooth functioning of the social system.[12] Therefore, they are naturally focused on the what of education, that is, content of teaching. Their curriculum is filled with behavioral objectives and measurable competencies, crucial markers to evaluate whether the taught contents were learned or not.

What to teach is a critical component of education. However, treating content as the only or most crucial matter of teaching and learning results in unhealthy and sometimes dangerous learning experiences for people, particularly those who are at the margins of society. Such a view is based on a belief that education is a value-free activity and thus content taught at any educational context is neutral, fair to all, and universally applicable knowledge. Henry Giroux, a noted educational thinker and critical pedagogy scholar, argues that such an ahistorical understanding is originated from the long-lived bureaucratic business principles that have been dominating the

---

9. Pinar, "The Reconceptualization of Curriculum Studies."

10. Glatthorn, et al, *Curriculum Leadership,* 62–103.

11. Pinar, "The Reconceptualization of Curriculum Studies," 167–69; Glatthorn et al., *Curriculum Leadership,* 73, 75–79.

12. Pinar, "The Reconceptualization of Curriculum Studies," 167–69.

field of curriculum studies.[13] Reviewing the history of curriculum thoughts, he analyzes that the traditionalist approach, which is still prevailing in North American educational contexts, began for administrative convenience to efficiently manage, control and predict teaching and learning activities and results. As an example, he presents the four-chapter titles of Ralph Tyler's 1949 book, *Basic Principles of Curriculum and Instruction*,[14] which have become the prototype themes of curriculum development even to this day[15]: (1) What educational purposes should the school seek to attain? (2) How can learning experiences be selected that are likely to be useful in achieving these objectives? (3) How can learning experiences be organized for effective instruction? (4) How can the effectiveness of learning experiences be evaluated? These questions are focused on the efficiency of the knowledge transmission process as decided by the educational authority. There are no questions on who learners are, contexts they live in, and experiences they bring to their learning. In other words, the curriculum is assumed to be a depoliticized course of study, happening in ahistorical contexts, which Carol Azumah Dennis, a British educator, calls "disembodied neutrality."[16] Traditionalist approaches to the curriculum cannot aid educators to undo extreme violence as its main purpose is to guide educational "practices as it anticipates and attempts to control it." When goals and results of education are pre-determined by those who are in the position of power, education inevitably becomes a vital tool for social maintenance, and thus, directly and indirectly, contributes to systemic discriminations against the vulnerable and their grievances.[17] Many members of the society also tend to take systematic problems for granted, and even victims of the system internalize their oppression. Giroux and others, therefore, argue that to transform social inequality that perpetuates the status quo, a society's view of education and its curriculum first must change.

Pinar calls a group of scholars who try to improve the weakness of the traditionalists Conceptual-empiricists, and Glatthorn et al. name their theory a Process-oriented approach.[18] Compared to traditionalists, they take a more teacher and teaching-oriented approach to the curriculum by incorporating other disciplines, especially psychology, anthropology, and

13. Giroux, et al., *Curriculum and Instruction*, 3.

14. Tyler, *Basic Principles of Curriculum and Instruction*.

15. Giroux, et al., *Curriculum and Instruction*, 3–4.

16. Dennis, "Decolonising Education," 192.

17. Giroux, *On Critical Pedagogy*, 19–21.

18. Pinar, "The Reconceptualization of Curriculum Studies," 169–71; Glatthorn et al., *Curriculum Leadership*, 73, 79–84.

various social sciences. If traditionalists are exclusively focused on the what of education, that is, delivering contents themselves, conceptual-empiricists are concerned with how to deliver contents more efficiently to result in intended learning objectives and outcomes. In other words, their emphasis is on how to teach what needs to be taught, and for that process, they believe that conceptual and empirical research of social science could evoke significant outcomes in education.[19] Regarding this, Pinar, after analyzing a few representative scholars' works, says that they are "concerned with what the authors view as logically defensible content sequencing alternatives, and it is empirical in its allegiance to the view of empirical research."[20] In a traditionalist approach-based context, a typical teacher is expected to master selected contents, efficiently organize them for proper instruction, and evaluate whether their students master the contents. In a conceptual-empiricist based context, a teacher utilizes developmental psychology, educational theories, and other disciplines to create a learning process with diverse activities that are appropriate for their students' learning capacities and ages as informed by experts in other related disciplines. The research of other fields is used to transmit the pre-determined content as traditionalists did but in a way that is more age and needs appropriate for learners, which sets conceptual-empiricists apart from the traditionalists. The purpose of the careful designing of a learning process is, therefore, to result in the expected learning outcomes in measurable ways.

The conceptual-empiricist curriculum is filled with behavioral objectives that serve as measurement standards for whether or not students gained intended knowledge, skills, and attitude development.[21] Some of the examples of this approach include competency-based education models and experience-based learning center models, which are still popular. The following learning objectives of a competency-based education program for the teachers of the incarcerated show the emphasis that conceptual-empiricists put on measurable learning outcomes along with influences of other disciplines on this approach. Also, this list published almost four decades ago indicates that this conceptual-empiricist approach is still prevailing as the similar language of the objectives is commonly found in many contemporary models:

1. Describe the system of courts and legal justice with which alienated students and correctional clientele must deal.

---

19. Christodoulou, "Conceptual Empiricist Perspective," 140.
20. Pinar, "The Reconceptualization of Curriculum Studies," 152.
21. Wilson, "Critical Examination of Teacher Education," 57.

2. Demonstrate skills in using instrumentation and diagnostic techniques common to special education testing.

3. Show competence in individualized instructional skill atypical students to succeed in learning tasks.

4. Analyze personal and individual needs of clients incarcerated, or otherwise categorized outside the mainstream public education.[22]

Pinar assesses that like traditionalists, conceptual-empiricists also accept the existing social ordering as it is, and thus its curriculum is still oriented to educate the members of a society to function well within the system and continue to run it. Ideological assumptions behind the educational system and curriculum, as well as the larger society, are hardly challenged, but instead implicitly presented as neutral and universal.[23]

Despite their claims for neutrality, the curriculum and education understood by both traditionalists and conceptual-empiricists inevitably serve as the major tool to maintain the interests of the powerful in society. The traditionalist view does not address the question of who and where: who the learners are and what they bring to their learning, which is formed in their contexts. The conceptual-empiricists pay attention to learners, mainly how they learn, and yet there is hardly any analysis of ideological assumptions embedded in the knowledge being taught. In sum, both approaches explicitly and implicitly regard curriculum as the primary vehicle for the transmission of proper knowledge as deemed appropriate by the experts of the society who occupy "a privileged place of neutrality which assumes a universal forefront."[24]

Pinar calls a group of curriculum scholars, who challenge such ahistorical and universal notion of knowledge and education of the two approaches Reconceptualists, and Glatthorn et al. label them as those who take a Value-oriented approach.[25] With their great dissatisfaction with the prevailing curriculum's ahistorical character, reconceptualists employ critical theories, psychoanalytic theory, phenomenology, existentialism, and Marxist and neo-Marxist analyses. They pursue a more democratic educational system and ideology.[26] Michael Apple, utilizing the critical theories of Gramsci and Bourdieu, analyzes how dominant culture and economic

22. Wilson, "Critical Examination of Teacher Education," 59–60.

23. Pinar, "The Reconceptualization of Curriculum Studies," 173–74.

24. Dennis, "Decolonising Education," 196.

25. Pinar, "The Reconceptualization of Curriculum Studies," 171–73; Glatthorn et al., *Curriculum Leadership*, 73–75.

26. Pinar, et al., *Understanding Curriculum*, 38–39.

policy, ideological traditions, and curriculum interact to maintain and reproduce the unequal distribution of "correct" knowledge at schools. He then challenges educators to critically and honestly explore the ideological assumptions and understandings that shape their work and to confront how they are implicated in the reproduction and maintenance of the dominant structure and organization of schooling.[27] Reconceptualists suggest that educators put the foremost emphasis on the human subject, the who of education, and the importance of critical thinking to reveal the class conflict and the unequal power relationships existing in the larger society.[28] Concretely, Pinar presents the following nine characteristics of reconceptualist curriculum summarized by Paul Klohr:

> 1) A holistic, organic view is taken of humankind and his or her relation to nature; 2) the individual becomes the chief agent in the construction of knowledge; s/he is a culture creator as well as a culture bearer; 3) the curriculum theorist draws heavily on his/her own experiential base as method; 4) curriculum theorizing recognizes as major resources the preconscious realms of experience; 5) the foundational roots of their theorizing lie in existential philosophy, phenomenology and radical psychoanalysis, also drawing on humanistic reconceptualizations of such cognate fields as sociology anthropology, and political science; 6) personal liberty and the attainment of higher levels of consciousness become central values in the curriculum process; 7) diversity and pluralism are celebrated in both social ends and in the proposals projected to move toward those ends; 8) reconceptualization of supporting political-social operations is basic; and 9) new language forms are generated to translate fresh meanings-metaphors for example.[29]

These characteristics show that the purpose of reconceptualist education is the liberation of the people, especially the marginalized due to systematic exploitation and oppression. They believe that learning and teaching is a political act, and thus the curriculum should connect the subject matter with historical, economic, and other social issues of the global and domestic society. Comparatively putting, whereas traditionalists and conceptual-empiricists mostly focus on the what and how of education, reconceptualists start with the who, why, and where, and then move to what and how. They seek an education that helps students pursue meaning by asking critical

---

27. Apple, *Curriculum and Ideology*.

28. Glatthorn et al., *Curriculum Leadership*, 72–73.

29. Pinar et al., *Understanding Curriculum*, 224.

questions about the world and establish their sense of identity as agents to build a more just world. These ideological challenges are translated into the following concrete questions that reconceptualist educators must explore as a foundation for curriculum development:

- In what ways do the schools replicate the power differentials in the larger society?

- What is the nature of a truly liberated individual, and how does schooling inhibit such liberation?

- How do schools consciously or unwittingly mold children and youth to fit into societal roles pre-determined by race and class?

- As curriculum leaders determine what constitutes legitimate knowledge, how do such decisions reflect their class biases and serve to inhibit the full development of children and youth?

- In what ways does the schools' treatment of controversial issues tend to minimize and conceal the conflicts endemic to the society?[30]

Through unearthing educational ideologies premised on the dominant group's interests, reconceptualists argue that the school based on the traditionalists and conceptual-empiricist curriculum serve as the instrument of social control, and yet it can be transformed into a place to create a more democratic social order.

Reconceptualist Theological and Religious Curriculum to Undo Violent Extremism: What and How to Teach?

What are the challenges of these different approaches to theological and religious studies in undoing violent extremism? Alan Glatthorn et al. raise concerns about the tripartite classification of Pinar and others following his work because there are many scholars whose work can fall under more than one category.[31] I agree with their assessment that education that emphasizes content alone without considering the process is problematic. Likewise, paying attention to values and ideologies underlying the curriculum alone cannot help students be critical thinkers either. Notwithstanding that, to undo extremist violence in theological and religious

---

30. Glatthorn et al., *Curriculum Leadership*, 74.
31. Glatthorn et al., *Curriculum Leadership*, 72.

education, I still propose that the reconceptualist approach be the leading frame for such a curriculum.

As articulated by Eleazar Fernandez in his chapter of this book, some of the key contributing factors to extreme violence are the unequal systems that are presented as fair for everyone when in reality, these systems serve the interests of the powerful. Communal, political and social grievances, economic inequality, and the cycle of poverty, oppressive systems that blame victims for their suffering in contemporary society, are based on multifaceted hierarchical ideologies such as white supremacy, neoliberalism, and colonialism. Such thoughts are also embedded in the education system and curriculum of a particular society, and the school serves as the main tool to keep social ordering. Reconceptualists argue that before considering what and how to teach, analyzing problematic ideologies embedded in education is critical for the creation of an equality and equity-based society. Therefore, in the following section, I will explore the challenges and implications of the reconceptualist approach to education for theological and religious education in undoing violent extremism.

Reconceptualists challenge teachers of theology and religion to prioritize the person and social milieus and to critically analyze ideologies embedded in the knowledge we teach. They concretely demand us (1) to know what the foundational ideologies are of knowledge/contents we teach; (2) to investigate how and by whom such ideologies were formed; (3) to analyze who are benefited from the knowledge, and whose voices are left out and ignored; and (4) to explore alternative perspectives from which we should teach for equity and equality. Similar questions have been asked by scholars who pursue decolonial education, which tries to disentangle education "from all power which is not constituted by free decisions made by free people. It rejects the academic and pedagogic posture, premised on colonialism, that assumes that the mainstream (that which is Western, colonial or Eurocentric) is global and universal and others – indigenous, local knowledges are a deviation."[32] Dennis provides the following concrete guidelines for reconceptual and decolonial education:

1. Establish a space within which it is possible to speak about decolonisation. This may require a rejection of the most readily and easily available spaces, necessitating the deliberate cultivation of an undercommons, or an otherwise space.

32. Dennis, "Decolonising Education," 201.

2. Recognise and reflexively explore your own implicatedness within the structures you critique. It is possible that this might not feel empowering.

3. Interrogate the existing cultural interpretive monopoly of European knowledges, assumptions and methodologies.

4. Identify those too frequently unexplored ways of being that are of most interest to you; imagine the shape of a curriculum driven by them.

5. Acknowledge the curriculum in its breadth, as including not only the specific content taught but also the way it is taught and the enactment of particular sorts of pedagogic relationships.

6. Refuse a single authoritative voice, perspective or approach. Remain within indeterminacy, accepting all conclusions as tentative, all settlements as temporary – including this suggestion. This may be uncomfortable.

7. Place the disciplinary founding fathers of philosophy and social sciences in their place: contextualize them and their ideas as emergent from a specific time and place rather than universal.

8. Locate unheard, silenced or trivialized voices relevant to your discipline – exemplify and amplify them, placing them alongside orthodox voices in an implicit motion of critique.

9. Explore and identify the political implications of specific pedagogic approaches. These may not be the ultimate drivers of your pedagogy but they are its inescapable by-products.

10. Extricate your curriculum from all power which is not constituted by free decisions made by free people and use the resources of imagination, organizing, opposition and resistance in pursuance of that end, pausing only when it is accomplished.[33]

Simply put, theological and religious teachers must remember the historicity of our discipline and content we teach as they are located in time, space, and specific cultures. Also, our education is to help students think critically, embrace diverse voices, and engage in respectful dialogue to commit to co-creating a just world, "drawing on our collective resources rather than falling prey to competitive self-interest."[34] This means that educators must center the multiplicity of meaning and "[accept] the 'cacophony of voices', where the risk

---

33. Dennis, "Decolonising Education," 202.
34. Dennis, "Decolonising Education," 200.

of disintegration is preferable to selective silencing."[35] Without it, we cannot dismantle the universalism of the dominant group.

In theological education, there have been several people who have done similar work. For example, R. S. Sugirtharajah, a renowned post-colonial biblical scholar, shows how such pedagogy can be practiced in a biblical studies class. In his book, *Postcolonial Criticism and Biblical Interpretation,* Sugirtharajah demands that biblical teachers scrutinize the ideologies the Bible embodies and that are entrenched in it.[36] He presents multiple biblical pedagogical methods that help students decode ideologies embedded in the Bible and interpreted texts. The following is my summary of one of his pedagogical examples:

> Utilizing different biblical hermeneutical methods and commentaries, find out which empire is in the scene?
>
> - What kind of political, economic, cultural, social, ideological, religious values are present in the text?
>
> - Are they people listed? Who are they? What kinds of values do they represent? Who are missing?
>
> Select a few commentaries written in different times (during and after colonialism, contemporary, etc.).
>
> - How have commentators interpreted the text? What conventional (political, economic, social, cultural) values do they bring to the interpretation of the text?
>
> - How are the marginalized portrayed in connection with the text and the time of the commentator? Whose values and ideologies are they advocating?[37]

Sugirtharajah emphasizes that contemporary biblical students must unearth imperial/colonial ideologies already embedded in the Bible itself as it was written, edited, redacted, and canonized in various ancient imperial contexts. Moreover, colonial motives of commentators of the West should not be freed from the exegetical process either. It is imperial ideologies of the text and colonial motives of the West together that create colonizing and oppressive lenses for readings that justify violence, wars, hierarchy, patriarchy, and other forms of subjugation. These are some of the critical causes of the communal grievances experienced by the marginalized.

---

35. Dennis, "Decolonising Education," 197.

36. Sugirtharajah, *Postcolonial Criticism and Biblical Interpretation,* 79.

37. Sugirtharajah, *Postcolonial Criticism and Biblical Interpretation,* 79–85.

What Sugirtharajah offers for biblical classrooms, which is in line with reconceptualist and decolonial pedagogy, has helpful pedagogical insights for what and how to teach to undo violent extremism in other theological and religious studies classes. First, it challenges theological educators to examine the history of knowledge we teach as the canon: the process of canonization, the power dynamics behind the process and dominant ideological assumptions that shaped the decisions, and voices that were silenced and excluded. This history needs to be taught to help our students understand the illusion of neutrality and universality that may have costed the most vulnerable of our society. Some of the critical root causes of various grievances experienced by the marginalized have been reinforced through a society's educational ideologies and systems, as reconceptualists argue. According to Henry Giroux, in the last three decades, neoliberalism has forcefully pushed to reduce the role of higher education to that of the production of technical personnel, frontline managers, and professionals, rather than helping people to be "critically engaged citizens—citizens who can engage in debate, dialogue and bear witness to a different and critical sense of remembering, agency, ethics and collective resistance."[38] Therefore, teaching and learning about the ideological assumptions of canonized knowledge are critical and fundamental in undoing violent extremism. Teaching such history also requires that we theological educators should critically examine our assumptions, biases, and sometimes un-checked claims for neutrality.

Second, theological educators need to take our students' life contexts and lived experiences as equally important texts as the printed materials we teach. Students' experiences and life context must be the starting point of education, not a site of implication. Starting with their own experiences helps them critically analyze their assumptions as well as their experiences with the dominant society. Their lives, in conversation with the rigorous studies that include an ideological analysis of their learning subjects, could help them foster their leadership for social change. Paulo Freire, a Brazilian educator, insists that the purpose of education is to help people uncover causes of human suffering by raising their critical consciousness so that they can engage in communal transformative actions to build more just and equitable life conditions for themselves and others. To do that, Freire proposes a problem-posing method designed to interrogate critical issues in people's lives, especially oppressive and divisive social phenomena, through dialogical inquiry between the teachers and students, and among students, who together as a learning community analyze identified problems, and make

38. Giroux, "Angela Davis."

constructive action plans for change.[39] Zeus Leonardo, a critical pedagogy scholar, assesses that this dialogical inquiry process guides the participants of learning to detect and disrupt the unequal and oppressive power dynamics of class, race, sexuality, gender identity, and other hegemonic agendas hidden both in schools and in the greater society.[40]

Third, reconceptualist pedagogy also challenges theological educators to pursue communal and intersectional learning and teaching as well as global solidarity. Violent extremism is a multifaceted and complex belief system that cannot be separated from tangled global and local political and economic systems as my students and I witnessed in Colombia. Global injustices are deeply connected to domestic oppressions and vice versa, and they both contribute to the perpetuation of the status quo, that is, if they are not tackled together. Thus, new and emancipatory knowledge should be generated through a communal process in both literal and metaphorical senses. In our teaching, we need to continually ask ourselves and our students whether or not our old and new knowledge of justice is gained at the cost of persons or communities. This was a critical element for my students to learn in Colombia. Most of them came from dominant and privileged contexts compared to people we encountered there, despite their lived experiences of discrimination in the United States. They were mostly inclined to focus on justice for their community alone, without paying attention to the fact that their unacknowledged privileges could harm invisible others. The biggest lesson we gained there was the necessity of global solidarity in our efforts to undo injustice and violent extremism. Our curriculum should include empathy for people who are different or live under different conditions.[41]

Even in the U.S. context, Andrea Smith, in her short but powerful article, "Heteropatriarchy and the Three Pillars of White Supremacy,"[42] probes that any efforts to undo oppression including violent extremism mandates serious solidarity work. She names the three dominant logics of white supremacy which are the foundation and driving force for all the oppressions we know: 1) slavery, underpinning capitalism, which is expressed in a form of anti-black racism; 2) racial slaughter which enables and strengthens the ongoing colonial and imperialism which Native Americans continually experience; 3) Orientalism, which rationalizes the militarism and the necessity of war to continue and maintain the interests of imperialism which targets

39. Freire, *Pedagogy of the Oppressed*, 71–86.

40. Leonardo, *Race, Whiteness, and Education*, 19.

41. Gereluk, *Education, Extremism and Terrorism*, 16–17.

42. Smith, "Heteropatriarchy," 69–73.

Muslims and immigrants of color. Irrespective of race, immigration history, economic class, and other statuses, Smith argues that every American is entangled in the system of heteropatriarchal white supremacy. For example, Korean American women, who are victims of the orientalism that discriminates against immigrants of color, are a part of an anti-black racist structure founded on capitalism while also being inhabitants of the land taken away from Native Americans. Without communal endeavors and solidarity, each minoritized people can continue to perpetuate others' sufferings. One minoritized group's lives are inherently connected and intertwined with others. Their privileges and oppressions, resistance and healing, self-reflection, and solidarity are concurrently formed and evolving in tangled, interwoven, and overlapping locations. Therefore, without solidarity-based and intersectional education, we cannot cut the chain of oppression, which also cause people's grievances feeding for extremist ideology formation.

Education in any given society serves as the primary tool for the ideological formation for its members as well as an essential site of new or alternative worldviews.[43] Educators aiming to undo violent extremism must examine and expand their definitions of curriculum. Theological and religious education that does undo violent extremism will significantly benefit from the reconceptualist approach to the curriculum. It requires educators to recognize the political nature of teaching and learning and to demystify the false notion of neutrality and universalism embedded in educational structure and ideologies. It also commands any educator to respect each human's communal nature that leads to the communal learning process through which new knowledge toward justice is generated in communal and intersectional ways. This approach also asks educators to go beyond the handed-down canon and the teacher, to students' life contexts and experiences as critical sites of authority. The education that undoes violent extremism can be achieved by moving away from a culture of unquestioning to one of empowering people to generate hope and action for shared lives as members of a global community.

Bibliography

Apple, Michael. *Curriculum and Ideology*. 4th ed. New York: Routledge, 2018.
Bruner, Jerome. *The Culture of Education*. Cambridge: Harvard University Press, 1996.
Christodoulou, Nikoletta. "Conceptual Empiricist Perspective." In *Encyclopedia of Curriculum Studies*, edited by Craig Kridel, 139–140. Thousand Oaks, CA: Sage, 2010.

43. Bruner, *The Culture of Education*, 1–8.

Dennis, Carol Azumah. "Decolonising Education: A Pedagogic Intervention." In *Decolonizing the University*, edited by Gurminder Bhambra, Dalia Gebrial, and Kerem Nişancıolu, 190–207. London: Pluto, 2018.

Freire, Paulo. *Pedagogy of the Oppressed*. New York: Continuum, 1970.

Giroux, Henry. "Angela Davis, Freedom and the Politics of Higher Education." *Huffington Post*, April 10, 2013. https://www.huffingtonpost.com/henry-a-giroux/angela-davis_b_3055913.html.

Giroux, Henry. *On Critical Pedagogy*. New York: Continuum, 2011.

Giroux, Henry, Anthony Penna, and William Pinar, eds. *Curriculum and Instruction*. Berkeley, CA: McCutchan, 1981.

Gereluk, Diane. *Education, Extremism and Terrorism: What Should Be Taught in Citizenship Education and Why*. New York: Continuum, 2012.

Glatthorn, Allan A., Floyd Boschee, Bruce M. Whitehead, and Bonni F. Boschee. *Curriculum Leadership: Strategies for Development and Implementation*. 5th ed. Thousand Oaks, CA: Sage, 2019.

Harvey, David. *A Brief History of Neoliberalism*. New York: Oxford University Press, 2007.

Leonardo, Zeus. *Race, Whiteness, and Education*. New York: Routledge, 2009.

Litonjua, M. D. "Third World/Global South: From Development to Globalization to Imperial Project." *Journal of Third World Studies* 27 (2010) 107–32.

McGregor, Sue. "Neoliberalism and Health Care." *International Journal of Consumer Studies* 25 (2001) 82–89.

Pinar, William. "The Reconceptualization of Curriculum Studies." *Journal of Curriculum Studies* 10 (1978) 205–14. Reprinted in Flindersis, David and Stephen Thornton, eds. *The Curriculum Studies Reader*. 5th ed., 167–76. New York: Routledge, 2017.

Pinar, William, William Reynolds, Patrick Slattery, and Peter M. Taubman. *Understanding Curriculum: An Introduction to the Study of Historical and Contemporary Curriculum Discourses*. New York: Lang, 2006.

Schirch, Lisa. *The Ecology of Violent Extremism: Perspectives on Peacebuilding and Human Security*. Lanham, MD: Rowman & Littlefield, 2018.

Smith, Andrea. "Heteropatriarchy and the Three Pillars of White Supremacy." In *The Color of Violence: The Incite! Anthology*, edited by Incite! Women of Color against Violence, 69–73. 2006. Reprint, Durham, NC: Duke University Press, 2016.

Sugirtharajah, R. S. *Postcolonial Criticism and Biblical Interpretation*. Oxford: Oxford University Press, 2002.

Thompson, Franklin, and William Austin. "The Impact of Revisionist History on Pre-Service and In-Service Teacher Worldviews." *Education* 132 (2011) 39–53.

Tyler, Ralph. *Basic Principles of Curriculum and Instruction*. Chicago: University of Chicago Press, 1949.

Wilson, Donald. "Critical Examination of Teacher Education from the Perspective of Curriculum." *Canadian Journal of Education* 6 (1981) 55–64.

4

Undoing Violence with the Brain in Mind

—RODOLFO R. NOLASCO JR.

Introduction

How can the interior ground of the heart yield both fruits of heartfelt praise to God and thorny thistles of exclusion, alienation, and—worse—violent extremism toward those who bear the same image of God as we? More pressingly, how might theological education engage in the work of undoing cruelty and violence through its teaching practices and pedagogies? What follows is an analysis, albeit provisional, of these confounding questions using the hermeneutical perspectives of evolutionary psychology, brain science, and, later, the anthropological process of scapegoating. But why this route, one may ask? The answer is simple if we come to think of it. Religious beliefs and commitments, especially those (re)formed in seminary classrooms, do not float in the air detached from the body that feels, thinks, and behaves. In other words, beliefs that we hold about human persons, God and other divine matters are grounded in our body. They can be understood as concrete and localized expressions of a brain and mind created to adapt to the environment around it. Hence, questions posed early on require that we pay close attention to the operations of the brain—the primary site of students' cognitive, affective, and bodily learning.

The Development of the Moral Brain[1]

At its core, evolutionary psychology considers "behavior, belief, emotions, thinking and feelings are all functions of a fully embodied brain. As the brain is a physical organ, it, like all other physical organs, has an evolutionary history. . . the product of evolutionary process that shaped this organ in response to environmental selection pressures."[2] Over a long period of time, the brain has gradually evolved into a "collection of task-oriented and problem-solving mental tools"[3] as a way of navigating a challenging, unpredictable, and ancient environment. To many evolutionary psychologists, this specialized and instinctual neural wiring is etched deeply into the brain and has left an indelible mark on contemporary behavioral and cognitive or learning patterns, which are now being revealed with fascinating detail by cognitive sciences.[4]

With this discovery we can now approach the religious mind and explore our propensity to produce in one seamless and uninterrupted movement the most profound spiritual insights and the most horrendous ideations and acts of cruelty and religious violence against others. More particularly, what triggers the neural activation of this ancient brain system that propels deeply committed believers as learners to act with such intention against those who hold different and divergent views? How might religious beliefs accrued over the years of seminary education induce and condone inhumane treatment of others? And how have we come to hold such beliefs that run contrary to the message of love and compassion that is central to Christian teaching in the first place?

Acknowledging the strain of violence embedded in the deepest level of religious imagination,[5] but ignored mostly in religious education, is a good place to start. This is in no way desacralizing our religious tradition. It only exposes this strain that "flows naturally from the moral logic inherent in many religious systems," including Christianity, and is "grounded in our evolved psychology."[6] But what is the nature of this moral logic that is capable of producing both religious morality and religious violence?

In its basic form, morality is concerned with "judgments about right and wrong, good or bad, as these terms are used to judge interpersonal

1. Original version of this article can be found in Nolasco, *Compassionate Presence: A Radical Response to Human* Suffering.

2. Teehan, *In the Name of God*, 2.

3. Teehan, *In the Name of God*, 2.

4. Teehan, *In the Name of God*, 2.

5. Juergensmeyer, *Terror in the Mind of God*, 6.

6. Teehan, *In the Name of God*, 147.

relations."[7] According to cognitive scientific study these judgments are instinctual and often the result of "intuitive, emotionally based reactions to
social interactions,"[8] which are then given rational justifications.[9] In other
words, morality is not solely the domain of reason as often claimed by
moral philosophers, nor is it simply a prescribed list of behaviors generated from sacred texts. Numerous functional magnetic resonance imaging
(fMRI) studies reveal a much more complex scenario where both emotion
and cognition are implicated in the process of making moral judgments.[10]
Hence, when faced with moral dilemmas, human beings make quick and
instinctual responses that emanate "below the horizon of consciousness"
and are caused by a complex network of "neurally-based cognitive and
affective systems."[11] This innate moral grammar that lies outside of conscious awareness and shapes moral judgments is believed to have evolutionary origins. That is, it evolved out of necessity to meet the "demands
faced by individuals pursuing their reproductive fitness"[12] amidst a socially
demanding and challenging environment. It comprised such elements as
kin selection, reciprocal altruism, indirect reciprocity, among others, and
is emotionally charged and powerful in navigating and shaping human
interactions.[13] Over time, this moral grammar developed into a coherent
moral system that is found in all culture.

> If a society is to function at a level beyond the clan it must
> develop a system to effectively encourage and reward coopera-
> tion, and to discourage and punish defectors and cheats. This
> is what moral systems are designed to do: to establish a code
> of behavior that promotes and rewards behavior necessary to
> cohesive social functioning, while condemning and punishing
> behavior contrary to cohesive social functioning . . . To the ex-
> tent that a moral code taps into this evolved moral sense it gains
> great intuitive and emotional appeal. It can move people to act
> because it triggers the cognitive and emotional predispositions
> that generate behavior.[14]

7. Teehan, *In the Name of God*, 15.

8. Teehan, *In the Name of God*, 16.

9. Teehan, *In the Name of God*, 16.

10. Green, "Emotional engagement in moral judgment."

11. Teehan, *In the Name of God*, 19.

12. Teehan, *In the Name of God*, 41.

13. Teehan, *In the Name of God*, 41.

14. Teehan, *In the Name of God*, 42.

Religion, being one of the most enduring and powerful cultural institutions, is a potent force in promoting group cohesion. Through the lens of evolutionary psychology, religion is considered as a potent force in "regulating human behaviors in a pro-social manner by triggering evolved cognitive/emotional mechanisms."[15] As religion codifies behavior through a series of moral imperatives, it divides people into two groups with distinguishable codes and ethic—the in-group or those who adhere to its moral codes and the out-group or the outsiders who are less, if at all, invested and committed to the group. Social cohesion is established within a group by promoting pro-social behavior marked by reciprocation among members of the group.[16] However, this social expectation has a dim outcome. It is exclusionary in nature in that if you do not belong to a clan "then you are an outsider . . . have less motivation to cooperate or to reciprocate cooperation and, therefore may pose a danger to the community. For all the constructive morality found in religion, we find an equally prominent place for warnings against outsiders."[17] Being excluded is not only a marker, at its worst; it merits unwanted and sometimes injurious or fatal consequences. For this to happen the out-group is not only excluded, they are also "otherized,"[18] subjected to various forms of cruelty and violence.

The otherization of certain individuals or groups is infused by an overestimation of self and the degradation of others because they adhere to a belief that is different and contrary to the established norm and values of the in-group[19] and the attribution of the "essence trap."[20] Here, their misdeeds or ill-conceived choices are considered to be reflections of their flawed nature, their character or essence. Consequently, a clear demarcation is drawn by emphasizing their marked difference from the in-group, "pushing the unpleasantness away to a more comfortable psychological distance and pushing the person away with it . . . purely because we have beliefs about other people which lead us to push them into hated outgroups."[21]

Beliefs gain their strength when delivered and heard repeatedly causing stronger synaptic connections and neural patterning in the brain to occur.[22] The classroom is exactly the laboratory where this happens. To be

---

15. Teehan, *In the Name of God*, 42.

16. Teehan, *In the Name of God*, 148.

17. Teehan, *In the Name of God*, 148.

18. Taylor, *Cruelty: Human Evil and the Human Brain*, 8.

19. Taylor, *Cruelty: Human Evil and the Human Brain*, 8.

20. Taylor, *Cruelty: Human Evil and the Human Brain*, 9.

21. Taylor, *Cruelty: Human Evil and the Human Brain*, 9.

22. Taylor, *Cruelty: Human Evil and the Human Brain*, 149.

more specific, "this strengthening tends to happen when the neurons they connect repeatedly co-activated. This may occur when one neuron triggers the second, or when other signals trigger both at once."[23] This explains partly why it is extremely difficult to give up or change beliefs that for long have been held dearly because neurologically they are intricately embedded or sculpted in the brain's neural networks. More so, beliefs also gain a foothold when they induce fierce and clear patterns of neural activity that fit nicely with neural patterns already in place and comes with "emotional boosters to help carve their impression into the cortex."[24] They are also likely to produce unwavering commitment when these accepted beliefs are uncomplicated, consistent, and easy to understand and decisively support the personal and communal narrative and identity of their followers.[25]

This anatomy of belief, albeit brief, provides the necessary conditions for otherization and violent extremism to happen. Hate speech heard in the classroom may be varied and casually rendered, yet in its basic form it propagates a very clear and simple story with three over-arching beliefs—"people are different, disgusting, not like you; these people want to harm you or have already harmed you or people like you; removing these people will solve your problems."[26] These core messages are couched in a familiar and compelling story and in a language the fits the context of their listeners. The effect of such skillful otherization is alarmingly predictable in that these key ideas ease more gently and deeply into the brain, especially when paired with an effective use of strong emotions to back up their claims.[27]

One such emotion is disgust. Disgusting stimuli evoke a powerful combination of physical and behavioral reactions—from changes in breathing and distinct facial expression to nausea and vomiting.[28] These aversive reactions to disgusting stimuli are innate or pre-programmed so as to allow for "early detection and avoidance of disgust-threats."[29] They have also evolved as a way of protection from perceived or actual threat.[30] Triggers include food, body products, sex, animals, interpersonal contamination, and moral offence,

23. Taylor, *Cruelty: Human Evil and the Human Brain*, 149.

24. Taylor, *Cruelty: Human Evil and the Human Brain*, 149.

25. Taylor, *Cruelty: Human Evil and the Human Brain*, 149.

26. Taylor, *Cruelty: Human Evil and the Human Brain*, 149.

27. Taylor, *Cruelty: Human Evil and the Human Brain*, 150.

28. Taylor, *Cruelty: Human Evil and the Human Brain*, 131.

29. Taylor, *Cruelty: Human Evil and the Human Brain*, 131.

30. Kazen, *Emotions in Biblical Law,* 93.

among others.[31] When confronted by these triggers people walk away in haste without much thought or provocation.

On a neuronal level, these reactions are complex, automatic, fast, and highly choreographed involving the stomach, the vagus nerve, and the brainstem, among others, to elicit a disgust response. Otherization relies on the repetition of the core message of difference and the accompanying emotion of disgust that one should feel toward the outsiders. The more disgusted we feel about the person or group the greater avoidance tactic is assumed. The disgust response can even go as far as eliminating the source of this aversive reaction.

As said previously, a signal of commitment and reciprocal cooperation are important elements of social cohesion. Any deviation from this incurs exclusion, particularly when beliefs, ideas, or views are divergent and incompatible with what the in-group holds to be true. To justify the otherization of the out-group, the in-group re-labels these ideas to make them appear more dangerous and threatening. The metaphor of ideas as pathogens and infectious succeed in eliciting counter measures to block the out-groups' ideas from spreading.[32] In effect, what they are really saying is that "people who have wrong ideas are plague-being organisms and ought to be eliminated for the sake of public health."[33] Not only are the ideas dangerous, the people who hold them are disgusting and therefore must be kept at bay and avoided at all cost. Thus, the chasm between the in-group and out-group widens and the animosity between the two groups is intensified.

Empathic Brain

Individuals who are always on high alert to mitigate actual or perceived threat are in danger themselves. The chronic activation of the stress-threat response can damage the body and can pose undue risk in matters of interpersonal relations. The latter takes the form of deficits in empathy quotient.

Empathy is the ability to inhabit the world of another to gain a fuller understanding of and appreciation for their thoughts and feelings and ways of being in the world. It is non-judgmental, sensitive, open, curious, and hospitable to the uniqueness of the person's internal world without losing one's own. It fosters genuineness, respect, honesty, and vulnerability in human relationships. Through it, minds meet and hearts commune in unity without sacrificing each other's differences and singularities. It promotes

31. Kazen, *Emotions in Biblical Law*, 93.

32. Taylor, *Cruelty: Human Evil and the Human Brain*, 158.

33. Taylor, *Cruelty: Human Evil and the Human Brain*, 149.

pro-social behavior, reciprocity and cooperation, which help facilitate the growth and flourishing of human society. In fact, our species is a rich reservoir of empathy by virtue of our shared experiences as human beings. Our commonality far outweighs our differences, which makes empathy readily accessible and available (in the absence of pathology).

Empathy is mediated by "mirror neurons" or brain cells that light up when we watch someone perform an action (e.g., moving a hand) and then having the inkling to do the same and the understanding of their intentions.[34] This "motor empathy" is intertwined with cognitive empathy or theory of mind (i.e. the ability to infer thoughts, beliefs, and perspectives based on the behaviors of others) and affective empathy (i.e. the ability to detect the feeling of another). These three coalesce together to form a wonderfully orchestrated manner of social engagement that relies on the "fundamental statistical facts of brain function: the correlations which ensure that similar events, on the whole, produce similar neural patterns."[35]

These psychological events occur in the right hemisphere of the brain.[36] The ability to see the interconnection of things, curiosity, interest and identification with others, self-awareness, and empathy are largely dependent on right hemisphere resources.[37] Particularly, when we try to put ourselves in the shoes of another, "we are using the right inferior parietal lobe, and the right lateral prefrontal cortex, which is involved in inhibiting the automatic tendency to espouse one's own point of it."[38] This means that the activation of this section of the brain makes possible the openness to divergent views and the willingness to be convinced of positions that have not been previously supported.[39]

In a broader sense, the right hemisphere has great affinity when it comes to emotional receptivity and expressiveness.[40] It is faster than the left hemisphere at detecting facial expression of emotion, reading subtle information that comes from the eyes, and understanding the emotional subtext of language.[41] It also plays a crucial role in animating the face and the prosody or intonation of voice to express emotions.[42] This is not to

---

34. Vittorio, "Action recognition in the premotor cortex," 593–609.

35. Taylor, *Cruelty and the Human Brain*, 180.

36. McGilchrist, *The Master and His Emissary*, 57.

37. McGilchrist, *The Master and His Emissary*, 57.

38. McGilchrist, *The Master and His Emissary*, 57.

39. McGilchrist, *The Master and His Emissary*, 57.

40. McGilchrist, *The Master and His Emissary*, 58.

41. McGilchrist, *The Master and His Emissary*, 59.

42. McGilchrist, *The Master and His Emissary*, 61.

say though that the left hemisphere has no part in the understanding and expression of emotion. The difference lies in the fact that the left hemisphere is more involved in the conscious representation of emotion, whereas the right hemisphere is more directly involved in the immediate even unconscious reception, expression, and processing of emotion.[43]

The hemispheric difference between the right and left side of the brain becomes starker when it comes to attention. In this context, attention is much more than a mental function alongside reasoning, memory, and acquisition of information.

> The kind of attention we bring to bear on the world changes the nature of the world we attend to . . . Attention changes what kind of a thing comes into being for us: in that way it changes the world . . . Attention also changes who we are, we who are doing the attending. Through the direction and nature of our attention, we prove to ourselves to be partners in creation, both of the world and of ourselves. In keeping with this, attention is inescapably bound up with value. Values enter through the way in which those functions are exercised: they can be used in different ways for different purposes to different ends.[44]

The right hemisphere sees the world more as a whole; it prioritizes context and the interrelatedness of things and people, and attends more acutely to the bigger picture.[45] The left hemisphere has a more focused and narrower attention, it sees mostly the individual parts and not the whole, and attends with much precision.[46] Both hemispheres function differently out of necessity. Together they need to bring to bear two incompatible types of attention on the world at the same time; one narrow, focused, and directed by our needs, and the other broad, open, and directed toward whatever else is going on in the world apart from ourselves.[47] This has ensured our survival and eventual success in navigating this complex and challenging world to our own benefit and advantage.

Though the two hemispheres differ in what they attend to, the right hemisphere does not have to know what the left hemisphere knows for that would compromise its ability to have the big picture view.[48] Neither should the left hemisphere be privy to the activities of the right hemisphere

43. McGilchrist, *The Master and His Emissary,* 62.

44. McGilchrist, *The Master and His Emissary,* 28.

45. McGilchrist, *The Master and His Emissary,* 27.

46. McGilchrist, *The Master and His Emissary,* 27.

47. McGilchrist, *The Master and His Emissary,* 27.

48. McGilchrist, *The Master and His Emissary,* 207.

because "from inside its own system, from its point of view, what it believes it has created appears complete."[49] Here lies its weakness, especially if the knowledge gained is not re-integrated back to the right hemisphere, which provides a complete and panoramic vista and more socially meaningful information about the self and the world.

The value of the left hemisphere is making the implicit explicit, "but this is a staging post, an intermediate level of the processing of experience, never the starting point or end point, never the deepest or the final level."[50] Unfortunately, the left hemisphere has become its own master instead of an emissary.[51] A world that is dominated by the left hemisphere is described as mechanical, abstract, disembodied, distanced from feelings, pragmatic, overconfident of its own view on reality, and lacking insight into its problems.[52] It is primed for competition and power[53] and when it forgets its function and place in light of the whole it offers a world that is stunningly familiar to what we have now. The current Western zeitgeist privileges rationality and empirical evidence as the only legitimate source of truth. It craves power and control and encourages abstraction and detachment from feelings, relationships, and community, and leaves us more isolated, disconnected, and divisive than ever before.

Consequently, this left hemisphere bias dampens the ability to form meaningful bonds with others. The empathy circuit, which is largely a function of the right hemisphere, is turned off, so to speak. As a result, this failure to make empathic connection makes otherization inevitable, especially in cases where the line between who is in and who is out has already been drawn. The left hemisphere can be co-opted to serve the purpose of otherization. Its narrow and limited focus can render members of the out-group purely as threats or objects to be avoided or eliminated and not appreciated as persons just like them—with feelings, families, and foibles. Its penchant for power and competition can be redressed as a way of justifying the all-too-consuming desire to win at all cost, even if that may mean taking the life of another. Its propensity to privilege reason or a particular way of reasoning can be co-opted or manipulated to rationalize various forms of cruelty and violence believing that somehow, they are deserving of such horrific acts because they exercise self-agency and dance to the beat of a different drummer. The tie that can bind one to another is cut-off such that the pain and suffering

49. McGilchrist, *The Master and His Emissary,* 207.
50. McGilchrist, *The Master and His Emissary,* 209.
51. McGilchrist, *The Master and His Emissary,* 428.
52. McGilchrist, *The Master and His Emissary,* 428.
53. McGilchrist, *The Master and His Emissary,* 428.

displayed by those who are otherized is obscured. The in-group is indifferent and unaffected by the suffering of their counterpart. They can be deaf to their cries of anguish and blind to their harrowing plight.

These empathic failures are not only expressed behaviorally through acts of avoidance, indifference, and non-response toward the suffering of the out-group. The brain reflects or captures these behavioral responses as well in fine detail as revealed through various fMRI studies.[54] For example, in a recent study of racial bias it is revealed that the "out-group members— merely by virtue of who they are and not anything they have done—reliably elicit diminished perceptions of suffering and fail to elicit equivalent physi- ological and affective empathic responses. More concerning is that these dampened empathic responses are related to less helping."[55] This is quite disconcerting and yet so true and rampant in today's society. Hence, it is all the more important that we educate students not only on the neural cor- relates of empathy but on ways of nourishing it so we can begin to mitigate the growing panacea of sacred violence.

Scapegoating[56] and Extremist Violence

The ubiquity of suffering that springs from and is sustained by violent extremist ideologies can also be explored through the age-old practice of scapegoating. Passing blame onto someone as a way of avoiding personal responsibility or culpability is a frequent occurrence in my work with cli- ents in therapeutic contexts. Too often, a "problem child," a "rebellious teenager," or the "black sheep" in the family heaps up blame for marital conflict or familial discord. By pointing fingers at the vulnerable and dependent offspring within the marital-familial hierarchy an exit door is swung wide-open, leaving behind a mess of emotional entanglements, unresolved conflicts, and enduring threat-based response patterns for the "weakest link" to clean up. As in most, if not all cases, this gets messier and locks everyone in a never-ending cycle of "blame game," which bears the fruits of further psychic and relational wounding and instability. The difficult, painful, but rewarding work of addressing the core issue or prob- lem is sacrificed in the altar of scapegoating that offers momentary gains expressed in a false sense of familial unity.

54. Avananti, "Racial bias."

55. Cikara, "Us and Them: Intergroup failures of empathy."

56. The original version of this part of the essay is found in Nolasco, *God's Beloved Queer: Identity, Spirituality, and Practice.*

Peering into the hidden dynamics of scapegoating, at least on a psychological level, reveals a "two-dual motive model,"[57] which usually operate outside of one's awareness. This defensive and self-serving maneuvering induces a sense of a stable perception of "personal moral value" as a way of minimizing guilt over one's contribution and responsibility for a negative outcome.[58] In the case of the "problem child," for example, inordinate negative attention is placed on him or her—from staying up late with friends to unpredictable behaviors, to adjustment challenges that come with this age-group—as a way of thwarting an acknowledgment of their own culpability for the family breakdown. The child is sent to therapy, which doubles as a confirmation of their collective projection, and everyone feels good about themselves for doing something right to "fix the problem." And then the cycle of blame rears its ugly head and this time either the same person is scapegoated again, or another family member is sacrificed on the altar of guilt purification. Related to this motive is the mechanism's efficacy in providing a sense of stable perception of "personal control"[59] in the midst of a weakening family structure. Everyone stands on shifting ground and with it comes discomfort and dis-ease of unknowing and a prospect of total collapse of the system. To assuage this, a scapegoat is enlisted as the bearer of misfortunes in the family who offers a convenient explanation and acts as a dispenser of control for an otherwise layered and complicated scenario. In a sense, a scapegoat is a person actively "destabilized" so as to achieve familial "stability" so that everything can go back to "business as usual" again.

The momentary triumph and release that is wrought by sacrificing "one" on behalf of the "many" signals an evolved ontological and cultural artifact that is not only embedded in all human relations but operates *ad finitum* whose life-negating consequences are grievous offenses to human worth, value, and dignity. It gets even more iniquitous and demonic, not in a supernatural sense, when the scapegoat mechanism, which underpins rampant extremist violence, is legitimized by co-opting the sacred and make it appear as a divine initiative.

In recent memory and on a much larger scale, we see this same mechanism yields atrocious and horrifying outcomes in the scapegoating and subsequent extermination of six million European Jews in Nazi Germany, the mass slaughter of Tutsis in Rwanda, and the on-going ethnic cleansing of Rohingya people in Myanmar. Each had been credited as the sole culprit behind the economic collapse, social stress, and political instability that

57. Rothschild, "A Dual-Motive Model of Scapegoating."
58. Rothschild, "A Dual-Motive Model of Scapegoating."
59. Rothschild, "A Dual-Motive Model of Scapegoating."

blanketed their nations, and consequently bore the brunt of the dominant group's "crimes against humanity." Close to home, the continuing violence inflicted upon black and brown bodies, hate crimes against Muslims, and the portrayal of immigrants as criminals and rapists give witness to the instinctual response to scapegoat a particular group, usually of minority status, to assuage collective guilt and fear of losing autonomy and project an illusory image of brute strength, power, and control. And since the cycle of injurious behaviors humans do to each other seems unyielding and hard to break, one cannot help but wonder if the scapegoat mechanism is more than just a psychological and collective defense but an anthropological reality—a feature of the human condition and by extension of human relating.

Religion, of course, is not immune to this reality. The religious undercurrent of the scapegoat mechanism finds its genesis in the Old Testament. In Leviticus 16, we read the pivotal role of the "goat of Azazel" in carrying all the sins of Israel upon itself on the day of Atonement. In a highly ritualized manner, the priest transfers the guilt of the Jewish people onto the escaping goat, which is then beaten, dispatched, and driven out into the wilderness. This highly choreographed but violent and bloody ceremony secured salvific efficacy for the community. This, of course, foreshadows the same mechanism deployed against Jesus, but not for the reason we normally think. The Old Testament account provides the genesis of scapegoating while the Gospel account of the Passion of Jesus serves to undo this very same mechanism and subsequently offers us a radical way of conducting our life together.

Scapegoating and Mimetic Desire

The cross as a symbol of the undoing of the scapegoat mechanism is elucidated by the French literary critic, anthropologist, religious scholar, and philosopher René Girard. His perspicacious description and revelatory analysis of the culture constructing and culture sustaining of the victimage mechanism[60] is connected to his ontological claim that human beings desire according to the desire of another. The finer details of his theory are not within the scope of this essay; however, it is important to provide a compendium of his theory particularly its religious and theological ramifications and relate them to hidden dynamics of the scapegoating of those otherized.

According to Girard's interdividual psychology, human desire does not originate from within the agential and isolated subject, independent from external influences or promptings. Instead, as mimetic individuals, our human

60. Girard, *Things Hidden*, 3.

112   TEACHING IN A WORLD OF VIOLENT EXTREMISM

desires, whether of temporal, relational, ideological, even religious or spiritual in nature, are borne out of imitating the desires of another.

In Girard's own words, "man [sic] is the creature who does not know what to desire, and he turns to others in order to make up his mind. We desire what others desire because we imitate their desires."[61] In other words, we have no clue as to what we want for our lives, oblivious to what is worthy and valuable and therefore rely on others to fill this existential void. This lack of being causes us to look elsewhere and this becomes our passage into what may resemble a sense of self that is derivative of the imitation of others. We are initiated into this dynamic imitative process during early childhood development, which also coincides with rapid growth in neural development and intense activation of mirror neurons that underlie and support our innate mimetic capacities.

In his theological appropriation of Girard's mimetic theory, James Alison states that "all of these things are received by us in patterns that are pre-shaped by the desires of others."[62] These ready-made patterns of desires are mediated by our models who reflect or mirror back to us who or what to desire, and in the process, conferring upon these objects of desires a sense of worth, value, and significance.

Incipient in mimetic desire is the potential for violence. Since two or more people are desiring the same object, there ensues mimetic rivalry, with the other seen as an obstacle to the acquisition or possession of the desired object. In this reciprocal, contentious, and rivalistic exchange, the intrinsic worth and value of the object recedes into the background and what takes center stage is the removal of the obstacle-model by whatever means necessary. As Girard asserts, ". . . violence is the process itself when two or more partners try to prevent one another from appropriating the object they all desire through physical or other means."[63] The single minded intent and intensity to eliminate the rival spreads like a contagion, drawing people into this matrix of violence or "mimetic crisis"[64] that teeters into an all-out-war-against-all, threatening to tear apart social cohesion and unity. To thwart this social collapse, a sinister plot is conjured up by these warring camps by pointing their collective fingers randomly at someone, usually considered by them as a weakling or a social misfit and make them responsible for the unfolding conflict. In other words, a scapegoating mechanism is activated, which is a convenient way of releasing and transferring their guilt onto another

61. Girard, "Generative Scapegoating."

62. Alison, *The Forgiving Victim*, 29.

63. Williams, *The Girard Reader*, 9.

64. Girard, *Things Hidden*, 287.

and secures the collective unanimity against the chosen victim. What starts out as an all-against-all is transformed into all-against-one punctuated by a cathartic resolution ending in peace. Of course, the peace that comes upon this newly reconstituted community is the offspring of violence and a victimage mechanism "built upon the lies about the guilt of the victim and the innocence of the community."[65] Hiding this truth in plain sight is reinforced further by divinizing the chosen victim or scapegoat through the attribution of "double transference,"[66] where they are considered to be both the cause of the conflict and therefore must be driven out and killed, and the cause of peace since the victim's expulsion re-calibrates their social standing, relation, and sense of unity.[67] In other words, the resolution of mimetic crisis mediated by the victim turns them into a divine figure, a god, who bears both the transgression of the community-turned lynch mob and the transgression of making him or her the bearer of their sins.[68]

In an effort to ensure and forestall a repetition of mimetic contagion prohibitions are instituted and rituals and myths are enacted and observed. But far more than just mitigating violence, this social regulatory device is meant to conceal sacred violence committed against an innocent victim, the account of which is told only by the victimizers themselves.[69] With this in place, the community is afforded with unrestricted resources to create, develop, sustain, and then regulate human communities while hiding in plain sight the fact that the evolution of human culture is founded on controlling violence with violence.[70] Sadly, not much has really changed. This social mechanism is still at work, with the "face" of the victim going through numerous iterations over time. Hence, we get this eerie and dreadful sense that somehow, we are still standing on shaky ground that is threatened constantly by a potential mimetic breakout. Again, from where does our help come?

Religion? Perhaps! But let us not be quick to assume that it is the panacea for this intractable predicament. In fact, the converse is also true. Religion has been and is used to otherize and inflict violence on various minority groups,[71] those considered to be falling outside and resisting, challenging, deconstructing established dogmas and prescribed practices. This

65. Colloquium, "What is Mimetic Theory."

66. Hammerton-Kelly, *Sacred Violence*, 26.

67. Hammerton-Kelly, *Sacred Violence*, 26

68. Hammerton-Kelly, *Sacred Violence*, 27.

69. Girard, *Things Hidden*, 28.

70. Girard, *Things Hidden*, 115.

71. See, for example, Bailie, *Violence Unveiled*; Cobb, *God Hates Fags*; Teehan, *In the Name of God*; Juergensmeyer, *Terror in the Mind of God*.

gives credence to Girard's claim that religion is not a response to a divine lure, or the "experience of the a priori Sacred, understood as ontologically prior to the individual or society,"[72] as most of us tend to believe, but is given birth by society as a protective response against mimetic delirium through the institution of prohibitions, rituals, and myths. It is "the sum of human assumptions resulting from collective transferences focused on reconciliatory victim at the conclusion of mimetic crisis,"[73] hence, "violence is the heart and secret soul of the Sacred."[74]

The task ahead for theological educators remains—how might we participate in the undoing of extremist violence in our own classrooms in light of the preceding discussion? What pastoral images, familiar and new, might offer fresh directions as we respond to this call?

Summarily, a contemplative and positive mimetic approach that gazes mindfully upon the Triune God, who is for us and over against nothing or no one at all, might be a good starting point. This mutual gazing creates an attitude of spaciousness and hospitality that mirrors the kenotic example of Jesus Christ, the forgiving victim, who we imitate as a mediator or model of non-acquisitive desire. Through following his gaze, we are empowered to live by his example of unconditional love that champions the inherent sacredness of all persons.

Bibliography

Alison, James. *Jesus the Forgiving Victim: Listening for the Unheard Voice.* Glenview: Doers, 2013.

Avananti, Alessio, et al. "Racial Bias Reduce Empathic Sensorimotor with Other Race-Pain." *Current Biology* 20 (2010) 1018–20.

Cikara, Mina, et al. "Us and Them: Intergroup Failures of Empathy." *Current Directions in Psychological Science* 20.3 (2011) 149–53.

Colloquim. "What is Mimetic Theory?" https://violenceandreligion.com/mimetic-theory/.

Girard, Rene. *Things Hidden Since the Foundation of the World.* Palo Alto: Stanford University Press, 1987.

———. *Violence and the Sacred.* New York: Norton, 1979.

Green, Joshua, et al. "An fMRI Investigation of Emotional Engagement in Moral Judgment." *Science* 293 (2001) 2105–8.

Hammerton-Kelly, Robert. *Sacred Violence.* Minneapolis: Fortress, 1992.

Juergensmeyer, Mark. *Terror in the Mind of God: The Global Rise of Religious Violence.* Los Angeles: University of California Press, 2001.

72. Hammerton-Kelly, *Sacred Violence*, 28.

73. Girard, *Things Hidden*, 42.

74. Girard, *Violence and the Sacred*, 31.

Kazen, Thomas. *Emotions in Biblical Law: A Cognitive Science Approach.* Sheffield: Sheffield Phoenix, 2011.

McGilchrist, Ian. *The Master and His Emissary: The Divided Brain and the Making of the Western World.* New Haven: Yale University Press, 2012.

Nolasco, Rolf. *Compassionate Presence: A Radical Response to Human Suffering.* Eugene, OR: Cascade, 2016.

———. *God's Beloved Queer: Identity, Spirituality, and Practice.* Eugene, OR: Wipf & Stock, 2019.

Rothschild, Zachary K., et al. "A Dual-Motive Model of Scapegoating: Displacing Blame to Reduce Guilt or Increase Control." *Journal of Personality and Social Psychology* 102 (2012) 1148–63.

Taylor, Kathleen. *Cruelty: Human Evil and the Human Brain.* Oxford: Oxford University Press, 2009.

Teehan, John. *In the Name of God: The Evolutionary Origins of Religious Ethics and Violence.* Oxford: Wiley-Blackwell, 2010.

Vittorio, Gallese, et al. "Action Recognition in the Premotor Cortex." *Brain* 119 (1996) 593–609.

Williams, James. *The Girard Reader.* New York: Crossroad, 1976.

5

Theological Ethics in a World of Violent Extremism

—Ellen Ott Marshall

Introduction

This chapter begins with critical reflection on two familiar approaches to teaching about violent extremism. The first is a case study approach that analyzes instances of religious violent extremism from a distance. The second is an understanding approach that frames religious violent extremism as the outlier that misrepresents a religious tradition. In the first approach, teachers address religious violent extremism by understanding the function of religion as it interacts with social, political, and economic factors in a particular context. In the second approach, teachers address religious violent extremism by shifting the learners' attention to more "authentic expressions" of the tradition. This chapter adds another approach, internal critical engagement. Writing as a white Christian in the U.S., I argue that theological ethics in a world of violent extremism requires that those in dominant positions teach through practices of internal critical engagement. Concretely, this means that we study the ways in which our own faith tradition (rather than another) is weaponized in the very contexts we occupy (rather than from a distance). It also means that our classrooms become spaces intentionally oriented toward disarming the religious violent extremism perpetuated by our own faith traditions through critical examination, constructive confrontation, and creative transformation. This immediate, internal critical engagement does not replace the case study or understanding approaches, but it is a crucial companion to them.

Two Established Approaches

In the first approach, teachers address religious violent extremism by understanding the function of religion as it interacts with social, political, and economic factors in a particular context.[1] Syllabi that reflect this approach examine religious dimensions of violent conflict through case studies in familiar hot spots like Israel/Palestine, Northern Ireland, Nigeria, or Sri Lanka. They often utilize the work of Scott Appleby, *The Ambivalence of the Sacred*, to provide a theoretical frame for understanding the relationship between religion, violence, and peace. They may also study profiles of terrorist organizations and individuals, often using Mark Juergensmeyer's *Terror in the Mind of God*. The resources for a course like this have grown exponentially in the last twenty-five years, and there are many variations. But the primary organizing mechanism is the case study, which helps students understand religion in relation to other contributing causes to violence.

The case study approach is necessary for understanding the interaction between religion and other social, economic, and political causes of violence. It also teaches students about important historical moments, ongoing conflicts, significant organizations and actors that should be a part of religious studies. Oftentimes, these courses also articulate the objective of equipping students to reflect critically on their own religious traditions. However, there are contextual and methodological gaps that students must maneuver between case study and critically reflective practice. The case study approach provides essential information about the role of religion in contexts of conflict and violence; but it also maintains a distance between learner and the object of study. It does not, therefore, provide the learner with resources and practices necessary for critical reflection on their own contexts and traditions.

The second pedagogical approach frames religious violent extremism as the outlier that misrepresents a religious tradition. In these courses, teachers address religious violent extremism by shifting the learners' attention to more "authentic expressions" of the tradition. These courses often serve to fulfill world religions requirements, and the discussion of religious violent extremism serves as a way for teachers to correct misperceptions about supposedly violent religions. Classes that utilize this pedagogical

---

1. These observations are based on syllabi collected by the American Academy of Religion and the Wabash Center for Teaching and Learning in Theology and Religion (https://www.wabashcenter.wabash.edu/syllabi-topic/Religion-and-violence/). I also draw on my own experience teaching a course in Religion, Violence, and Peacebuilding and participating in a seminary collaboration focused on interfaith peacebuilding, which brought faculty and students from different theological schools to attend the Parliament of the World's Religions.

approach emphasize the ways in which religions contribute to peace and justice and encourage students to distinguish between the violent actors and the true religion. Drawing on books like *Religion and Peacebuilding* (Smith and Coward, 2004) and *Subverting Hatred* (Smith-Christopher, 2007), this approach promotes interreligious understanding and identifies peacebuilding resources within each religious tradition.

The understanding approach is essential to correcting misperceptions and to resisting Islamophobia, in particular. However, it does not provide the resources and practices for critical engagement with the violent dimensions of one's own tradition. It is so keen to correct misperceptions that it leaves students ill-equipped to grapple with the ways in which a religious tradition (their's or another's) may well contribute to violence. A pedagogical approach that fosters understanding toward other religions is essential, and it needs to be supplemented by teaching that critically engages ethically complex religious material.

The case study and understanding approaches are essential to courses in religious violence and religious peacebuilding, and I have used them myself. However, they do not provide what we need for teaching theological ethics in the context of religious violent extremism. The case study method frames religious violence as an object to study at a distance rather than part of one's own theological world. The understanding approach invites defense mechanisms (such as distinguishing between my good religion and those bad actors) that inhibit a confessional criticism of one's own belief and faith community. As Fernandez explains, "violent extremism is a belief system that may justify acts of terror." Teaching Christian theology in this context requires critical reflective practice on one's own tradition, constructive conflict with one's faith community, and the capacity to reconstruct theologies for peace and justice. Therefore, I add internal critical engagement as the pedagogical method best suited to teaching Christian theological ethics in the context of religious violent extremism.

A Third Approach: Internal Critical Engagement

This third approach emerges most concretely from my own experience of teaching Christian Ethics and Peace and Conflict Studies, which I have done for more than twenty years now. I began teaching Christian theology and ethics at a college that offered a minor in Peace and Conflict Studies. For eighteen years, I have been teaching graduate students in theological schools committed to forming religious leaders to deal constructively with conflict in diverse contexts of ministry. Emory University, where I have taught for eleven years, also offers a concentration in Religion, Conflict, and Peacebuilding for doctoral students in the Graduate Division of Religion. Although my master's level work in Peace and Conflict Studies and my doctoral work in Christian Ethics were not well integrated, my teaching rests on the conviction that every course in a theology school should contribute to religious peacebuilding.

After a rather slow start, the interdisciplinary conversation between peace and conflict studies and theology and religious studies is now robust and varied.[2] In the *Oxford Handbook of Religion, Conflict, and Peacebuilding*, Atalia Omer offers a comprehensive and carefully structured account of the literature in the field of religious peacebuilding. She credits Scott Appleby's text, *The Ambivalence of the Sacred*, for creating space for a more constructive engagement with religion in contexts of violence and thus opening the door for literature on religious peacebuilding. We now have a critical mass of material on theologies, texts, rituals, and religious convictions that "make for peace." We also have a healthy and growing supply of ethnographic studies of religious actors, organizations, and communities that contribute to the work of peacebuilding in particular socio-historical contexts.[3] We see religion, conflict, and peace intersecting in a variety of ways within scholarly organizations and journals.[4] And we have several graduate programs now preparing a new generation of scholars who are trained in religious studies/theology and peace and conflict studies.[5]

What counts as religious peacebuilding also continues to expand. In the 2010 volume *Strategies of Peace*, Gerard Powers uses the phrase "religious peacebuilding" to describe "the beliefs, norms, and rituals that pertain to peacebuilding, as well as a range of actors . . . for whom religion is a

2. See also Susan Hayward, "Religion and Peacebuilding: Reflections on Current Challenges and Future Prospects." *United States Institute of Peace Special Report* 313 (August 2012). Hayward's essay focuses on the increased presence and activity of religious organizations and agencies.

3. James W. McCarty III and Joseph Wiinikka-Lydon, "Resources in Religion, Violence, and Peacebuilding," *Practical Matters* 5 (Spring 2012), http://practicalmattersjournal.org/issue/5/teaching-matters/resources-in-religion-violence-and-peacebuilding.

4. For example, the "Religion, Social Conflict, and Peace" and the "Religion and Violence" units of the American Academy of Religion; *Journal of Religion, Conflict and Peace* published by the Plowshares consortium of Earlham College, Goshen College, and Manchester University in Indiana.

5. For example: The University of Notre Dame offers a PhD in Peace Studies and Theology. Emory University's Graduate Division of Religion offers a concentration in Religion, Conflict, and Peacebuilding for doctoral students. George Mason University's Institute on Conflict Analysis and Resolution contains a Center for Diplomacy, World Religions, and Conflict Resolution.

significant motivation for their peacebuilding."[6] Powers provides an overview of religious resources for peacebuilding, including beliefs and ideas that reflect "hermeneutics of peace" (David Little's phrase), peacebuilding practices engaged by individuals and institutions, local community organizations with a global reach, and sheer "people power" (or the capacity of religious communities to mobilize). Powers' chapter also asserts several arguments that are worth repeating and building upon. First, he insists that integration is key to strategic religious peacebuilding, and he describes several kinds of integration. Peacebuilding must be integrated into one's set of religious commitments, or, better yet, emerge organically from them. So, he affirms the integration of theology, ethics, and praxis. Such integration contributes to sustainability of peacebuilding work and also mitigates the instrumental use of religion. Powers also commends a form of institutional integration that maintains a balance between depth in terms of formation, identity, and community *and* breadth in terms of outreach and collaboration. Lastly, he connects this vertical and horizontal integration to an integration of different types of peacebuilding, and he offers examples of religious leaders taking on a variety of tasks: "observation and witness, education and formation, advocacy and empowerment, and conciliation and mediation," and speaking to multiple publics at different social levels.[7]

To contribute to religious peacebuilding from the context of theological education means that we engage in the work of integration that Powers describes and we also draw on the history of peace education for pedagogical practices that not only cover material but also develop capacities. In their 2019 volume, *Peace and Justice Studies: Critical Pedagogy*, Margaret Groarke and Emily Welty assert that the interdisciplinary field of peace and justice studies no longer insists upon a canon given the wide-ranging resources necessary to understanding conflict and pursue peace and justice. Rather, it focuses on cultivating certain habits of mind and heart. Seeking to educate students to advocate for peace and justice, Groarke and Welty argue, means helping them to cultivate "critical thinking, and ethos of solidarity, optimism, and activism."[8] In a similar way, I aim to design courses that develop capacities more so than to cover content and often select content that helps students develop capacities. Moreover, continuing in the tradition of peace education, I recognize that education is not value neutral. Course content, learning goals, and pedagogical practice reflect and communicate values,

---

6. Powers, "Religion and Peacebuilding," 322.

7. Powers, "Religion and Peacebuilding," 332.

8. Groarke and Welty, *Peace and Justice Studies*, "Rejecting the Canon" (Kindle version, loc 396).

whether teachers make them explicit or not. One of the central features of peace education has been to make values explicit. In that spirit, I make explicit my intention to teach practices essential to building more peaceful and just societies. I believe that teaching and learning should be part of the work of religious peacebuilding, which includes practicing as well as studying peacebuilding. Practicing peacebuilding, given the reality of religious violent extremism within our own faith traditions, requires the cultivation of habits of internal critical reflection. Put another way: to be a religious peacebuilder and not just a religious practitioner (that is to say, a believer) requires that one adopt practices of critical reflection about his or her religious convictions. This is the form of religious peacebuilding reflected in these teaching and learning practices: religious peacebuilding as development of dispositions and capacities related to internal critical engagement. From this teaching commitment, I identify two over-arching goals for teaching Christian theological ethics in the context of religious violent extremism: to understand the ways in which our faith tradition is weaponized and to create classrooms where faith is disarmed.

Weaponized Faith

I describe internal critical engagement as an important supplement to the first two approaches, because case studies keep faith at an objective distance in a religious studies model, and because the understanding approach often functions as a defense mechanism that inhibits critical reflection. The case study approach does not invite confessional-critical reflection, though it signals clearly why it is necessary. Internal critical engagement needs the evidence provided by case studies: that our faith tradition also includes an ambivalence that lends itself to violence as well as to peace. The supplemental pedagogical move is to take Appleby's analytic language and internalize it such that one lives as a person of faith ever-aware of the ways in which one's own faith tradition may lend itself to violence. This also means that we resist the defense mechanism offered by the second approach, namely to position ourselves as wholly apart from the extremists who misrepresent the faith. It is certainly important to clarify the ways in which Christian extremist violence distorts the message of the gospel, for example. But the impulse to correct, to clarify, and to distinguish good Christians from bad Christians may also function as a problematic defense mechanism. Christians must also develop the capacity to confess the ways in which violence pervades our past and present.

Teaching Christian theological ethics in the context of religious violent extremism requires that we develop the capacity to reckon with violence as a persistent feature within the Christian tradition rather than to cast it as an outlier or anomaly. This is the first goal of internal critical engagement: to increase awareness of the ways in which one's own religious tradition contributes to violence. The first approach accomplishes this goal most often through case studies that demonstrate the ways in which particular Christian beliefs motivate violent actors. Internal critical engagement supplements the case study approach with contextual education, asking students to focus their attention on contexts that they know and occupy.

This contextual approach draws on liberative and critical pedagogies and on theological models such as the Kairos document, and I will discuss these below. However, I begin in the classroom because the pedagogical strategies I describe emerge most concretely from my experience revising a course that utilized the first two approaches described above (case study and understanding). For a few years, I taught a survey course titled Religion, Violence, and Peacebuilding. In every way, this course covered too much content. I tried to provide students with a variety of case studies in a variety of geographical contexts examining different features of the relationship between different religious traditions, various forms of violence, and a variety of religious peacebuilding practices. As I say, I attempted to include too much content! But the feature of the course that I want to highlight here is that it framed religious traditions as distant objects of study. When I revised the course, I removed a good deal of content, and I shifted the nature of the course so that it could serve as a contextualized education elective (CEE). CEEs at Candler School of Theology, where I teach, require assignments that connect students' contextual education site to the discipline-specific content of the course. Rather than learning via case studies from a distance, students were now asked to conduct a conflict analysis within their context of ministry. And they needed to think about and articulate the ways in which Christian texts, traditions, and/or practices contributed to this conflict. These changes meant that the course became less about content and more about disposition. The assigned materials, such as John Paul Lederach's *Moral Imagination* and Leah Gunning Francis's *Ferguson and Faith*, demonstrate social and contextual analysis and provide examples of critical reflection by religious leaders. Students focused on learning practices of ministry that involve ongoing critical reflection on the relationship that their faith tradition has to conflict in their immediate context.

This practice of ongoing critical reflection is no small thing. It requires a broad understanding of violence, the ability to attend to impact without defensively naming intentions, and a posture of humility. It may seem odd to encourage a broad understanding of violence as a pedagogical response to violent extremism, in particular. However, religions contribute to violence in a variety of different ways, and a strict focus on one form of violence may well excuse other forms of violence as not worth critical theological reflection. On the other hand, if we exercise the muscles of critical reflection and practice a disposition of humility, then we are better equipped to understand the connections between extremist violence and other forms of violence.

The teaching practice that I use to expand students' understanding of violence is collaborative. We begin by brainstorming examples of violence. As examples appear on the board, we see that they illustrate different kinds of violence: physical, emotional, psychological, structural, and spiritual. Considering this variety of actions and categories, we attempt to craft a working definition that encompasses them. This proves to be an exceedingly difficult task, and students frequently question its value. Their challenge helps me to articulate the purpose of the exercise, which is not to arrive at a definition but to broaden our understanding so that we enter into contextual analysis listening for what arises rather than looking for actions that fit a definition. Attempting to craft a definition out of the variety of words and categories before us also sparks a conversation about what makes an experience violent.

The question of what makes something violent shifts the landscape for the course considerably. To put it simply, we find ourselves listening for impact rather than focusing on intention. Regardless of the intention of a believer, their belief and the practices attached to it may have a violent impact in the church and/or community. Regardless of intention, the belief may indeed justify terror. The shift to focus on impact more than intention grants epistemological privilege to those affected, to those who experience an impact that they describe as violent. To receive this information and grant authority to those impacted requires listening without defensiveness, which again is no small thing.

Contemporary anti-racism training provides important resources for attending to impact and for keeping defensiveness in check while listening. Robin DiAngelo's term, white fragility, is a particularly apt description of the dynamics that diminish the capacity to receive information about one's own role in perpetuating injustice. "[W]hite fragility is a state in which even a minimum amount of racial stress in the habitus becomes intolerable, triggering a range of defensive moves. These moves include the outward display of emotions such as anger, fear, and guilt and behaviors such as argumentation, silence, and leaving the stress-inducing situation."[9] DiAngelo provides a long list of defensive claims and underlying assumptions that accompany white fragility and then names ways that white fragility functions. In my view, these observations do not only apply to white Christians confronted with our racism; they also apply to Christians more generally when we are confronted with extremist beliefs within our tradition. When we Christians are confronted by the reality of homophobic violence, anti-Semitic violence, anti-immigrant hate crimes, and Christian white supremacy, we utter variations of the defensive claims that DiAngelo names: you can't judge Christianity according to the actions of a few bad people; I am a good Christian, not like them; but Christians are persecuted in some parts of the world too.[10] These claims reflect our efforts to deny the presence of extremist beliefs (beliefs that may justify terror) within our faith tradition and faith communities. Like white fragility (which is certainly entwined with Christian fragility), these defensive impulses "close off self-reflection," "trivialize the reality of racism," and "protect a limited worldview."[11] Being aware of the dynamics of fragility begins a process of developing a different set of reactions, which include "reflection, apology, listening, processing, [and] seeking more understanding."[12]

In *Backlash*, George Yancy describes the vitriol of white defensiveness by sharing letters he received from white readers of his *New York Times* editorial, "Dear White America." The letters were graphically violent, and Yancy's response to them was unyielding. He insists that white people in America relinquish any reference to intention and acknowledge that they (we) cannot avoid benefiting from whiteness. White people must acknowledge "the complex and insidious ways in which white racism has become embedded within your [my] white embodied self."[13] This does not mean that white people cannot do anything about racism, Yancy argues. Rather, he provides "the grounds for a more robust sense of white humility and conceptual clarity regarding the complexity of white racism; [he issues] a call for risking the white self—to tell the truth to yourself and to others."[14] Yancy, DiAngelo, and many other contemporary anti-racism scholar-practitioners make clear that addressing racism absolutely requires that white people listen to the truth about the impact of our whiteness. This kind of

9. DiAngelo, *White Fragility*, 103.

10. DiAngelo, *White Fragility*, 119–20.

11. DiAngelo, *White Fragility*, 122.

12. DiAngelo, *White Fragility*, 141.

13. Yancy, *Backlash*, 79.

14. Yancy, *Backlash*, 81.

listening cannot happen as long as the defense mechanisms dominate our behavior. And, Yancy argues, one way to cultivate different kinds of behavior is through the disposition and practices of humility.

In her article, "Christian Education, White Supremacy, and Humility in Formational Agendas," Katherine Turpin traces the ways that Christian education contributes to beliefs and practices of white supremacy. She draws on the work of Willie James Jennings, Musa Dube, and James Cone to document the connections and to set the stage for alternative pedagogical practices guided by humility. As an Anglo focused on the responsibility of Anglo Christian educators, Turpin writes, "embracing humility means being willing to tell these stories [of racist violence and oppression] and accept responsibility for their legacy. It means teaching these histories, accepting the charges of participation in cultural decimation, and honestly seeking to discover where we are still participating in this kind of educational venture."[15]

Humility is also frequently named as a virtue in the work of religious peacebuilding and interreligious dialogue. As a disposition it shapes the believer to remain open to learning from others, to receive challenging information without defensiveness, and to envision new possibilities. For example, consider the work of John Paul Lederach and Catherine Cornille. In their texts, *The Moral Imagination* and *The Im-Possibility of Inter-Religious Dialogue*, respectively, Lederach and Cornille recognize the place of techniques and skills but draw attention to disposition and disciplines as more foundational to peacebuilding and dialogue.

"How do we transcend the cycles of violence that bewitch our human community while still living in them?" This is the over-arching question that motivates Lederach's text. His response pushes against the "technique-oriented" approach that dominates professional conflict resolution.[16] He notes the importance of skills and processes, but he also draws the reader's attention to another plane of experience and another kind of practice. Lederach suggests that transcending violence requires the moral imagination, a phrase that he uses to capture the "potential to find a way to transcend, to move beyond what exists while still living in it."[17] Four disciplines give shape to this form of the imagination: "the capacity to imagine ourselves in a web of relationships that includes our enemies; the ability to sustain a paradoxical curiosity that embraces complexity without reliance on dualistic polarity; the fundamental belief in and of the creative act; and the acceptance of the

15. Turpin, "Christian Education," 414.

16. Lederach, *The Moral Imagination*, 52.

17. Lederach, *The Moral Imagination*, 28.

inherent risk of stepping into the mystery of the unknown that lies beyond the far too familiar landscape of violence."[18]

Lederach's explicit discussion of humility occurs in the context of his reflections on "web watching," a metaphor that he takes from the careful practices of observation exercised by scientists who study spiders. He uses this image, web watching, to describe disciplines of attentiveness that are essential to building peace. Related to social and conflict analysis, web watching attends to a different plane, what Lederach refers to as "matters of the soul."[19] For example, whereas conflict analysis requires that we determine conflict roles, understand the history of the conflict, and perform an initial assessment of needs, web watching directs attention to deeper questions about identity, personhood, and place. Lederach suggests that this search for the "soul of place" engenders humility as we come to see ourselves as "a small part of something really big."[20] He also describes a kind of epistemological humility as essential. In his words, "learning and truth seeking are lifelong adventures."[21] Humility, as the recognition that there is always more to learn, is required for adaptation and transcendence. Without humility, we cannot change.

Catherine Cornille makes a similar argument in the context of interreligious dialogue, which requires humility not only toward other religious traditions but about one's own religion. She refers to this form of humility as "epistemic or doctrinal humility," which she defines as "recognition of the constant limitation and therefore endless perfectibility of one's own religious understanding of the truth."[22] Partial human knowledge, imperfect understanding, the contingency of language, and the limitations of symbols all call for "humility about the way in which ultimate truth is grasped and presented in doctrinal formulations" as well.[23] Cornille notes that her own Christian tradition has more often encouraged humility in the face of doctrine, but she argues that humility *about* doctrine is essential to dialogue and to learning and growth. Humility, along with commitment (to one's faith), empathy, a sense of interconnection, and hospitality, then emerges as a central virtue for those engaging in interreligious dialogue if

18. Lederach, *The Moral Imagination*, 5.

19. Lederach, *The Moral Imagination*, 103.

20. Lederach, *The Moral Imagination*, 106–7.

21. Lederach, *The Moral Imagination*, 107.

22. Catherine Cornille, *The Im-Possibility of Interreligious Dialogue*, 10.

23. Cornille, *The Im-Possibility of Interreligious Dialogue*, 33.

such dialogue is to contribute to a genuine pursuit of truth and not simply an accumulation of facts about the other.[24]

The genuine pursuit of truth requires a posture of listening and openness, even to information that implicates our faith tradition and ourselves in acts of violence. Of course, the work of teaching and learning theology in the context of extremism does not end with this listening posture and critical examination. The approach of internal critical engagement includes two other pedagogical practices as well: constructive confrontation and creative transformation. Both of these practices help to disarm faith.

Disarming Faith

Like the practices discussed thus far, these teaching strategies are informed by theory and literature and emerge from my own experiences in the classroom. In particular, I am drawing on courses that I regularly teach at the master's level in a theological school: Introduction to Christian Ethics, Contemporary Christian Ethics, and Conflict Transformation Skills.

There are many ways to teach Christian ethics, of course. My approach to the introductory course focuses on methods of moral discernment and requires students to complete a scaffolded writing project in which they (a) craft a moral question, (b) analyze moral sources that inform discussions of their question, (c) represent fully and fairly a point of view with which they disagree, and (d) craft their constructive response. In the Contemporary Christian Ethics course, students also identify a social problem, deconstruct theological material that exacerbates it, and offer a constructive theological-ethical response. These assignments reflect a particular method in theological ethics, one that evaluates theological claims according to ethical criteria.[25] This is not a new method; indeed it dates back to the emergence of Christian social ethics in the nineteenth century as theologians were grappling with the implications of an historical understanding of religion. Once believers perceive religion to develop historically (rather than to remain encapsulated in a-historical kernels of dogmatic truth), then we understand the work of faith to involve active wrestling with beliefs in light of human experience. If I learn that a belief I hold may justify an act of terror, then deconstructing

24. Cornille, *The Im-Possibility of Interreligious Dialogue*, 3.

25. This method receives regular criticism from theologians and ethicists who perceive it as anthropocentric insofar as it makes human issues the central concern and even criteria for theology. I address these concerns and more fully explain and defend the method in *Introduction to Christian Ethics: Conflict, Faith, and Human Life.*

that belief becomes an act of faith as well as a mode of theological education and scholarship.

I suggest that teaching theological ethics in the context of religious violent extremism requires that we equip students to re-evaluate theological assertions in light of their justification of terror and that we help students to understand this theological work as a practice of faith. Fortunately, we have many illustrations of faithful theological criticism in contexts of violence. Foremost among these is the Kairos movement, which began during the height of apartheid in South Africa and now finds expression in a variety of contexts around the world. Informed by Latin American liberation theology, South African theologians utilized a method of contextual analysis to craft a theological criticism of state theology and of church theology and to articulate a prophetic theology in the context of apartheid. Although the South African Kairos document was drafted thirty-five years ago, it continues to inspire prophetic theology from contexts of violence today. Felipe Gustavo Koch Buttelli underscores this point in an essay that describes the "Kairos Way of Doing Theology." The *Kairos Document* reflects the commitment of "'concerned Christians in South Africa to reflect on the situation of death in our country.'"[26] They identified theologies related to different positions on apartheid and offered poignant criticism of the theology that justified the terror of apartheid (state theology) and the theology that maintained the status quo by offering only a moderate criticism of apartheid (church theology).[27] In contrast to these two theologies, the *Kairos Document*, articulates and practices a prophetic theology that begins with social analysis from which it brings a new hermeneutic to Scripture to discern "a new understanding of how social relations should be constructed."[28] The *Kairos Document* and the Kairos movement more broadly offer us a model for how to do theology in the context of religious violent extremism. In the documents produced, we find examples of theologians challenging beliefs that justify terror and proposing alternative theologies for social relationships marked by peace and justice.

At the beginning of this section, I described assignments structured according to this method of constructive Christian ethics. With the mention of the Kairos movement, I suggest that we prepare students for assignments like this by assigning reading that models the method of deconstructing violent theologies and constructing theological alternatives.

---

26. Buttelli, "Public Theology," 93. Buttelli is quoting the preface of the *Kairos Document*.

27. Buttelli, "Public Theology," 93–94.

28. Buttelli, "Public Theology," 95.

Thus far, however, the pedagogical practices for disarming faith have only involved work with texts, be it through reading or writing. These are crucial practices of internal critical engagement, to be sure. However, believers do not live alone with books and papers but rather live in community. Therefore, disarming faith also requires developing the capacity to challenge one's faith community and creatively transform the practices that shape church and community. Teaching theological ethics in the context of violent extremism requires that we equip students to reflect critically on texts and traditions and also to work constructively with conflict in Christian communities where beliefs are enacted.

In an effort to equip religious leaders to deal with conflict constructively in their varied contexts of ministry, Candler offers courses every semester in conflict transformation. Conflict transformation is the latest in a lineage of approaches to conflict. It is distinguished from its immediate predecessor, conflict resolution, by insisting that conflict itself is not necessarily a problem to be solved. Without trivializing the true costs of conflict, the transformation approach insists that conflict is a natural and necessary element of life and can be a catalyst for constructive change in personal lives, relationships, communities, and churches. The task, therefore, is to engage conflict constructively for purposes of positive change.[29] These classes introduce students to conflict dynamics, conflict analysis, mediation, and circle facilitation. The purpose is to bring these capacities into the arts of ministry. I draw on these courses to identify pedagogical practices for constructive confrontation and creative transformation.

My proposal is to utilize conflict transformation practices in our classrooms and congregations while doing the work of challenging beliefs that may justify terror. Internal critical engagement entails conflict with one's own beliefs and community. Perhaps the most striking contrast to the case study and understanding approaches is that this one demands considerable interpersonal and emotional labor. Theological critique and construction often feel like an assault on faith and identity. And, as the work on white fragility indicates, people employ defense mechanisms of all kinds when they feel accused of participating in injustice and violence. Thus, we need pedagogical practices for challenge and transformation that take the whole body into account and that help people understand disarming faith as shared, ongoing work.

Since the election of President Trump, college and university classrooms have become increasingly contentious places. This is not because

---

29. I provide an introduction to the emergence of conflict transformation practices and literature in *Conflict Transformation and Religion*. See also Lederach, *Little Book of Conflict Transformation*.

students are "snowflakes," but because their identities have been under assault. Under-represented minority students, Dreamers, gay and gender nonconforming students, and international students experience emotional, psychological, and structural violence on a daily basis. Moreover, as white supremacy, nativism, homophobia, and misogyny shape domestic and foreign policy, students of all kinds experience the transgression of core values and commitments they hold dear. It is no secret that most professors are ill-equipped to deal with emotion in the classroom. We remain stuck in a frame that perceives emotion as contrary to reason and thus an impediment to clear thinking. And, of course, emotion is profoundly shaped by culture, which means that the range of publicly acceptable emotions varies from context to context depending on the cultural make up of participants and particularly the cultural identity of those who hold power in the space. However, when we are dealing with contentious issues—like beliefs that may justify terror—we must be prepared to work constructively with the emotions that arise in the classroom.

We can begin this work by understanding emotion as a source of knowledge. Emotions, particularly strong emotions, signal values. If we can open up spaces in our classrooms to work constructively with emotions that arise, then we can learn more about what our students value, what they fear losing or already grieve, what transgression of principles they perceive, and what object of hope they are protecting. Emotions give us information about ourselves and about others; they are an essential element of communication, especially when the stakes are high. When we are addressing beliefs and violence, the stakes are very high and students have an emotional investment in the subject matter. Indeed, we should worry if they do not. The first pedagogical practice is simply to make these points clearly to students. We create space for emotion in the classroom, first, by articulating its value to our students. On matters of belief and violence, emotions are part of the learning experience, not an impediment to it.

Creating space for emotions in the classroom requires more than rearranging the furniture, though that is also necessary. Everyone present, students and faculty alike, need to feel that what they share will be honored by the group. They do not need the promise of comfort, but they do need to know that they will be supported in their discomfort. The classroom needs to be a place where students can risk vulnerability. In the words of Catherine Meeks, it needs to be a brave space more so than a safe space.[30] Teachers create brave spaces through agreements and guidelines that set expectations

---

30. Rev. Dr. Catherine Meeks is the Executive Director of the Absalom Jones Center for Racial Healing in Atlanta, Georgia. "Brave space" is language that she uses in anti-racism trainings and workshops.

for dialogue and by helping all participants to hold one another accountable to those agreements. We also create brave spaces by modeling behavior, by also sharing our emotions and our reflections on them, by being honest, by demonstrating care and respect, by honoring what is risked by our students, and by holding them accountable to one another.[31]

One way that we honor what students share and incorporate their contributions into the process of teaching and learning is by asking good, open questions. Open questions do not convey judgement and are invitational in nature. Posing open questions in response to strong emotions not only enhances the possibility of working with them constructively in the moment but also signals that emotions are part of the learning process rather than something to deal with before getting on to the real material. Open questions also foster the kind of non-defensive listening discussed earlier.[32]

As is often the case with effective pedagogical practices, their purpose extends beyond the classroom. Working with emotions, creating brave space, crafting guidelines and practicing accountability, and posing open questions that integrate emotions into the process of learning foster dispositions that contribute to the work of building peaceful and just communities. When we practice them in the classroom, we not only create spaces that are more conducive to teaching and learning, but we also help students develop capacities to create such spaces for others. These spaces make constructive confrontation and creative transformation possible.

By constructive confrontation, I mean the capacity to enter into conflict with someone who holds a belief that may justify terror. Skeptics often dismiss this difficult and important work by quipping that you can't mediate with a terrorist. Such quips ignore the reality that extremist beliefs are ubiquitous rather than concentrated in a terrorist individual or organization, and the work of challenging them occurs not in the moment of violent attack but through ongoing efforts of resistance and dialogue. Gary Mason, a British Methodist pastor from Belfast, describes his relationships with former paramilitaries as critical friendship. Over years, Mason comes alongside these "men of violence," as he calls them, to accompany them through a process of repentance, healing, and perhaps reintegration into society.[33] Mason's example of challenging someone while remaining

---

31. This claim reflects a central insight of transformative mediation, namely that parties in a mediation process most need recognition and empowerment. They need to feel seen and they need to experience agency. See *Transformative Mediation* by Baruch Bush and Folger.

32. For more on open questions, see Schirch, *The Little Book of Dialogue for Difficult Subjects.*

33. Mason, "Serving as a Critical Friend," 52.

in relationship with them provides a model for religious leadership in contexts of religious violent extremism. Teaching theological ethics in the context of religious violent extremism requires us to equip our students to practice relationships like this. Especially if our students intend to be religious leaders, they need to be equipped to come alongside those whose beliefs may justify violence. They need to have the knowledge and the disposition to challenge effectively. In less dramatic contexts, we have occasions to practice this kind of relationship, although our increasingly polarized societies make it increasingly difficult.

Mason's language of coming alongside is also significant. One of the key insights from conflict resolution and conflict transformation is that parties move toward understanding and perhaps agreement when they begin to see the problem as shared, when they can perceive common needs beneath their different positions. In my experience of working with Christians who disagree, I have noticed a similar thing. The turning point in the process is most often related to a moment when the participants in the conversation begin to come alongside one another to address a challenge rather than position themselves against each other fighting over a problem. The presence of Christian beliefs that may justify terror is a problem that all Christians share. I do not teach with the delusion that all Christians will disarm their faith and rid the Christian tradition of violence. But I do teach with the hope that study and practice can contribute to the presence of less violence. I do teach with the hope that moments of creative transformation break through.

By creative transformation, I do not mean a dramatic conversion but rather the ongoing work of creating new possibilities in every moment. It is not something that occurs at the end of a linear process of critical engagement and constructive challenge. Rather, the possibilities for transformation break through as we facilitate these different modalities of teaching and learning. I have come to think of transformation as the eruption of familiar patterns of behavior and thought by the awareness of new possibilities. As teachers, our job is to facilitate processes through which these eruptions might occur and to support students in responding to the possibilities by changing their thoughts and behavior. This value-neutral description of a process of transformation needs to be qualified in the context of religious violent extremism, however. In the tradition of peace education, theology teachers must intentionally design learning processes that disrupt the logics of theologies that justify terror and create possibilities for alternative voices and practices that contribute to peace and justice.

In the revised Religion, Violence, and Peacebuilding course I referenced earlier, I ask student to follow up their contextual conflict analysis with a peacebuilding assets project. The idea is to utilize the resources of deep listening and asset-based analysis to locate resources for peace and justice already present in the site where they are working. I encourage them to cast a wide net and to think about peace as broadly as they have thought about violence. I am consistently inspired by their findings, which include trusted individuals, local artists, unearthed traditions, surprising friendships, walking meditations, creative buy-back programs, community gardens, and lots of food. These inquiries and investigations do not produce definitive solutions to community violence, but they surface community practices for building peace and pursuing justice even in the context of ongoing violence. In Lederach's language, they elicit examples and practices of the moral imagination. In my understanding, the peacebuilding assets project helps us to see and celebrate moments of creative transformation.

In this chapter, I have suggested that this kind of teaching and learning requires attention to knowledge and to disposition. We need the knowledge to correct violent misuse of scripture and tradition, and we need a humble disposition willing to critically examine our own beliefs in light of their violent impact on others. We need the knowledge to deconstruct violent theologies, and we need the prophetic disposition to proclaim and advocate for nonviolent and just theological alternatives. We need to know how theology impacts the lives of people, and we need a disposition to listen without defensiveness and respond with commitment. We need to know about models and methods of constructive, liberative theologies, and we need the disposition to practice deconstruction and reconstruction as an act of faith.

Conclusion

One of my teaching practices on the first day of a new class is to draw on a recent, current event to introduce the subject matter and to convey its relevance outside of the walls of the classroom. In preparing to write this chapter, I looked through my notes from several classes and found a sobering pattern.

- Summer of 2015, Mother Emmanuel AME Church in Charleston, SC
- Summer of 2016, Pulse Nightclub in Orlando, FL
- Summer of 2017, Unite the Right Rally in Charlottesville, VA
- October of 2018, Tree of Life Synagogue in Pittsburgh, PA
- Summer of 2019, Walmart in El Paso, TX

The current events that launched our class (or, in the case of fall 2018, paused our class) involved violence by white supremacists. Not all of these perpetrators identified as Christian, but the links between Christianity and white supremacy are established enough to prompt serious critical reflection by Christians. Courses in Christian theological ethics must respond to violent extremism by forming Christians—especially those called to positions of religious leadership—to practice internal critical engagement. Internal critical engagement means that we study the ways in which our own faith tradition (rather than another) is weaponized in the very contexts we occupy (rather than from a distance). It also means that our classrooms become spaces intentionally oriented toward disarming the religious violent extremism perpetuated by our own faith traditions through critical examination, constructive confrontation, and creative transformation.

In this pedagogical approach, students turn a critical eye to their own beliefs, attending to the ways in which those beliefs may "justify acts of terror." They also attend to the beliefs held by fellow Christians past and present and learn how to deconstruct them. They also practice the interpersonal and emotional labor required to constructively challenge fellow believers who still hold theologies demonstrated to have violent implications. Finally, students learn how to practice the ongoing work of creative transformation, which involves cultivating a commitment and a capacity for faithfully reconstructing beliefs and practices according to a hermeneutic of nonviolence. In addition to case studies that help students understand the dynamics between religion, violence, and peace, and in tandem with resources that correct misperceptions of religious traditions other than their own, internal critical engagement helps Christian theology students develop capacities essential to religious peacebuilding in the context of violent extremism.

Bibliography

Bush, Robert A. Baruch and Roger Folger. *The Promise of Mediation: A Transformative Approach to Conflict*. San Francisco: Jossey Bass, 2005.

Cone, James. *The Cross and the Lynching Tree*. Maryknoll, NY: Orbis, 2011.

Cornille, Catherine. *The Im-Possibility of Interreligious Dialogue*. New York: Crossroad, 2008.

DiAngelo, Robin. *White Fragility: Why It's So Hard for White People to Talk about Racism*. Boston: Beacon, 2018.

Francis, Leah Gunning. *Ferguson & Faith: Sparking Leadership and Awakening Community*. St. Louis: Chalice, 2015.

Groarke, Margaret, and Emily Welty. *Peace and Justice Studies: Critical Pedagogy*. New York: Routledge, 2019.

Harvey, Jennifer. *Raising White Kids: Bringing Up Children in a Racially Unjust America.* Nashville: Abingdon, 2017.

Jennings, Willie James. *The Christian Imagination: Theology and the Origins of Race.* New Haven: Yale University Press, 2010.

Lederach, John Paul. *Little Book of Conflict Transformation.* Brattleboro, VT: Good Books, 2003.

Lederach, John Paul. *The Moral Imagination: The Art and Soul of Building Peace.* Oxford: Oxford University Press, 2010.

Marshall, Ellen Ott, ed. *Conflict Transformation and Religion: Essays on Faith, Power, and Relationship.* New York: Palgrave MacMillan, 2016.

Marshall, Ellen Ott. *Introduction to Christian Ethics: Conflict, Faith, and Human Life.* Louisville: Westminster John Knox, 2018.

Omer, Atalia. "Religious Peacebuilding: The Exotic, the Good, and the Theatrical." In *Oxford Handbook of Religion, Conflict, and Peacebuilding,* edited by Atalia Omer, Scott Appleby, and David Little, 3–32. Oxford: Oxford University Press, 2015.

Powers, Gerard. "Religion and Peacebuilding." In *Strategies of Peace: Transforming Conflict in a Violence World,* edited by Daniel Philpott and Gerard Powers, 317–52. Oxford: Oxford University Press, 2010.

Schirch, Lisa. *The Little Book of Dialogue for Difficult Subjects: A Practical Hands-On Guide* Intercourse, PA: Good Books, 2015.

Sims, Angela. *Lynched: The Power of Memory in a Culture of Terror.* Waco, TX: Baylor University Press, 2016.

Turpin, Katherine. "Christian Education, White Supremacy, and Humility in Formational Agendas." *Religious Education* 112/4 (2017) 407–17.

Yancy, George. *Backlash: What Happens When We Talk Honestly about Racism in America.* Lanham, MD: Rowman & Littlefield, 2018.

6

Religious Extremism in the History of Early Christianity

—J. Samuel Subramanian

Introduction

Religious extremism is often associated with a particular religious group that supports a radical agenda in politics. It engenders negative stereotypes toward particular religious groups among the public opinion. Sometimes it is associated with terrorism which leads to misunderstanding of people practicing a particular religion. Religious groups are extremely diverse in beliefs and practices, whereby religion or even religious extremism is expressed in many different ways. Religious extremism is multidimensional and it has to be understood in a broader context.

There are many factors in each religion that contribute to religious extremism. People express different beliefs and practice diverse rituals and adhere to several religious texts. Religious extremism may manifest in the ways beliefs and practices are regulated. One needs to look at the root cause that funds religious extremism and eventually leads to all forms of violence. Any basic dimension of religion may constitute beliefs, practices, and organizations. Various expressions of religious forms slowly contribute to the growth of religious extremism. For instance, religions share theological beliefs and try to oppress other beliefs as heretical. One religious group may involve women in the practice of ministry and the other religious group may reject them altogether. Likewise, conflicts arise among various religious groups over the organizational structures. In this essay I would like to explore four categories in the history of early Christianity up to the fourth century CE that might have sown seeds to the rise of religious extremism. They are: 1. Church Government, 2. Canonization of the New Testament,

3. Christological Controversies, and 4. Women in Ministry. Then I would like to draw implications for teaching religious extremism.

Church Government

The word, "Church" (Gk: *ekklēsia*), stands for the sociological community of Christianity. The church represents the community of organization which regulates the beliefs and practices of Christianity. The word "Church" is used four times in the first canonical Gospel of Matthew (Matt 16:18; 18:15–20). It is the earliest occurrence during the life and ministry of Jesus Christ. First, it appears in the context of Peter's confession at Caesarea Philippi where Jesus alludes to building his church upon the rock which is Peter: "And I tell you, you are Peter, and on this rock I will build my church, and the gates of Hades will not prevail against it" (Matt 16:18). But nothing is said about the organization of the church. It is only assumed that Peter would serve as an instrument for founding the church but not Christianity. On the day of Pentecost, Peter preached the gospel and as a result of that more than three thousand people were admitted through baptism to a newly formed religious community which is the church (Acts 2:37–42). Second, the three uses of church in Matthew are found in the context of settling a dispute among the believers (Matt 18:15–20). Here the church represents a body of believers with no hierarchical structure. Jesus seems to suggest that the act of disciplining a member of the church belongs to the entire Christian community: "If the member refuses to listen to them, tell it to the church, and if the offender refuses to listen even to the church, let such a one be to you as a Gentile and a tax collector" (Matt 18:17).

During the early history of the church, some kind of church government began to develop. In the Acts of the Apostles, a new group of leaders known as "elders" (Gk: *Presbyteroi*) appears alongside the apostles to decide matters of dispute (Acts 15:6). The elders, along with the apostles, had the responsibility to make decisions regarding ethical and doctrinal issues. These elders had oversight of the church (Acts 20:20) and were thus responsible to provide supervision for the church (cf. 1 Tim 5:17; Titus 1:5). They were set apart by the apostles by laying hands on them (cf. Acts 6:6). Eventually the elders became the successors to the apostles. The order of deacons was created to assist the elders (cf. 1 Tim 3:8–13). In the Pastoral epistles, there is another title used for church leadership. It is spoken of the office of bishop (Gk: *episcopos*) who seems to oversee the affairs of the church (1 Tim 3:1; Titus 1:7; cf. Phil 1:1). It is not clear whether the office of elders is distinct from the office of a bishop.[1] The Pastoral epistles were written toward the end of Paul's life, around 64 CE or toward the end of first century or even early in the second century CE when Pauline authorship is called into question.

In most of the Pauline churches, church leadership is based on spiritual gifts (Gk: *charimata*). These spiritual gifts seem to emerge from the Spirit and the believers are called to exercise their God-given gifts. Paul says, "Now there are varieties of gifts, but one same Spirit; and there are varieties of services, but the same Lord; and there are varieties of activities, but it is the same God who activates all of them in everyone" (1 Cor 12:4–6). It seems to suggest that everyone worked together in service to God's Kingdom without a mono leader. In that context the leaders of the church are not based on superiority but on ranking of gifts: "And God has appointed in the church first apostles, second prophets, third teachers; then deeds of power, then gifts of healing, forms of assistance, forms of leadership, various kinds of tongues." (1 Cor 12:28). Paul's understanding of church leadership seems to be egalitarian and non-hierarchical.[2]

As the hierarchical structure began to develop toward the end of the first century or early second century, charismatic leadership was suppressed. It is evident in 3 John, an epistle written by the elder to Gaius. This epistle was probably composed toward the end of the first century or early second century. In that epistle the elder seems to exercise authority over Diotrephes who was probably a charismatic leader in one of the Johannine churches. The author of 3 John writes, "I have written something to the church; but Diotrephes, who likes to put himself first, does not acknowledge our authority" (3 John 9). The tension between the two forms of church government, one headed by the elder and the other headed by a charismatic independent leader, seems to create tension and dissension in the early church. The elder in 3 John seems to accuse Diotrephes of disrespecting the authority of the elder. Ecclesiastical authority seems to underlie the early church government which planted the seed for religious extremism. It created division and enmity.

Early in the second century, Ignatius, bishop of Antioch (30–108 CE), laid the foundation for episcopacy. Arrested by the Roman empire and condemned to die, Ignatius wrote a series of letters to various churches while in route to his martyrdom in the arena of Rome. Bishop Ignatius

---

1. Merkle, "Hierarchy in the Church?", 32–49, argues that the early church was initially governed by only two types of office: Elders/Bishops and Deacons. A three-tiered order (Bishops, Elders, and Deacons) is a later development which is seen in the writings of Bishop Ignatius in the second century.

2. Clarke, *A Pauline Theology of Church Leadership*, 89–95.

wrote to the churches about adherence to their bishop. Baptism and communion were placed under the authority of a bishop. In his *Epistle to the Smyrnaeans*, Bishop Ignatius wrote about the authority of a bishop over the sacraments: "Let no one do anything that has to do with the church without the bishop. Only that Eucharist which is under the authority of the bishop (or whomever he himself designates) is to be considered valid. Wherever the bishop appears, there let the congregation be; just as wherever Jesus Christ is, there is the catholic church. It is not permissible either to baptize or to hold a love feast without the bishop."[3] Bishop Ignatius seems to invoke human authority as a visible sign of divine authority. He writes, "It is good to acknowledge God and the bishop. The one who honors the bishop has been honored by God; the one who does anything without the bishop's knowledge serves the devil."[4]

In his *Epistle to the Ephesians*, Bishop Ignatius called the obedience to the bishop: "Therefore whoever does not meet with the congregation thereby demonstrates his arrogance and has separated himself, for it is written: 'God opposes the arrogant.' Let us, therefore, be careful not to oppose the bishop, in order that we may be obedient to God."[5] In his *Epistle to the Trallians*, Bishop Ignatius drew attention to the deacons, presbyters, and bishops as constitutive of the church: "Similarly, let everyone respect the deacons as Jesus Christ, just as they should respect the bishop, who is a model of the Father, and the presbyters as God's council and as the band of the apostles. Without these no group can be called a church."[6] The *Shepherd of Hermas*, an apocalyptic book that enjoyed canonical status in some areas of the church, issued a strong warning for the church officials. The author writes, "Now, therefore, I say to you officials of the church, and occupants of the seats of honor: do not be like sorcerers. For the sorcerers carry their drugs in bottles, but you carry your drug and poison in your heart."[7] The struggle to establish hierarchy and the struggle to oppose hierarchy came to collide with one another.

During the persecution of the church in Carthage in the Roman province of Africa, Cyprian, bishop of Carthage (200–258 CE), refused to readmit those who obtained the certificates (*libeli*) without actually offering sacrifices to the Roman gods in order to avoid persecution. Cyprian demanded that the lapsed should undergo some kind of public penance

3. *Ign. Smyrn.* 8.16–21.

4. *Ign. Smyrn.* 9.1.

5. *Ign. Eph.* 5.3.

6. *Ign. Trall.* 3.1.

7. *Herm. Vis.* 17.7.

before being restored to church.[8] Novatian, a presbyter in Rome (200–258 CE), supported the authority of excommunication of those who lapsed to be reconciled. The ecclesiastical hierarchy became so powerful in excommunicating people who wanted to be reconciled to church. The council that met in Carthage in 251 CE took a stringent policy to punish the offenders and declare baptisms officiated by the heretics as invalid.[9]

By the end of the fourth century when Christianity was officially declared as the legal religion of the Roman empire, bishops gained sole religious authorities in cities. The canons of Nicaea (325 CE) affirmed the authority of bishops on doctrinal and ecclesiastical matters. As E. Glenn Hinson remarks, "Whereas early on bishops presided over small flocks like shepherds, some especially in areas where there were few episcopates, now became powerful executives whose main duty was to direct other clergy and to represent their churches in the public arena."[10] For instance, Ambrose, bishop of Milan (339–394 CE), not only supervised the churches and fought against heresies, but also functioned as a public figure.[11] John Chrysostom, archbishop of Constantinople (347–407 CE), emphasized the authority of priests to forgive sins.[12] In all, ecclesiastical authority in the form of church government contributed to schisms, exclusions, and excommunications.

2. Canonization of the New Testament

The New Testament contains twenty-seven books. The word, "canon" is derived from a Hebrew and Greek word meaning a "reed" or "cane." When it is applied to the Christian Scriptures, it came to denote authoritative rule used to regulate the church's doctrine and practice. The New Testament Canon did not exist during the time of the New Testament writings. Sometimes it is argued that the author of 2 Timothy refers to the Scriptures as the Canon of the New Testament. The author writes, "All scripture is inspired by God and is useful for teaching, for reproof, for correction, and for training in righteousness, so that everyone who belongs to God may be proficient, equipped for every good work" (2 Tim 3:16). The epistle was probably written in the first century CE and the books of the New Testament were not collected. The author seems to refer to the Jewish Writings (the Old Testament) as "Scripture" and does not seem to point to any books of the New Testament.

8. Hinson, *The Church Triumphant*, 108.

9. Hinson, *The Church Triumphant*, 109.

10. Hinson, *The Church Triumphant*, 194.

11. See Gilliard, "Senatorial Bishops," 153–175.

12. Hinson, *The Church Triumphant*, 194.

The definition of the New Testament Canon sought not only to include the authoritative writings but also to exclude other Christian writings which were contemporary to the New Testament writings.[13] Exclusion became the norm of constituting the New Testament Canon.

Irenaeus, bishop of Lugdunum in Gaul (130–202 CE), is traditionally credited with the founding of the New Testament canon. He was the first church father to make a collection of the books of the New Testament and he was the first to claim inspiration and divine authority of its books. At the close of the second century, the Christian community was divided into several groups having their own Christology. Irenaeus and others conceived the plan of uniting these groups, or the more orthodox of them, into one great catholic church, with Rome at the head. Rome at this time became the largest and most influential of all Christian churches. In his treatise on *Adversus Haereses* ("Against Heresies"), Irenaeus wrote, "For it is a matter of necessity that every Church should agree with this Church, on account of its preeminent authority, that is, the faithful everywhere, inasmuch as the apostolical tradition has been preserved continuously by those [faithful men] who exist everywhere."[14] Irenaeus asserted the authority of the apostles as found in the apostolic tradition which is the Scripture.

The order of the books as listed in the New Testament has varied in their placement in various stages of the church throughout its history. But the Gospels—Matthew, Mark, Luke, and John always stand at the head of the order. Other gospels, such as the Gospel of Thomas, the Infancy Gospel of Thomas, the Gospel of Mary, the Gospel of Peter, and the Gospel of Judas were used in the ancient church, but they were excluded in the Canon of the New Testament.[15]

In the work of establishing the catholic church and the New Testament canon, Irenaeus was succeeded by Clement of Alexandria (150–215 CE) and Tertullian (155–240 CE). Clement of Alexandria was a Christian theologian, having taught at the catechetical School of Alexandria. Tertullian was a prolific early Christian author from Carthage in the Roman province of Africa. They adopted the books made by Irenaeus. The books adopted by these fathers were selected from a large number of Christian writings, then extant— forty or more gospels, nearly as many Acts of the Apostles, a score of books of Revelation, and several epistles.

---

13. For a list of scriptures that were excluded from the New Testament Canon, see Ehrman, *Lost Scriptures.*

14. Irenaeus, *Haer.* 3.3.2.

15. For a list of non-canonical gospels, see Ehrman and Pleše, *The Apocryphal Gospels.*

Most Christians believe that all of the books of the New Testament, and only the books of the New Testament, have been accepted as canonical by all Christians. And yet, how far from this is the truth! In the early age of the church, there have been Christians, eminent for their piety and learning, who either rejected some of these books or who accepted as canonical books not currently contained in the New Testament. Origen (184-253 CE) was a scholar and early Christian theologian from Alexandria. He doubted the authority of the Epistle to the Hebrews, of the Epistles of James, of Jude, of the Second Peter, and of the Second and Third John, while at the same time he was disposed to recognize as canonical certain apocryphal books, such as those of the Shepherd of Hermas and the Epistle of Barnabas. In addition to the apocryphal books named, Origen also accepted as authoritative the Gospel of the Hebrews, the Gospel of the Egyptians, the Acts of Paul, and the Preaching of Peter.[16]

Eusebius, a celebrated church historian (260–340 CE), was the bishop of Caesarea. In his most valuable writing, *Ecclesiastical History*, Eusebius provides three lists of the (i) acknowledged; (ii) disputed; and (iii) rejected books of the New Testament.[17] Eusebius excluded most of the Christian writings with a stern warning: "They ought, therefore, to be reckoned not even among spurious books but shunned as altogether wicked and impious."[18] Jerome (347–420 CE) was a Scripture scholar from Stridon in Dalmatia. He translated the Bible into Latin, called *Vulgate*. Although he included in his canon all the books of the New Testament, he admitted that Philemon, Hebrews, 2 Peter, 2, 3 John, Jude, and Revelation were of doubtful authority.

The first church synod which acted upon the question of canonicity was the Synod of Laodicea which met in 363 CE. In this Synod, on the question of Biblical Canon, the sixtieth canon listed the books, with the New Testament containing twenty-six books, omitting the Book of Revelation, and the Old Testament including the twenty-two books of the Hebrew Bible plus the Book of Baruch and the Epistle of Jeremy. The third council of Carthage which met in 397 CE admitted the Book of Revelation and the apocryphal books or the extra-canonical books of the Old Testament (except

---

16. See Eusebius, *Hist. eccl.* 6.25.

17. Eusebius, *Hist. eccl.* 3.25.1–7. Of the acknowledged book, Eusebius lists: Four Gospels, Acts of the Apostles, Thirteen Letters of Paul, 1 John, 1 Peter, and Revelation of John. Of the disputed books, he states: James, Jude, 2 Peter, 2, 3 John, Acts of Paul, Shepherd of Hermas, Revelation of Peter, Epistle of Barnabas, Institutions of the Apostles, Revelation of John, and Gospel according to the Hebrews. Of the rejected books, he classifies: Gospel of Peter, Gospel of Thomas, Pseudo-Matthew and other Gospels, Acts of Andrew, Acts of John, and other writings.

18. Eusebius, *Hist. eccl.* 3.3.7.

Lamentations). The early church did not make any effort to authorize the use of the apocryphal books for public worship.

Athanasius, bishop of Alexandria (298–373 CE), was very influential in defining the Canon of the New Testament. In his thirty-ninth *Festal Epistle* written around 367 CE, Athanasius listed all the twenty-seven books as current in the New Testament.[19] Since then, the canonical books of the New Testament remain intact without any attempt on the part of the church to include other early Christian writings. As David L. Dungan observes, "In terms of the history of Christianity, a canon of scripture, properly so called, did not appear until church officials, acting under the guidance of the highest levels of the Roman government, met together on several specific occasions to create a rigid boundary around the approved texts, forever separating them from the larger 'cloud of sacred books.'"[20] The rigid boundary set by the church silenced the voices of many early Christian writers who genuinely sought to express the faith.

Since the discovery of a cache of relatively early Christian texts bound in leather as codices, at Nag Hammadi in 1945, an increasing number of the apocryphal texts have been made known to the public and they remain a focal point for scholarly interest and study.[21] But those Christian texts are kept outside the boundary of the Canon of the New Testament until today. Recently Hal Taussig published a book that contains not only the traditional New Testament canonical books, twenty-seven in number, but also ten apocryphal Christian writings.[22] The included texts are: Prayer of Thanksgiving, Gospel of Thomas, Odes of Solomon, Thunder: Perfect Mind, Gospel of Mary, Gospel of Truth, Prayer of the Apostle Paul, Acts of Paul and Thecla, Letter of Peter to Philip, and Secret Revelation of John. Taussig provided those books to the general public for study and reflection.

The persistent challenge seems to be whether the church is willing to revisit the issue of canonicity and include additional books in the New Testament Canon. Hans von Campenhausen insists, "Without adherence to the Canon, which—in the widest sense—witness to the history of Christ, faith in Christ in any church would become an illusion."[23] It is true that adherence to the Canon is required to keep the church intact. But strict adherence to the Canon seems to have left out a broader understanding of Jesus Christ. Limiting the Canon of the New Testament only to the twenty-seven books

---

19. Athanasius, *Ep. Fest.* 39.5.

20. Dungan, *Constantine Bible*, 3.

21. See Meyer, *Nag Hammadi Scriptures*.

22. Taussig, *A New New Testament*.

23. von Campenhausen, *The Formation of the Christian Bible*, 333.

constrains the revelation of God in Jesus Christ and excludes the voices of many people who called themselves "Christians."

Christological Controversies

Christology is primarily concerned with the identity of Jesus Christ. The early church assumed both the humanity and the divinity of Jesus Christ based on the confession of Peter at Caesarea Philippi. Peter confessed that Jesus is "the Messiah, the Son of the living God." (Matt 16:16). The author of 1 Timothy provides one of the earliest doctrinal confessions on the identity of Jesus Christ: "Without any doubt, the mystery of our religion is great: He was revealed in flesh, vindicated in spirit, seen by angels, proclaimed among Gentiles, believed in throughout the world, taken up in glory" (1 Tim 3:16). A greater understanding of this evangelical confession of Jesus Christ grew as church fathers were compelled to respond to erroneous views that did not well align with orthodoxy. As such, the early church created more enemies than followers of Jesus Christ. While the confession of Christ's divinity and humanity is pivotal to the faith of the infant church, christological doctrine began to develop in light of various false teachings that arose from the earliest days of the church.

The earliest christological controversies in early Christianity include Ebionism and Docetism. The Ebionites were a type of Jewish-Christian sect that flourished in the late and early second centuries. They maintained the authority of the Jewish Scriptures and held a strict adherence to the Torah. They argued that God adopted Jesus at his baptism, thus rejecting his preexistence and virgin birth. Eusebius notes, "The first Christians gave these the suitable name of Ebionites because they had poor and mean opinions concerning Christ. They held him to be a plain and ordinary man who achieved righteousness merely by the progress of his character and had been born naturally from Mary and her husband."[24] A similar view was exposed by a teacher named Cerinthus (50–100 CE) who lived in Asia Minor. The early church fathers deemed him heretical. Cerinthus denied virginal conception and taught that Jesus was an ordinary human who was empowered by the spirit at his baptism. Irenaeus remarks, "He [Cerinthus] represented Jesus as having not been born of a virgin, but as being son of Joseph and Mary according to the ordinary course of human generation, while he nevertheless was more righteous, prudent, and wise than other men."[25] Quoting from Gaius, Eusebius writes, "Moreover, Cerinthus, who

24. Eusebius, *Hist. eccl.* 3.27.1–2.
25. Irenaeus, *Haer.* 1.26.1.

through revelations attributed to the writing of a great apostle, lyingly introduces portents to us as though shown him by angels, and says that after the resurrection the kingdom of Christ will be on earth . . . . He is the enemy of the scriptures of God and in his desire to deceive says that the marriage feast will last a thousand years."[26] In the name of orthodoxy, the early thinkers began to attack those who held views contrary to the doctrine of the church. Instead of embracing different christological understandings of Christ, the early church set to drive away those who also sought to express their faith in the personhood of Christ.

Another early christological controversy to arise within the church was Docetism, which disputed the full humanity of Christ. The author of 1 John warns against this belief, noting that many false prophets refused to acknowledge Jesus Christ came in the flesh (1 John 4:1–3). Raymond E. Brown comments, "For the secessionists the human existence was only a stage in the career of the divine Word and not an intrinsic component in redemption."[27] Somehow the author of 1 John seems to reject those who held a different view of the incarnation of Jesus Christ.

Bishop Ignatius warns against that erroneous doctrine when he writes his *Epistle to the Ephesians*. He cautions, "Now Onesimus himself praises your orderly conduct in God, reporting that you all live in accordance with the truth and that no heresy has found a home among you. Indeed, you do not so much as listen to anyone unless he speaks truthfully about Jesus Christ."[28] Bishop Ignatius seems to uphold the view that Jesus Christ took on human flesh and suffered. He states, "There is only one physician, who is both flesh and spirit, born and unborn, God in man, true life in death, both from Mary and from God, first subject to suffering and then beyond it, Jesus Christ our Lord."[29] Instead of accommodating every possible view on the personhood of Jesus Christ, the early church sought to attack and suppress different christological understandings.

Another major christological controversy was set against Gnosticism. Some of the apocryphal gospels, such as the Gospel of Thomas and the Gospel of Mary are deemed to be gnostic. An early form of Gnosticism promoted a doctrine that Christ came in spirit to impart knowledge (Gk: *Gnosis*) to only a select few. The proponents of Christian Gnosticism in the early church included Valentinus of Rome (100–160 CE) and Marcion of Sinope (85–160 CE). Marcion dismissed the Jewish Scriptures and

26. Eusebius, *Hist. eccl.* 3.28.1–2.

27. Brown, *The Community of the Beloved Disciple*, 113.

28. *Ign. Eph.* 6.2.

29. *Ign. Eph.* 7.2.

edited ten letters of Paul and a fragmentary Gospel of Luke. Marcion was eventually excommunicated from the church of Rome. Both Irenaeus and Tertullian provided extensive refutations of Gnostic understanding of biblical Christology. Contrary to the Gnostics who distinguished between heavenly Christ and earthly Jesus, Irenaeus affirmed that "Our Lord Jesus Christ being one and the same, as He Himself the Lord doth testify, as the apostles confess, and as the prophets announce, ..."[30] Using the Gospel of Luke, the only gospel Marcion possessed in edited form, Tertullian exposes Marcion's error. In his treatise on *Adversus Marcionem* ("Against Marcion"), Tertullian defends that "that Gospel of Luke which we are defending with all our might has stood its ground from its very first publication; whereas Marcion's Gospel is not known to most people, and to none whatever is it known without being at the same condemned."[31] Again, the early church fathers strived to forcefully confront differing christological views in their attempt to establish orthodoxy.

In the second and third centuries, the early church was debating with Noetus of Smyrna and Sebellius of Rome who taught that the Father, Son, and Holy Spirit were not distinct persons, but different ways (*modi*) of acting of the one God. They denied the unique role and personhood of each member of the Trinity in order to preserve the *monarchia* or oneness, of God. Tertullian engaged in a thorough defense against those differing views on the personhood of the godhead. In his treatise on *Adversus Praxean* ("Against Praxeas"), Tertullian vigorously defends the doctrine of Trinity. Tertullian asserts that the Father, the Son, and the Holy Spirit are three persons (*personae*), "not in condition, but in degree; not in substance, but in form; not in power, but in aspect; yet of one substance, and of one condition, and of one power, inasmuch as He is one God, from whom these degrees and forms and aspects are reckoned, under the name of the Father, and of the Son, and of the Holy Ghost."[32] Tertullian establishes the doctrine of Trinity as the rule of faith: "Bear always in mind that this is the rule of faith which I profess; by it I testify that the Father, and the Son, and the Spirit are inseparable from each other, and so will you know in what sense this is said."[33] Those who were able to articulate a different understanding of Trinity found themselves at odds

30. Irenaeus, *Haer.* 3.17.4.

31. Tertullian, *Marc.* 4.5.

32. Tertullian, *Prax.* 2. Commenting on Tertullian's chief argument of Trinity, Eric Osborn observes, "God is three persons and one substance. The tension between the three and the one points to relative disposition or substantial relation. God is one God; but father and son are mutually necessary to each other, and never identical. Identity would destroy them; their difference is the ground of their unity." Osborn, "Tertullian," 146.

33. Tertullian, *Prax.* 9.

with powerful church leaders. They were excommunicated from the church and condemned to be heretics.

In the fourth century, the major christological controversy was Arianism. Arius, presbyter in Alexandria (256–336 CE), began to teach that Jesus was created rather than being the co-equal eternal Son of God with the Father from the beginning. Arius and his followers believed that if the Son were co-equal to the Father, there would be more than one God. The early church dealt with this controversy at the Council of Nicaea in 325 CE, a council convened by the emperor Constantine. They declared that Jesus Christ is "God from God, Light from Light, true God from true God, begotten not made, consubstantial (*homoousios*) with the Father, by whom all things were made."[34] The Council of Nicaea eventually produced a creed known as the Nicene Creed which is used in the church today. The Nicene Creed is a revised version from the Council of Constantinople (381 CE). The Council of Nicaea anathematized Arius and his adherents and the emperor sent Arius and his followers into exile. The early church wanted to define the tenets of Christian faith in a way that put aside many forms of expression of one's faith in Jesus Christ. The type of Christianity that emerged from the Council of Nicaea and the subsequent church councils that followed became more interested in establishing orthodoxy than in embracing different dogmas.

Women in Ministry

It is no surprise that women were actively involved in ministry in the early church. From the very beginning—the birth, ministry, death, and resurrection of Jesus Christ—women were significantly visible. In fact, women were the major witnesses of Jesus's crucifixion and resurrection (Matt 27:55; Mark 15:40; Luke 23:49; Matt 28:9). In John's Gospel, the Risen Jesus appears to Mary Magdalene who went and proclaimed the message of Jesus's resurrection to the male disciples (John 20:18). The early church considered Mary Magdalene an "apostle of the apostles" (*Apostolorum apostola*).

In the first few decades of the infant church, a number of women served as leaders of the house churches that emerged in the cities of the Roman empire—the list consists of Priscilla, Chloe, Lydia, Apphia, Nympha, and possibly the "elect lady" of 2 John.[35] In his letter to the Romans, Paul includes a long list of women who served as leaders in the churches. He mentions Phoebe, a deacon of the church in Cenchreae (Rom 16:1); Prisca along with her husband Aquila as co-workers (Rom 16:3); Mary as a hard

34. Hall, *Doctrine and Practice*, 130.

35. See Wood, *The People Paul Admired*.

worker (Rom 16:6); Junia as a prominent figure among the apostles (Rom 16:7); Rufus's mother as a mother to Paul (Rom 16:13); and Julia, probably a prominent house church member along with her husband Philologus and sister of Nereus (Rom 16:15). The four daughters of Philip the evangelist appear in Acts 21:9 as prophetesses. Eusebius regarded Philip's daughters and their ministry as the bench mark of "apostolic succession." He attests, "Among those who were famous at this time was also Quadratus, of whom tradition says that he shared with the daughters of Philip the distinction of a prophetic gift. And many others beside them were well known at this time and take the first rank in the Apostolic succession."[36]

Women's leadership was highly commended at the beginning years of the early church. Bishop Ignatius acknowledges women's leadership and sends greetings. He recognizes, "I greet the household of Gavia, and pray that she may be firmly grounded in faith and love both physically and spiritually. I greet Alce, a name very dear to me, and the incomparable Daphnus, and Eutecnus and everyone else individually. Farewell in the grace of God."[37] Polycarp, bishop of Smyrna (69–155 CE), mentions the sister of Crescens who deserved special commendation when she and her brother came to Philippi to deliver the letter. In his *Epistle to the Philippians*, Polycarp writes, "I am writing these things to you via Crescens, whom I recently commended to you and now commend again, for his conduct while with us has been blameless, and I believe that it will be likewise with you. And you will consider his sister to be commended when she comes to you."[38] Women were commended for their leadership role in the church along with their male counterparts.

The role of women in church leadership was tarnished as the church began to express disapproval of women leadership. The author of 1 Timothy echoes a marked ambivalence toward women. The author instructs Timothy to follow this mandate: "Let a woman learn in silence with full submission. I permit no woman to teach or to have authority over a man; she is to keep silent" (1 Tim 2:11–12; cf. 1 Cor 14:34–35). In light of the organized ecclesiastical structure, women were restricted from holding an official position in church. Throughout the early centuries, church authorities continued to rule against the leadership of women. Only men were engaged in establishing doctrinal standards of the church.

Some of the church fathers' perception of women as the weaker sex probably led to women's oppression in ministry. As Hannelie Wood

36. Eusebius, *Hist. eccl.* 3.37.1.

37. *Ign. Smyrn.* 13.2.

38. *Pol. Phil.* 14.

observes that "women" in the writings of the church fathers, "were not only regarded as the cause of all sin, they were also seen as inferior and weak in both mind and character and also as not having been created in the 'image of God.'"[39] Irenaeus writes, "Why was it, that when these two (Aaron and Miriam) had both acted with spite towards him (Moses), the latter alone was adjudged punishment? First, because the woman was the more culpable, since both nature and the law place the woman in a subordinate condition to the man."[40] It is unheard of women being in authority over men in the early church. Tertullian's views on women went extreme. In his treatise on *De Cultu Feminarum* ("The Apparel of Women"), Tertullian states, "And do you not know that you are (each) an Eve? The sentence of God on this sex of yours lives in this age: the guilt must of necessity live too. You are the devil's gateway . . . you are the first deserter of the divine law; you are she who persuaded him whom the devil was not valiant enough to attack."[41] Tertullian seems to express profound anti-feminine feelings.

In his treatise on *De Praescriptione Haeretocorum* ("Prescription against Heretics"), Tertullian maintains that the church has the sole authority to declare what is considered to be and what is indeed not, of an Orthodox Christian constitution. He states, "The very women of these heretics, how wanton they are! For they are bold enough to teach, to dispute, to enact exorcisms, to undertake cures—it may be even to baptize. Their ordinations, are carelessly administered, capricious, changeable."[42] The role of women in ecclesiastical matters was one such practice that he opposed. In his work on *De Baptismo* ("Baptism"), Tertullian notes in dismay that a woman was teaching and baptizing. He says, "But the woman of pertness, who has usurped the power to teach, will of course not give birth for herself likewise to a right of baptizing, unless some new beast shall arise like the former; so that, just as the one abolished baptism, so some other should in her own right confer it!"[43]

Tertullian understood that many of his contemporaries were grounding their actions and ideas on the *Acts of Paul and Thecla* which gave women authority to teach and baptize.[44] He stated that under no circumstances

39. Wood, "Feminists and Their Perspectives," 4.

40. Irenaeus, *Frag.* 32.

41. Tertullian, *Cult. fem.* 1.1.

42. Tertullian, *Praescr.* 41.

43. Tertullian, *Bapti.* 17.

44. Tertullian rejected the Acts of Paul and Thecla, a second-century apocryphal book. He reported that the presbyter who wrote the book in the name of Paul was removed from his office. According to the work, Thecla accepts Christ as a result of Paul's preaching in Iconium. She is condemned to die by fire, but is rescued by a sudden

should the work be used to inspire women to claim the right to teach and baptize. Tertullian seems to deny the sacramental rights to women. He comes to the conclusion that the apostle Paul who wrote 1 Cor 14:34–35 would never have permitted a woman to teach or baptize, and he sought to forbid this. Tertullian writes, "For how credible would it seem, that he [Paul] who has not permitted a *woman* even to *learn* with over-boldness, should give a *female* the power of *teaching* and of *baptizing*! 'Let them be silent,' he says, 'and at home consult their own husbands.'"[45] The act of prohibition in itself however, bears testimony to the possibility and likelihood that women were engaged in teaching and baptism in some places.

Early church fathers did not consider gender to be an important theological concept but rather gender was understood by them in apophatic assertions. Women were involved in ministry in the early years of the apostolic church. As the church became hierarchical, women were not recognized as suitable material for the priesthood with the result that the church never appointed them as presbyters or priests or bishops. In most cases women were placed in a subordinate role to assist male clergy. As Wood notes, "If these historical viewpoints about women reflect women's subordination and oppression, they force women to discover their roots and their past. With this comes the right to redefine, to decide and to act upon freedom from oppression, and to ultimately create emancipation."[46] History, especially early church history, teaches that the church should redefine the view of women in order to actively involve women in every life of the church including ordaining women to priesthood.

Implications for Teaching Religious Extremism

The early church history of Christianity in the first four centuries reveals the struggles the early church faced. The early church began to define orthodoxy and, as a consequence of it, several facts contributed to religious extremism which continued to divide the church throughout the centuries. Teaching the history of early Christianity should point out both the dangers that tarnished the witness of the early church and the means to overcome

---

cloudburst which extinguishes the flames pointing to divine providence. In Antioch she is condemned to fight against wild beasts, but is once again delivered from danger at which time she baptizes herself by plunging into a ditch full of water in the amphitheater (see *Acts Paul*, 34).

45. Tertullian, *Bapti.* 17.

46. Wood, "Feminists and Their Perspectives," 9.

religious extremism. Past history can help us to stop fueling religious extremism and to promote religious inclusivism.

1. The early church began as a charismatic movement which was largely dependent on the spiritual gifts people possessed, rather than on formal leadership. Early apostles, including Paul, recognized the gifts of new believers and effectively used them in building up the church. As the church began to grow, leaders were selected by the people and given authority by the laying on of hands. Soon after New Testament times, the office of elder/bishop bifurcates into elder and bishop. Beginning with Bishop Ignatius, the church promoted the threefold ministry of deacon, elder, and bishop. The charismatic leadership disappeared in the main stream church that became catholic orthodoxy. The apostles and prophets had been replaced by bishops and the gifts of the Spirit by elect officials. Ecclesiastical hierarchy assumed power to decide on doctrinal matters. It continued down through the centuries and caused many schisms within the church.

The rigid form of church government does not allow room for charismatic ministry and is perceived by many as a form of religious extremism. We are faced, then, with a serious dilemma. On the one hand, church government is necessary to regulate the ordering of ministry in the church. On the other hand, placing ministry under the appointive leadership is an equally great danger. When I taught a course on the New Testament Church, I encouraged students to explore different models of church leadership. I invited students to consider church leadership based on ministry. A ministry-focused leadership may perhaps help us move the focus from an extreme, rigid form of church government to a more flexible structure which seeks to embrace the gifts of the people.

2. The early church did not, at first, form a "canon" of books to begin with. The process of canonization of Christian Scriptures was gradual and very complex. Not all the books of the present New Testament were not considered canonical in the early church. The four Gospels, the book of Acts, and the epistles of Paul, John, Peter, and James were considered as legitimate writings of the New Testament. Some of the apocryphal books, such as the *Shepherd of Hermas*, the *Epistle of Barnabas*, the *Gospel of the Hebrews*, the *Gospel of the Egyptians*, the *Acts of Paul*, and the *Preaching of Peter* enjoyed canonical status for a while. When the church became more ecclesiastical, a list of authoritative books became a necessity. In 367 CE Bishop Athanasius took the chance afforded him and included in his *Festal Epistle* of that year what he declared to be canonical texts: the very New Testament we now have (Four Gospel, Acts, Twenty-one Epistles, and Revelation). Other Christian writings, roughly from the New Testament times, were left out.

The closing of the Canon of the New Testament was an ecclesiastical decision made in the post apostolic age. By limiting the Canon of the New Testament to twenty-seven books, this automatically excluded the apocryphal books of Christian origins. The Christian apocryphal writings represent various trends of the Gospel of Jesus Christ. The first thing I talk about in my New Testament class is the Canon of the New Testament. I try to show the canonical validity of both the New Testament books and the apocryphal writings. Just like the apocryphal writings, the New Testament books also present a diverse understanding of Jesus Christ. Perhaps studying the apocryphal books along with the New Testament books may greatly help students use all of the early Christian writings in teaching and preaching. In this way one can seek to overcome religious extremism and embrace a body of Christian literature that represents the ongoing revelation of Jesus Christ.

3. The early church was engaged in many christological controversies. The controversies arose because of critical questions regarding the relationship between the divinity and the humanity of Jesus Christ. The early church defended the doctrine of Christ so vigorously because it believed that the gospel itself was at stake. Early church fathers sought to establish a gospel that would uphold both the divine and human nature of Jesus Christ. They thought that the views expressed in Ebionism, Docetism, Gnosticism, and Arianism attempted to divide the personhood of Jesus Christ. Instead of acknowledging the existence of various forms of expression of faith, the early church took an extreme position to settle the christological doctrines for the catholic church. The early church declared that any other doctrine that affirms a place for Jesus Christ, without asserting his full divinity and humanity, is erroneous. Early Christians who held a different view of the personhood of Jesus Christ were condemned as heretics and excommunicated from the church.

The early church did a good job of setting good boundaries which protected both the full divinity and the full humanity of Jesus Christ. Because of the boundaries determined by the early church, early Christianity gave rise to religious extremism. The doctrines of the church established in the name of Jesus Christ began to exclude those Christians who also genuinely sought to convey the biblical Christology. Teaching a course on Early Christianity should focus on two factions of the church as a genuine expression of Christology, rather than emphasizing the early church's Christology as orthodox and the splinter group's Christology as heterodox. The Christology that strived to split the personhood of Jesus Christ is as good as the Christology that attempted to unify the personhood of Jesus Christ. Perhaps unification of various expressions of Christology may bring everyone to continuously articulate the mysteries of Jesus Christ.

4. In the early years of the apostolic church women were held in high esteem and considered as co-partners in ministry with the apostles and the followers of the apostles. Some of the church fathers spoke very highly of women who administered the affairs of the church along with their male counterparts. As the church began to be grounded in hierarchy, women were slowly silenced in the church. Early church fathers attempted to restrict women's involvement in church affairs. Women were not only blamed for sin but also perceived by the church fathers as the weaker sex and inferior to men. The church fathers forbade women to teach, baptize, and become priests. Women were not allowed to take part in the church councils that constituted the doctrines of the church. Most of the early Christian writers were men. The early church refused to consider the *Gospel of Mary* and the *Acts of Paul and Thecla* as canonical, because those writings affirmed the role of women in ministry.

The church fathers' view of women led to women's subordination and oppression in ministry. Women were only allowed to assist the male priests, but never as priests or bishops or archbishops. Early church history teaches that the apostolic church fully recognized the gifts of women in the early development of early Christianity. Only the inferior understanding of women pushed the early church to become exclusively a male-centered ecclesiology. Teaching the importance of the role of women in the early formation of the early church may create awareness of women's effectiveness in ministry. Teaching human sexuality, particularly women's sexuality as a God-given gift to the world may pave the way for women's equal involvement in church ministry. Including women in every aspect of the church including making decisions on doctrinal matters may change the way the church functions today.

Conclusion

Religious extremism expresses itself in various dimensions of religion. The four categories discussed in this essay broadly identify the marks of religious extremism in the history of early Christianity. It is important to understand the consequences and damages done to religion as a result of religious extremism. It will be of great help in developing a viable pedagogy in academic teaching. Past history may shed light on the way religious extremism continues to manifest in multiple dimensions of religion. Perceiving the multidimensionality of religion in the context of religious extremism may help researchers, teachers, and students of religion articulate trajectories of systemic change.

Bibliography

Beeley, Christopher, A. "The Early Christological Controversy: Apollinarius, Diodore, and Gregory Nazianzen," *Vigiliae Christianae* 65 (2011) 376–407.

Brown, Raymond E. *The Community of the Beloved Disciple*. Mahwah, NJ: Paulist, 1979.

Campenhausen, Hans von. *The Formation of the Christian Bible*. Translated by J. A. Baker. Philadelphia: Fortress, 1972.

Charteris, Archibold Hamilton. *Canonicity: A Collection of Early Testimonies to the Canonical Books of the New Testament, Based on Kirchhofer's "Quellensammlung."* Edinburgh: Blackwell, 1880.

Clarke, Andrew D. *A Pauline Theology of Church Leadership*. London: T. & T. Clark, 2008.

Dungan, David L. *Constantine Bible: Politics and the Making of the New Testament*. London: SCM, 2006.

Ehrman, Bart D. *Lost Scriptures: Books That Did not Make It into the New Testament*. Oxford: Oxford University Press, 2003.

Ehrman, Bart D., and Zlatko Pleše. *The Apocryphal Gospels: Texts and Translations*. Oxford: Oxford University Press, 2011.

Eusebius. *Ecclesiastical History, Books 1–5*. Translated by Kirsopp Lake. LCL. Cambridge: Harvard University Press, 1926.

Eusebius. *Ecclesiastical History, Books 6–10*. Translated by J. E. L. Oulton. LCL. Cambridge, MA: Harvard University Press, 1932.

Geljon, Albert C., and Riemer Roukema, eds. *Violence in Ancient Christianity: Victims and Perspectives*. Leiden: Brill, 2014.

Gillard, Frank D. "Senatorial Bishops in the Fourth Century," *Harvard Theological Review* 77 (1984) 153–75.

Hall, Stuart G. *Doctrine and Practice in the Early Church*. Grand Rapids: Eerdmans, 1991.

Hinson, Glenn E. *The Church Triumphant: A History of Christianity up to 1300*. Macon, GA: Mercer University Press, 1995.

Lightfoot, J. B., and J. R. Harmer, eds. and trans. *The Apostolic Fathers: Greek Texts and English of Their Translations*. 2nd ed. Grand Rapids: Baker, 1992.

McDonald, Lee M., and James A. Sanders, eds. *The Canon Debate*. Peabody, MA: Hendrickson, 2002.

Merkle, Benjamin L. "Hierarchy in the Church? Instruction from the Pastoral Epistles Concerning Elders and Overseers." *Southern Baptist Journal of Theology* 7 (2003) 32–43.

Osborn, Eric. "Tertullian." In *The First Christian Theologians: An Introduction to Theology in the Early Church*, edited by G. R. Evans, 143–49. Oxford: Blackwell, 2004.

Roberts, Alexander, and James Donaldson, eds. *Ante-Nicene Fathers*, Vol. 1. Peabody, MA: Hendrickson, 1999.

Roberts, Alexander, and James Donaldson, eds. *Ante-Nicene Fathers*, Vol. 3. Peabody, MA: Hendrickson, 1999.

Roberts, Alexander, and James Donaldson, eds. *Ante-Nicene Fathers*, Vol. 4. Peabody, MA: Hendrickson, 1999.

Siootjes, Daniëlle. "Bishops and Their Position of Power in the Late Third Century CE: The Cases of Gregory Thaumaturgus and Paul of Samosate." *Journal of Late Antiquity* 4 (2011) 100–115.

Taussig, Hal, ed with commentary. *A New Testament: A Bible for the 21st Century Combining Traditional and Newly Discovered Texts.* New York: Houghton Mifflin Harcourt, 2013.

Wood, Beulah. *The People Paul Admired: The House Church Leaders of the New Testament.* House of Priscilla and Aquila Series. Eugene, OR: Wipf & Stock, 2011.

Wood, Hannelie. "Feminists and Their Perspectives on the Church Fathers' Beliefs Regarding Women: An Inquiry." *Verbum et Ecclesia* (online) 38 (2017) 1–10.

7

Teaching Revelation and Questions of Violent Extremism

—TAT-SIONG BENNY LIEW

O ne of the most well-known and most horrendous cases of violent extremism was the Holocaust. Calling the Jews "a dangerous bacillus," "subhuman," and "lower than vermin,"[1] Hitler and his Third Reich attempted an extermination program literally to eliminate the Jews. After the atrocities of the Holocaust, many have called for the need to reread Scriptures, given, among other reasons, how some German Protestant scholars and church leaders collaborated with Hitler's regime and justified its systematic murder of Jews with particular readings of the Bible.[2]

Sadly, the Bible itself is not devoid of violent extremism. God orders the Israelites in Deuteronomy 7, for example, not only to invade and take over the land of others but also to annihilate the inhabitants there and their heritages in an act of total—that is, both physical and cultural—genocide. Worse, this divine command is based on "chosenness" and conditioned on obedience. Deuteronomy 7 states more than once that the Israelites were chosen by God to be holy and hence set apart (Deut 7:6–7); in fact, the emphasis on the Israelites' victory over and final destruction of these other(ed) peoples, despite being outnumbered by them, comes across somewhat perversely as a proof of their chosen status (Deut 7:7–8). At the same time, the text is clear that the Israelites themselves will be punished,

---

1. See, for example, Koonz, *The Nazi Conscience*, 24, 252, 260–61; and Herzstein, *The War That Hitler Won*, 309.

2. For a sobering account of how German Protestant leaders collaborated with the Third Reich, see Heschel, *The Aryan Jesus*. For attempts to re-read the Bible after the Holocaust, see, for instance, Fackenheim, *The Jewish Bible after the Holocaust*; Linafelt, *Strange Fire*; and Sweeney, *Reading the Hebrew Bible after the Shoah*.

even rejected and destroyed, if they fail to carry out God's genocidal command (Deut 7:4, 9–11, 26).

In light of the history of the Holocaust, especially how the New Testament has been used as a justification, I will look at the last book in the New Testament canon—the Apocalypse of John/Book of Revelation—and use it as a case study to talk about how I may teach this biblical text in particular and biblical studies in general, given this problem of violent extremism.[3] This is of particular importance with my own teaching context in the United States of America, which was founded on violent extremism: namely, the genocidal attempt against the native peoples.

Questions in Reading Revelation

John's violent rhetoric in Revelation is obvious and well known; whether it falls into the category of violent extremism is more debatable. Its frequent and adamant emphasis on purity— readers must "come out of" the impure whore of Babylon and abandon teachings of "false" teachers if they are to escape God's violent destruction and be given entry into the New Jerusalem (Rev 2:6, 9, 14–16, 20–23; 3:9; 18:4–8; 21:1–2, 26–27; cf. Rev 14:1– 5)—certainly seems to divide people into two camps with consequences of either everlasting life or eternal death (Rev 20:11–15). Is this radical and rigid emphasis of "purify"-or-perish not a clear case that dissenters and opponents must be violently excluded and eliminated, and hence a glaring example of violent extremism?

Who Initiated the Violence?

In his introduction to this volume, Eleazar Fernandez differentiates violent extremism from a conditional violence that is necessary to protect the life of one's own group from another aggressive and attacking group. In one sense, the book of Revelation does present the cosmic "battle" or "war" (Rev 2:16; 9:7, 9; 11:7; 12:7, 17; 13:7; 16:12, 14; 17:14; 19:11, 19; 20:8) between followers of Christ/God and followers of the Dragon/Satan (Rev 12:9) as being initiated by the Dragon and its Beasts. Since God is credited as the Creator (Rev 4:11; 10:6; 14:7) with Jesus as "the origin [or the beginning] of God's creation" (Rev 3:14), the very early reference to Jesus being "pierced" (Rev 1:7) and the repeated statements that "the earth" is being "destroyed" and

---

3. For a study that looks at how violence might have been related to not only the Bible but also the Quran, see Avalos, *The Reality of Religious Violence*.

"corrupted" (Rev 11:18; 19:2) imply nothing less than an assault on God's creation.[4] The same is true of the attacks being launched—including those on humans, even but not exclusively God's special witnesses and other saints— by monstrous-looking troops (Rev 9:1–11, 16–19); by the two "beasts" (Rev 11:1–10; 13:1–7a); by Satan, the "great red dragon" (Rev 12:1–6; cf. Rev 12:9; 20:2); or by the "great whore" of Babylon (Rev 17:1–6; cf. Rev 18:24; 19:2). The devil and its beasts will kill anyone who refuses to be coerced to worship them (Rev 13:15). The influence of the Babylonian whore is shown to be not only thoroughly wicked by the thrice-repeated use of the word "every" (Rev 18:2), but also all-pervasive by the reference to "all the nations," as well as kings and merchants "of the earth" (Rev 18:3). Furthermore, both the description of and the charge against Babylon's economic exploits end with a reference to the negative implications on human lives (Rev 18:13, 24). The violence unleashed by these evil forces destroys not only the faithful in particular but also the human race in general.[5]

What I am getting at is how Revelation repeatedly depicts offensives being taken—first?—by the "enemies." In other words, there is textual evidence to suggest that the violent acts done by Revelation's God and Christ are "conditional"—that is, defensive and perhaps even moral—in nature.[6] The martyrs' cry for God to judge and avenge their blood (Rev 6:10) seems to communicate that whatever God does is a response to the evil and violence that were initiated by God's opponents. As the angel declares after the pouring of the third bowl of God's wrath, "You are just, O Holy One; . . . because they shed the blood of saints and prophets, you have given them blood to drink. It is what they deserve!" (Rev 16:5–6). Moreover, not only does the praise hymn of the twenty-four elders in heaven make it clear that God is just in "destroying those who destroy the earth" (Rev 11:18g), but the large heavenly choir, in response to the angel's concluding proclamation that "in [Babylon] was found the blood of prophets and of saints, and of all who have been slaughtered on earth" (Rev 18:24) and at the sight of Babylon's destruction, also sings in unison that God's "judgments are true and just; [God] has judged the great whore who corrupted the earth with her fornication, and [God] has avenged on her the blood of [God's] servants" (Rev 19:2). As if these heavenly songs are not enough, John will say again regarding Christ as the rider on a white horse that "in

4. Decock, "Images of War and Creation," 189.

5. Bauckham, *The Bible in Politics*, 85–102. We know that many oppressed peoples had read Revelation to sustain their hope for justice and for a better world. See, for example, Blount, *Can I Get a Witness*; Boesak, *Comfort and Protest*; Richard, *Apocalypse*.

6. See, for example, Decock, "Images of War and Creation," 195.

righteousness he judges and makes war" (Rev 19:11). The warring—and, yes, violent—activities of the divine are, the book of Revelation seems to suggest, ethical replies to or returns for the bloody violence first initiated by the devil, Babylon, or the Roman Empire.

While saying "You started it" is often associated with childish fights and hence viewed as a silly argument to defend or excuse one's participation in them, the book of Revelation is depicting a cosmic war. Having said that, "You started it" is actually also used in serious business. As I am writing this, I am hearing from the radio President Donald Trump's explanation for his decision to authorize the controversial killing of the Iranian commander Qassem Soleimani: "We took action last night to stop a war. We did not take action to start a war." Is it always easy to tell who or which party initiated a conflict? Or, is it not true that, as the popular saying goes, "It takes two to tango"?

Not Following Christ, or Not Following Christ in the Same Way?

This question is especially important since we cannot be sure when Revelation was written or whether there was widespread persecution when the book was written.[7] As many scholars have pointed out, Revelation's clear concern is that Christ-followers do not become too comfortable and assimilated because of a failure to recognize evil. The Roman Empire, for example, is represented by the whore of Babylon to show that what appears to be appealing, attractive, and enticing is impious, impure, iniquitous, and injurious in reality. Evil in Revelation, however, involves both external and internal threats; there is not only the "pagan" Roman Empire that attacks the church from the outside but also "false" teaching that tries to corrupt the church from within. The messages for the seven churches clearly display that the biggest problems, as far as Revelation is concerned, are: (1) indifference, as is the case in Ephesus and Laodicea (Rev 2:4; 3:15–16); and (2) toleration of what should not be tolerated, whether it is the teaching of Balaam or of the Nicolaitans in Pergamum (Rev 2:14–15; cf. Rev 2:6), the teaching of "Jezebel" in Thyatira (Rev 2:20), or the dismissal or disobedience of the "original" teachings in Sardis (3:1–4). What Revelation praises and recommends, as we

---

7. See, for example, Beal, *The Book of Revelation*, 33–40, for the two primary suggestions about Revelation's date of composition: namely, (1) after the death of Nero and during or shortly after the First Jewish-Roman War in the late 60s or the early 70s; or (2) during the reign of Domitian in the 90s. For the first view, see, for instance, Marshall, "Collateral Damage," 37–38; for the second, see Thompson, *The Book of Revelation*.

see in the case of the churches in Smyrna and in Philadelphia, is a vigilant faith that perseveres even in the midst of difficulties, trials, and sufferings (Rev 2:9–10; 3:8–11), especially given the presence of "a synagogue of Satan" made up of fake Jews (Rev 2:9; 3:9).

Following not only the growing scholarly consensus that Christ-followers remained within Judaism much longer than we first thought, but also the reference to the problem of committing fornication and eating "food sacrificed to idols" in both Pergamum and Thyatira (Rev 2:14, 20), Elaine Pagels recently summarized the argument that the so-called fake Jews in Revelation were none other than Christ-followers of the Pauline ilk.[8] Paul had adamantly stated in his letter to the Galatians that, because of Jesus Christ, circumcision was not necessary for Gentiles to become children of Israel's God, and hence members of the Jewish faith. He, as we know from his first letter to the Corinthians, was also much less bothered by the idea of consuming food sacrificed to idols (1 Cor 8:4–6), or by the continuation of marriages between a Christ-follower and an "unbelieving partner" (1 Cor 7:12–16). "False" teaching in Revelation, according to the argument, refers therefore to understanding of the Christ faith as taught by the great apostle to the Gentiles and his followers.

We know that there were a lot of internal disagreements among early Christians about what it meant to follow Christ and to follow God, as well as accusations between different factions of spreading "false" teachings or "heresies." It certainly sounds astounding, though we may not be able to ascertain this particular argument, that Paul's teachings could be connected with those of Balaam, who was willing to collaborate with a Moabite king for material gains (Rev 2:14; cf. Num 22–24; Deut 23:3–5); those of Jezebel, who oppressed Yahweh's prophets and instituted the worship of Baal (Rev 2:20–21; cf. 1 Kgs 16:29–34; 19:1–3); and even those of Satan the devil (Rev 2:9; 3:9). How may this thought that John's primary targets

---

8. Pagels, *Revelations*, 53–64. The idea that disputes among early Christ-followers might be partly the background of Revelation does not mean that one needs to remove the Roman Empire from one's consideration in reading this book. It also does not mean that these early Christ-followers had necessarily differentiated and separated themselves from Judaism. On both of these points, see Marshall, "Collateral Damage" (though Marshall dates the book earlier to the time of Nero and the First Jewish-Roman War, which, for Marshall led to John's concern over questions of cultural purity and cultural assimilation). The Jewishness of Revelation can be clearly seen by the way John "recycles" great chunks of materials from Hebrew Scriptures, including Daniel (see Beale, *The Use of Daniel in Jewish Apocalyptic Literature and in the Revelation of St. John*) and Ezekiel (see Ruiz, *Ezekiel in the Apocalypse*), to name just a couple of examples. John's use of Hebrew scriptures also speaks against any attempt to justify a supersessionist reading of Revelation with John's "synagogue of Satan" phrase (Rev 2:9; 3:9).

included other Christ-following teachers and groups with whom he disagreed, whoever they might actually have been, change our thinking about this book and violent extremism? Is John too extreme in his separatist stance? Is John too rigid in his view that his way and his way alone is right? Would one's judgment of John not largely depend on what Revelation has to say about the fate of those whom John attacks at the final and victorious coming of God's kingdom?

Is the "Conditional" Proportional?

Even if readers are ready to agree that God's warring activities in Revelation are meant to redress the violence started by the devil and those under its commands (including those who spread "false" teachings inside the church), they must consider what exactly God does in return. What is God going to do to the devil, its followers, and the "false" teachers? Are God's actions only for the purpose of protecting God's saintly and faithful followers?

Revelation is clear that the devil will be defeated. However, the book is also clear that the devil, along with its two beasts, will then be "thrown into the lake of fire and sulfur," and "be tormented day and night forever and ever" (Rev 20:10; cf. 19:20). Is this eternal torment or torture proportional to, or reasonable as, a form of defense or protection? Careful readers may notice that the devil in Revelation is not one who will give up its assaults just because of defeats. After being thrown out of heaven and onto the earth for its failed attempt to devour the Christ child who will "rule [or shepherd?] all the nations with a rod of iron" (Rev 12:1–9; cf. 19:15), it goes after the mother who gave birth to this child and, when that attempt also fails, it starts a war against the woman's other children—namely, those who follow Jesus (Rev 12:13–17)—with and through its two beasts (Rev 12:18—13:18). Similarly, we see the devil resuming its aggressions immediately upon its release from its thousand-year imprisonment in the pit (Rev 20:2–3, 7–9a). Is its eternal burning merely a way to keep the devil down (without killing it?), so to speak, especially since the devil has shown itself to be unrepentant even after a thousand years of imprisonment? At the same time, John is clearly aware that an ongoing torment can in many ways be more painful than death (Rev 9:5–6).

It is one thing to be more severe with the leader(s) of a violent "destruction" or "corruption" (Rev 11:18; 19:2) of God's creation; it is quite another to do what God will do to those who follow these destructive and corrupt leader(s), especially if these followers have been "deceived" (Rev 18:23; 19:20; 20:8, 10). There is, however, a hint that these followers will not repent and change their behaviors even if they have to face God's "just judgment" (Rev 16:1–21).[9] Christ, with a sharp sword of execution in his mouth against the nations, "will [therefore?] tread the wine press of the fury of the wrath of God the Almighty" (Rev 19:15), a wine press that, according to an earlier chapter, will be used to extract an unimaginable amount of blood: "as high as a horse's bridle, for a distance of about two hundred miles" (Rev 13:20). As a follow-up on this mass killing, God will have birds eat the flesh of the deceased bodies of these followers (Rev 19:17–21) in what the book calls "the great supper of God" (Rev 19:17) or "the marriage supper of the Lamb" (Rev 19:9). We further read from the next chapter in Revelation that when the dead are judged, "anyone whose name was not found written in the book of life was thrown into the lake of fire," which is characterized as the site for "the second death" (Rev 20:14–15; cf. Rev 2:11; 20:6; 21:8). Given Revelation's symbolic nature and cyclical structure, one does not need to quibble if this death is a "second" or a third death to recognize the clear emphasis that a single physical death will not be enough to punish those who do not follow God and Christ. John actually doubles down on the emphasis that God will double the harm to the whore of Babylon for whatever harm she has caused—"Render to her as she herself has rendered, and repay her double for her deeds; mix a double draught for her in the cup she mixed" (Rev 18:6).

Any doubt about this emphasis should dissipate with an angel's announcement that those who follow the wrong leaders

> will be tormented with fire and sulfur in the presence of the holy angels and in the presence of the Lamb. And the smoke of their torment goes up forever and ever. There is no rest day or night for those who worship the beast and its image and for anyone who receives the mark of its name (Rev 14:10–11).

The presence of the angels and of the Lamb in this scene seems to imply a kind of vengeful or even sadistic enjoyment in witnessing the suffering of others. Commenting on these verses, a biblical scholar writes, "Had such a statement been written about the beast, commentators would no doubt have described it as the epitome of malice, vindictiveness, and evil."[10] Should the same not be said of the divine decision to kill children because of their parents' "adultery" (Rev 2:22–23)?

Regardless of who is responsible for starting this cosmic war or who may be among John's "opponents," is there not enough textual evidence to

---

9. Barr, "Doing Violence," 98.

10. Moyise, "Does the Lion Lie Down with the Lamb," 182.

suggest that the God of Revelation not only escalates violence but also practices and promotes violent extremism?

Who Performs the Violence?

David L. Barr proposes a different reading of God's violence in Revelation.[11] Pointing to a call for the saints to endure in faith—"If you are to be taken captive, into captivity you go; if you kill with the sword, with the sword you must be killed" (Rev 13:10)—Barr suggests that the violence experienced by the enemies of God in Revelation is not performed by God; instead, it is generated by and a result of the enemies' own violence. That explains why the horrific violence that comes upon the whore of Babylon—being stripped naked, devoured, and burnt—is said to come from the beast with its ten horns or ten kings on which she rides, even though she is also said to be ruling over all the kings and her destruction is also said to be purposed by God (Rev 17:16–18). "Those who seek to dominate others will themselves be devoured in the process," Barr writes; this is "what God has ordained."[12] In other words, it is built within the universe that God has created that those who try to dominate through violence will self-destruct by the very violence that they employ. God does not commit any violent act directly against these enemies.

Can the same be said for other passages in the book of Revelation that Barr does not discuss, assuming in the meantime that one will interpret the clause "[f]or God has put [the violent punishment of the Babylonian 'whore' in Rev 17:16] into their [the two beasts'] hearts" (Rev 17:17) as Barr does rather than reading it as attributing to God or "crediting" God with the ultimate agency and responsibility for the violence? After the three cries of "woe" by an angel (Rev 8:13), the actual woes that follow are not carried out directly by the angels themselves. Instead, they only seem to give permission for the evil forces to run their courses. One angel gets the key to open "the shaft of the bottomless pit" (Rev 9:1–3), and another is told to release four (evil?) angels who were previously bound (Rev 9:13–15). Does this not support Barr's suggestion that God's violence is really nothing more than God *allowing* the violent forces of evil to self-destruct?

What about when Christ appears as a fiery-eyed divine warrior leading "armies of heaven" out to battle on a white horse (Rev 19:11–16)? Since this passage mentions Christ wielding "a sharp sword" to "strike down the

---

11. Barr, "Doing Violence," 100–102, 104–5. See also Boxall, *The Revelation of St. John*, 249.

12. Barr, "Doing Violence," 104.

nations" and treading "the wine press of the fury of the wrath of God the Almighty" (Rev 19:15), the blood that soaks or stains his robe may well be the blood of his enemies. In fact, Revelation is clear that besides the two beasts, "the rest were killed by the sword of the rider on the horse" (Rev 19:21). Having said that, since Christ is also repeatedly portrayed as a Lamb that had been slaughtered (Rev 5:6, 12; 13:8) and had bled (Rev 7:14; 12:11), the violence of the Lamb's death could also be the reason for Christ's blood-soaked or blood-stained robe. Or is it not conceivable that his robe is soiled by both his own blood and his enemies' blood, so that Christ in Revelation is not only slaughtered by others but also a slaughterer of others?

It is strange, however, that Christ's sharp sword is not in his hand but from his mouth (1:16; 2:12, 16; 19:15, 21). Is this merely a metaphorical way to refer to Christ's "sharp" words of judgment, given the explicit reference to his name as "The Word of God" (Rev 19:13)?[13] What makes Christ worthy to open the scroll with seven seals is, as John makes clear, the fact that he is the lamb that had been slaughtered (Rev 5:1–3, 9–10). When John describes the new heaven, the new earth, and the new Jerusalem, the most consistent portrayal of the Christ in victory is not that of a divine warrior but that of a lamb (Rev 21:9, 14, 22–23; 22:1–5). Those who follow Christ clearly are said to "have conquered . . . by the blood of the Lamb and by the word of their testimony, for they did not cling to life even in the face of death" (Rev 12:11; cf. Rev 2:24–27; 14:12–13). Do these emphases not point to an understanding that God's and Christ's victory in Revelation comes through a neutralization of violence and an exhaustion of the devil's violence rather than their direct use of violence?[14]

In addition, the two witnesses in Revelation 11 are also said to have fire coming out of their mouths to kill anyone who wants to harm them (Rev 11:1–6), but they, like Christ the lamb, only end up being killed somehow (Rev 11:7–9). Are these two references to killing of two different natures? At the same time, the text affirms that their deaths cause much rejoicing because they were "a torment to the inhabitants of the earth" (Rev 11:10) before they were killed. "Torment" can of course also be violent; in fact, it can be even more violent than ending one's life, as we have discussed earlier regarding the torment with fire and sulfur (Rev 14:11; 19:20; 20:10; 21:8; cf. Rev 9:5–6). In addition to how one may read these oral weapons of mass destruction in Revelation, there is also the question of how to read Christ's role in the humongous bloodbath that results from *his active treading* in

13. See, for example, Blount, *Can I Get a Witness,* 76, 82.

14. See, for example, Blount, *Can I Get a Witness,* 81–82; Decock, "Images of War and Creation," 191–92, 198.

God's wrathful wine press. What about the angel's call to the birds to eat the flesh of the corpses (Rev 19:17–18, 21)? Do these passages not portray God and God's allies as also acting violently in Revelation?

Martyrs who long for God's judgement and avenging are given white robes and are told to wait until their numbers are completed by the arrival of the rest of the faithful (Rev 6:9–11). Later, the armies of heaven on white horses that follow Christ the divine warrior into battle are described as wearing "white and pure" linen clothing (Rev 19:14; cf. Rev 7:14). This battalion of riders thus seems to be the same assembly of martyrs mentioned earlier. Does this mean that Christ-followers will and should *one day*—after their resurrection?—follow Christ's example and be active in committing this violence of destruction and annihilation?[15] Or are they merely "following" to reap the benefits or the harvests of Christ's and God's violent retributions (Rev 14:14–20) without committing any violent acts themselves? In the end, does it make any real difference if the violence in Revelation is performed by God, by Christ, by angels, and/or by Christ-followers, especially if the violence is of the extremist sort?

What Are the Differentiations and Connections between Violent Words and Violent Acts?

The question about the potential to kill through one's mouth, whether we are talking about the mouth of Christ or those of the two witnesses (Rev 11:5; 19:21), is related to an issue that has been central in the scholarly debates about Revelation and to my purposes here: namely, the use and effects of words and metaphors.

While some scholars reject the words and metaphors in Revelation as endorsing and promoting violence, others argue that the admittedly troubling words and hyperbolic portrayals in Revelation should not be taken too literally and at face value, because both are pointing to a different and deeper meaning in this highly figurative book (such as the ultimate victory of God and Christ over all evil), not to mention that the book is literarily following a particular tradition (such as that of the prophets of the Hebrew Bible or the combat myth of the ancient Near East).[16] At the risk of oversimplification, let me say that this interpretive debate is tightly connected with debates over whether one should read the whore of Babylon in Revelation as either a woman (Rev 17:3–6) or as a city (Rev 17:18); while those in the former camp tend to reject the whore metaphor as entailing harmful

15. See, for instance, Middleton, *The Violence of the Lamb*.
16. Hylen, "Metaphor Matters," 777–9.

implications for flesh-and-blood women, those in the latter camp emphasize that the point of the whore metaphor is actually not to abuse women but to critique imperial Rome.[17]

The once popular saying, "Sticks and stones may break my bones but words will never hurt me," has generally been discredited, especially in this age of cyber bullying. If we have learned anything from postmodern understandings, it would be the power of language to create reality.[18] There is also the risk, perhaps even the likelihood, that people will take metaphors literally, especially those found within the Bible.[19] The following example may be extreme, but it did take place in history. For Joseph Goebbels, one of Adolf Hitler's closest associates, the building and the work of the Third Reich corresponded to what he read in Revelation:

> It can hardly be disputed that Joseph Goebbels' understanding of faith corresponds with the structure of Revelation. The relationship between present and future is decisive. The future has the quality of salvation and means "the Third Reich." The decisive Initiator is God. The opposing party, which corresponds with God, is Satan. With him corresponds certain collaborators. The "world enemy," as Goebbels also said, has "Antichrist" as qualification. The war against the "Antichrist" is driven by violence which has a supernatural character ("half God, half human"). The destruction of Evil, that is, "the evil ones" precedes the condition of salvation.[20]

At the same time, postmodern sense and sensibilities about not only ideology but also power differential should help us to become sensitive to and think about the social location of John.[21] While John's self-representation as a persecuted exile on the island of Patmos because of Christ's gospel (Rev 1:9) may or may not be factual, he was indeed on the margins in the

---

17. For arguments critiquing Revelation's portrayal of Babylon as a woman, see, for example, Pippin 1992. For arguments that such gender-critical critiques of Revelation risk missing the book's anti-imperial emphases, see, for example, Schüssler Fiorenza 2007: 130–48. For a succinct summary of the debate between Pippin and Schüssler Fiorenza, see Smith 2014: 73–90.

18. See, for example, García-Osuna, *Borges, Language and Reality*; and Caputo, *Hermeneutics*, 2018.

19. See, for example, Ipsen, *Sex Working and the Bible*, 190.

20. Cited in Nicklas, "The Eschatological Battle According to the Book of Revelation," 228.

21. See, for example, Feuerwerker, *Ideology, Power, Text*. That is not to say that power differential was not recognized by people before the dawning of the postmodern. The marginalized have always been aware of power differentials; see, for instance, Dubey, "Contemporary African American Fiction and the Politics of Postmodernism."

sense that he wanted to separate himself from the socioeconomic power and benefits of the Roman Empire and he called others to join him. Since I mentioned cyber bulling earlier, let me ask if there is any difference between the threatening words spoken by a bully and those spoken by the one who is bullied? In other words, does it make a difference if and when threats of violence are articulated, to release frustration and aggression, by people who are oppressed but who have no power to actually carry out the violence?[22] What if the violent words are spoken by people who have no power to do anything about their oppression, but their oppression is "perceived" rather than "real"?[23] What about when someone powerful (such as Goebbels) reads and identifies (for whatever reason) with the words (of both hurt and hate) first written by someone who did not have power, and decides to act out those threats of violence? Moreover, how does one tell who has and who does not have power? Is the equation or arithmetic to calculate more and less power ever clean and easy? Who can make judgments about the difference between "perceived" and "real" crisis? What may be the relations between violent words and violent acts? Are these relations necessarily stable or consistent? Or are they fluid and contingent?

Given the repeated calls to repentance in Revelation's letters to the seven churches (Rev 2:5, 16, 21–22; 3:3, 19), including for those who have gone astray after "false" teachings, may one not read the violent words and even the violent acts in the book as rhetorical ploys to provoke, scare, or traumatize people into following Christ and God? Is that why the gates of the New Jerusalem are said to be always open, and "the nations" and "the kings of the earth" appear there (Rev 21:22–26) even though they previously have been guilty of fornicating with Babylon (Rev 18:3)? Revelation is clear that those violent punishments described in the book are reserved only for those who refuse to repent (Rev 9:20–21; 16:8–11). Does it make a difference if the violence or violent extremism in Revelation "is focused on conversion of the nations and not their extermination"?[24]

Issues in Teaching Revelation

My readers will notice that all of my subsection headings above are in the form of questions, and that each of those subsections also ends in questions. In other words, I actually do not provide any definitive answers to the main questions being posed, despite the fact that I do provide various

22. See Yarbro Collins, *Crisis and Catharsis*.

23. See Thompson, *The Book of Revelation*.

24. De Villiers, "Unmasking and Challenging Evil," 224.

bits and pieces of information and observations about the text of Revelation. This is, in fact, how I would teach Revelation in particular and biblical studies in general, especially regarding the question of violent extremism. Let me elaborate and explain.

Preference for Constructivist Education

As a teacher, I have become convinced over the years that a constructivist practice is more conducive to teaching and learning.[25] Simply put, those who practice constructivist education facilitate an active learning process for students to explore, discover, assess, and create knowledge for themselves. This approach is a response to what Paolo Freire has famously called a "banking" model of teaching: namely, one in which the teacher is the active supplier of knowledge and information, and students are passive recipients.[26] Instead of being told by a master-teacher what they need to learn, students in a constructivist classroom reflect on what they observe or what they experience to discover not only what they know but also how to learn. My role as a teacher in this case—to use a couple of admittedly overused descriptions—is less that of a "sage on the stage" and more that of a "guide on the side" who provides primarily inquiry-based activities for students to engage and formulate their own ideas.[27] Since this kind of education is centered on students' discoveries and not on them receiving information or "answers" from teachers who appear to know everything, it also means that education is an ongoing process of discoveries rather than something that a person "finishes" by taking a particular course or going through a particular curriculum.

Let me give an example to help concretize what I may do when I teach Revelation. In the beginning of a course on Revelation, I often show students a set of ten political cartoons, including a few that are from outside of the United States of America, and ask them what they think each of those cartoons is about.[28] When students are able to identify some but

25. For an example that provides empirical data to argue for the benefits of constructivist teaching and learning, see Ambrose et al., *How Learning Works*. For a handbook on constructivist learning, see Pelech and Pieper, *The Comprehensive Handbook of Constructivist Teaching*. See, in the case of teaching religion and theology, Harris, *Teaching and Religious Imagination*. I am indebted to colleagues who are experts in the field of religious education for first introducing me to these books; these colleagues include Boyung Lee, Mai-Anh Tran, and Lynne Westfield.

26. Freire, *Pedagogy of the Oppressed*, 71–86.

27. King, "Sage on the Stage to Guide on the Side."

28. I am indebted to Marianne Meye Thompson for this exercise, though I have

unable to do the same with those that are more obscure to them, I ask them why they think this is the case. They can generally respond by pointing out that, because some of the cartoons are more distant from them in terms of geography, time, or context, their meaning is harder to discern. This exercise indirectly helps students to understand something about the genre of Revelation, as well as realize some of the reasons why they have such difficulty in making sense of this book. While the genre of apocalypse is similar to that of political cartoons with its use of exaggerated word pictures for political purposes, the contextual difference and distance make it challenging for students to interpret the words. On the issue of violence or violent extremism in Revelation, I ask students to think and talk about what they see as the functions or influences of political cartoons, particularly if any kind of violence depicted in them may result in actual violence. This discussion, even if it takes place early in a semester, will help prepare students for a more substantial conversation later about if and how violent words may lead to violent acts.

Dynamics of Interpretation

This kind of inquiry-based and student-centered pedagogy may also enable students to experience and understand what happens in the interpretive process. While the historical-critical methods generally assumed that there was an original meaning readers should seek when they read the Bible, feminist criticism and reader-response criticism helped clear the space for scholars in biblical studies to recognize the significant role and influence of a reader—a recognition that gradually led to the emphasis on "social location" within the discipline.[29] Besides readers' social locations, texts themselves are, to use the vocabulary of Mikhail Bakhtin, "heteroglossic."[30] Put simply for our purposes here, heteroglossia refers to the existence of multiple viewpoints—and, hence, tensions—within a single text. In Revelation, as we have seen, there is an emphasis on love and non-violence: the Lamb is made worthy by death (Rev 5:1–3, 9–10), and Christ waits patiently and lovingly outside the door to seek admission inside a human heart (Rev 3:20). On the other hand, we

---

tweaked it for my own purposes; see her "The Symbolism of the Apocalypse through Political Cartoons."

29. For feminist criticism of the Bible, see, for example, Koosed, *Reading the Bible as a Feminist*. For reader-response criticism, see, for example, Fowler, *Let the Reader Understand*. For the significance of "social location" in biblical studies, see Segovia and Tolbert, eds., *Reading from This Place*.

30. Bakhtin, "Discourse in the Novel."

also find in Revelation a harsh and terrifying Christ whose appearance is more frightening than falling mountains and rocks that kill (Rev 6:12–17), as well as a God whose reign comes with destruction of all dissenters (Rev 11:15–18; 19:11–21). By pointing to different data or features in various parts of Revelation, as I did in raising particular questions about Revelation and the issue of violence, I hope that students will come to realize, as they read and discuss with each other, that diverse and even contradictory interpretations may result as readers focus on different parts or aspects of the book. Biblical texts are complex—and, yes, inconsistent—enough that readers can make different senses and meanings out of them. I often use inkblots in my biblical studies courses for students to experience and discover the reality of multiple interpretations. All I have to do after the inkblot exercise is to remind them that words, like other marks or signs put on paper, can also be construed or read in various ways.

To help students consider and gain understanding of not only the issue of violence in Revelation but also the interpretive process, I give examples of different meanings readers have made of Revelation and ask students why and how these diverse readings came about.[31] For instance, many—including Bernard of Clairvaux from the eleventh century, the Hussite Taborites from the fifteen century, and, as already mentioned earlier, Goebbels of the Third Reich—have read Revelation as a mandate for war and for the murder of non-Christians,[32] while others insist that Revelation is a book of non-violence.[33] Instead of limiting what students may read and think about this book like a demigod or a colonial master, I prefer to help students find out what they think about Revelation and why they think the way they do. As teachers, we must remember that experiences and processes of teaching and learning can themselves be violent, perhaps at times even violently extremist. Identifying "indoctrination" as one form of violence in education, Conrad Hughes points out that authors of postcolonial literature "have made it clear that they felt alienated by the cultural message that was being thrust on them."[34] Making a single reading of Revelation the only right—and often white—way to read this book is alienating to, and perhaps even annihilating of, different readers or readers of difference.

---

31. For a helpful cultural history of how Revelation has been read and used, see Beal, *The Book of Revelation.*

32. De Villiers, "The Violence of Non-Violence in the Revelation of John," 190 n.5.

33. See, for example, Barr, "Doing Violence"; and Rossing, *The Rapture Exposed,* 109–22.

34. Hughes, "Addressing Violence in Education: From Policy to Practice."

The Problem of the Singular Definitive

In many ways, violent extremism is a problem of the singular definitive. That is to say, there is only one way and one truth, and that is mine. Anyone or anything that does not abide by this singular definitive must be erased or eliminated. At its core, violent extremism is an inability and an unwillingness on the part of the powerful to live with difference.

In teaching biblical studies, I often show students a Ted-Talk video, "The Danger of a Single Story" by Chimamanda Ngozi Adichie.[35] According to Adichie, telling only a single story at the exclusion of all others denies—and, worse, erases—the complexity of people and of life. Since Adichie is a writer, I assume she will agree with me that singular definitive also denies the complexity of texts.

In that sense, violence against the devil and its followers, whether extremist or not, also cannot be the singular story in our teaching and reading of Revelation. Whatever meaning students may end up creating with this book, they need to attend to the gender dynamics of the text, in which women are given a single definitive choice between being either a "heroine" or a "whore."[36] While the former—represented in the figure of the woman clothed with the sun (Rev 12:1–17) and that of the bride of New Jerusalem (Rev 19:6–10; 21:1–2)—is protected and praised, the latter will be punished through portrayals of sexual violence and violation, as we see in not only the whore of Babylon (Rev 17:1–19:2) but also the prophet/teacher "Jezebel" (Rev 2:20–23). In addition, all this violence will be accompanied by ecological destruction. For example, the two witnesses are given the power and authority to cause drought, to make waters undrinkable, and to "strike the earth with every kind of plague, as often as they desire" (Rev 11:6). With the opening of the sixth seal, after the fifth seal and the anxious cries for God's judgment and avenging by Christ-followers (Rev 6:9–10), we read:

> [T]here came a great earthquake; the sun became black as sackcloth, the full moon became like blood, and the stars of the sky fell to the earth as the fig tree drops its winter fruit when shaken by a gale. The sky vanished like a scroll rolling itself up, and every mountain and island was removed from its place. (Rev 6:12–14).

35. Adichie, "The Danger of a Single Story." I am indebted to Jung Choi for introducing me to this Ted-Talk video.

36. Pippin, "The Heroine and the Whore: The Apocalypse of John in Feminist Perspective."

Again, with the blowing of the seven trumpets, we learn that basically a third of the natural world will be destroyed (Rev 8:6–12); with the pouring of the seven bowls, we have poisoned water sources, scorching heat, shattered landscape, and extreme weather (Rev 16:1–21). Finally, there is fire coming out of heaven to consume the dragon and its troops (Rev 20:7–9). Students will need to factor this kind of ecological destruction into their consideration of what constitutes God's "just judgment." Does the repeated emphasis that (only?) one-third of the natural world (Rev 8:6–12) would be destroyed imply restraint, and hence God's protection of the environment?[37] Or is this destruction the inevitable end-result of evil attacks on God's creation? They also have to keep in mind that this same book also pronounces the coming of a new heaven, a new earth, and a New Jerusalem "coming down out of heaven" (Rev 21:1, 10), and consider how they should read the ecological and ethical implications of this climatic announcement. While some scholars would see the book as ecologically conscious and committed,[38] Stephen D. Moore measures the dimensions of the New Jerusalem as given in Revelation (Rev 21:9–21) and argues that, despite the promise of water and the presence of the tree of life (Rev 21:6; 22:1–2), building a continental-sized city cannot be good for the environment.[39] To prevent telling a single story of Revelation's meaning, I introduce students to not only the complexity of Revelation but also to various scholarly readings of Revelation so they can come up with their own interpretive reasons and decisions.

Authority of the Bible

In addition to interpretations by scholars, I also bring into my course popular readings of Revelation even if they are not scholarly. For instance, I discuss John Hagee's use of Rev 6:12 and other verses from the Bible (Joel 2:31; Acts 2:20) to predict the beginning of the end times with his talk of four "blood moons."[40] I do that not only to pluralize the story about reading Revelation but also to facilitate a conversation with students regarding how they understand the Bible. For people such as Hagee, the Bible is a secret code about the future of the world; it is also a kind of sorcery book in which verses from different biblical books written by different authors in different periods of time can cohere with one another to give the same

37. Woodman, *The Book of Revelation*, 210.

38. See, for instance, Woodman, *The Book of Revelation*, 209–12; and Kiel, *Apocalyptic Ecology*, 57–110.

39. Moore, "Ecotherology."

40. Hagee, *Four Blood Moons*.

message. Others may see the Bible as a timeless blueprint or set of rules that dictates how we should live, a documentary of history that provides factual information, a constitution for the church, or something else altogether. Students in biblical studies classes must consider how they understand the Bible and its authority. After all, no matter what they decide to be the meaning of Revelation regarding violence and violent extremism, the most basic question comes down to what they are supposed to do with "what the Bible says." What if they think that Revelation really advocates violent extremism? Should they then go and do likewise?

In my biblical studies classes, I always make a point to stress to students that the Bible is actually not a single book, but a library of books. In fact, as we have discussed, even a single book such as Revelation may also contain diverse materials on, say, the subject of violence. This characteristic of heteroglossia makes it difficult to simply do "what the Bible says," since the Bible, as we have seen with our example of Revelation, often says different and even contradictory things about a given topic.[41] What does one do with Revelation's condemnation of consuming food sacrificed to idols (Rev 2:14, 20) when Paul sees no real problem with the food itself (1 Cor 8:1–13), for example? How do I "follow the Bible" if it tells me to do contradictory things? If the Bible says several different things about a topic and I choose to do one but not do the others, by what criteria do I make that choice? And am I merely following the Bible when I do so? Or is the Bible giving me different positions and possibilities so I have to decide and take responsibility for what is best to do and not to do?

Another point that I often remind students in my biblical studies classrooms is the fact that, as we know, the biblical canon actually did not come about until the fourth century. It is, of course, well known that there were a lot of heated arguments about whether the book of Revelation should be included in the New Testament canon.[42] Instead of focusing on Revelation here, I want to point out that the late establishment of today's biblical canon means that many in the first three centuries were following Christ without it. If so, what may this imply about the authority of the Bible in terms of one's own ethical decisions today, even or especially if one claims to be a follower of Christ?[43] Although the canon is established today, I want students to see that there is still an evolution, elasticity, or even instability about this library of books because of not only the manuscript transmission and translation

41. For an exceptionally good and helpful account of the Bible's diverse contents, as well as how the same passage may be read in different ways, see Stone, *Practicing Safer Texts.*

42. Pagels, *Revelations*, 2, 160–8.

43. See, for example, Martin, *Biblical Truths*, 71–110.

process but also the publishing industry. Given the existence of different manuscripts with incongruent readings for the same biblical book or passage, various English and other language translations, as well as differently formatted and packaged Bibles (such as children's Bibles with truncated contents but illustrative pictures, or Study Bibles with detailed commentary in the form of "notes"), some scholars have correctly suggested that we can only talk about Bibles in the plural and never *the* Bible in the singular definitive.[44] Again, what would this plurality imply about the authority of "the Bible" and my choice of what to do and not do?

Conclusion

Since many view the U.S. Constitution as an ultimate authority—a secular Bible, if you will—I tell students about two Supreme Court Justices and their opposing views of this Constitution: while the late Antonin Scalia insisted that we need to know and follow the original intentions of the Constitution's authors, the late Ruth Bader Ginsburg argued that the Constitution is an imperfect step in our continuous commitment to strive for a more perfect union. I ask students to consider both the desirability and feasibility of these two views and explain why they prefer one over the other.

Justice Ginsburg's view of the Constitution is similar to what Krister Stendahl has said about Scriptures. For Stendahl, Scriptures contain insights that the biblical writers themselves did not always live up to.[45] As a result, Scriptures often contain both noble ideas and hideous thoughts, and responsible readers of Scriptures have to be honest enough to acknowledge this reality and vigilant enough to serve as a kind of "Public Health Department" to avoid harmful consequences.[46] While I do not want to dictate in any ways how my students interpret Scriptures, I will always want them to think about what their interpretations imply and what they should do with their interpretations. It is one thing for students to say that, after careful consideration, they have decided Revelation is "a text that is permeated by an agonistic spirit aiming at excluding, othering, and demonizing those who do not share its ideology"[47]; it is quite another

---

44. See, for instance, Beal, *The Rise and Fall of the Bible*; Beal, *The Book of Revelation*, 4–8; Stone, "Bibles That Matter."

45. Stendahl, "Ancient Scripture in the Modern World," 208.

46. Stendahl, "Ancient Scripture in the Modern World," 205. See also Stone, *Practicing Safer Texts*, 1–22; and Hylen, "Metaphor Matters."

47. De Villiers, "The Violence of Non-Violence in the Revelation of John," 200.

for them to say that readers of Revelation should commit acts of violent extremism simply because Revelation teaches it.

Bibliography

Adichie, Chimamanda Ngozi. "The Danger of a Single Story." *TED: Ideas Worth Spreading*. https://www.ted.com/talks/chimamanda_ngozi_adichie_the_danger_of_a_single_story?language=tt.

Ambrose, Susan A., et al. *How Learning Works: Seven Research-Based Principles for Smart Teaching*. San Francisco: Jossey-Bass, 2010.

Avalos, Hector. *The Reality of Religious Violence: From Biblical to Modern Times*. Sheffield: Sheffield Phoenix, 2019.

Bakhtin, Mikhail. "Discourse in the Novel." In Mikhail Bakhtin, *The Dialogic Imagination: Four Essays*, edited by Michael Holquist, 269–422. Translated by Caryl Emerson and Michael Holquist. Austin: University of Texas Press, 1981.

Barr, David L. "Doing Violence: Moral Issues in Reading John's Apocalypse." In *Reading the Book of Revelation: A Resource for Students*, edited by David L. Barr. Atlanta: Society of Biblical Literature, 2003.

Bauckham, Richard. *The Bible in Politics: How to Read the Bible Politically*. 2nd ed. London: SPCK, 2010.

Beal, Timothy. *The Book of Revelation: A Biography*. Princeton: Princeton University Press, 2018.

———. *The Rise and Fall of the Bible: The Unexpected History of an Accidental Book*. Boston: Houghton Mifflin Harcourt, 2011.

Beale, G. K. *The Use of Daniel in Jewish Apocalyptic Literature and in the Revelation of St. John*. 1984. Reprint, Eugene, OR: Wipf & Stock, 2010.

Blount, Brian K. *Can I Get a Witness? Reading Revelation through African American Culture*. Louisville: Westminster John Knox, 2005.

Boesak, Alan A. *Comfort and Protest: The Apocalypse of John from a South African Perspective*. Louisville: Westminster John Knox, 1987.

Boxall, Ian. *The Revelation of St. John*. New York: Continuum, 2006.

Caputo, John D. *Hermeneutics: Facts and Interpretation in the Age of Information*. New York: Pelican, 2018.

De Villiers, Pieter G. R. "Unmasking and Challenging Evil: Exegetical Perspectives on Violence in Revelation 18." In *Coping with Violence in the New Testament*, edited by Pieter de Villiers and Jan Willem van Henten, 201–25. Studies in Theology and Religion 16. Leiden: Brill, 2012.

———. "The Violence of Non-Violence in the Revelation of John." *Open Theology* 1 (2015) 189–203.

Decock, Paul B. "Images of War and Creation, of Violence and Non-Violence in the Book of Revelation." In *Coping with Violence in the New Testament*, edited by Pieter de Villiers and Jan Willem van Henten, 185–200. Studies in Theology and Religion 16. Leiden: Brill, 2012.

Dubey, Madhu. "Contemporary African American Fiction and the Politics of Postmodernism." *NOVEL: A Forum on Fiction* 35 (2002) 151–68.

Fackenheim, Emil L. *The Jewish Bible after the Holocaust: A Re-reading*. Bloomington: Indiana University Press, 1990.

Feuerwerker, Yi-tsi Mei. *Ideology, Power, Text: Self-Representation and the Peasant "Other" in Modern Chinese Literature.* Stanford: Stanford University Press, 1998.

Fowler, Robert M. *Let the Reader Understand: Reader Response Criticism and the Gospel of Mark.* Minneapolis: Fortress, 1991.

Freire, Paolo. *Pedagogy of the Oppressed.* 50th ann. ed. London: Bloomsbury Academic, 2017.

García-Osuna, Alfonso J. *Borges, Language and Reality: The Transcendence of the Word.* New York: Palgrave Macmillan, 2018.

Hagee, John. *Four Blood Moons: Something Is About to Change.* Brentwood: Worthy, 2013.

Harris, Maria. *Teaching and Religious Imagination: An Essay in the Theology of Teaching.* San Francisco: Harper & Row, 1987.

Herzstein, Robert Edwin. *The War That Hitler Won: Goebbels and the Nazi Media Campaign.* New York: Paragon, 1987.

Heschel, Susannah. *The Aryan Jesus: Christian Theologians and the Bible in Nazi Germany.* Princeton: Princeton University Press, 2008.

Hughes, Conrad. "Addressing Violence in Education: From Policy to Practice." *Prospects* (2019). doi:10.1007/s11125-019-09445-1.

Hylen, Susan E. "Metaphor Matters: Violence and Ethics in Revelation." *Catholic Biblical Quarterly* 73 (2011) 777–96.

Ipsen, Avaren. *Sex Working and the Bible.* New York: Equinox, 2009.

Kiel, Micah D. *Apocalyptic Ecology: The Book of Revelation, the Earth, and the Future.* Collegeville, MN: Liturgical, 2017.

King, Alison. "Sage on the Stage to Guide on the Side." *College Teaching* 41 (1993) 30–35.

Koonz, Claudia. *The Nazi Conscience.* Cambridge: Harvard University Press, 2003.

Koosed, Jennifer L. *Reading the Bible as a Feminist.* Biblical Interpretation Series. Leiden: Brill, 2017.

Linafelt, Tod. *Strange Fire: Reading the Bible after the Holocaust.* New York: New York University Press, 2000.

Marshall, John W. "Collateral Damage: Jesus and Jezebel in the Jewish War." In *Violence in the New Testament,* edited by Shelly Matthew and E. Leigh Gibson, 35–50. London: T. & T. Clark, 2005.

Martin, Dale B. *Biblical Truths: The Meaning of Scripture in the Twenty-First Century.* New Haven: Yale University Press, 2017.

Middleton, Paul. *The Violence of the Lamb: Martyrs as Agents of Divine Judgment in the Book of Revelation.* London: T. & T. Clark, 2018.

Moore, Stephen D. "Ecotherology." In *Divinanimality: Animal Theory, Creaturely Theology,* edited by Stephen D. Moore, 196–209. New York: Fordham University Press, 2014.

Moyise, Steve. "Does the Lion Lie Down with the Lamb?" In *Studies in the Book of Revelation,* edited by Steve Moyise, 184–94. New York: T. & T. Clark, 2001.

Nicklas, Tobias. "The Eschatological Battle According to the Book of Revelation: Perspectives on Revelation 19:11–21." In *Coping with Violence in the New Testament,* edited by Pieter de Villiers and Jan Willem van Henten, 227–44. Studies in Theology and Religion 16. Leiden: Brill, 2012.

Pagels, Elaine. *Revelations: Visions, Prophecy, and Politics in the Book of Revelation.* New York: Penguin, 2012.

Pelech, James, and Gail Pieper. *The Comprehensive Handbook of Constructivist Teaching*. Charlotte: Information Age, 2010.

Pippin, Tina. *Death and Desire: The Rhetoric of Gender in the Apocalypse of John*. Louisville John Knox, 1992.

———. "The Heroine and the Whore: The Apocalypse of John in Feminist Perspective." In *From Every People and Nation: The Book of Revelation in Intercultural Perspective*, edited by David Rhoads, 127–45. Minneapolis: Fortress, 2005.

Richard, Pablo. *Apocalypse: A People's Commentary on the Book of Revelation*. Maryknoll, NY: Orbis, 1995.

Rossing, Barbara. *The Rapture Exposed: The Message of Hope in the Book of Revelation*. New York: Basic, 2004.

Ruiz, Jean-Pierre. *Ezekiel in the Apocalypse: The Transformation of Prophetic Language in Revelation 16,17–19,10*. New York: Lang, 1989.

Schüssler Fiorenza, Elisabeth. *The Power of the Word: Scripture and the Rhetoric of Empire*. Minneapolis: Fortress, 2007.

Segovia, Fernando F., and Mary Ann Tolbert, eds. *Reading from This Place: Social Location and Biblical Interpretation in Global Perspective*. Minneapolis: Fortress, 1995.

Smith, Shanell T. *The Woman Babylon and the Marks of Empire: Reading Revelation with a Postcolonial Womanist Hermeneutics of Ambiveilance*. Minneapolis: Fortress, 2014.

Stendahl, Krister. "Ancient Scripture in the Modern World." In *Scripture in the Jewish and Christian Tradition: Authority, Interpretation, Relevance*, edited by Frederick E. Greenspahn, 202–14. Nashville: Abingdon, 1982.

Stone, Ken. "Bibles That Matter: Biblical Theology and Queer Performativity." *Biblical Theology Bulletin* 38 (2008) 14–25.

———. *Practicing Safer Texts: Food, Sex and Bible in Queer Perspective*. New York: T. & T. Clark, 2005.

Sweeney, Marvin A. *Reading the Hebrew Bible after the Shoah: Engaging Holocaust Theology*. Minneapolis: Fortress, 2008.

Thompson, Leonard L. *The Book of Revelation: Apocalypse and Empire*. New York: Oxford University Press, 1990.

Thompson, Marianne Meye. "The Symbolism of the Apocalypse through Political Cartoons." In *Teaching the Bible: Practical Strategies for Classroom Instruction*, edited by Mark Roncace and Patrick Gray, 389–90. Atlanta: Society of Biblical Literature, 2005.

Woodman, Simon. *The Book of Revelation*. London: SCM, 2008.

Yarbro Collins, Adela. *Crisis and Catharsis: The Power of the Apocalypse*. Philadelphia: Westminster, 1984.

8

Fundamentalism as Toxic Spirituality

Exploring the Psycho-spiritual Structure and Dynamics of Violent Extremism

—DANIEL S. SCHIPANI

T his chapter is an exercise in Practical Theology with a pastoral and spiritual care focus.[1] It addresses the challenge of violent extremism by focusing on fundamentalism with a twofold thesis: most forms of fundamentalism foster toxic spirituality because they are closed systems that harm the human spirit in recognizable ways; and fundamentalisms tend to nurture and support diverse forms of violence[2] and violent extremism in particular. Readers can keep in mind the following three goals: to identify main features of fundamentalism from a spiritual health science perspective; to test the claim that most forms of fundamentalism foster spiritual toxicity; and to encourage interdisciplinary and inter-religious dialogue and collaboration concerning ways to assess, engage, and transform fundamentalist toxic spirituality in both education and spiritual care practice.

---

1. The epistemological structure and methodological dynamic of Practical Theology consist of four movements or functions, as follows: observation (empirical descriptive function), analysis (interpretive or hermeneutic function), evaluation (normative function), and application (pragmatic-strategic function). Osmer, *Practical Theology*.

2. Violence is here defined as the human exercise of physical, emotional, spiritual, social, or technological power which results in injury or harm to others or oneself. Further, from a theological standpoint, all forms of human violence thus defined are expressions of evil.

Introduction: Understanding Fundamentalism(s)

For the last several decades, "fundamentalism" has been a news cycle buzzword. In the vernacular of the United States, the term is often associated with white, "Bible-thumping" Christians in the southern states and extremist Islamist movements throughout the Middle East, but these are not the only groups to whom the media have assigned the sullied label. Such a seemingly widespread phenomenon merits further discussion. While fundamentalisms vary, their causes, manifestations, and consequences are similar across the Abrahamic religious traditions and beyond.

The term "fundamentalism" was coined in the United States in the early twentieth century, and, since its beginnings a century ago, it has come to be woven into the religious vocabulary of various faith traditions.[3] Conservative American Protestants, looking to reform the rapidly modernizing Christian church in the country, began to harken back to what they viewed as "The Fundamentals"[4] of Christian faith and practice.[5] It should be acknowledged that fundamentalist thought has been not simply the continued following of tradition; rather, it continues to be a deliberate effort to regenerate tradition and make it socially significant again. Therefore, fundamentalism as such, it is not a thing of the past but "a form of engagement with the modern world."[6]

The 1960s brought about a new wave of fundamentalism among Protestants in the United States. Many conservative Christians believed that the nation was declining into a kind of moral corruption and upside-down society that, to them, signaled the onset of the End Times. By the late 1970s, fundamentalists in the United States became fully aware of their own number and of their power with the Moral Majority. This was a political interest group, comprising largely of fundamentalists and other white conservative Christians, which became part of the New Christian Right. They have fought a number of causes related, among others, to Cold War appeasement, "second amendment" rights, gay rights, feminism, and abortion.[7]

3. Lechner, "Fundamentalism," 197.

4. Journalist Curtis Lee Laws introduced the term "Fundamentalism" into the U.S.-American vernacular in 1920 when he named the movement spurred by a series of periodicals called *The Fundamentals*, published by Lyman and Milton Stewart, Presbyterian brothers. They sought to combat what they saw as "the growing laxity in faith and morals," in the first two decades of the twentieth century. Biblical inerrancy was the basis for the other "fundamentals" (virgin birth of Jesus, substitutionary atonement of sin through Jesus, a resurrection with the same body, and second coming of Jesus).

5. Lechner, "Fundamentalism," 197.

6. Lechner, "Fundamentalism," 198.

7. See Karen Armstrong documentation and helpful discussion of these

The call to return to the fundamentals of religious tradition as a response to modern secular culture has not remained isolated within Christianity. The late-twentieth and early-twenty-first centuries have witnessed the expansion of "fundamentalism" to radical conservatism outside Protestant Christianity in the United States.[8] However, for traditions outside of the United States, it has not so much been modernity as secular Western hegemony against which the fundamentalists have reacted.[9]

Abrahamic traditions lend themselves to fundamentalism because of the emphasis on orthodoxy and orthopraxy—right belief and right action.[10] In other words, they center on the idea of scriptural norms for doctrine, ethics, politics and society.[11] Those Abrahamic traditions work from a place of "scriptural revelations" that, for them, have political, moral, and social implications and "form the corpus of demands."[12] Other-than-Abrahamic religious traditions do not hold scriptural or doctrinal allegiance at the center of their organization or ideology and tend to instead uphold "national or cultural purity" in religious-political movements.[13] For example, certain Buddhist, Sikh, and Hindu groups aggressively and sometimes violently emphasize nationalistic political ideologies rather than doctrinal religious-political ideologies.[14]

In all cases it is important to realize that fundamentalist movements have come about through different historical experiences and reactions. At the same time, the overarching claim has been made that what those movements have in common is that they have turned the *mythos* of their religion into *logos*, either by insisting that their dogmas are scientifically true or by transforming their complex mythology into a streamlined ideology. Karen Armstrong concludes that fundamentalist movements are rooted in a fear of imminent annihilation.[15] Reflecting on the documentable reality of the tendency of Abrahamic traditions to undergird and foster diverse forms of violence, she laments: "When they created these alternative societies, fundamentalists were demonstrating their disillusion with a culture which could not easily accommodate the spiritual. Because it was so embattled,

developments, *The Battle for God,* 136–311.

8. Partridge, *Fundamentalisms,* 6.

9. Armstrong, *The Battle for God,* 270, 259.

10. Partridge, *Fundamentalisms,* 7.

11. Partridge, *Fundamentalisms,* 16.

12. Partridge, *Fundamentalisms,* 11.

13. Partridge, *Fundamentalisms,* 10–11.

14. Partridge, *Fundamentalisms,* 10–11.

15. Armstrong, *The Battle for God,* 366–68.

this campaign to re-sacralize society became aggressive and distorted. It lacked the compassion which all faiths have insisted is essential to the religious life and to any experience of the numinous. Instead, it preached an ideology of exclusion, hatred, and even violence."[16]

In this chapter we will keep in mind the valuable contributions to understanding "fundamentalism" from various perspectives as summarized above. From a spiritual health science viewpoint, our presentation will focus on the structure and dynamics characteristic of all forms of fundamentalism, as follows: a markedly strict literalism as applied to specific scriptures, dogmas, or ideologies; a strong effort to maintain in-group and out-group distinctions; and, in many but not all cases, an assertive and sometimes violent "missional" impulse.

The remainder of this chapter follows the fourfold pattern of practical-theological reflection. The next section considers four case studies that illustrate the violent nature of religious extremism. Then follows an interpretive analysis of fundamentalism's toxicity with interdisciplinary lenses. The section on evaluation explains the threefold collapse that characterizes fundamentalisms as closed systems; it also describes key features of toxic authoritarian leadership. Finally, the section on application focuses on understanding transformation as the overarching goal of healing.

Observation: Cases of Fundamentalism and Violence

This section illustrates the manifold manifestations of violent extremism, beginning with the New Testament accounts of the religiosity of Saul of Tarsus and his conversion experience. It then presents other personal testimonies related to the three so-called Abrahamic faith traditions followed by a reference to the tragic saga of the Peoples Temple.

Saul of Tarsus: Portrait of a Religious Zealot

In the Book of Acts, Saul appears for the first time as a young witness to the stoning of Stephen (7:58). In the following chapter we are told that a severe persecution began against the church in Jerusalem and that he "was ravaging the church by entering house after house; dragging off both men and women, he committed them to prison" (8:3). Later on, right before Saul's conversion experience, his religious zeal is described as, "still breathing

16. Armstrong, *The Battle for God*, 370–71.

threats and murder against the disciples of the Lord, [Saul] went to the high priest and asked him for letters to the synagogues at Damascus, so that if he found any who belonged to the Way, men or women, he might bring them bound to Jerusalem" (9:1–2). Testimonial personal reference to Saul's violent religious extremism are then found in the account of his defense after the arrest in the temple in Jerusalem:

> I am a Jew, born in Tarsus in Cilicia, but brought up in this city at the feet of Gamaliel, educated strictly according to our ancestral law, being zealous for God, just as all of you are today. I persecuted this Way up to the point of death by binding both men and women and putting them in prison, as the high priest and the whole council of elders can testify about me. From them I also received letters to the brothers in Damascus, and I went there in order to bind those who were there and to bring them back to Jerusalem for punishment (22:1-5).

Again, during his defense before King Agrippa, now "Paul" says,

> . . . I have belonged to the strictest sect of our religion and lived as a Pharisee. And now I stand here on trial on account of my hope in the promise made by God to our ancestors . . . Indeed, I myself was convinced that I ought to do many things against the name of Jesus of Nazareth. And that is what I did in Jerusalem; with authority received from the chief priests, I not only locked up many of the saints in prison, but I also cast my vote against them when they were being condemned to death. By punishing them often in all the synagogues I tried to force them to blaspheme; and since I was so furiously enraged at them, I pursued them even to foreign cities" (26:9-11).

Finally, Paul alludes to his religious convictions and behavior before his conversion experience in his letters to the churches (e.g., 1 Cor 15:9; Phil 3:6):

> You have heard, no doubt, of my earlier life in Judaism. I was violently persecuting the church of God and was trying to destroy it. I advanced in Judaism beyond many among my people of the same age, for I was far more zealous for the traditions of my ancestors" (Gal 1:13–14).

Many authors have studied Paul's conversion experience. They all agree that it was transformational and life-changing.[17] It consisted of a sharp discontinuity between past and present yet not necessarily a

17. Loder, *The Transforming Moment*, 21–26.

conversion from Judaism to "Christianity."[18] In a nutshell, that conversion involved a new way of seeing and knowing, a new way of being in community, and a new vocation and life project. Further, the deconstruction of his fundamentalist religiosity and his overarching existential reorientation process necessitated the welcoming embrace of a witnessing, supporting, interpreting, and guiding community.

The following three testimonies represent people in very different social and religious contexts and family circumstances. They have in common having "lost" their toxic religious faith, as poignantly revealed in their own words.[19]

Megan Phelps-Roper (Ex-member of the Westboro Baptist Church)

My first memories are of picketing ex-servicemen's funerals and telling their families they were going to burn in hell. For us, it was a celebration. My gramps was the founder of the Westboro Baptist Church, so it wasn't just our religion–it was our whole life . . . I was allowed to mix with other kids early on, but over time my world shrank.

We believed it was a Good vs. Evil situation: that the WBC was right and everybody else was wrong, so there was no questioning. It was a very public war we were waging against the "sinners." I asked a lot of questions as I got older, but there's a big difference in asking for clarification and actually questioning the beliefs you're taught. I spent so much time reading the Bible, trying to see the world through this very particular framework, that to have truly considered [it was wrong] was inconceivable . . . and the thought of ever leaving the church was my worst nightmare.

The WBC loves and thrives on publicity, so I joined Twitter in 2009 to run the church's account. I was very zealous and adamant that my beliefs were the truth, but I began to realize that the 140-word limit meant I had to drop the throwaway insults or conversations would die. Over time, I found I was actually beginning to like people: to see them as human beings rather than people to condemn. For the first time, I started to care about what people outside the WBC thought of me. As

18. Gaventa, *From Darkness to Light*, 147–52.

19. The three were published in *The Guardian*, April 10, 2016. https://www.theguardian.com/world/2016/apr/10/losing-my-religion-life-after-extreme-belief-faith.

my feelings towards my faith wavered I'd boomerang between thinking "none of this makes sense" to "God is testing me and I am failing . . .

Leaving was unbearably sad . . . I still momentarily flinch when I come across someone or something the WBC would disapprove of. Two men kissing on the street, a drag queen— anything that takes me back to what I believed for so long. I still encounter those old feelings and then I have to process it: "That's what the old me would have felt"—it's an ongoing process of deep deprogramming.

I see the world in split screen now. I remember feeling like we at WBC were a persecuted minority, triumphant in the face of evil people "worshipping the dead" as we picketed funerals or rejoiced at the destruction of the Twin Towers. But beside that memory is the one where I weep thinking about how callous and unmerciful I was to so many people who'd just lost a son or a daughter. I'm ashamed of that now, and it's still really difficult to think about the harm I caused. It's overwhelming sometimes

Megan has significantly re-oriented her life. She is now a spouse and a mother, and an advocate for freedom from religious extremism and authoritarian leadership.[20]

Deborah Feldman (ex-Satmar Hasidic Jew)

The Satmar sect of Hasidic Judaism I was born into was founded by Holocaust survivors who wanted to reinvent the Eastern European *shtetl* in America. Before I learned anything else, I learned the Holocaust had happened because Jews were bad and that the way we lived was different from the rest of the world because if we didn't, the Holocaust would happen to us again.

Growing up in such a strict community meant we had no contact with the outside world. It still amazes me to think that was and is possible in the Bronx. The only time I'd get a glimpse was if I were ill. Tonsillitis meant a car journey to the doctor, where I'd watch, from the window, people living their lives freely.

I hit my teens and figured out what I needed to do to survive in the community. I'd drawn the wrong sort of attention to myself as a young girl. I'd been rebellious. Asking "why?" was forbidden and I'd be yelled at, ostracized; kids stopped talking to me at school. Women and girls belonged in the kitchen, my grandfather often reminded me. Soon I figured out how to live

20. Phelps-Roper, *Unfollow.*

a double life: I had the version of me that fitted in with the community, and then I had my interior life that no one knew about. As soon as I pretended I was going along with it all, things got easier for me. I got married to someone from the sect when I was 17 and had my son. The most difficult thing was the constant lying. By denying who I really was, I was slowly killing myself. I lived a double life: I had the version of me that fitted in with the community, and then I had my interior life.

Leaving wasn't about courage or strength for me. It was all much more practical than I thought it would be. Some of it was perhaps biological: as soon as my son was born I had this driving instinct to get him out. It took three years of planning and at the very end, when I had everything lined up—money in the bank, a small network of friends on the outside, a divorce lawyer working on the custody of my son—I still couldn't quite cross the boundary. I was too scared.

What happened next was fate. I was in a car accident I shouldn't have survived and I walked away without a scratch. As I got out of the car, the Jewish girl in me thought: "God is punishing me and telling me I shouldn't go," but as I walked away from the wreck, I thought: "Hang on, if I can survive this, I can survive leaving."

I have no contact with my family now. The backlash was immense. My family wrote me threatening letters, and later on when I wrote a book about my experiences,[21] the community said I was a hysteric, a liar. I don't know that I'll ever be fully deprogrammed. I didn't just leave a religion, I left a sect that was based on inherited trauma and incorporated antisemitism. Many of the [antisemitic] ideas my grandparents heard in Europe got integrated into their beliefs about themselves and then passed on to their children. I grew up believing we were genetically inferior. They didn't see that as a bad thing—they'd sit me down and explain: "We're special to God. Our souls are special, but our genes are inferior, just like they said about us." How do you even begin to unstitch that?

Deborah's life has been transformed. Her autobiography tells the story of her escape from an ultra-religious community that values silence and suffering over individual freedoms.

---

21. Feldman, *Unorthodox*.

Imad Iddine Habib (ex-Salafi Muslim)

I was born on a Friday at prayer time, which was seen as an auspicious sign in my community. Growing up in Morocco I was constantly told I was to become a religious scholar. My name is translated as "pillar of religion." I was enrolled into a Salafi Koranic school at four, but I had trouble reading and reciting verses of the Koran, as I was so dyslexic. This was seen as a big disappointment in my family, so I learned most of the Koran by heart to save myself any grief. By the time I left the Koranic school at 13, I knew I didn't believe.

Our lives were based around a single version of a much bigger religion. Disagreements were frowned upon. We weren't to voice questions. I couldn't understand why no one debated or discussed the opinion of the scholars and imams—we were expected to blindly follow. Many of the students from my school went to Afghanistan and Syria—that had been their life's purpose, and though I was interested in Islam as a religion from an academic viewpoint, I knew I wasn't a Muslim. I was scared, but I also felt it was my duty.

My faith finally ruptured at 14. I told my parents I didn't believe, and I also came out as pansexual. I felt, and still feel, that I was looking at the bigger picture, but they weren't open to it. I couldn't be a part of a faith that kept changing the rules depending on the situation. My family's reaction was typical: a lot of violence and threats initially, and when that didn't work, my mum got "sick" for 40 days, saying I was being banished from heaven and making her suffer. I was resolute, so they kicked me out. I became homeless and I've not seen or heard from them since. In a way I feel I may have shut the emotion of losing my family away somewhere. I try not to feel. There are vivid moments where I miss my mother: her face, her cooking, knowing what she is thinking about, but I can't afford to get emotional about it.

I moved from place to place and stayed with friends. I got an education: I have a baccalaureate in Islamic sciences and I then founded the Council of Ex-Muslims of Morocco. The resistance is small, but we have a voice. I have had to live in hiding and have received countless death threats. In Morocco, Islam is the state religion, and the state considers you a Muslim by default. You can be jailed for eating in public during Ramadan, so you can imagine what my future there looked like. There is a wide belief that all apostates should be killed.

I attended a public conference in 2013 and spoke out about my beliefs. I was scared, but I also felt it was my duty. I called Islam a virus, which I knew would be inflammatory. Secret services began investigating me and I heard that they contacted my family and questioned my father. I was asked to attend court. My father would later testify against me on the count of an apostasy charge. When it all got too heavy, I knew I had to [go] to England as a refugee and start over. Not long after I arrived here, I was sentenced to seven years in prison in absentia. I gave up everything and everyone I know, but I'm free.

Imad's story is another dramatic illustration of conversion. He rejected a way of life under the strict imposition of the beliefs and practices of a religious tradition and was willing to pay the price. He has continued to play a leading role in the Council of Ex-Muslims advocating for the rights and interests of non-religious, secular persons of Muslim heritage who have left Islam.

"Religious Trauma Syndrome"

The cases of Megan, Deborah, and Imad clearly fit the description of Religious Trauma Syndrome (RTS). This constellation of symptoms refers to the experience shared among many who have escaped cults, fundamentalist religious groups, abusive religious settings, or other painful experiences with religion. While not an official psychiatric diagnosis, RTS is a function of both the chronic abuses of harmful religion and the impact of severing one's connection with one's faith and faith community. The trauma consists in a huge systemic shock on personal, family, and communal levels. As illustrated in those three cases, RTS is the condition experienced by people who struggle with leaving an authoritarian, dogmatic religion and must cope with the damage of indoctrination and harmful practices. They typically go through the shattering of a personally meaningful faith and/or breaking away from a controlling community and lifestyle. Indicators of RTS may include, among others, the following: confusing thoughts and reduced ability to think critically; negative beliefs about self, others, and the world; trouble making decisions; feelings of depression, anxiety, grief, anger, lethargy; a sense of feeling lost, directionless, and alone; a lack of pleasure or interest in things one used to enjoy; a loss of a community (family, friends, and romantic relationships); and feeling isolated or a sense of not belonging. Recovery always involve a laborious re-orientation and healing process.[22]

22. Pasquale, *Sacred Wounds*.

The following case was chosen as illustrative of the potentially lethal outcome of religious violent extremism. It also highlights the significant role of authoritarian leadership complicated and enhanced by a serious mental disorder.

The Case of the Peoples Temple

The congregation known as the Peoples Temple was founded by the Rev Jim Jones in Indianapolis in 1956 and was associated originally with the Disciples of Christ denomination. It was conceived as an integrated church with a strong communitarian vision and a focus on caring and advocating for oppressed people. Jones developed the ideology of "apostolic socialism" by combining tenets of the Christian prophetic tradition with socialist ideals. He also blended social concerns with faith healing and "charismatic" worship services drawn from the black church experience. In the 1960s he moved the congregation to California where he established several locations gathering thousands of followers. In 1974, after a number of significant achievements and public recognitions as well as political conflicts, scandals, and adverse publicity, Jones and his team decided to move to Guyana, in South America. The vision was to create the "Peoples Temple Agricultural Project" in the area informally renamed "Jonestown." It was meant to become a utopic sanctuary and socialist paradise. In reality, Jones' leadership became more and more authoritarian as his mental health continued to deteriorate. The testimony of surviving followers includes the record of diverse forms of physical, emotional, and spiritual violence. Eventually, violence perpetrated against suspected outsiders and those seeking to escape also engulfed the whole community in a final act of self-destruction.

On November 18, 1978, 919 people died in Jonestown. The toll included 276 children. Except for U.S. Rep. Leo Ryan and the party who accompanied him to Guyana in a fact-finding mission and were killed by armed Temple members, the rest died in what had been planned and described by Jim Jones as "revolutionary suicide." The event marked the collapse of an ill-fated project fashioned under the banner of apostolic socialism. It was the largest and most notorious murder-suicide in American (that is, is Latin America and United States) history.

There have been numerous studies focusing on that tragedy. All of them highlight the lethal effect of consistently fostered toxic spirituality among people searching for significance, belonging, and a sense of life purpose. Ultimately, their fate was sealed under Jim Jones's megalomaniac, paranoid, and authoritarian leadership.[23] It is painfully ironic that people longing for personal dignity would have their lives ended by poisoning while their leader was addressing them with the words, "Die with a degree of dignity. Lay down your life with dignity; don't lay down with tears and agony . . . I tell you, I don't care how many screams you hear, I don't care how many anguished cries . . . death is a million times preferable to ten more days of this life. If you know what was ahead of you, you'd be glad to be stepping over tonight . . ."[24]

Analysis: Spiritual Toxicity and Fundamentalism

The psychological and spiritual dimensions of our lives can be viewed as integrated and inseparable as well as distinguishable. Directly related to our concern about toxic religiosity and religious fundamentalism in particular, the following observations are therefore in order.

First, the conditions of mental health, emotional maturity, and wellness, make it possible to experience spirituality more freely (for example, less fearfully, compulsively, or obsessively) and to express it verbally and otherwise more authentically than in the case of mental illness. Second, mental disorders and emotional immaturity always affect the subjective experience as well as the visible expressions of spirituality and spiritual health in some way and degree.[25] Third, mental health and emotional maturity are necessary but not sufficient conditions for spiritual health and maturity. Progress in treatment, or the restoration of mental health, does not automatically enhance people's spirituality and spiritual health; the spiritual dimension must be engaged intentionally in spiritual direction, education for spiritual formation, counseling or psychotherapy.[26]

A fourth critical observation is that all kinds of toxic spiritualities express themselves in terms of beliefs, attitudes, relationships, and practices with different degrees of toxicity. Further, they also include a measure of violence and, often, a form of power or abuse that harm or injures self and/or others. Such violence can be emotional, spiritual or moral, and, sometimes, physical, including sexual violence. Further, those dimensions

---

23. Guinn, *The Road to Jonestown*, 451–60.

24. Jim Jones last speech. https://www.youtube.com/watch?v=Jr9WnQxZu64.

25. Griffith, *Religion that Heals, Religion that Harms*; Pargament, *Spiritually Integrated Psychotherapy*; Scazzero, *Emotionally Healthy Spirituality*.

26. Spiritual caregivers representing diverse religious traditions and Humanism share this claim in terms of their particular theoretical framework. See, Schipani, *Multifaith Views in Spiritual Care*.

and degrees of violence can be appraised on a spectrum in which harm goes from relatively minor to lethal.

As illustrated in the case studies, spiritual toxicity undermines emotional/mental health, and it does so without exceptions. Further, family systems and faith communities severely affected by toxic spirituality usually show habitual patterns of behavior that can be characterized as "hamster wheel syndrome", describable as "running in circles."[27] It must be also acknowledged that both religious and nonreligious spiritualities[28] can become toxic.

Abrahamic faith traditions appear to supply particular "content" to toxic spiritualities. In fact, the Fundamentalism Project's summary statement on the genus and species of fundamentalisms reads: "The similarities in religious tradition attributable to a common heritage explain the association of fundamentalism . . . with Christianity, Islam, and Judaism. We speak of movements sharing in these characteristics, in these religious traditions, as Abrahamic fundamentalisms." And the researchers conclude: "We have established that the first three types of oppositional movements, descended from the Abrahamic tradition, share close ideological and organizational family resemblances. We also suggest that these common ideological and organizational characteristics tend to cohere, to require one another, in a functional logic."[29]

In the last several years there have been numerous important contributions regarding assessment of spirituality from a psychological and social science perspective.[30] Those resources are necessary, indeed indispensable;

27. See the insightful testimony of Engelmann, *Running in Circles: How False Spirituality Traps Us in Unhealthy Relationships*. See also the comprehensive study from an Islamic perspective, Isgandarova, *Muslim Women, Domestic Violence, and Psychotherapy: Theological and Clinical Issues*.

28. For example, my ongoing work with training prison and hospital chaplains in Cuba regularly includes the appraisal of an ideologically appropriated, secularized spirituality consistently promoted by the government in the public education system of that country. Christian chaplains must therefore develop intercultural and interfaith competence in order to adequately engage care receivers spiritually in their own terms. See Bidwell and Schipani, "Interregious Care in Totalitarian Contexts: Learning from Vietnam and Cuba."

29. Marty and Appleby, eds., *Fundamentalisms Comprehended*, 416–23. This book is the fifth of the series of texts that document and reflect on the findings of The Fundamentalist Project (1987–1995) edited by Martin E. Marty and R. Scott Appleby. Marty and Appleby viewed fundamentalism primarily, although not exclusively, as the militant rejection of secular modernity. The Fundamentalism Project is a major comparative study of anti-modernist, anti-secular militant religious movements on five continents and within seven world religious traditions resulted in multiple influential publications.

30. See, for instance, Hodge, *Spiritual Assessment in Social Work and Mental Health Practice*.

however, they are not sufficient. It is also necessary to evaluate spirituality explicitly from theological or another normative worldview perspective, particularly although not exclusively in terms of the theory and practice of pastoral and spiritual care.

Analysis: Interdisciplinary Lenses

An interdisciplinary approach that works with psychological and theological norms finds that, consistently, fundamentalist spiritualities can never be "healthy" even when they are psychologically (including psycho-sociologically) functional. That was precisely the original situation in each of the case studies presented in the first part of this essay. The following chart helps us to visualize four possibilities with interdisciplinary lenses. It may also help to visualize the process from fundamentalist oppression to healing.

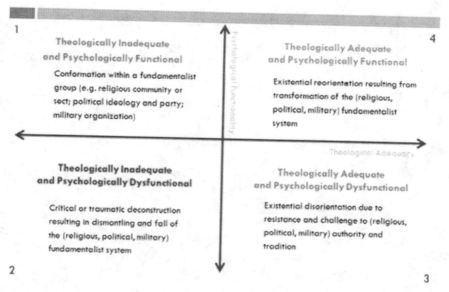

Quadrant 1 represents the case of psychological functionality and theological inadequacy, the latter so judged by those leaving the community or tradition, or militant group. The psychological functionality consists in the multiple benefits of belonging to a certain group such as an extreme Islamist organization. The decision to leave the system, however, always involves a major collapse understandable in terms of psychological dysfunctionality and theological inadequacy, as indicated in quadrant 2. Moving away physically and ideologically, typically results in measures of dysfunctionality-existential disorientation-related to the loss of former integration; in addition, there follows rejection, punishment or persecution by those remaining in the system, as suggested in quadrant 3. Finally, existential reorientation can happen as people move toward and find a place within a healthier communal-social environment (quadrant 4).

Spiritual care providers must be able to assess spirituality and help people access their spiritual resources in the direction of healthy integration. They must be able to work with a normative framework, both psychological and theological (or theologically neutral ethical-philosophical) while engaging care receivers in their own terms, especially when the care receivers' normative frameworks are deemed problematic or totally opposed to their own. Competent caregivers will normally find creative ways to make available safe and sacred spaces for care and healing to happen regardless of ideological incompatibility.

It is therefore essential for caregivers to be clear and consistent regarding their frames of reference and values while remaining open to challenge and correction by care receivers and colleagues alike. The following section presents my normative views about human spirit and spirituality in a way that will further illumine the nature of violent fundamentalism and the way to transformation.

Interlude: A Model of Human Spirit and Spirituality[31]

Simply stated, we are humans because we are spiritual beings. The spirit is the essential dimension of being human; hence the Judeo-Christian claim about being created in God's image, according to the words of Genesis 1:26–27. So, in terms of this model, spirituality is understood as how our spirit manifests itself in ways of searching for, experiencing ("inner" sense), and expressing ("outer" manifestations) in three interrelated domains: meaning-truth, (wisdom, faith); relatedness and communion with others, nature, the Divine, oneself; and purpose-life orientation. The claim that those three dimensions of spirituality—meaning, communion, and purpose—name fundamental experiences and expressions of our human spirit is based on consistent and converging confirmation stemming from various sources such as these: clinical work and supervision; analysis of sacred texts, cultural anthropology, and comparative studies including literature in the

---

31. This section follows closely Schipani, "Pastoral and Spiritual Care in Multifaith Contexts", 125–35.

fields of pastoral and spiritual care; and spiritual direction, in particular. The reference to "searching for" connotes a process of deep longing, that is, a fundamental need as well as potential.

With these notions in mind, it is possible to identify a wide and rich variety of religious and non-religious spiritualities, including diverse streams within a given tradition. For example, in the case of the Christian tradition, a plurality of spiritualities can be identified, such as contemplative, evangelical, charismatic, prophetic, and others.[32] The construct of *spirit* is therefore inseparable from that of *psyche*, so the content of the former's "longing" or "searching for" must be viewed in continuity with ongoing psychological process and content.

It should be clear that this is assumed to be a transcultural model of the human spirit, that is, non-culturally specific in terms of both structure and dynamics. In other words, "transcultural" here means universal. The explicit anthropological claim is that, considered at their (spiritual) core, human beings demonstrate (contextually and particularly, to be sure) the need and potential for meaning, communion, and purpose. At the same time, it is imperative to recognize that the human spirit expresses itself uniquely within specific socio-cultural contexts and (religious and nonreligious) faith traditions in particular. Further, we must also keep in mind that the spirit is always in process (as implied with the emphasis on "longing" and "searching for").

The *spiritual* self can be visualized analogously as having three interrelated expressions that I have chosen to name "Vision," "Virtue," and "Vocation." Thus, the following drawing may be viewed as a functional model of the wholesome human spirit. "Vision" connotes ways of seeing and knowing reality, both self and world. Fundamentally, it names the need and potential for *deep perception* and *meaning*. Growth in Vision necessitates deepening dispositions and behaviors, such as heightened awareness, attentiveness, admiration and contemplation, critical thinking, creative imagination, and discernment.

"Virtue" connotes ways of being and loving; fundamentally, it is *being in communion* grounded in love and community. Growth in Virtue may be viewed as requiring a process of formation and transformation shaping one's inmost affections and passions, dispositions and attitudes (i.e., "habits of the heart").

"Vocation" connotes a sense of life's *purpose* and existential orientation and *destiny*. It is about investing one's life, energies, time and human potential in creative, life-giving, and community-building ways.

32. Foster, *Streams of Living Water.*

In the case of Christian theology this model can be understood in light of Trinitarian anthropological conceptions articulated and developed through the history of Christian thought, from Augustine[33] to Catherine LaCugna and Leonardo Boff.[34] Further, from a theological perspective we can also posit a direct connection between these facets of the spiritual self and the gifts of Faith, Love, and Hope, as represented in the diagram below.

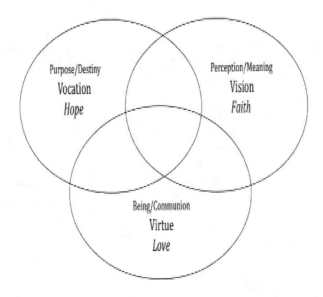

Threefold expression of the wholesome spiritual self
(within family, social, global, cosmic contexts)

Pastoral and spiritual caregivers from other traditions, including Humanism, can also broadly consider the (theological and non-theological) categories of faith, love, and hope, as potentially helpful to name three main sets of existential experiences or conditions concerning spirituality and the spiritual self as such.

The next section consists in an evaluation of fundamentalism in light of the framework and model outlined above. It demonstrates the nature of the harm to the human spirit in a way that may help to better understand

---

33. Augustine included such view in his classic *De Trinidade* (Treatise on the Holy Trinity).

34. LaCugna, *God for Us: The Trinity and Christian Life*, 293; Boff, *Trinity and Society*, 149.

the illustrations provided while also pointing to the way forward for transformation and healing.

Evaluation: Fundamentalism's Grave Spiritual Impairment

Not all toxic spirituality is fundamentalist strictly speaking.[35] However, all kinds of fundamentalism engender and sustain some measure of toxic spirituality. In this section and the next we will explore, first, the essential structure and content of fundamentalism as epistemology, ethics, and politics; and, second, we will consider the key traits of leadership that promotes and sustains fundamentalism. I thus hope to illumine the claim that fundamentalism can cause irreparable damage and even death because it gravely impairs the human spirit. The case of Rev. Jim Jones and the Peoples Temple supplies a clear illustration. It can be represented with another diagram in light of that model of the human spirit with its three closely related dimensions—meaning, relatedness, and purpose.

35. For instance, a geographically and socio-culturally isolated religious community that focuses on self-sufficient survival, can generate spiritual toxicity without engaging in aggressive proselytism. It may be argued that such is the case of many Amish communities that combine Jesus-focused biblical literalism, culturally non-conformed segregation, and an internally enforced ethic. See, Kraybill, et al., *Amish Grace: How Forgiveness Transcended Tragedy;* and *The Amish Way: Patient Faith in a Perilous World.* On the Amish and fundamentalism see also, Hood, Jr., et al., *The Psychology of Religious fundamentalism,* 133–54.

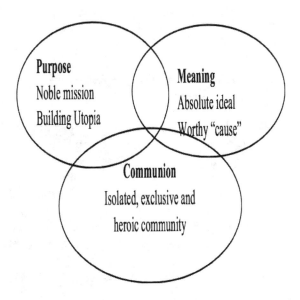

A model of the spirit applied to Peoples Temple's spirituality

Features of Toxic Fundamentalist Spirituality

This model can help us understand the challenge of fundamentalism from an interdisciplinary perspective. That is the case because it identifies the three collapses—the three-dimensional reductionism—that define fundamentalism, namely, the collapse of meaning, collapse of communion, and collapse of purpose. It should be kept in mind that those essential features of fundamentalism must be considered as closely interrelated.

The *collapse of meaning* can be characterized in terms of *dogmatism* as an epistemological structure and content with recognizable features such as these: absolute certainty regarding "fundamental" normative convictions; suppression of curiosity and questioning (e.g. suspicion, critique, doubt, new questions); eclipse of imagination and creativity; underestimation of mystery; logic incapacity to deal with paradox (i.e., the opposite to a great truth can be another great truth); and so on. Such collapse defines the epistemological failure of fundamentalism. Therefore, we can conclude that fundamentalism, especially in its religious expressions, fosters a caricature of faith.

The *collapse of communion* can be characterized in terms of *sectarianism*. Religious and other types of fundamentalism include the pretense of moral integrity and purity of the selected company of those groups self-defined and identified by the corresponding ideological (religious, political, philosophical) dogmatism. The kind of communion that fundamentalism promotes is necessarily exclusive and excluding; those who do not fit or accommodate become "strangers", adversaries or even enemies. Such collapse reveals personal as well as social, ethical and moral failure. Therefore, we can conclude that fundamentalism fosters a caricature of love.

The *collapse of purpose* can be characterized in terms of *proselytism* in the sense of crusades that create and distribute a radical politics based on the illusion of a certain, assured time to come. According to fundamentalist ideologies, the future is pre-determined; they thus offer a pseudo-utopian vision of a life project necessary to proclaim in order to persuade or "convert" the outsiders, and to defend that project with the most effective means possible. Such collapse reveals fundamentalism's political failure. Therefore, we can conclude that fundamentalism fosters a caricature of hope.

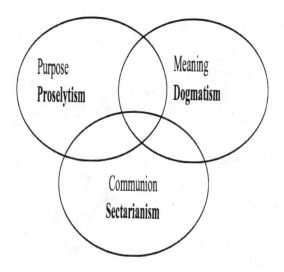

Model of the spirit applied to fundamentalist religion and spirituality

Key Traits of Fundamentalist Leadership

It is well known that fundamentalism can become a seductive and fascinating alternative for entire groups of people especially during times of significant cultural and socio-economic challenges.[36] It is attractive and persuasive especially in the face of life's ambiguities and vulnerabilities exacerbated in times of crisis and difficult transitions coupled with spiritual and political weakness. Together with those factors that determine susceptibility regarding such ideological, moral, and political alternative it is also necessary to identify the main characteristics of the kind of leadership that promotes and sustains fundamentalism. We will do that while taking into account the contribution of the French author Pierre Bourdieu concerning the dynamics of power[37] manifested in human interaction in terms of *mauvaise reconnaissance* (misrecognition). When that contribution is integrated with our model of the human spirit and toxic spirituality connected with fundamentalism, it is possible to identify key traits of leadership that promotes and sustains it: (a) unappealable positional authority that is both admired and feared; (b) technical competence as a special, unquestionable knowledge; and (c) a radical politics that determines and propels mission. We can retrospectively recognize those traits in Rev. Jim Jones's leadership; they are also obviously present always among certain militant groups and military leadership.

Positional authority refers to the status and roles that define authoritarian leadership necessary to promote the development of fundamentalism and indispensable in order to sustain it. These leaders have and use *power over* their followers. That power can be manifested not only with openly authoritarian attitudes and practices but also with paternalism and manipulation as well. Further, such leadership necessarily involves *power against* internal and external opposition. Authority is assumed and conferred by the institutions represented and the followers as well; it is not appealable and, therefore, it is both admired and feared at the same time. That leadership promotes a sense of solidarity within the community whose borders remain clearly defined and are faithfully defended.

36. At the time of this writing, fundamentalist religion—Christian, Hindu, Buddhist—is dangerously connected with political power in diverse countries such as Brazil, India, and Myanmar, respectively, among others. Those forms of fundamentalism clearly inspire and support violent extremism.

37. Pierre Bourdieu (1930–2002) is a recognized philosopher, sociologist, and anthropologist, especially as a creative thinker in connection with his theory of power and social practice. In this theory, misrecognition denotes a false, imaginary, or incorrect understanding of the social world.

The *competence of knowledge*, in the twofold sense of knowing and practical action (knowing how), is the second key trait of this leadership. Leaders function according to fundamentalism's epistemological-ethical-political structure; they demonstrate or claim the recognition of a seemingly superior and unquestionable knowing that is essential. This is obviously the case when it comes to interpretation of reality and the interpretation and application of the sacred texts that define the philosophic, religious or political ideology of fundamentalism.[38] Obviously, this core competency correlates with the collapse of meaning (dogmatism, false certainty, etc.) mentioned above.

Radical politics that determines and propels mission is the third key trait in our model. The logic of all forms of fundamentalism necessary leads to some kid of "missional" project. The leadership that fundamentalism calls for must articulate a certain (pseudo)utopian vision of an alternative reality, that is, a better world in the midst of history or beyond history. It must stimulate vocation at the service of such dream together with a program that promises or even guarantees its future realization. This is especially the case of religious fundamentalism particularly, although not exclusively, in its Christian and Muslim versions. It is imperative, therefore, to recruit and educate (indoctrinate, really) faithful followers in order to carry out the mission.

Application: A Constructive Proposal for Understanding *Transformation*

As already indicated, "transformation" is the main aspiration and goal of spiritual care in the face of fundamentalism and all forms of toxic spirituality. Transformation can be considered as a process of systemic change detectable on different *levels* and within three *dimensions* in the lives of those who receive spiritual care.

First and foremost, strictly speaking, transformation is second-order change, or "revolution." In short, transformation consists in radical change. Whereas a change within a given system is a "first-order change," systemic change consists in the change of the system as such and can be called "transformation." Therefore, we reserve this term to personal conversion

38. It is interesting that some philosophical and scientific associations, such as Marxist and psychoanalysis societies, can also develop fundamentalist tendencies as described in this chapter, that is, concerning "orthodox" knowledge, exclusive membership, and assertive participation in the battle of ideas. Ironically enough, Marx and Freud, great masters of suspicion, as Paul Ricoeur would call them, created valuable resources to unveil, analyze and critique religious and other forms of fundamentalism!

experiences such as those of Saul of Tarsus, Megan, Imad, and Deborah, as briefly discussed above.

Second, transformation can be identified and appraised on three inter-related levels—intrapersonal, interpersonal, and community. In addition to what individual or group therapy can accomplish intra- and interpersonally, successful strategies and approaches confronting fundamentalism can have a positive communal and social effect as well. That includes, of course, the potential transformation of religious communities.

Third, genuine transformations take place within three dimensions. Those systemic changes happen when (or, to the extent that) the follow-ing inter-related outcomes are met: (a) contextual appropriation of new insights, for example, related to sacred texts, results in revelatory *mean-ing* and paradigm/perspective change; (b) the *experience* of community, solidarity and integrity is enriched (e.g., a new sense of belonging and communion); and (c) empowerment and re-orientation with movement toward creative, liberating, or healing community *action* (e.g., devising healing and reconstruction strategies, reconciliation, and others). In short, the kind of transformation hoped for can be experienced and witnessed as a revolution in three dimensions, loosely named a new "orthodoxy", a new "orthopathy", and a new "orthopraxis." The following paragraph explicates what this revolution entails.

Transformation at the *existential or spiritual* level. The question of the shape and content of transformation can be further illuminated by the sig-nificant analogy detectable between what clinical research and empirical evidence show between intercultural and interfaith spiritual care[39] and the process and dynamics of intercultural Bible reading.[40] It is in that light that transformation can be appreciated as a process that reshapes the human *spirit*, as follows: (a) from deception, falsehood, illusion, denial and mean-inglessness to a new vision and understanding in which "truth" is construct-ed and revealed afresh—FAITH (Meaning, a new "orthodoxy" with humbly held conviction and openness to mystery); (b) from isolation and exclu-sion, alienation, condemnation, division and enmity, to connectedness and communion; community and solidarity are strengthened—LOVE (Com-munion, a new "orthopathy" or "orthokardia"); and (c) from mis-placed vocation, inertia, resignation, disorientation, despair and hopelessness, to re-orientation and empowerment for justice and peace—HOPE (Purpose, a

---

39. See, Schipani, "The heart of the matter: Engaging the *spirit* in spiritual care," *Multifaith Views in Spiritual Care*, 149–66.

40. Schipani, "Transformation in intercultural Bible reading."

new "orthopraxis"). Further, it is obvious that these three dimensions must be considered as dynamically interrelated.

Empirical evidence is abundant, including countless personal testimonies like the ones reviewed,[41] and those of disparate groups such as Fundamentalists Anonymous and veterans recovering from moral-spiritual injury after war.[42] That evidence also points to the fact that dismantling and deconstructing psycho-spiritual and epistemological-ethical-political structures of fundamentalism as toxic spirituality requires participation in communities of support and discernment. In fact, without such enfolding support, people can quickly fall into a vacuum of meaninglessness, self-condemning isolation, and self-destructive fatalism with the suppression of all life projects, as documented in the large percentage of war veterans that die by suicide.[43] An alternative is, of course, to move content-wise, so to speak, from one fundamentalism to another, but that cannot be considered as transforming change according to the criteria we have discussed.

In light of the model of human spirit presented in this essay, the following diagrams suggest that the "content" observable, for instance, in Islamist militant groups and all kinds of militaristic spirituality resembles what was highlighted concerning the Peoples Temple.

41. See, for example, Nawaz, *Radical: My Journey Out of Islamist Extremism*.

42. In light of the argument presented in this essay, I prefer to use the term moral-spiritual injury. The following resources are nevertheless very helpful: Brock and Lentini, *Soul Repair*; Meagher, *Killing from the Inside Out*; and, Graham, *Moral Injury*.

43. I include regular armed forces among the groups that require and operate with a fundamentalist system and its characteristic structure in terms of ideology and leadership. In fact, I argue that those military forces cannot function unless its authoritarian leadership structure is consistently supported by military versions of dogmatism (nationalism, patriotism), sectarianism (good people clearly separated from and against evil people), and mission (heroic vocation to destroy "evil" in specific ways). However, it must be clear that in no way do I posit moral equivalence between, say, radical Islamist militias and regular armed forces. In any event, the moral-spiritual dilemmas faced by military chaplains who, in the case of the United States, must be military officers, is beyond the scope of this essay.

Application of the model to Islamist extremism and militaristic spirituality

The kind of training and indoctrination necessary to sustain such spiritual configuration must include the goal of fostering in the recruits and followers the appropriation of values and development of certain competencies in integrated and integrating ways. In other words, recruits and followers must conform to the system along the lines represented below.

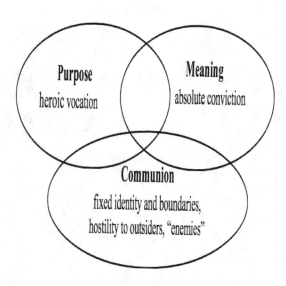

**Spirituality features of followers and recruits *before* the collapse
of the fundamentalist system**

Clinical and other studies demonstrate that, when the fundamentalist system is no longer viable, for example in the face of the atrocities
witnessed or perpetrated in combat, a major and potentially traumatic
disruption takes place. This is precisely the condition identifiable in the
studies of and approaches to both the "religious trauma syndrome" and
"moral (and spiritual) injury."[44] On the spiritual level, those syndromes
present multidimensional faces of existential anxiety.[45] The corresponding
representation follows.

44. Moral-spiritual injury normally includes a number of symptoms also found in
Post-Traumatic Stress Disorder, such as these: anger, depression, anxiety, insomnia,
nightmares, and self-medication with alcohol or drugs. In addition, moral-spiritual
injury typically includes sorrow, grief, regret, shame, and a sense of alienation.

45. Paul Tillich insightfully identified and described main features of existential
anxiety in terms of the threefold threat of nonbeing, namely, emptiness, condemnation,
and annihilation. And he further suggested that existential anxiety is precisely a focus
of theoretical concern and practical involvement of pastoral counselors and chaplains.
See, Tillich, *The Courage to Be*, 32–77. He was a theologian interested in, among other
things, the converging fields of psychology and health. He wrote that book as a philosopher of being by proposing ontological categories mediating between psychological
and theological concepts.

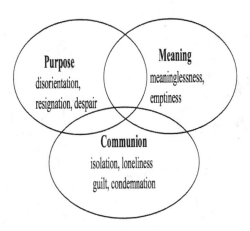

Spirituality features of followers and recruits *after* the collapse of the fundamentalist system

Our discussion suggests that the goals of transformation must be articulated as spiritual reorientation, that is, as systemic change at the spiritual or existential level as described above. Using psychiatric language, in the case of pastoral and spiritual care, those goals pertain especially in secondary and tertiary prevention[46] while caring for people in need to recover from all types of religious trauma and moral-spiritual injury. It is clear that they must also be included in any "primary prevention" approach designed to strengthen psycho-spiritual health at all possible levels. In other words, our concern to effectively address the challenges of all forms of fundamentalism necessitate comprehensive educational endeavors. Therefore, pastoral and spiritual caregivers as well as educators can consider adopting and adapting integrated goals related to the fundamental questions of meaning, communion, and purpose, in connection to both ministerial and professional formation and competent caregiving and educational practice.

---

46. "Secondary prevention" is understood as timely care offered and received at the onset of a crisis. The term "tertiary prevention" is applied to care offered and received after the crisis, during the phase of further recovery. See, Caplan, *Principles of Preventive Psychiatry.*

Main goals for spiritual or existential formation and transformation

Conclusion

The overarching purpose of the project leading to this book is understanding and undoing violent extremism. Within that umbrella subject, this chapter addressed fundamentalism from a pastoral and spiritual care perspective as a system that tends to foster and support violent extremism. It did so as an exercise in practical theology with its descriptive, interpretive, evaluative, and strategic dimensions. The discussion centered on the twofold thesis that fundamentalisms foster toxic spirituality because they are closed systems that harm the human spirit in recognizable ways; and that fundamentalisms support the activity of groups that employ violence. Although written from a Christian viewpoint, it is hoped that this essay will invite further reflection focused on finding common ground and collaborative ways to assess, engage, and transform fundamentalist toxic spirituality in both education and spiritual care practice.

Bibliography

Armstrong, Karen. *The Battle for God: A History of Fundamentalism.* New York: Random House, 2000.

Antoun, Richard T. *Understanding Fundamentalism: Christian, Islamic, and Jewish Movements.* 2nd ed. New York: Rowman & Littlefield, 2008.

Bidwell, Duane R., and Daniel S. Schipani. "Interreligious Care in Totalitarian Contexts: Learnings from Vietnam and Cuba." In *Navigating Religious Difference in Spiritual Care and Counseling,* edited by Jill L. Snodgrass, 115–34. Claremont: Claremont Press, 2019.

Brock, Rita Nakashima, and Gabriella Lentini. *Soul Repair: Recovering from Moral Injury after War.* Boston: Beacon, 2012.

Caplan, Gerald. *Preventive Psychiatry.* New York: Basic Books, 1964.

Engelmann, Kim. *Running in Circles: How False Spirituality Traps Us in Unhealthy Relationships.* Downers Grove, IL: InterVarsity, 2007.

Feldman, Deborah. *Unorthodox: The Scandalous Rejection of My Hasidic Roots.* New York: Simon & Schuster, 2012.

Foster, Richard J. *Essential Practices from the Six Great Traditions of Christian Faith.* San Francisco: Harper & Row, 1998.

Gaventa, Beverley Roberts. *From Darkness to Light: Aspects of Conversion in the New Testament.* Philadelphia: Fortress, 1986.

Graham, Larry. *Moral Injury: Restoring Wounded Souls.* Nashville: Abingdon, 2016.

Griffith, James L. *Religion that Heals, Religion that Harms: A Guide for Clinical Practice.* New York: Guilford, 2010.

Gritsch, Eric W. *Toxic Spirituality: Four Enduring Temptations of Christian Faith.* 2nd ed. Minneapolis: Fortress, 2009.

Guinn, Jeff. *The Road to Jonestown: Jim Jones and the Peoples Temple.* New York: Simon & Schuster, 2017.

Hodge, David R. *Spiritual Assessment in Social Work and Mental Health Practice.* New York: Columbia University Press, 2015.

Hood, Ralph W., Jr. et al. *The Psychology of Religious Fundamentalism.* New York: Guilford, 2005.

Isgandarova, Nazila. *Muslim Women, Domestic Violence, and Psychotherapy: Theological and Clinical Issues.* New York: Routledge, 2019.

Khatab, Sayed. *Understanding Islamic Fundamentalism: The Theological and Ideological Bases of al-Q'ida's Political Tactics.* Cairo: American University in Cairo Press, 2011.

Koenig, Harlod G., Dana A. King, & Verna Benner Carson. *Handbook of Religion and Health.* 2nd ed. Oxford: Oxford University Press, 2012.

Kraybill, Donald B. et al. *Amish Grace: How Forgiveness Transcended Tragedy.* San Francisco: Jossey-Bass, 2007.

Kraybill, Donald B. et al. *The Amish Way: Patient Faith in a Perilous World.* San Francisco: Jossey-Bass, 2010.

LaCugna, Catherine Mowry. *God for Us: The Trinity and Christian Life.* San Francisco: Harper, 1991.

Lechner, Frank J. "Fundamentalism." In *Encyclopedia of Religion and Society,* edited by William H. Swatos, Jr. et al., 197–200. Walnut Creek, CA: Alta Mira, 1998.

Marty, Martin E., and R. Scott Appleby, eds. *Accounting for Fundamentalisms: The Dynamic Character of Movements.* The Fundamentalism Project. Chicago: University of Chicago, 1994.

———, eds. *Fundamentalisms and Society: Reclaiming the Sciences, the Family, and Education.* The Fundamentalism Project 2. Chicago: University of Chicago, 1993.

———, eds. *Fundamentalisms and the State: Remaking Polities, Economies, and Militance.* The Fundamentalism Project 3. Chicago: Uni-versity of Chicago, 1993.

———, eds. *Fundamentalisms Comprehended.* The Fundamentalism Project 5. Chicago: University of Chicago, 1995.

———, eds. *Fundamentalisms Observed.* The Funda-mentalism Project 1. Chicago: University of Chicago, 1991.

Meagher, Robert Emmet. *Killing from the Inside Out: Moral Injury and Just War.* Eugene, OR: Cascade Books, 2014.

Nawaz, Naajid. *Radical: My Journey Out of Islamist Extremism.* Lanham, MD: Rowman & Littlefield, 2013.

Nelson, Anne. *Shadow Network: Media, Money, and the Secret Hub of the Radical Right.* New York: Bloomsbury, 2019.

Pargament, Kenneth I. *Understanding and Addressing the Sacred.* New York: Guilford, 2007.

Pargament, Kenneth I., et al. *APA Handbook of Psychology, Religion, and Spirituality.* Washington, DC: American Psychological Association, 2013: Volume I, "Context, Theory, and Research"; Volume II, "An Applied Psychology of Religion and Spirituality."

Partridge, Christopher H., ed. *Fundamentalisms.* Carlisle, UK: Paternoster, 2001.

Pasquale, Teresa B. *Sacred Wounds: A Path to Healing from Spiritual Trauma.* St. Louis: Chalice, 2015.

Phelps-Roper, Megan. *Unfollow: A Memoir of Loving and Leaving Westboro Baptist Church.* New York: Farrar, Strauss & Giroux, 2019.

Ramsay, Nancy J., and Carrie Doehring. *Military Moral Injury and Spiritual Care: A Resource for Religious Leaders and Professional Caregivers.* St. Louis: Chalice, 2019.

Scazzero, *Emotionally Healthy Spirituality.* Updated ed. Grand Rapids: Zondervan, 2017.

Schipani, Daniel S., ed. *Multifaith Views in Spiritual Care.* Kitchener, ON: Pandora, 2013.

———. "Pastoral and Spiritual Care in Multifaith Contexts." In *Teaching for a Multifaith World,* edited by Eleazar S. Fernandez, 124–146. Eugene, OR: Pickwick Publications, 2017.

Schipani, Daniel S. "Transformation in Intercultural Bible Reading: A View from Practical Theology." In *Bible and Transformation: The Promise of Intercultural Bible Reading.* Edited by Hans de Wit and Janet Dyk, 99–116. Atlanta: SBL Press, 2015.

Tillich, Paul. *The Courage to Be.* New Haven: Yale University Press, 1953.

Winell, Marlene. *Leaving the Fold: A Guide for Former Fundamentalists and Others Leaving Their Religion.* Oakland: New Harbinger, 1993.

9

Spiritual Practice and Formation in a World of Violent Extremism

—RUBEN L. F. HABITO

Introduction

A t this writing, the pandemic called COVID-19, also known as coronavirus, is wreaking havoc and sweeping over the face of our earth,
upturning many of the conventional ways of thinking and of doing things
that we had taken for granted up to recently. We are all still uncertain as
to how this contagion will play out in the short and the long-term future
of our global society. The gravity of the situation is not to be gainsaid, but
our collective and focused attention to this pandemic is tending to overshadow a matter that continues to be a significant threat to our collective
lives on Earth: this is the spectre of violent extremism that pervades our
contemporary global society.

The effects of this pandemic could putatively bring about a change
of heart and change in the way of life for a critical mass of humanity, but
short of that, our time-worn, ego-centric and tribalistic ways of thinking
and living may get the better of us, aggravating our situation and woefully
dragging us further in the destructive path of violent extremism.

A prominent event that brought this reality of violent extremism into
our collective attention is what we refer to as 9/11, an abbreviation for September 11, 2001, when a group of nineteen terrorists undertook four coordinated attacks by four hijacking planes, with two succeeding in destroying the
Twin Towers in New York City. The other two, one aiming for the Pentagon,
and another for Washington, D.C., were foiled in their goals, crashing along
the way and killing the passengers and the perpetrators aboard. The overall
tally included nearly three thousand victims killed along with the suicide-bent

perpetrators, and over 25,000 people injured. This widely publicized notorious event became the trigger as well as the reference point for so many other occasions of violence, directly or indirectly connected, in so many other locations in our twenty-first century global society.[1]

This is by no means to say that violent extremism began with that fateful event of 9/11. One could effectively argue that it has been with us since the beginning of our human history, with Cain's murder of his brother Abel. And it goes without saying that violent extremism has been a feature of human societies throughout our collective history on Earth. But the technological advances we have accomplished in our day have given us such powerful instruments of violence and weapons of mass destruction as never before. And now it may not be an exaggeration to say that with violent extremism on the rise from different directions, compounding the ecological destruction already impinging upon us, our very survival on Earth is in the balance.

Extremism, following the working definition provided by J. M. Berger[2] and as laid out in the introductory chapter of this volume, is based on a frame of mind characterized by a "belief that an in-group's success or survival *can never be separated* from the need for the hostile action against an out-group . . ." The frame of mind that leads to animosity and violent action against "the other," which often also implicates and inevitably brings harm upon oneself, is precisely this view that separates "us" against "them," the "in-group" from "those outsiders" who do not belong or who are refused admission to this in-group.

Another term closely akin to extremism is "tribalism," referring to a mindset informing attitudes and behavior that stem from devotion and loyalty to one's own in-group at the concomitant exclusion or elimination of those others who do not belong to this group. Some noted authors rightly argue that this tribalistic mentality lies at the root of the major problems faced by our world today, not to mention throughout our common human history.[3]

The question we address in this essay is this: how can spiritual practice and spiritual formation be carried out and taught in ways that would not only alleviate and mitigate but also possibly overcome and eliminate violent extremism and its effects upon human society and our Earth community as a whole? This may sound like an idealistic dream, but this essay is offered

---

1. See Fernandez, chapter 1 of this volume, providing yearly statistical figures of terrorist attacks from 2001 to 2017.

2. Berger, *Extremism*.

3. See Rozenblit, *Us Against Them*; and Wright, *Why Buddhism Is True*, 18.

as a contribution toward laying the groundwork for "a more beautiful world our hearts know is possible."[4]

What Is Spiritual Practice, and Spiritual Formation?

By "spiritual" here we will take the working definition provided by a multivolume series under the common title *World Spirituality*, with individual and dual volumes devoted to the spirituality of particular religious traditions, including Judaism, Christianity, Islam, Buddhism, and Hinduism, with volumes also on African, South and Meso-American Indigenous, Classical Mediterranean, Modern Esoteric, and also Secular Spirituality.[5] A common preface to these volumes points out that the "*spiritual core is the deepest center of the person. It is here that the person is open to the transcendent dimension; it is here that the person experiences ultimate reality* . . ."[6] We may add that it is at this deepest center of the person where one experiences *an intimate connectedness with all beings.*

This understanding of "the spiritual" is in contrast with some ways this term is usually taken, pointing to a realm *distinguished* from the physical or bodily, from the material dimension of our existence. This latter, a dualistic view separating "the spiritual" from "the material," is a predominant one in Western culture, which has also influenced much of Christian "spiritual" literature. In this view, a turn to "the spiritual" can be construed as a way of escaping from the undesirable and dissatisfactory realities in this concrete world of ours, toward a "higher dimension." A spiritual pursuit in this context may refer to seeking solace in some ethereal realm separate from the concrete world of our day to day life. This dualistic mindset makes a sharp dividing line between the spiritual as the "heavenly," "pure," and "eternal" realm, in contrast to our physical existence as "worldly," "impure," and "despicable" domain, with the rejection, denigration, and intended flight from the latter. This is *not* what this essay is about.

The understanding of the spiritual that we are taking as the basis of this essay, one that is in consonance with recent findings in the sciences, notably

---

4. Eisenstein, *A More Beautiful World.*

5. Green, et al., *World Spirituality.*

6. There are currently 18 volumes published, with a few more under preparation. Ewert Cousins, late Emeritus Professor of Theology at Fordham University, is the author to this common Preface, based on a consensus of all the editors of the volumes of the series.

quantum physics,[7] avoids this dualistic pitfall separating the spiritual from the physical world. Rather, it is presented as a holistic view that integrates and brings unity and wholeness to the disparate aspects of our humanity and our being. What we refer to in this essay as the "spiritual" is not a separate realm from our life in this concrete day to day world, but a living center which opens us to the Holy, the transcendent, permeating our entire existence, and which incorporates and embraces the physical, psychological, social, ecological, and in fact, all dimensions of our existence.

This essay addresses how may we activate and enhance an awareness of this spiritual core of our being, wherein we may overcome the gap, the separation, the tension and consequent animosity between "us" and "them." This overcoming may happen in opening ourselves to the transcendent dimension (whatever one may choose to name it) and experiencing the intimate connectedness with everyone and everything at the core of our being.

How may we envision the formation of attitudes, values, and behavior in individuals and communities that highlights the cultivation and activation of this awareness of the spiritual core of our being? How may we go about this in a way that this awareness grounds the conduct and the maintenance of our lives on the individual, social, economic, political, and ecological dimensions? From another angle, what would it take to form individuals and communities who nurture, cultivate, activate, and habitually embody a frame of mind of "we together" rather than an "us vs. them" mentality, referring not just to the human family but to the entire Earth community?

Spiritual practice is the intentional cultivation of attitudes and actions to nurture, cultivate, activate, and habitually embody a frame of mind and way of being that issues forth from this innermost core. Spiritual formation is the process by which this frame of mind and way of being is inculcated, developed, and deepened in individuals and integrated in one's entire life, including the personal, social, political, economic, ecological dimensions of our being.

In laying out the key points of our theme, we will take the Buddha's Four Ennobling Truths as a framework, modeled on a method of healing derived from ancient Indian Ayurvedic tradition. This involves four interrelated steps: describing the symptoms and manifestations of the illness; tracing and analyzing the root causes; providing a prognosis for recovery and return to a state of well-being; and prescribing steps toward this recovery through uprooting of the root causes.[8] We will also refer to resonating Christian themes that will serve to shed light on our main thesis.

7. See Bohm, *Wholeness and the Implicate Order*, among others.

8. The Buddha's core teaching of the Four Ennobling Truths lays out a description of

Mapping the Symptoms: Global Dysfunction

"Violent extremism" covers not only the blatant acts of terrorism perpetrated in different parts of the world that we read or hear about in the media, or may experience directly or indirectly ourselves, but also to the many levels of violence, including direct *physical* violence, through the use force that results in harming others, as well as *structural* and *ecological* violence that deprive people of or diminish the quality of their lives and impute harm on their and the entire Earth's well-being. These are a *result of attitudes and actions assumed or taken by human beings individually and collectively that draw a sharp demarcation between one's "in-group" on the one hand, and an out-group on the other*, whereby the latter, either by intention or default, become the objects or victims of violence.

A survey of our global situation, with an eye to the eruptions or manifestations of violent extremism, is in order.

A UNICEF website, in a report dated September 18, 2018, notes that "an estimated 6.3 million children under 15 of age died in 2017, or 1 every 5 seconds, mostly of preventable causes . . ."[9] There are several other websites that report statistics of global trends, and in the years since the beginning of this millennium, the reported numbers of children's deaths due to hunger and malnutrition have varied, from 3.1 million to 9 million annually. If we take the UNICEF figure of 6.3 million annually as our indicator, that would be approximately 17,000 children dying daily due to *mostly preventable causes.* The tragedy is compounded by the fact that if we take this *daily* death toll as a gauge, it is almost six times more than the number of fatalities in that single day of the 9/11 event, and this is ongoing, yet rarely causes a ripple in the popular media.

Given the advances in agriculture, science, technology, communication, and other areas of human endeavor that we can be proud of having accomplished up to this point of our history, the fact of 17,000 children dying around the world on a daily basis through malnutrition and hunger, disease and other related causes—factors that would have been prevented—is a scandal of major proportions for all of us living in the twenty-first century. Lamentably, we, collectively, could have taken this issue as

---

the human condition as dis-eased (*dukkha*), goes on to pinpoint the root causes of this dis-ease, and having laid out a scenario of healing and well-being, goes on to prescribes an eightfold path to this healing. See Habito, *Experiencing Buddhism*.

9. https://www.unicef.org/press-releases/child-under-15-dies-every-five-seconds-around-world-un-report.

affecting all of us and could have taken significant steps toward its resolution, but this has not been the case.[10]

One may ask how this kind of structural violence would fall under "violent extremism," if this term, by definition, involves "hostile action" against "the other." Further, one might argue that even those who unwittingly or knowingly contribute to the structural violence of our consumeristic lifestyles, in our implicit or explicit support of exploitative practices of corporations as we purchase their products, etc., including many or most of us, may feel sympathy or compassion for the "starving children" and for the countless victims of structural violence all over the world (of which we ourselves may also acknowledge as being part of the cause).

In response, although the direct or indirect perpetrators of this structural violence (which would arguably include most of us who maintain more or less of a middle class lifestyle and continue benefiting from the current global economic structures) may not *feel* hostility toward the victims, there is nevertheless "hostile action" against them, in the very deprivation of their right to life, in not having the necessary food, sanitary water, health care, and so on, to maintain their existence. For all too many of us, "those (pitiable) children dying of hunger daily" remain on the level of "them," of whom we may think about every now and then, as we send a check to some charitable agency to mollify our conscience somewhat, but still do not enter into our field of concern in a way that challenges us to transform our lifestyle or ways of seeing and doing.

This scandalous fact of the loss of lives of thousands of innocent children and so many others day in and day out through preventable causes stares at us in the face, as violence of the structural kind. The key argument here is that as long as "those poor victims" remain "other" to us, the term "violent extremism" applies.

In a website presenting data on various global issues,[11] a column with links to other sites provides current or recent reports on specific themes, and the following headings are listed (in alphabetical order), among others: Arms Control, Arms Trade, Biodiversity, Causes of Poverty, Climate Change and Global Warming, Conflicts in Africa, Corporations, Environmental issues, Geopolitics, Human Rights, International Criminal Court, Iraq Crisis, Middle East, Nuclear Weapons, Palestine/Israel, Third World Debt, War on Terror, World Hunger and Poverty.

10. This is not to neglect or belittle the efforts of those groups and agencies, both governmental and non-governmental, who have been tackling these issues for decades now, but is only a statement of lament that it has not caught the attention of a critical mass of the population to make a significant difference.

11. www.globalissues.org.

As we examine and reflect on the meaning and implications of each of these headings, we are able to recognize that these headings can be taken as the "nodes" of the irruptions and manifestations of symptoms of our global malaise, having to do with violent extremism in one way or the other, some more obvious than others.[12] Let us take a brief overview of how this is so.

"Arms control" and "arms trade," needless to say, are all about the instruments that are used in the violence perpetrated by human individuals and groups against other individuals and groups, including those sanctioned by national states against those they put forth as their "enemies." Another heading, "Conflicts in Africa" is an issue that directly reflects the cases of violent extremism in that continent and not unrelated to issues of arms trade. Issues pertaining to the Iraq Crisis, Middle East, Palestine/Israel, likewise pertain to the acts of violent extremism being perpetrated from all sides involved in those specified areas.

The statistical report on biodiversity is about the ongoing loss and extinction of species due to climate change and related factors—violence perpetrated on many different forms of non-human life, leading to their disappearance from this earth. "Causes of Poverty" lays out the factors that contribute to the loss, or diminishment of the quality of life, of countless children and adults as well. "Climate Change and Global Warming" is about the gradual loss of ecological balance of our Earth's ecosystem that leads to the rapid rates in the extinction of species, described in the Biodiversity report.

"Corporations" may be a more subtle heading and may raise questions among readers as to whether this belongs on this list of issues that relate to violent extremism. We will not go into the particulars of the argument here, beyond suggesting a reading of David Korten's 1995 book, *When Corporations Rule the World*, with a twentieth anniversary edition published in 2015, which will provide the rationale and background arguments for this claim that "corporations," with the inherent value system and principles by which they operate, do relate intricately to the structural violence that victimizes multitudes of our global population.

"Environmental issues" are about the violence being done to our Earth's ecosystem, threatening the ongoing subsistence of millions of species of living beings. As long as "the Earth" is regarded as "the environment," that is, "the surroundings and conditions within which we living beings maintain our

12. There may be questions and criticisms about the particular data indicated in this website, as with any other website, and without taking sides in the argumentation or going into detail into the background of the data, this is simply to highlight the very headings themselves as marking the significant issues that affect our global community.

life," it remains on the level of "them," that is, as outside of "us," albeit providing us with what we need for our biological life.

Geopolitics is about the powerplay among nations and its leaders and powerbrokers with varying levels of responsibility in making decisions that influence the lives of the populace and the course of our events in global society. This powerplay is driven by an "us vs. them" mentality that affects the social, economic, political, and ecological arenas of our global society and brings about outcomes that wreak havoc on the lives of millions of people. The emergence of tens of millions of refugees in different parts of the world who are forced to leave their ancestral homes simply in search for a place conducive to living a decent human life with their families in some corner of this earth is one outcome of this geopolitical powerplay. Here again, "those poor refugees," "those poor victims of violence," or "those people of this or that country" remain on the side of the "them" that may cause some concern in "us," but the gap between "us" and "them" is not bridged.

The issue of Human Rights comes up to the fore in the light of the blatant violations of these rights resulting from actions and attitudes of human beings who operate on an "us versus them" mentality, pushing forth actions and policies detrimental to segments of the human community.

Third World Debt and World Hunger and Poverty are interrelated issues that directly relate to the diminishment of the quality of life, not to mention the death, of a large segment of the world's population.

We take the above-named issues in their own specific ways as indicators, outcomes, manifestations of different forms of violent extremism on a global scale.

We can now summarize three main categories of "violence" as underlying the global issues outlined above. One is the actual *physical violence* being perpetrated against human beings by other human beings, on individual and collective levels, which we are made keenly aware of through the media. This kind of violence is felt in escalating measure, breeding fear and insecurity in people across our global society, causing mass migration and increasing numbers of refugees in different places of the world.

Another is *structural violence*, based on the ever-widening gap between the "haves" and the "have nots" in our human community, maintained and reinforced by unjust political, social, and economic institutional structures on a grand scale, resulting in the dehumanization and loss of lives of a major segment of the world population. This structural violence is behind the death of millions of children from hunger and malnutrition and related causes, cited above, as well as widespread hunger and poverty that characterize the lives of major segments of the world population.

A third is the *ecological violence* being perpetrated upon our ecosystem, in ways that are compounded with the physical violence and structural violence in our human society, and resulting in the ongoing extinction of countless living species from the planet, not to mention the loss of human lives occasioned by ecological deterioration.

We refer back to our working definition of extremism as "belief that an in-group's success or survival *can never be separated* from the need for the hostile action against an out-group . . ." In short, it is this "us versus them," "in-group versus out-group" mentality that is somehow or other behind all the violence on these different levels, resulting in the hostile and harmful *action* (through direct human intervention, or as a result of structural social realities and ecological conditions). In tracing the root causes of our global dysfunctional condition in these manifestations of violence, the finger points to this extremist, tribalistic frame of mind.

As one steps back and surveys our Earth community wracked in pain from these levels of violence in different degrees of intensity, and takes to heart the fact that not only considerable numbers of human lives but also those of countless species are being extinguished from this earth from this violence, and that we are heading in the direction of further deterioration, one comes to a rude awakening that *there is something untenable in our current situation*—a dysfunctional condition of global proportions. Coupled with this is the realization that "we cannot go on living like this."

This realization corresponds to the First Ennobling Truth that the Buddha realized and taught—the recognition of our human condition as *dukkha,* often translated as a "state of suffering," but which more properly is understood as a sense of dissatisfaction, dis-ease, a dysfunctional state of being. The Buddha's insight into the individual human condition can be transposed into collective level, as *dukkha,* or dysfunction on a global scale.

There are a number of possible ways individual human beings may react to such an overwhelming scenario of global violence, dis-ease and dysfunction. One would be closing one's mind in outright denial. "No, this cannot be," and one may go on with one's "normal" routine of life without taking such a scenario into account or continuing to block it away from one's consciousness by turning to pursuits of pleasure, possessions, power, things that would occupy one's mind and drive one to relentless and directionless activities. One would be to impute blame on persons or institutions from which one can distance oneself and be able to wallow in one's own feigned innocence: "It's those narrow-minded fundamentalists of this (or that) religion that foment all this hatred!" Or, "It's those evil governments!" Or "It's those multinational corporations!" Or "it's the radical right (or left)!" or whoever one may have in mind as "the culprit" to blame.

Or one could react with a pessimism that would render oneself power-less from doing anything. "The world is in a mess, and there's nothing you or I can do." This then can become an excuse for going on to the useless pursuits noted in the first kind of reaction above (denial). Another would be a reaction of revolutionary activism, with a resolve to engage in all kinds of activities possible to "help the victims" and "prosecute the perpetrators," with a sense of self-righteousness that propels the projected activities.

Or, one could step back and, while grieving and bemoaning with the world in pain, seek ways in which one might be able to address the situation toward healing, beginning with one's own life choices and lifestyle, so that one could at least minimize those areas within one's own control, like one's choice of work, one's ways of relating with others, one's ways of consuming and dis-posing of waste, for example, seeking new ways whereby one could become less of a factor in perpetrating the violence, whether personal, structural, or ecological. Moving forward in this direction, the next step, taking cue from the Buddha, is to examine the root causes of the malady.

Examining the Root Causes of Our Global Malaise

The thesis we are exploring here is that violence in the world caused by hu-man agency (as opposed to natural calamities that take their toll on lives like tornadoes, landslides, earthquakes and the like) comes from an "us versus them" mentality, the hallmark of what we call "extremism." A term synony-mous with this type of mentality is "tribalism," which can be defined as "be-havior and attitudes that derive from staunch loyalty to one's own tribe or social group,"[13] "putting one's own group above every other consideration, even kindness, and justice," a state of mind that "can lead to bigotry, racism, and, when taken to extremes, even war."[14]

In *Us Against Them: How Tribalism Affects the Way We Think,* author Bruce Rozenblitt clarifies that this is a term that is not meant to denigrate indigenous tribal societies, but is used rather to describe a particular human predisposition, linked to the natural evolution of our biology, that shapes our thoughts and behavior.[15] Robert Wright, best-selling author who writes about history, politics, society and religion, describes how tribalism is manifested in "the discord and even open conflict along religious, ethnic,

13. https://www.google.com/search?client=firefox-b-1-d&q=definition+of+tribalism.

14. https://www.vocabulary.com/dictionary/tribalism.

15. Rozenblitt, *Us Against Them.*

national, and ideological lines," and observes that "more and more, it seems, groups of people define their identity in terms of the sharp opposition to other groups of people."[16] These are suggestive pointers indeed for our exploration of the root causes of the violence that continues to threaten and wreak havoc on our global society.

Those who carry on their lives with a tribalistic frame of mind may remain isolated within their own social nexus, and as long as their interactions with those outside their tribe remain minimal, they can maintain relatively stable and non-violent ways of life. But in a pluralistic, multicultural, multiethnic, multinational global society, it is now hardly possible to remain in isolation from others who differ in many aspects from oneself and one's in-group, with the exception perhaps of monastic and other semi-reclusive communities bound together by a commitment to remain within their inner circle for religious, ideological, or other reasons. This inevitability of interaction with others outside one's own tribe with their different ways of thinking and behaving is what generates friction and conflict, and violent attitudes and actions can ensue. From the tribalistic standpoint, the encounter with, even the very presence of, "the other" becomes perceived as a threat to oneself, causing one to be fearful and insecure and unsettled in one's identity.

This tribalistic mentality then, easily turns into extremism when, in order to forestall or mitigate this threat, sense of insecurity, and challenge to one's identity, one begins to feel a sense of animosity and a necessity for hostile action against "the other."

In our exploration into the root causes of our global dysfunctional situation, the Buddha's description of the Second Ennobling Truth can serve as further angle of reference. Behind the *dukkha* (dis-ease, dysfunction) of the human condition is "craving (*tanhā*)," which manifests itself in the "three poisons" of greed, ill will, and delusion. This craving stems from one's deepest frustration in thinking of my "self" as separate from the world that I am in and from everything that exists. This illusory sense of self, accompanied by a sense of "lack" at the heart of my being based on that separateness, is what drives me to do things that attempt to mitigate or alleviate this deep frustration, "trying to identify with and become attached to something in the world, in the belief that it can make me whole and complete."[17] I want possessions, I want power, I want pleasure, and more and more of them. And yet the more I have of these, the more I seem to be frustrated. In my quest to fill in my inner lack, I look at others around me and tend to regard them as

16 Wright, *Why Buddhism Is True*, 18.

17. Loy, "Three Institutional Poisons," 6.

competitors, as rivals, or enemies who may take what I want from me, and thus ill will is generated against "those others."

This is an oversimplified description of the root cause of the dissatisfactory, dysfunctional condition of the individual human being, tending to thoughts, words and actions that only aggravate this condition all the more. It is based on the illusion of a separate self that sees itself as alienated from the rest of the world to which it inherently belongs and is intimately interconnected. Transposing this into the collective, institutional level will provide us insight into the dysfunctional state of our global society.

Here I refer to David Loy's analysis of our global society, as he points to institutional greed, institutional ill will, and institutional delusion as the root causes of our global dysfunction.[18] Institutionalized greed manifests itself in the way our societies are run based on merging of the consumerist credo, "I am what I consume," and the corporate principle of "Profit above all" that propels the global economic system. Human beings are relegated to the role of consumers, and the corporations, whose main purpose of existence is to generate profit for its shareholders and executives, not only to provide the products that consumers want and need, but also devise whatever means available, through advertising ploys, etc., to make the consumers want or think they need those products.

Institutionalized ill will is personified in the global military industrial complex, which finds profit in actual armed conflicts being waged in different parts of the world. It supports the glorification and escalation of armed conflicts in the name of some declared principle of "righteousness," against those who are demarcated as "enemies of righteousness." Military expenditures are on top of annual budgets of many nation-states, all in the name of "national defense and security." Global military expenditures have risen to $1.8 trillion a year (2018), with the United States spending around half of that amount,[19] overshadowing amounts spent for education, health care, and other projects meeting basic needs of the populace. Institutionalized ill will is also manifested in attitudes and actions based on discrimination the basis of religion, ethnic origin, gender, physical or mental ability, and other factors demarcating certain segments of the populace from others.

Institutionalized delusion is personified in the media, the key player "responsible for moulding our collective sense of self."[20] Major media outlets, having become mega-corporations themselves, are also "profit making

---

18. Loy, *The Great Awakening*; Loy, "Three Institutional Poisons."

19. https://www.sipri.org/media/press-release/2019/world-military-expenditure-grows-18-trillion-2018.

20. Loy, "Three Institutional Poisons," 6.

institutions whose bottom line is advertising revenue, (and whose) main concern has to do with whatever maximizes those profits."[21] The corporate media's concern in keeping this "bottom line" would sidetrack the various outlets from their mission of conveying the truth to the public, of the dissemination of news "without fear or favor."[22] Loy continues,

> It is never in their own interest to question the grip of consumerism. Thanks to clever advertisements, my son can learn to crave Nike shoes and Gap shirts without ever wondering about how they are made. I can satisfy my coffee and chocolate cravings without any awareness of the social conditions of the farmers who grow those commodities for me, and, even more disturbingly, without any consciousness of what is happening to the biosphere: global warming, disappearing rainforests, species extinction, and so forth.[23]

In the context of our globalized pluralistic society, where diversity has become the norm, and different views about ultimate reality (the sphere of religion), politics, economics, society, and human behavior are in an open market competing for adherents and allegiance of the populace, persons with a tribalistic mindset may be liable to fear, insecurity, and a loss of a sense of identity. They will turn to those specific media outlets that tend to reinforce their preconceived ideas or belief systems about society and about reality, and regard "those others" who hold other views with animosity and hostility.

One might object here that Loy is overly harsh in pointing to the media as the sole culprit in "institutional delusion" of the populace. This collective delusion is of course fostered and fed by the propensity of many of us to want to be left undisturbed and unperturbed in continuing to do the things we are used to do, and prefer not to be exposed to facts or scenarios that challenge us and upset us from our conventional ways of living our middle class lives. In fairness, there are a good number of initiatives from various sectors and small outlets that seek to provide more reliable and accurate informative reports about what is behind the scenes in our concrete world, and there are investigative journalists who risk lives and career to uncover sensitive issues and offer their reports in such outlets. So those who are earnest in finding out what is really going on should have the means of getting access to these sources of information, which may not appear in the popular and more lucrative media outlets.

21. Loy, "Three Institutional Poisons," 6.
22. Echoing a declared motto of the *New York Times*.
23. Loy, "Three Institutional Poisons," 6.

A Christian perspective would also shed light on our global dysfunction from a different angle. In Christian understanding, it is *human sinfulness*, understood as condition of separateness from God, the source and fount of our being and wellbeing, to which we can attribute the root cause of our communal dysfunction and dis-ease. This alienation from our source of being and wellbeing can be seen as including three levels. One is the alienation from our true self as created in the image of God, as mirroring God's goodness, truth, and beauty. In short, we have become a warped mirror that does not properly reflect that divine image we are endowed with by grace. This is what is meant when we speak of our "fallen humanity."

A second dimension is our alienation from our fellow human beings, from the human community, as we tend to hold of one another at arms-length, or regard our fellow humans as "other" to us. This kind of alienation is what breeds animosity, rivalry, competition, conflict among human beings. We tend to demarcate those who are "with us" or "for us," from those who are not, those who are therefore "against us." It is the tribalistic mentality that we have described above.

A third level of our separation is our alienation from the rest of creation, from the natural world, the Earth's ecosystem upon which we depend for our very life and sustenance. We have tended to regard the natural world as objects for human exploitation and subjugation, using our religious scriptures as justification. "Let them have dominion over the fish of the sea, over the fowl of the air, over the cattle, and over all the earth, and over every creeping thing that creepeth upon the earth."[24]

In the Christian view, it is these three levels of separation that lie behind the propensity of human beings to think, say, and do things detrimental and harmful to others, to the natural world, and to one's own self, and are thus the root cause of our dysfunctional state as individuals and as a global community.

Summarizing the above, we have explored how, from a Buddhist perspective, the tribalistic mentality of "us versus them" is based on an illusion of a self that is seen as separate from the world but, in reality, is intimately interconnected, a fundamental delusion which thereby begets greed and ill will. Transposed to the collective level, this illusory sense of self is what propels the institutional greed of the consumeristic, corporation-dependent global society; the institutional ill will personified in the military industrial complex and in the attitudes and actions that foster and

---

24. Genesis 1:26. This is the passage, and the historical effects it has had on the industrial revolution and aftermath, that has been pointed out in a well-cited article by Lynn White Jr., denouncing Christianity as the "culprit" behind the global ecological crisis. See White, "On the Historical Roots of our Ecologic Crisis," in *Science*.

foment discrimination based on religion, race/ethnicity, gender, ability, and other factors; and the institutional delusion promoted by corporate media, feeding the populace with news coverage and images with subtle messages that serve their interests in keeping their bottom line, rather than providing access to the facts and giving coverage of events and themes that really matter. The three poisons, in their personal and institutionalized manifestations, comprise the root causes of our global malaise and are behind the physical, structural, and ecological violence that destroys lives and threatens the very Earth's ecosystem.

From a Christian perspective, the tribalistic mentality is a consequence of our sinful human condition of being estranged from our Source—we have come to be alienated from our true selves made in God's image, from one another as brothers and sisters belonging to the same family deriving the same source of life and wellbeing from God, and from the rest of God's creation, given to us all for the glorification of our common source in God. This separation in these three levels is what drives us to attitudes, thoughts, words, and actions that individually and collectively tend to our own harm and eventual destruction, and cause the three levels of violence described above, characteristics of our global dis-ease.

In short, we return to where we began, in pinpointing the tribalistic mindset, seen from different religious perspectives, as behind the dis-eased world of violent extremism in which we are all enmeshed. In beholding all of this, one asks in earnest, "where is the hope?" Is there a way for us to find our way to a world that is less violent, less destructive, and more conducive to the well-being of all of us as fellow inhabitants of our beautiful and wondrous Earth, rendered vulnerable and threatened with destruction through our own human greed, ill will, and delusion?

Envisioning a Different World

The somber picture of our world as depicted above may make us feel powerless and weighed down to a state of impasse or paralysis. We need to step back, and engage in some imagining, some dreaming, to find our way out of this mess that we have made our world into.

John Lennon sang, "Imagine all the people living life in peace! . . . Imagine all the people sharing all the world!" Martin Luther King Jr. proclaimed, "I have a dream . . . ." We want to imagine a world that is different from our contemporary global society as depicted above. A world wherein no child dies of hunger or malnutrition or preventable causes, and whereby every precious human life born on this earth is given a viable opportunity and suitable conditions to live the fullness of that life. A world wherein human beings do not think, say, or do things harmful to one another, and no one has to die a violent death from actions perpetrated by their fellow human beings. A world wherein all the Earth's inhabitants live together in peace and harmony with one another. A world wherein our Earth's riches and bountiful gifts of nature are shared by and with all living beings. As the song goes, indeed, what a wonderful world this would be. For us mired in the reality of this world of violent extremism, is such a world possible at all?

In the scriptural texts of early Buddhism, there is a passage describing a person who has mastered the path of peace:

> This is what should be done by one who is skilled in goodness, and who knows the path of peace:
>
> Peaceful and calm and wise and skillful, not proud or demanding in nature.
>
> Let them not do the slightest thing that the wise would later reprove.
>
> Wishing: In gladness and in safety, May all beings be at ease.
>
> Whatever living beings there may be,
>
> whether they are weak or strong, omitting none,
>
> The great or the mighty, medium, short or small, the seen and the unseen,
>
> Those living near and far away, Those born and to-be-born—
>
> May all beings be at ease!
>
> Even as a mother protects with her life, her child, her only child,
>
> So with a boundless heart should one cherish all living beings;
>
> Radiating kindness over the entire world, spreading upwards to the skies,
>
> And downwards to the depths, Outwards and unbounded,
>
> Freed from hatred and ill-will.
>
> Whether standing or walking, seated or lying down
>
> Free from drowsiness, one should sustain this recollection.
>
> This is said to be the sublime abiding.[25]

In this passage, the "sublime abiding" is an English translation of a Sanskrit (and Pāli) term, *brahmavihāra*, which can also be rendered as

---

25. *Metta Sutta*, Scripture on Lovingkindness, from the *Sutta Nipāta*, in Habito, *Experiencing Buddhism*, 19.

"divine dwelling." Lovingkindness (*mettā*), as laid out in this passage, a heart which cherishes all living beings "as a mother . . . (toward) her only child," is one of the four features of the divine dwelling that mark the state of mind and heart of one who is "skilled in the path of peace," that is, who has awakened and who now lives in the light of that awakening. The other three are compassion (*karunā*), or a boundless heart with the capacity of bearing the suffering of all beings; sympathetic joy (*muditha*), a heart that rejoices with every joy of every being whoever they may be; and equanimity (*upekkhā*), a peaceful heart able to take things as they are with acceptance, humility, and gratitude.

The message here is that if everyone in the world were able to live in this way, as an awakened one, there would be no wars, no animosities or enmities, no unjust dealings, no exploitation, no violence. So here we are given a key to bringing about such a world of our hopes and dreams. It begins with every human being, taking stock of one's own life, and living out its potential in awakening to one's true self, embodying this awakening in a way of life suffused with lovingkindness, compassion, sympathetic joy, and equanimity.

The Second of the Four Ennobling Truths points to craving, which plays out in the three poisons of greed, ill will, and ignorance, as the root cause of the dis-eased condition of our human existence and of our global society. We imagine an overturning of this root cause, and are able to envision a different world. What kind of life, what kind of world would it be, to overturn craving, and realize *contentment?* What if greed could be converted into *generosity?* What if ill will could be converted to *goodwill?* What if delusion could be overturned and give way instead to the *wisdom of seeing things as they are?*

These are the features that come to be realized in a person who follows the way of the Buddha. It is not about a nirvana in the afterlife but a way of being that can be realized in this very human life of ours.

What would it be if all this could also be transposed and applied to the communal, institutional levels of our being? What would it take? These are questions calling on all of us who care about bringing about peace and harmony in our global community and sustainability in our Earth's ecosystem, who are called to address and cooperate with one another in tackling. These are challenges facing us on a major order, beginning with each and every one of us, and bringing us together into communities of spiritual practice and formation, for mutual support.

Turning to a Christian perspective, we are offered an invitation to enter into a different world, a different way of being, right here in this very context of our human life on Earth, in the Good News of Jesus Christ. A recurring theme of the message of Jesus is an invitation for a change of hearts and minds (*metanoia*) *now*: "The Reign of God is at hand!" (Matt 3:2). Those who profess to follow the way of Jesus begin by confessing their sinfulness, acknowledging their state of having been alienated from the image of God that is inherently their's from the start through grace; separated from their neighbor in living a self-centered life; separated from the rest of God's creation, in looking at creation as an object to be used and exploited for one's own self-centered purposes. To undergo a *metanoia* is to turn around from such a state of alienation from one's Source of life, and to reconnect with this Source. This entails reclaiming one's divine image, as mirroring the goodness and truth and beauty that is God's; reconnecting with one's neighbor, loving one's neighbor as one's own self; reconnecting with creation, receiving its gifts as a way of glorifying their Source, and becoming a faithful steward.

Above we have briefly examined Buddhist and Christian perspectives of a different world, visions of a different way of being right in this very world in which we continue to live as human beings. What these have in common is a point of conversion in a human being's experience. In the Buddhist story, from a way of life characterized by craving, driven by the three poisons of greed, ill will, and delusion, to a life that is now awakened and characterized by contentment, and subverting the three poisons into their opposites of generosity, goodwill, and wisdom. In the Christian story, from a life of separateness and alienation from God, and consequently from one's own self as created in the divine image, from other human beings, and from the natural world, through a *metanoia*, a turning to God, with the concomitant healing of the three levels of separation, that is, the reclaiming of one's divine image, reconnecting with one's neighbor now seen and loved as one's own self, and reconnecting with creation, with the natural world, in partnering toward the glorification of their common source in God.

What would it mean to transpose these conversions, from the individual, personal level, to the communal, institutional levels of our being? The challenge before us here is thus twofold: to bring about such a conversion on the individual, personal level of our being, and simultaneously (rather than subsequently, or consequently), to bring this also to the social, communal, institutional dimensions in which we live our human lives in this global society.

Buddhist, Jewish, and Christian resources cited above envision a different world, a world we are all called to help in birthing, through a conversion, a transformation in our way of seeing and way of being.

In *A More Beautiful World Our Hearts Know Is Possible*, Charles Eisenstein calls our attention to such a vision coming from the deepest longing that lies in all of us as human beings.

> I knew that millions were not supposed to be starving, that nuclear weapons were not supposed to be hanging over our heads, that the rainforests were not supposed to be shrinking, or the fish dying, or the condors and eagles disappearing. I could not accept the way the dominant narrative of my culture handled these things, as fragmentary problems to be solved, as unfortunate facts of life to be regretted, or as unmentionable taboo subjects to be ignored.[26]

Listening from the depths of his own being, reflecting and examining resources from history, sociology, psychology, philosophy, and yes, religion, though not in a sectarian but in a generic way, what Eisenstein offers is "a guide into a new story . . ." addressing readers and inviting them to be agents of transition, from the old story, to a new one that lays out "nothing less than a transformation in the experience of being alive . . . nothing less than a transformation of humanity's role on this earth."[27]

Eisenstein's vision begins with a description of the old story of human existence as Separation, which resonates with the above depictions of the tribalistic mentality, the "us versus them" attitude that has characterized our human existence that has brought us to our current malaise of rampant physical, structural, and ecological violence. As we see these destructive forces of violence hemming in around us, we acknowledge that we are now in the midst of a Breakdown from the society built on the old story.

The violent extremism manifesting itself on all fronts in our global society, erupting in mass migrations and surging of the refugee population of the world, the poverty and dehumanization of multitudes, and the ecological destruction that we are facing together, are indicators of this Breakdown. The story of Separation is no longer tenable as a way of living together, as a way of understanding our role on earth, and in the universe. We are facing either a path to utter devastation, or are being led to a transition to a new age. Eisenstein then describes what is now emerging as the new Story of Interbeing, ushering in an emerging Age of Reunion which overcomes and heals the Separation that is causing our current predicament.

He lays out some of the principles of this new story, this different world that our hearts know is possible. These include the principles

- that my being partakes of your being and that of all beings

- that, therefore, what we do to one another, we do to ourselves.

- that each of us has a unique and necessary gift to give to the world

26. Eisenstein, *A More Beautiful World*, 2.
27. Eisenstein, *A More Beautiful World*, 2.

- that the purpose of life is to express our gifts.

- that every act is significant, and has an effect on the cosmos.

- that we are fundamentally unseparated from each other, from all beings, and from the universe

- that every person we encounter and every experience we have mirrors something in ourselves

- that humanity is meant to join fully the tribe of all life on Earth, offering our uniquely human gifts toward the wellbeing and development of the whole

- that purpose, consciousness, and intelligence are innate properties of matter and the universe.[28]

Eisenstein's description of an emerging story of Interbeing, bringing about an Age of Reunion that would overcome the separation that is at the root of our current malaise, involves a personal and also necessarily a communal, societal, and institutional dimension.

How then are we to proceed in making this transition to this New World in the making? This is where spiritual practice and spiritual formation come in.

Spiritual Practice and Formation: Birthing a New World in the Making

What we can offer here is a bare outline that will take much more to lay out than what this essay allows. The question for us is, what kind of concrete practical steps can we take so we may become an agent of transition from the old story to the new? What can we do in practical terms to put behind us the story of Separation, which has brought about this world of violent extremism that we decry, and welcome and bring about a New World in the Making, one that will be marked by a healing of that separation and usher in world of peace and harmony among all of Earth's inhabitants, celebrating and living together under the principle of the mutual interdependence of all beings? How can we be agents who may activate the new story of Interbeing and its implications not only in our individual personal lives but also in our collective institutional lives, in the social, economic, political, and ecological dimensions of our being for our entire global community?

28. Eisenstein, *A More Beautiful World*, 15–16.

In Buddhist terms, how do we make the transition from a deluded, self-preoccupied way of being that is characterized by dis-ease and dysfunction, driven by craving that manifests itself in greed, ill will and delusion, to an awakened way of being marked by lovingkindness, compassion, sympathetic joy, and equanimity?

In Christian terms, what is involved in the *metanoia*, a total transformation of heart and mind, from a sinful mode of existence that thinks, says, and does things harmful to others and to oneself, marked by three degrees of separation (from one's true self as made in the image of God, from one's neighbor, and from the rest of Creation that is the natural habitat for all life), to a graced and redeemed way of life, reunified with God, the source of life in whose image one is created, reunited with one's neighbor, that is, all human beings as fellow partakers in the same divine life, and reconciled with Creation with whom one lives in harmony together in giving glory to God?

The key to all the above and the path we are being led to pursue is spiritual practice and spiritual formation. Referring back to our working definition of "the spiritual" spelled out in the beginning of this essay, this is an intentional and deliberate turn inward, connecting to the innermost core of our being, where we encounter the transcendent, the holy, and where we also discover our interconnectedness with one another.

This inward turn a person is drawn to may be occasioned by the dissatisfaction and disgust at the violence and destruction that characterizes our present world, generating a search for a different world, another way of being. For the Buddha, this inward turn was triggered by his rude awakening to the fact of *dukkha,* the suffering and dissatisfaction brought about by a way of life driven by craving, by greed, ill will, and delusion. For Christians, the realization of one's sinfulness, causing dissatisfaction and disgust with oneself as alienated from one's own divine image, from one's neighbor, and from the rest of creation, may be the occasion for the inward turn back to God.

Various religious traditions offer their own specific ways of cultivating and nurturing the spiritual realm in making this inward turn, based on their particular views and teachings on the problematic of the human condition, their understanding of ultimate reality and ultimate destiny, their prescriptive guidelines for the realization of that ultimate destiny, and the modes of social expression embodying their belief system.[29] There are also spiritual forms of practice offered from non-religious sources, such as from the Mindfulness Based Stress Reduction movement inspired

---

29. These are four key features of "religion" that figure in a working definition proposed by Streng, *Understanding Religious Life.*

by Buddhist meditative traditions, or some New Age varieties of spirituality that include meditative or contemplative practice. These can be taken on their own merit as resources for this inward turn described above, and individuals may find one or other suited to their own needs and particular angles of interest more than others.

Within the Christian tradition there are different schools of spiritual practice and cultivation issuing forth from our rich two thousand-year history, with their own particular approaches to and prescriptions for experiencing the holy and actualizing this in one's day to day life. We cannot go in detail into any one of these rich traditions, with their own particularities, but will simply lay out the bare bones of an approach to spiritual practice explicitly or implicitly contained in many existing traditions.

A recommended form of contemplative practice involves: (a) taking a posture conducive to stillness, (b) paying attention to the breath, and (c) allowing the mind to calm down and come to rest in the present moment.[30] One may begin by taking a few minutes on a daily basis, from five to ten, and then extending the time frame one gives to this practice in one's regular schedule, to half an hour, or more.[31] One may also enter into an intensive mode of this practice from time to time, going to a retreat center, for a weekend, a week, an entire month, with a groups, or by oneself in consultation with a spiritual guide, one's heart beckons.

When posture, attentive breathing, and calmed mind are in place, we are ready to plunge into the depths, into the silence. As we go further and further into the depths in this cultivation of stillness, at a ripe moment, when our mind is still, and our heart is open, what awaits is an experience, of touching, or being touched, and moved, by something or other we are not able to name, from that innermost core of our being. *This is an experience that takes us beyond the conventional dichotomy of subject-object perception, beyond the separation of "self" and "other."*

We may call this an "aha moment," a touch of the Holy, a glimpse of a new dimension of being that enters into our awareness. In such a moment or moments, *we are brought into an entirely different level of being*, and are

30. Various forms of meditative or contemplative practice, including Buddhist Insight meditation, Tibetan *Dzog Chen* practice, Zen, and also Transcendental Meditation, Passage Meditation, as well as Christian forms as Centering Prayer, or meditation or contemplation in the Carmelite tradition of St. John of the Cross or St. Teresa of Avila, and the Spiritual Exercises of St. Ignatius, are possible paths that may be taken in this regard. In examining these various forms, and in taking up any one of them, the threefold structure of posture, breathing, and calmed mind can be applied.

31. Prescriptive guidelines for dealing with and realigning an easily distracted, or "monkey" mind can be found in different books on meditation and/or contemplative practice.

enabled to see through the wall that separates "myself" and "the world," and overcome that separation. One way of describing this is precisely the activation of the capacity to bridge that gap that separates subject and object, "myself" versus "other selves." One enters a realm beyond such oppositional concepts as "us versus them," and realizes, in a singular and transformative moment, a oneness with all that exists, and awareness that embraces all: *You are that* (*Upanishads*); or, *Just this.* (Zen); or, "*Be still and know that I am God*" (Ps. 46:10).[32]

Those who are graced with such an experience may interpret it or articulate it in different ways, from the context of their religious background or belief system.[33] But the proof of the pudding is in the eating, as the saying goes, and the test of genuineness of such an experience is in whether and how the individuals reporting it make that turnaround, from a life of self-centered preoccupation, to one that has now found inner peace and acceptance with oneself and with the world. And further, such a person now looks at the world, and other persons around, no longer as "other" to oneself, but precisely as manifestations of one's own bigger Self, to whom one now aspires to give one's life in loving service.

Such a person is now someone able to hold the world in one's heart, place oneself in the shoes of everyone else, and think, say, and do things out of lovingkindness and compassion toward all, "as a mother, toward her only child." Someone who has been able to see through the utter destitution and untenability of a tribalistic mentality, and with an open heart be able to welcome and embrace those who had formerly been regarded as from "other tribes" now seen as inherently belonging to one's own. Such persons are now able to turn their lives around, seeking to live no longer for themselves, but in service of a wounded world that is wracked by violence from all sides, caused by the extremism that separates "us" against "them" that they have now been able to see through and overcome.

This turn-around, brought about by a transformative moment for which spiritual practice can lay the ground, is a momentous but also a momentary experience, a holy moment wherein the barrier between self and other is dissolved. It has also been reported to happen to individuals in

32. For an elucidation of spiritual practice along the lines described in this essay that focuses on the implications of this line from the Psalmist, see Habito, *Be Still and Know*.

33. In elucidating this further, I recommend an essay by Sarvepalli Radhakrishnan (1888–1975), writer and intellectual who served in public capacities including president of his country, India, and who wrote many books interpreting Hindu thought and religion for Westerners, "Personal Experience of God," originally published in Radhakrishnan and Moore, *A Sourcebook in Indian Philosophy*, and excerpted in Stewart, *Exploring the Philosophy of Religion*, 16–27.

spontaneous and random moments, without the individual's having had any intentional preparation for it.[34]

If that glimpse of "the whole" comes only in a fleeting moment, it can remain only as a memory of a wondrous experience to cherish, a past experience one can recount to others when occasion arises. It is through a follow up of *spiritual formation* that will foster, nurture, expand, deepen, render current and operative, and bring to maturation, that momentary glimpse of a world of non-separation. That fleeting experience of oneness, fleeting though it may have been, contains the power to usher in an entire life characterized by lovingkindness, compassion, sympathetic joy, and equanimity, in loving service to others, through intentional cultivation. Spiritual formation then is a lifelong process that will require ongoing attention and solicitude, bolstered by a rhythm of life that maintains and sustains spiritual practice as its constant and ever accessible source of nourishment.

In order to be effective not just in transforming individuals in the way they live their personal lives, but also to enable such individuals to become agents in the transformation of institutional structures that run our global society, such spiritual formation must also include skills for engagement in social, political, economic, ecological and other dimensions of our communal lives.[35] Expounding this matter in greater detail could easily take volumes, and there are a good number of works one could turn to deriving from different religious traditions, on how spirituality is conceived and how spiritual formation is conducted in those traditions.[36]

An established and widely accepted movement of spiritual practice and formation derives from *The Spiritual Exercises of St. Ignatius*.[37] This

---

34. As an example, see Shukman, *One Blade of Grass*.

35. There are a good number of published volumes on "socially engaged spirituality" from Buddhist, Christian, and multifaith perspectives that we can turn to for guidelines in this area. For some examples, Jon Sobrino, *Spirituality of Liberation: Toward Political Holiness*, Sallie King, *Socially Engaged Buddhism*, Gregory C. Stanzak, *Engaged Spirituality: Social Change and American Religion,* and a host of others. There are also educational institutions that offer certificates or Master's Degrees in Socially Engaged Spirituality, including Naropa University in Boulder, Colorado, Saybrook University in Pasadena, California, and others.

36. Here the multivolume series on World Spirituality published by Crossroads, including volumes on Jewish, Christian, Muslim, Hindu, Buddhist, New Age, Secular, and other forms of spirituality, is a valuable resource. See Green et al., *World Spirituality*.

37. Ignatius of Loyola started his career as a soldier and cavalier with worldly ambitions, was wounded during a battle, and during his time of recuperation, underwent a process of spiritual transformation, emerged as an earnest follower of Jesus, offered himself in service to the world of his day and time. He recorded his experiences during this process in notes that he later presented as a booklet to guide others in their spiritual journey. Ignatius went on to establish a religious order, the Society of Jesus, or

school of spirituality has had significant influence and continues to have wide appeal among Christians worldwide, and has recently come to be offered beyond Christian circles, for spiritual seekers of different backgrounds and religions.[38]

Taking practitioners through a process of purgation (or purification), illumination, and union, a significant point to highlight in the Ignatian (and Jesuit) school of spiritual practice and spiritual formation is that its eventual outcome is not a so-called "spiritualized being" with eyes toward heaven and feet above the earth, someone who has left behind concerns with this world and its travails, but is precisely one who has now been empowered and charged with a vision and mission to offer oneself to the world in service in different ways toward healing the world's woundedness. A person who has undergone the Ignatian Exercises and continues to be nourished by its practice in one's day to day life is called a *contemplative in action*, that is, one who is keenly attuned to the Divine in connecting to the spiritual core of one's being, and thus is inspired and empowered to engage oneself in the world as an instrument of God's healing action upon the world.

Transforming individuals from a life of self-preoccupation and self-glorification, confined in a tribalistic mentality, toward a life of selfless and loving service to the world, with a heart open to the world and to everyone, can be found in other traditions of spiritual practice and formation as well. For one, contemplative practice in the Zen tradition reveals similar key features and outcomes, and resonates closely with themes found in the Ignatian Spiritual Exercises.[39] There are other traditions of spiritual practice and formation that deserve further exploration and exposition along these lines, but this is now beyond the scope of this essay.

Conclusion

The question with which we began this essay is this: how can spiritual practice and spiritual formation be carried out, and taught, in ways that would not only alleviate and mitigate, but also possibly overcome and eliminate violent extremism and its effects upon human society and our Earth community as a whole?

---

the Jesuits, and spent the rest of his life guiding a band of men whom he initiated into his school of spiritual practice and formation.

38. Haight, *Christian Spirituality for Seekers*; Cline, *The World on Fire*; Habito, *Zen and the Spiritual Exercises*.

39. Habito, *Zen and the Spiritual Exercises*; *Healing Breath*.

This essay has offered observations on the state of our world belea-guered by violent extremism and examined its root causes in a tribalistic mentality and its related attitudes and factors (such as the "three poisons") that influence the thinking and behavior of people. It presented a vision of a different world than the one we have, and has offered steps in realizing that world through spiritual practice and formation.

An urgent task facing us from this point on is to widen the circle of those who have had a "rude awakening" as described above, and who acknowledge the impasse and untenability of our present violent world order. Not falling into a stance of denial, blame, or pessimism, such persons are thereby drawn to engage in spiritual practice and ongoing spiritual formation, not as an es-cape, but as an earnest search for inner resources that would enable them to be instruments in transforming themselves and the world.

The challenge and task are to overcome the tribalistic mentality that is at the root of all this, and take on a heart and mind that embraces the world, offering themselves in service toward its healing. Such persons who undergo an inner transformation and continue to deepen their connection to the innermost core of their being through ongoing spiritual formation will not keep their spirituality to their own private individual lives. As a natural outflow of that spiritual vision that they continue to nurture and uphold, they will precisely be drawn to engaging in the affairs of the world, working toward the transformation of society and its institutional struc-tures, toward mitigating, alleviating, eliminating the violence. As the circle of such persons grows and grows, and forms a critical mass in different parts of our global society, a New World in the Making, "a more beautiful world our hearts know is possible" is bound to emerge on the horizon.

Bibliography

Berger, J. M. *Extremism.* Essential Knowledge Series. Boston: MIT Press, 2018.

Cline, Erin. *The World on Fire: Sharing the Ignatian Exercises with Other Religions.* Washington, DC: Catholic University of America Press, 2018.

Eisenstein, Charles. *The More Beautiful World Our Hearts Know Is Possible.* Berkeley: North Atlantic, 2013.

Green, Arthur, et al. *World Spirituality: An Encyclopedic History of the Religious Quest.* New York: Crossroad, 1986–present.

Habito, Ruben L.F. *Experiencing Buddhism: Ways of Wisdom and Compassion.* Mary-knoll, NY: Orbis, 2005.

———. *Healing Breath: Zen for Christians and Buddhists in a Wounded World.* Boston: Wisdom, 2006.

———. *Zen and the Spiritual Exercises: Paths of Awakening and Transformation.* Mary-knoll, NY: Orbis, 2013.

Haight, Roger. *Be Still and Know: Zen and the Bible*. Maryknoll, NY: Orbis, 2017.

———. *Christian Spirituality for Seekers: Reflections on the Spiritual Exercises of Ignatius of Loyola*. Maryknoll, NY: Orbis, 2018.

King, Sallie B. *Socially Engaged Buddhism*. Dimensions of Asian Spirituality. Honolulu: University of Hawai'i Press, 2009.

Korten, David. *When Corporations Rule the World*. 3rd ed. Oakland: Berrett-Koehler, 2015.

Loy, David. *The Great Awakening: A Buddhist Social Theory*. Boston: Wisdom, 1997.

———. "The Three Institutional Poisons: Challenging Collective Greed, Ill will, and Delusion." *Insight Journal* (Winter 2006) 4–8. https://www.buddhistinquiry.org/article/the-three-institutional-poisons-challenging-collective-greed-ill-will-delusion.

Radhakrishnan, Sarvepalli, and Charles Moore. *A Source Book in Indian Philosophy*. Princeton: Princeton University Press, 2014.

Rozenblit, Bruce. *Us Against Them: How Tribalism Affects the Way We Think*. Kansas City, MO: Transcendent, 2008.

Shukman, Henry. *One Blade of Grass: Finding the Old Road of the Heart: A Zen Memoir*. Berkeley: Counterpoint, 2019.

Sobrino, Jon. *Spirituality of Liberation: Toward Political Holiness*. Translated by Robert R. Barr. Maryknoll, NY: Orbis, 1988.

Stanzak, Gregory C., *Engaged Spirituality: Social Change and American Religion*. New Brunswick, NJ: Rutgers University Press, 2006.

Stewart, David. *Exploring the Philosophy of Religion*. Englewood Cliffs, NJ: Prentice Hall, 2010.

Streng, Frederick J. *Understanding Religious Life*. Belmont, CA: Wadsworth, 1984.

White, Lynn, Jr. "On the Historic Roots of Our Ecologic Crisis." *Science*, 10 March 1967, vol. 155, no. 3767, 1203–7.

Wright, Robert. *Why Buddhism Is True: The Science and Philosophy of Meditation and Enlightenment*. New York: Simon & Schuster, 2017.

10

Local Peacebuilding in Response to Violent Extremism

—WENDY KROEKER

Introduction

The call for peacebuilding is as urgent as ever. The extent and severity of violence, whether it be state violence, or inter- and intra-state violence, revolutionary-nationalist violence, or what is termed violent extremism (VE) is alarming and fear inducing on many fronts. Local peacebuilding is a crucial dimension—alongside other interventions—of working toward peace in the contexts of "radical movements that employ violence."[1]

This chapter will examine the possibilities for local peacebuilding actors in a context of conflict and violence. In particular, it will begin with an exploration of the complexities of the current VE discourse and an examination of the deep structural dynamics that drive expressions of violence as direction-setting for solid contributions toward peacebuilding and community flourishing in contexts of conflict and violence.

The key theme of this chapter concerns the pivotal role of local peacebuilding efforts. The constructive entry point for religious and lay leaders will emerge from a place of understanding the context, stakeholders, and dimensions of violence and conflict in a given community impacted by violence. Understanding the complexities provides potential for developing competencies that will be helpful in leading congregations to become active in the work of building strong communities.

---

1. This is the preferred way of speaking of things now commonly dubbed "violent extremism" by Mindanao peacebuilder Maria Ida "Deng" Giguiento, in personal communication.

The particularity of the local context is an indispensable dimension in the examination of violent extremism. My reflections in this chapter draw from my direct connections to peacebuilding work and organizations in the Philippines, concentrated on the island of Mindanao. My family and I lived in the central region of the country for a number of years as I worked with a local peace center. This immersion into a particular community and set of peacebuilding actors frames my belief of the necessity for understanding contextual dynamics of conflict and violence toward peacebuilding efforts. My recent research has involved interviews with local peacebuilders seeking to find avenues for building resilience, and even flourishing, in a context where it appears that violence is rising. Despite that rise, many peacebuilders in the region struggle to name the parameters of the violence given the close-knit connections between communities and peoples and the understanding of the historical injustices that exist. From this standpoint, the chapter will examine relevance for ecclesial involvements—from the local context—and education interventions.

Assessing the Discourse of Violent Extremist (VE)

The language one employs in the pursuit of peace and justice must constantly be assessed. Though the terminology of VE and countering or preventing VE (CVE/PVE) is relatively recent, it has begun to dominate discourses in various settings, from states to civil society actors (educators, peacebuilders, for instance). A full genealogical analysis of this terminology still awaits.

Briefly, the terminology of VE and CVE came into prominence in the United States initially as the Bush administration's alternative terminology for terrorism and counterterrorism ("war on terrorism"), according to one security studies observer, as a "cosmetic replacement" for the latter terms.[2] For another observer, VE is thus "the latest, most-politically-correct label for (essentially Islamic) fundamentalism,"[3] even as other forms of violent extremism have been included within its orbit (e.g., white or green "extremism"). A broadening framework for this state-oriented, political use of CVE emerged in 2015, first at a "CVE summit" hosted by Barack Obama, with ministers from 70 countries in attendance, and then later that year in UN deliberations around the term "PVE." In both cases, the emphasis was on "softer" strategies to CVE and PVE (beyond militarized counterterrorism) which emphasized broad structural causes of VE in multiple contexts, and the outcome was the "UN Plan of Action to Prevent Violent Extremism,"

2. Frazer and Nünlist, "Concept of Countering Violent Extremism," 2.
3. Schomburg, "Countering Violent Extremism."

included among the UN's Strategic Development Goals (#16.a). The "concept" of this framework for what became increasingly termed CVE/PVE, however, had been emerging in the EU and within the UN since the mid 2000s in the aftermath of terrorist attacks.[4]

As a result of (a) this new predominant language in public discourse for a particular form of worrisome violence, (b) the broadening of the framework for CVE/PVE, and (c) government funding specifically tied to the language of CVE/PVE becoming available to non-state actors, those invested in the development, human rights, education, peacebuilding fields also increasingly became part of this broader discourse. But many active in these latter areas continue to be nervous about adopting the terminology and/or concept of CVE/PVE without careful qualification. Typical concerns revolve around (1) the close connection of CVE/PVE in some settings to traditional measures of counterterrorism which themselves can become drivers of VE; (2) concern about the stigmatization of communities labeled with VE, with CVE/PVE programs used as pretexts for surveillance operations; (3) CVE/PVE programs tending to be state-driven, often localizing the problem as simply those who oppose a state with some kind of violent means, and often forcing those involved in CVE/PVE initiatives to side with the government in any internal, intra-state conflict; (4) CVE/PVE programs tending to ignore the work of anti-violence local actors who may be considered to espouse "extreme" viewpoints outside the "mainstream"; and (5) the current structure of funding arrangements which make peacebuilding or development NGOs nervous about becoming "instrumentalized" in government-defined objectives.[5]

As a result, some peacebuilders seek to distance themselves from the prevailing discourse of VE and CVE/PVE, while others have resolved to work within the CVE framework, seeking to guide it in the best possible direction.[6] Some are more explicit in expressing concerns about the prevailing use itself of VE as the new key point of departure for peacebuilding work; others are willing to work with the terminology of VE, but argue that a new

4. For this overview, see Frazer and Nünlist, "Concept of Countering Violent Extremism," 1–3. The UN still maintains an "Office of Counterterrorism," which now includes PVE among its priorities; see https://www.un.org/counterterrorism.

5. See Frazer and Nünlist, "Concept of Countering Violent Extremism," 2–4; Brennan Center for Justice, "Why Countering"; Slachmuijlder, *Transforming Violent Extremism*, 4–6; Myers et al., *Peacebuilding Approaches*, 4–7; Ensor et al., *Peacebuilding and Violent Extremism*, 4–25.

6. Ensor et al., *Peacebuilding and Violent Extremism*, 9–21.

label and framework of "transforming and engaging VE" is needed, replacing the terminology of "countering and preventing VE."[7]

Inadequacies of terminology begins with "extremism" itself. While understandable as an effective (even if typically prejudicial) term in political discourse, it is a problematic term for social analysis and research. It is relativistic, context dependent (and subject to its own subjective or extreme use), and contrasts simply to the supposedly legitimate framework of those who might be "moderates, the majority, or the mainstream," but who are typically more precisely the "dominant." Those whose experience is only as a member of a majority framework or experience have a difficult time comprehending this. Martin Luther King Jr. illustrates the problem inherent in this term, retorting in his 1963 "Letter from a Birmingham Jail" after being labelled an "extremist": "So the question is not whether we will be extremist, but what kind of extremists we will be. Will we be extremists for hate, or will we be extremists for love? Will we be extremists for the preservation of injustice, or will we be extremists for the cause of justice?"[8]

In the context of VE discourse, some in the security studies sector have argued that the problem is "extremism" as such, and that the distinction between those embracing violence and nonviolence is simply fluid and incidental.[9] Others have argued that "extremism" as such is not the core issue; rather, the choice to engage in acts of violence and/or terror is the problem.[10] And the popular notion that "radicalization" is the conveyor belt that inevitably leads to VE runs against empirical evidence: many embracing what might be labeled "extreme" beliefs do not turn to violence, and terrorist violence is not always associated with "extreme" ideologies.[11] Peacebuilders are well aware that those labelled "extremists" often have lives intertwined with broader local community relationships and dynamics, making peacebuilding efforts challenging.

In this chapter, the term VE will nevertheless still be used, while recognizing that it emerged as a loose replacement for "terrorism" (itself notoriously difficult to define), and has since, given the imprecise and generalizing nature of definitions attached to it, resulted in a conceptual flattening of multiple forms of violence by association with the label. In the context of the protracted violent conflict in the Philippines, for instance, a judicious and

7. Austin and Giessmann, *Transformative Approaches*, iv–v; similarly Lederach, "Addressing Terrorism," 241–54.

8. King, "Letter," 4.

9. Schmid, "Violent and Non-Violent Extremism," 2; Alexander, "What Is Violent Extremism," 44.

10. Schomburg, "Countering Violent Extremism."

11. For instance, Brennan Center for Justice, "Why Countering Violent Extremism."

contextually appropriate use of the term VE would suit only a small amount of the varied forms of armed insurgency and social violence that have been the focus of broad-ranging peacebuilding efforts.[12]

Drivers of the Push toward VE

It is crucial to understand the drivers that push groups toward violence as the method for working with the issues causing injustices. The peacebuilding community must assist in developing a greater understanding of the causes of this violence and more localized responses to it. The decision to take up arms is never a simple decision, and is always a complex process that involves many actors caught in a wide range of conditions and evolving circumstances.[13] Groups espousing violence are also bound by families and communities, impacted by the problems plaguing many others.[14]

There are causes that are more proximate and those that are deeper. Given that the tools for understanding origins of violence and said causal factors are intertwined and layered—involving immediate, proximate, or ultimate causes—it is always difficult to state with certainty which causal factors are the most decisive. Yet, political violence and inequalities are key factors in the erosion of peaceful communities.

The causes of extreme violence are many and the theories of intrastate war or revolutionary insurgencies have highlighted differential treatment and group cultural identity,[15] crumbling nation states and economic inequalities,[16] lack of protection for land rights, poverty and myopic leaders,[17] strong religious adherence,[18] and the role of colonial

12. For a detailed description and analysis of "armed groups and human security efforts" in the Philippines, see Santos and Santos, *Primed and Purposeful*. For unease with the current labelling of VE, see also Cogoco-Guiam, "Terrorists are Made." Cogoco-Guiam is professor emeritus at Mindanao State University in General Santos City and former director of its Institute of Peace and Development in Mindanao. She is currently one of the convenors of the Independent Working Group of the Transitional Justice Dealing with the Past, which aims to organize a social movement to create a National Transitional Justice and Reconciliation Commission for the Bangsamoro in order to initiate the process of healing and reconciliation among conflict-affected communities in Mindanao.

13. Smith, *Trends and Causes*, 5.

14. Cogoco-Guiam, "Terrorists are Made."

15. Gurr, "Why Minorities Rebel."

16. Blin, "Armed Groups."

17. Blattman, "Civil War."

18. Toft, "Getting Religion?"

legacies[19] as significant factors in the research. Much of the research around conflict and violence causation has centered around the themes of greed and grievance.[20] Deep cultural clash—in contrast to a vision of an ideal community—is also a significant aspect to what drives groups to the use of extreme violence.

This analysis can be oversimplified, but to deny it is certainly problematic. These clashes arise in the modern world in contexts of many factors, such as migration, new group to group contact, or colonial legacies. The importance of understanding the perceptions of alienation, marginalization, deprivation or injustice, and viewing violent extremism in the context of revitalization movements that are nationalistic or framed as liberation, are crucial in regard to assessing the peacebuilding possibilities.

The question of why individuals become involved in actions of extreme violence is a complex one. Although there is no way to determine whether someone will engage in violence, there are factors—pushes and pulls—that can create vulnerabilities toward this likelihood.[21] The pushes toward engaging in violence emerge most significantly from structural conditions.[22] These can include issues of poverty, access to resources, grievances ensuing from circumstances of perceived injustices, or weak governance that build a sense of frustration and alienation. The pull factors involve the multiple ways in which friends and family, local leaders, or injustice-oriented messaging might convince an individual to violence as a course of action to meet the needs of marginalization. The following sections will explore some of the pushes toward violence in order to build the capacities of peacebuilders seeking to understand risk factors and build communication abilities toward reducing those impacts.

Root Causes

In 1835 Alexis de Tocqueville wrote that if one cleared away all of the secondary causes for upheavals in the world "you will almost always find the principle of inequality at the bottom."[23] Effective peacebuilding work is tied

19. Chalk, "Liberation Tigers."

20. Mac Ginty, *No War*, 69.

21. Much of the literature and current consultations are using the language of push and pull factors that in combination create dynamics of vulnerability toward extreme violence. See Holmer, "Countering Violent Extremism"; Slachmuijlder, *Transforming Violent Extremism*.

22. Holmer, "Countering Violent Extremism."

23. de Tocqueville, *Democracy in America*, 266.

to the ability to identify root causes. There are numerous lenses with which to understand the causes of political inequalities and violence. Societies organized so that segments of society are treated unequally and unjustly have strong possibilities of erupting into conflict, especially if the leaders are not perceived to represent all of the members of that society. Research in the area of causal factors requires depth of perception in order to add to the possibilities for re-framing dynamics constructively in contexts of protracted conflict. The analysis of root causes requires entry into the various "under bellies" that have shaped the current context.

Among my on-the-ground respondents in the Philippines, Bishop Efraim Tendero,[24] then Secretary-General of World Evangelical Alliance, stressed that:

> the Philippines is a nation where you see so much conflict. We are in so much unpeace. Then there's the lack of development. And, on the other hand, we also say that the lack of development is also part of the reason why there is also the unpeace situation. Therefore, if we want to really have an impact in our society, in our community, we need to be able to address these issues. So, what are the root causes of conflict? Why is there conflict? And how can we help provide both, let's say, an equitable and sustainable as well as a suitable peace for everyone?

He emphasized this in the context of analyzing the potential strategies for peacebuilding.

Many of the interviewees in my research commented on the need to seek out the root causes as part of the process for enabling justice and a sustainable peace to flourish. As conversations circled around the topic of structural dimensions of peace, emotions rose and they leaned forward to impress on me the vehemence they brought to their answers. Lyndee Prieto, a staff member of an international non-government organization and a peacebuilding activist from the context pronounced:

> We [Filipinos] have this history of decades of conflict and various experiences of exclusion and minority issues here. It's very important that at least peace is basically addressing the root causes of conflict because of this kind of reality that we have as a third world country. So, when you address that, you are able to put food on the table, you have jobs, respect members of the community, able to go to school, able to do a little bit

---

24. My peacebuilding research has focussed on interviewing local peacebuilding actors in the Philippines, primarily in the island of Mindanao; Kroeker, "Multidimensional Peacebuilding," 30.

of recreation. When you say this is our land and that land is shared, land is tilled by the farmers, crops and harvest being shared; and it doesn't go to international investors who are based in Makati [the business district of Manila] who are basically based around the world. So, the wealth should be, first and foremost, be shared with the people who offered their lives. It's addressing the root causes of conflict.[25]

Much of the causal research into intra-state extreme violence indicates that this is often initiated when there are significant asymmetries in terms of relative power.[26] The relative power that groups perceive themselves to have in large part determines their strategies and, of course, the possible avenues for peace.

The exploration of root causes requires the effort to uncover the injustices experienced. Mohagher Iqbal, one of the founders of the Moro Islamic Liberation Front (MILF), and active in the peace process between the government of the Philippines and the MILF, emphasizes the need to dig deep into the presenting issues:

> The absence of fighting does not necessarily mean that there is peace but my ultimate definition of peace is that peace is with justice. Unless there is justice then there can be no peace because peace and justice are parts of the same coin. The two faces of the coin: justice and peace. You cannot separate one from the other so it must go together. If you have peace, meaning there is no fighting, that is not peace. There has to be peace with justice.[27]

Given that the dominant push toward violence is structural at its core, it is a challenging task to redirect the energies of the marginalized communities. Years of mistrust easily eat away at any negotiated constructive steps if not based on a deeper analysis of the violence present. Peacebuilding interventions must exert the effort to discover the depths of frustrations for any movement forward.

Structural Dynamics and Critical Theory

An essential point of consideration in a discussion regarding the severity and role of violence is the impact of structural dynamics. Critical theorists concern themselves with politicizing social problems and seeking to

25. Kroeker, "Multidimensional Peacebuilding," 153.
26. Hultquist, "Power Parity," 623.
27. Kroeker, "Multidimensional Peacebuilding," 156.

place them within a social and historical context.[28] People are inextricably intwined within their social and geographic location. Elements and relationships within social structures are often hierarchical, dependent on attainment of power, and averse to change.[29] These dynamics shape the direction of responses to imbalanced structures.

Peace research scholar Johann Galtung argues that structural violence is built into the very fabric of our cultural and societal institutions. It focuses on the systematic ways in which regimes or states can institutionalize violence such as racism or sexism.[30] Social scientist Ralf Dahrendorf perceives social classes as the foundation for structural conflict. The specific ways in which a society is structured impacts the ways in which conflict is exhibited. He views power as the key determinant in the dynamics of a society, surmising that political forces are stronger than economic ones. If human beings are denied basic health care, education, or housing they become marginalized within a society. When structural imbalances are maintained through fear or coercive measures, they can go unchallenged for long periods of time. Counter to many other thinkers of his time, Dahrendorf believed that to consider it possible to counter structural imbalances with violence was only an illusion. His view was that the seat holders of power might change through violence but that the deeper issues would not be resolved. Change of a deeper nature must be sought.[31]

Structural tensions are warnings of likelihoods of outbreaks of violent conflict.[32] Thus, critical theory stresses the examination of culture. When people perceive that the injustice directed toward them is beyond what they can handle or accommodate, physical violence often erupts. In the peacebuilding field, Galtung was the first theorist to suggest that structural imbalances could be transformed through peacebuilding. Conflict transformation is an approach that seeks deep and more permanent levels of change with a bias toward systemic change as a way to accomplish re-structuring.[33] Structural inequalities must be analyzed to ascertain the sources and causes of the conflict for the purpose of determining appropriate points of change. Frequently the dynamics seem insurmountable since those benefitting from unjust structures will seek to maintain those structures.

28. Critical theorists such as the Frankfurt School, Karl Marx, Louis Althusser, Michel Foucault, and Edward Said have been influential in identifying structural dynamics as an essential aspect of social theory.

29. Botes, "Structural Transformation," 2008.

30. Jeong, *Peace and Conflict Studies*, 21.

31. Schellenberg, *Conflict Resolution*, 86.

32. Botes, "Structural Transformation," 362.

33. Botes, "Structural Transformation."

Culture, and Self-Determination, and Identity Theory

The analysis of violence impacted contexts would be inadequate if the impact of centuries-old colonial domination and the desire of a marginalized group for self-determination was ignored.[34] A discussion of culture and self-determination in light of identity theory is crucial to the analysis of this type of conflict dynamic. Group identity is awakened through a realization of social inequalities and marginalization.[35] Nationalism as an ideology asserts that nations or groups of people who share a common history and destiny have the right to a territory or state of their own. It is incompatible ideological convictions or a perception of some threat that can position a community for violence.

Identity theorists focus on the identity markers that create a sense of cohesion for a group, and points of demarcation in relation to the "other." Past experience, for example, is an important influence on a conflict's intractability. Groups may pass on the heritage of suffering and of enmities arising from historic traumatic events.[36] Through early identification with the key events of one's community, a sense of sameness develops and a commitment to the viewpoint of that group becomes solidified. The desire for an autonomous space can become a key driver for resistance movements. And when it comes to a point of identity and survival, people can go to great lengths to preserve their communities, even resorting to behavior that is outside of their usual standards.[37] Celia Cook-Huffman furthers the discussion in this area to argue that when deep-seated needs such as identity acknowledgement are not met, traditional conflict resolution methods might not be adequate for the situation.[38] The broad consensus in the peacebuilding field is that attention solely directed toward the proximate indicators will cause the deeper issues to simmer until points of violence and unrest.

Greed and Grievances

Unmet needs and lack of attention to structural injustices fuel the perception of communal grievances.[39] The peacebuilding field has recognized that

---

34. Jeong, "Structure," 182.

35. Jeong, *Peace and Conflict Studies*, 72.

36. Volkan, *Need to Have*.

37. Burton, *Conflict*, 36. Burton has contributed significant work on the connection between human needs, violence, peacebuilding.

38. Cook-Huffman, "Role of Identity in Conflict," 22.

39. Gurr, "Why Minorities Rebel," 188: "communal grievances have driven the most

key themes of violence in the intra-state category have emerged from what is termed "greed and grievances."[40] Ted Robert Gurr emphasizes that community grievances regarding unequal treatment in comparison with others, alongside a developed sense of cultural identity, "provide the essential bases for mobilization" and the ensuing tactics of the group's leaders.[41] Dan Smith's assessment is that economic factors are one of the greatest indicators of intra-state conflict.[42] These political and economic issues clearly matter if we want to tackle violent conflict. Yet, we do need to have caution regarding polarizing the conversation and thinking that it is indeed possible to determine the exact root cause of violent actions.

It is long-term and abiding inequities that can promote the high likelihood of moving toward serious conflict. Case studies suggest that group-based—or horizontal—inequalities can be deeply destabilizing.[43] Gurr's model is premised on the theory that protest and rebellion by communal groups are motivated both by deep-seated grievances about group status and by the political interests that they have for the group.[44] Grievances about differential and inequitable treatment and the pressure on the group's cultural identity frame the key bases for mobilization of the group as well as shaping the kinds of claims made by group leaders. If deep grievances exist and a strong sense of group identity is intact, along with the existence of coherent common interests, this will provide the materials necessary to fuel potentially violent actions when controls appear to have weakened. Groups that express strong demands for political rights typically have social and economic grievances based in economic disadvantages and cultural discrimination.

In addition to horizontal inequalities, the relative deprivation theory is one of the predominant theories linking a people's grievances with the conflicts that emerge. It focusses on existent vertical inequalities. Although there is debate in the field regarding the range of application for this theory, much of the work suggests that when the observation is made that a particular group is in a radically different situation than others the tensions rise considerably in that context.[45] Structural asymmetries make

---

persistent civil wars of the last 40 years."

40. Mac Ginty, *No War*, 69: "Academic debate on conflict causation [of civil wars] has crystallised around two [distinct] themes: greed and grievance."

41. Gurr, "Why Minorities Rebel," 167.

42. Smith, *Trends and Causes*, 6.

43. Stewart, *Horizontal Inequalities*; Brinkman, et al., "Addressing Horizontal Inequalities as Drivers of Conflict."

44. Gurr, "Why Minorities Rebel, 166–167.

45. See Cederman et al., "Horizontal Inequalities."

violent efforts much more likely and must be considered as a significant aspect of analysis of a violent context.

The potential drivers toward the use of extreme violence are numerous. But to ignore the uncomfortable analysis to ascertain and name these dynamics that push individuals and groups toward violence is to resist the collective responsibility to participate in building constructive communities.

The Framework of Peacebuilding

Given the complexities of violence, the work of envisioning constructive peacebuilding avenues is equally challenging. Yet, this is delicate and necessary work and will require a conflict sensitive lens. Conflict sensitive approaches seek to understand the conflict context and to operate constructively within that context.[46] Although a term utilized most by international development agencies in regard to the evaluation of projects in conflict zones, it has much to lend peace and conflict studies research with its attention to seeking processes that reduce violence, promote peace, and enhance the structure of relationships in the region. The key focus of a conflict sensitive approach is learning about the conflict context, acknowledging the differentials in each context, and responding to the factors that emerge.[47] The question emerges as to how intervention takes place in the context of extreme violence, without feeding into the conflict situation or exacerbating the already challenging dynamics. This section will explore the parameters for thinking about a vision for peace, the efforts required toward peacebuilding, and ways to frame potential entry points into the conflicted context.

Definitions of Peace

Just as violent extremism raises challenges for defining in ways constructive toward a helpful framework, so is the dilemma around defining peace. It might well be easy to assume that the term peace is clearly understood in the circles of church ministry and requires no further interrogation. Yet, as peacebuilding scholars assert, it is difficult to define what peace is without considering "who creates and promotes it and who peace is for."[48] Peace work is always situated in a particular time and context and, as such, can't be

---

46. Barbolet et al., "Utility and Dilemmas," 3.

47. Barbolet et al., "Utility and Dilemmas," 14.

48. Richmond, *Transformation of Peace*, 15.

"assumed to be monolithic and universal."[49] The contemplation of cultural, economic, political, and social conditions is required when considering the focus of the needed peace—this is the necessary work of deep analysis regarding the context in which we do our work. Without grappling with the parameters of peace, it is difficult to be visionary in our peace work.

Defining peace, on its own, as an isolated concept in the midst of conflict impacted communities is not assistive toward imagining transformative possibilities. Johan Galtung views peace as having two faces: negative peace and positive peace.[50] Negative peace, simply put, is the absence of violence. Positive peace, on the other hand, is oriented to social justice and the building of structures that enable society to flourish. Galtung's basic premise is that "[t]o work for peace is to work against violence" in its varied forms, from overt to covert, latent to manifest, and intra/inter-group to institutional.[51] Peace work requires analyzing the multiple drivers of the violence to next imagine potential actions for the prevention of that violence in order to achieve peace. Galtung is emphatic that the journey toward sustainable peace must be linked to the naming and analysis of violence.

Oliver P. Richmond observes that peace is a fluid, context based, value laden term and that many organizations expend very little effort in "conceptualizing the essential qualities of peace."[52] Is it possible to direct peacebuilding efforts without thinking about the kind of peace that is sought? John Paul Lederach explains that peace cannot be "just for a few" and that if peace is not pervasive it is only a mirage.[53] Religious leaders concerned about violence in their congregations and communities and seeking to enhance the local peace must consider how they define the terms of their work. In turn, this becomes the vision for the peace work.

In the face of fear created by violence it is crucial to consider the networks needed for a sustainable peace. Peace scholar Adam Curle's definition of peace emphasizes the importance of building relationships in contexts already impacted by violence. Curle views peace as "making changes to relationships so that they may be brought to a point where [flourishing] can occur."[54] Foundational to the work of achieving peace is the expectation that this entails working toward significant change in the dynamics of the relationships—addressing the drivers of violence—within the conflict situation. The

49. Richmond, *Transformation of Peace*, 16.

50. Galtung, "Violence, Peace," 167–91; Galtung, *Peace by Peaceful Means*.

51. Galtung et al, *Searching for Peace*, xiii.

52. Richmond, "Globalization of Responses," 136.

53. Lederach, *Building Peace*, 28.

54. Curle, *Making Peace*, 15.

work of peace requires a focus toward the transformation of relationships for the purpose of creating flourishing communities. Engagements seeking to be transformational can be recognized by an orientation toward seeking out the roots of the violence on both personal and structural levels.

Peacebuilding

When the stakes are high—when security seems paramount—clarity around what constitutes peacebuilding is also crucial. Lisa Schirch defines peacebuilding as that which "seeks to prevent, reduce, transform, and help people recover from violence in all forms."[55] Kevin Clements understands peacebuilding that holds a vision toward transformation as an engagement requiring significant "levels of collaboration," observing that societal stakeholders need to invest in being a vital part of the whole energies toward peace, along with development and conflict resolution experts and agencies.[56]

Peacebuilding is that work which utilizes all processes—and all potential stakeholders— in order to transform conflict and move toward peaceful relationships. Lederach describes this wide approach toward peacebuilding as a "dynamic social construct."[57] This new social construct has potential when the vision is inclusive and deep.

This deep work requires an investment in understanding the context of concern. Anthropologist Clifford Geertz argued that given the complexity of culture, the descriptions of people's interactions and lives needed to have sufficient depth. His term "thick description" came to mean the deliberate attention to the specifics of people's activities.[58] Thick descriptions emerge via intensive and focused examinations of communities and people's lives. When working with historical and entrenched conflict it is especially important to give sufficient attention to the details and deep values of the persons involved in the conflict. Peacebuilding plans must be holistically grounded in current realities, articulated by a range of voices and players, and be oriented toward building relationships.

Peacebuilding is complex work. As Kenneth Bush argues, it is a twofold project of "*deconstructing* the structures of violence and *constructing*

55. Schirch, *Little Book of Strategic Peacebuilding*, 9.

56. Clements, *Berghof Handbook for Conflict Transformation*, 14.

57. Lederach, *Building Peace*, 20.

58. Geertz, *Interpretation of Cultures*. Geertz's work is relevant to peacebuilding for the aid in examining complex community dynamics. He aimed to provide the social sciences with an understanding and appreciation of "thick description" as a way to urge an examination aware of its limits placed by one's own cultural cosmologies when attempting to offer insight into the cultures of other people.

the structures of peace."[59] The realization that these two aspects require simultaneous coordination is crucial. For peacebuilding work to have a chance of success, this axis provides the opportunity for a positive and constructive peace impact. The challenge for faith-based peacebuilding is to identify opportunities to "nurture the political, economic, and social spaces" and utilize various factors and resources that can assist in creating a positive peace.[60]

Multiple Entry Points and Horizontal-Vertical Integration in Peacebuilding

The work necessary toward a meaningful and transformative peace requires a critical peacebuilding lens that emphasizes analysis of underlying structures. Accordingly, maximizing efforts at different levels is key to building an integrative and sustainable peace.[61]

The work of peace scholar John Paul Lederach enhances this consideration. He approaches peacebuilding as work that necessitates an infrastructure that intertwines multiple dimensions. Lederach's "Pyramid of Actors" framework provides a springboard for identifying stakeholders and the directional aspect of their engagement with each other.[62] The peacebuilding space is vast and there are multiple roles for community actors and organizations to play in the areas of conflict prevention and peacebuilding. It is impossible for any one local group to address the immensity of societal needs and, thus, Lederach contends, it is important to identify the aspects necessary to nurture the assets that are already available and to partner with others to build a collaborative and sustainable approach. He identifies these potential engagement sectors for peacebuilding as: top, middle, and grassroots. Lederach's framework encourages vertical and horizontal networking between the different levels of stakeholders and organizations. With an integrated peacebuilding approach, coordination and stronger possibilities emerge for any given situation. Congregational efforts can be lodged for potential engagement in any of these levels and to work toward building assets vital for bridging work.

59. Bush, "Commodification," 25.

60. Bush, "Commodification," 25.

61. McCandless et al., "Vertical Integration," 1.

62. See Lederach, *Building Peace*, 39. For a visual representation and summary by Michelle Maise, Conflict Information Consortium, see online: http://www.beyondintractability.org/essay/hierarchical-intervention-levels.

Richmond asserts that Lederach has "made one of the most important theoretical contributions to the peacebuilding debate" by highlighting who local actors are and what the roles are for local actors toward
a particular "construction" of peace.[63] In large part it is Lederach's work
that has paved the way for the "development of multidimensional peace
operations" and diverse discourses on peacebuilding mechanisms.[64] This
diversity provides significant opportunities for imagining spaces for religious leaders as local actors.

What are the most effective strategic arenas? Lederach writes of an
alternative to the majority of counterterrorism approaches—a direction
oriented toward a transformative peace and local context efforts. Lederach
posits that since 9/11 what has emerged, in terms of countering terrorism, is
a divide "between two competing theories of change."[65] The theory that he
views as currently held as the base for the foreign terrorist list is that which
promotes effective change being a strategy served by isolation policies.

Lederach defines "isolation" as a framework for resisting extreme
violence that is enabled by identifying, targeting and limiting individuals
and groups who espouse violence defined as terrorism."[66] The focus is to
determine what actions or programs might limit the dynamics that enhance
a legitimate profile or bring about some aspect of success for the groups
utilizing violence as their method of change. Schirch's work on violent extremism has indicated that there is a link between violent extremism and
counterterrorism. For example, "drone warfare creates more terrorists than
it kills."[67] The isolation approach "has rarely clarified its formational theories of change" and it has had a profound impact in defining these arenas for
peacebuilding work as official and legal efforts.[68] The aim of this approach
certainly exudes intentionality toward reducing violence yet has challenges
in illuminating its desired results.

The second theory of change that Lederach denotes is engagement.
Looking toward a transformative peacebuilding theory, a theory of change
that embraces engagement would "require contact, consultation and
dialogue."[69] This theory espouses the importance of involving a broad range
of stakeholders—those outside of official processes and, as well, impacted

63. Richmond, *Transformation of Peace*, 103.
64. Richmond, *Transformation of Peace*, 105.
65. Lederach, "Addressing Terrorism," 241.
66. Lederach, "Addressing Terrorism," 241.
67. Schirch, *Ecology of Violent Extremism*, 8.
68. Lederach, "Addressing Terrorism," 241.
69. Lederach, "Addressing Terrorism," 241.

by the violence existent. The engagement theory of change takes a long view toward the reduction of violence and the transformation required toward building a sustainable peace.

The Turn to Local Peacebuilding

The best role for the peacebuilding community might well be to focus on building the capacities of the civil society as a way to reform the local context.[70] This section will turn to efforts to envision ways to practically address the theories and drivers regarding violent extremism in already conflict-impacted communities. Key to this, in addition to multiple other potential partners, is the engagement of local peacebuilders toward this vision. This means that no one-size-fits-all approach can alleviate the highly complex dimensions within the realm of impacted communities. Given the challenges—already expressed—regarding the framing of terms, local wisdom and memory is essential as part of efforts to build and rebuild flourishing communities.

Much of the work regarding the reduction of violent extremism emphasizes the vital need to include women and youth in the efforts.[71] Many of the pull efforts currently target these demographics and thus it is vital to understand the efforts made. And yet, it is women and youth who have exhibited inspiring examples of what it means to counter the violence emerging from within their communities.

Attention to economic and social empowerment is crucial in the face of frustration and marginalization emerging in many sectors and in many corners of the world. To shy away from naming the existent disparities will only serve to exacerbate the already painful perceptions of injustice. Allowing space to express the narratives of communities experiencing the pressures of violence as a solution is a crucial aspect of collective healing.

There are many entry points available to community and religious leaders living and working in disruptive contexts. And all of it is difficult work. It is important to think creatively, work across historical divides, view it as collective responsibility, and envision a path to inclusion and resiliency. One of many options to pursue is the possibilities that lie within educating for peace.

---

70. Holmer, "Countering Violent Extremism," 5–6.

71. See for instance Giscard d'Estaing, "Engaging Women"; Ensor et al, *Peacebuilding*, 26–27; UNDP, *Preventing Violent Extremism*, 5–6; UNESCO, *Teacher's Guide*, 14, 18, 32–33; UNESCO, *Preventing Violent Extremism*, 11–13, 43.

Educating toward Local Peacebuilding

What does it mean to consider teaching in a world of violent extremism? As discussed earlier, the conditions that nurture violence as a response to social injustices do not appear overnight. These dynamics are decades, even centuries, in the making. Choosing to engage in addressing the structural and contextual dimensions of violence and working towards a sustainably peaceful community requires broad-ranging strategies.

Peace education has emerged over the past few decades as a key tool of peacebuilding efforts in many violence-impacted contexts around the globe. As peacebuilding definitions have evolved and changed within the complex conflict landscapes and parties, the scope of peace education has been pushed and challenged.[72] In their work on peace education, Kenneth D. Bush and Diana Saltarelli argue that "the recognition that one size never fits all" is a crucial component to one's peace education work, especially in conflict impacted contexts.[73]

This necessitates an immersion into one's context for meaningful direction setting. In the face of challenges confronting violence-impacted communities, simplistic approaches for peacebuilding are inadequate. Education toward peacebuilding must commit to an upward-looking approach that builds on local experiences and wisdom of how to rebuild relationships. The present shift toward peace education that deliberately emphasizes building peace as an essential framework creates possibilities for imagining deep and structural change in complex conflict environments. This entails seeing peacebuilding education as rooted in relevant concrete ideas and activities. A commitment to this approach compels community leaders to consider cultural and political norms in the context and to engage in processes that give voice and control to local actors to ensure that the impacts connect to the context.

Ilan Gur-Ze'ev contends that it is not helpful for those in the peace education field to operate on the basis of the principle that "good will" defines the activities without the essential "conceptual work and reflection."[74]

---

72. Cheldelin et al., "Theory, Research"; Richmond and Franks, *Liberal Peace Transitions*; Richmon, "Globalization of Responses"; Richmond, *Transformation of Peace*; Aggestam and Björkdah, "Introduction"; Lederach, *Building Peace*; Jeong, *Peacebuilding*; Dibley, *Partnerships, Power and Peacebuilding*; Paffenholz, *Civil Society and Peacebuilding*; Schirch, "Strategic Peacebuilding"; Smith, "Strategic Framework for Peacebuilding," Zelizer and Rubenstein, "Introduction"; Clements, *Berghof Handbook for Conflict Transformation*; Chinkin and Charlesworth, "Building Women into Peace"; King and Matthews, "New Agenda for Peace"; Bush, "Commodification."

73. Bush and Saltarelli, *Two Faces of Education*, 25.

74. Gur-Ze'ev, "Philosophy of Peace Education," 315.

Working to reduce violence requires courageous contemplation of the causes and whole-hearted commitment for the long-term. For authors Michalinos Zembylas and Zvi Bekerman the peace education field must "reclaim its *criticality* [authors' emphasis]" toward questions of social justice, power, structural violence, and the ensuing responses to conflict in order to maintain the integrity of its educational endeavors and applicability in conflict situations.[75] Peace education needs to be about changed perceptions and ensuing action.

Helpful to this consideration of peace education as one avenue toward reducing violence is the work of Peter Pericles Trifonas and Bryan Wright who view this as needing to be about what they call a "curriculum of difference" that critically examines issues of peace and education in relation to questions of culture, identity, and meaning as needing to be at the forefront of our peace work.[76] Peace education holds potential as a vehicle to bring about multiple sectors for meaningful examination of perceptions and future visions. Paramount to this is that peace educators must become knowledgeable regarding the political and social contexts of the environment and be part of the local situation as an insider, or ally, to ensure that the educational effort is distinct and directly appropriate for the needs of the impacted community.

This is no ordinary approach to peace education. Bush and Saltarelli have articulated this approach to meeting the complex dynamics present in many conflict contexts as peacebuilding education, deliberately highlighting that the educational approach to working with a severity of violence needs, in its naming, to indicate that this is conscious work toward societal change.[77] Although skills training can enhance the existent capacities, it is vital to address the deeper, structural causes of the conflicts.[78] The task, then, of the educational context is not to homogenize but emerge from the "bottom-up" out of the proximate realities of the context.[79] This peacebuilding approach to education requires constructing and deconstructing relationships and narratives and an openness of the learning facilitator to examine their approach to the work.

The peacebuilding education approach requires depth. The *etic* and *emic* ethnographic research concepts from the field of anthropology can be helpful within this discussion of peace/peacebuilding education. Kevin Avruch

75. Zembylas and Bekerman, "Peace Education," 197.
76. Trifonas and Wright, "Introduction," 2.
77. Bush and Saltarelli, *Two Faces of Education*, 23.
78. Bush and Saltarelli, *Two Faces of Education*, 23.
79. Bush and Saltarelli, *Two Faces of Education*, 23.

describes the etic as that which yields the ability to "analyze distinctions."[80] The emic frame relies on capturing both "thick description and rich context" from the grassroots.[81] Peace is inextricably tied to ideas about sacred values, time-honored institutions, exemplary individuals, and ideal ways of handling differences within a context of shared community."[82] Peacebuilding education that emerges from the bottom-up frame—that is, from within the community—has the ability to transcend the trappings of the traditional and move toward essential linkages and change. Thick descriptions emerge via intensive and focused examinations of communities and people's lives. When working with historical and entrenched conflict it is especially important to give sufficient attention to the details and deep values of the persons involved in the conflict. Thick description techniques focus on this type of attention. These thick descriptions are the result of significant work and time spent in the context. The exploration of hidden layers will provide additional, and rich, information for the educational task.

Peace education design that is committed to the deep exploration of narratives and the courage to demonstrate solidarity with peoples traumatized by violence and oppressive legacies can enable constructive imaginations to emerge and participate with local peoples in these efforts. Approaches that consider the complexity of histories of political violence, power inequalities, colonial legacies, and trauma while, at the same time, contemplating particular social contexts and participants, will have the possibility of creating constructive opportunities for meaningful change in times of significant social dilemmas.

The non-government organization Muflehun created a peacebuilding workshop entitled ViralPeace.[83] This workshop was designed specifically for youth with the potential to be influencers in their communities to "learn strategies to push back against hate, extremism, and violence."[84] Key to this workshop was the capacity building toward learning to identify the "narratives that are used to incite hate and manipulate people toward violence" and to be able to design campaigns that could constructively serve their communities.[85]

The educational component to reducing violence extremism must lodge itself in the identification of the conditions that initiated the

80. Avruch, *Culture and Conflict Resolution*, 64.
81. Avruch, *Culture and Conflict Resolution*, 68.
82. Funk and Said, "Localizing Peace," 109.
83. Khan and Ansari, "Countering Violent Extremism Framework," 197–229.
84. Khan and Ansari, "Countering Violent Extremism Framework," 204.
85. Khan and Ansari, "Countering Violent Extremism Framework," 204.

vulnerability—namely, the drivers—in order to diminish the need for extremist responses.[86] Work within these deep spaces is crucial in the face of colonial legacies and the need to analyze dynamics of power. Sandra L. Bloom's work emphasizes the consistent and long-term work required to create safe spaces.[87] This emphasizes the crucial need for peacebuilding education to expand potential responses to conflict and violence. Religious leaders, attentive to context, become significant partners for constructive community building.

Conclusion

For leaders, thinking through how to navigate these complex arenas of people's lives need to ensure that they are willing to engage in the important questions surrounding people's lives.[88] One of the most useful directions is that of exposing the structural dynamics of relationships and the impacts that these structures have on the everyday dimensions of life. I find Lederach's discussion of the moral imagination as the "capacity to imagine something rooted in the challenges of the real world yet capable of giving birth to that which does not yet exist" a fitting and liberating challenge in the face of the obstacles faced in many communities.[89] This urges the imperative to think through the realities of what one already knows combined with the encouragement to move ahead, all the while considering the impacts of power in the shape of colonialism, trauma, and political inequalities. If one is rooted in the challenges facing a real situation, one's imagination can assist in provoking the creativity to move beyond the current reality and cultivate alternatives.

Bibliography

Aggestam, Karin and Annika Björkdahl. "Introduction." In *Rethinking Peacebuilding: The Quest for Just Peace in the Middle East and the Western Balkans*, edited by Karin Aggestam and Annika Björkdahl, 1–16. New York: Routledge, 2013.

86. Khan and Ansari, "Countering Violent Extremism Framework," 204.

87. Bloom, "Commitment to Nonviolence." Her model focuses on assisting people who have experienced deep trauma.

88. Tickner, "What Is Your Research Program," 5. As a feminist researcher, she argues that the "questions that are asked—or, more importantly, those that are not asked—are as determinative of the adequacy of the project as any answers that we can discover."

89. Lederach, *Moral Imagination*, 29.

Alexander, Audrey. "What is Violent Extremism?" In *Linking Security of Women and Security of States*, 42–45. Futures Without Violence, Policymaker Blueprint, May 2017. https://www.futureswithoutviolence.org/wp-content/uploads/FWV_blueprint_Final_web.pdf

Austin, Beatrix and Hans J. Giessmann, eds. *Transformative Approaches to Violent Extremism*. Berlin: Berghof Handbook Dialogue Series No. 13. Berlin: Berghof Foundation, 2018.

Avruch, Kevin. *Culture and Conflict Resolution*. Washington, DC: United States Institute of Peace Press, 1998.

Barbolet, Adam, et al. "The Utility and Dilemmas of Conflict Sensitivity." Berlin: Berghof Research Center for Constructive Conflict Management, 2005.

Blattman, Christopher and Edward Miguel. "Civil War." *Journal of Economic Literature* 48/1 (2010) 3–57.

Blin, Arnaud. "Armed Groups and Intra-State Conflicts: The Dawn of a New Era?" *International Review of the Red Cross* 93/882 (2011) 287–310.

Bloom, Sandra L. "Commitment to Nonviolence." The Sanctuary Model website. Online: http://sanctuaryweb.com/TheSanctuaryModel/THESANCTUARYMODEL FOURPILLARS/Pillar2SharedValues/CommitmenttoNonviolence.aspx

Botes, J. M. "Structural Transformation." In *Conflict*, 2nd edition, edited by Sandra Cheldelin et al, 358–379. New York: Continuum, 2008.

Brennan Center for Justice. "Why Countering Violent Extremism Programs are Bad Policy." Published Online, September 9, 2019: https://www.brennancenter.org/our-work/research-reports/why-countering-violent-extremism-programs-are-bad-policy.

Brinkman, Henk-Jan, et al. "Addressing Horizontal Inequalities as Drivers of Conflict." Presented at Addressing Inequalities: The Heart of the Post-2015 Development Agenda and the Future We Want for All, Global Thematic Consultation, February 2013.

Burton, John. *Conflict: Resolution and Provention*. New York, NY: St. Martin's, 1990.

Bush, Kenneth. "Commodification, Compartmentalization, and Militarization of Peacebuilding." In *Building Sustainable Peace*, edited by Tom Keating and Andy W. Knight, 23–46. Edmonton: University of Alberta Press, 2004.

Bush, Kenneth D., and Diana Saltarelli. *The Two Faces of Education in Ethnic Conflict: Towards a Peacebuilding Education for Children*. Florence, Italy: UNICEF, Innocenti Research Centre, 2000.

Cederman, Lars-Erik, et al. "Horizontal Inequalities and Ethnonationalist Civil War: A Global Comparison." *American Political Science Review* 105/3 (2011) 478–495.

Chalk, Peter. "The Liberation Tigers of Tamil Eelam Insurgency in Sri Lanka." In *Ethnic Conflict and Secessionism in South and Southeast Asia: Causes, Dynamics, Solutions*, edited by R. Ganguly and I. Macduff, 128–165. Thousand Oaks, CA: Sage, 2003.

Cheldelin, Sandra, et al. "Theory, Research, and Practice." In *Conflict*, 2nd edition, edited by Sandra Cheldelin et al., 9–38. New York: Continuum, 2008.

Chinkin, Christine & Hilary Charlesworth. "Building Women into Peace: The International Legal Framework." *Third World Quarterly* 27 (2006) 937–957.

Clements, Kevin. *Berghof Handbook for Conflict Transformation: Towards Conflict Transformation and a Just Peace*. Vol. 6. Berlin: Berghof Research Center for Constructive Conflict Management, 2004.

Cogoco-Guiam, Rufa. "Terrorists are Made, Not Born." *Philippine Daily Inquirer.* September 20, 2018. Online: https://opinion.inquirer.net/110403/terrorists-made-not-born.

Cook-Huffman, Celia. "The Role of Identity in Conflict." In *Handbook of Conflict Analysis and Resolution,* edited by Dennis J. D. Sandole et al., 19–31. London and New York: Routledge, 2008.

Curle, Adam. *Making Peace.* London: Tavistock, 1971.

de Tocqueville, Alexis. [1835] *Democracy in America.* Translated and edited by Phillips Bradley. New York: Vintage, 1954.

Dibley, Thushara. *Partnerships, Power and Peacebuilding: NGOs as Agents of Peace in Aceh and Timor-Leste.* New York: Palgrave Macmillan, 2014.

Ensor, Marisa O., et al. *Peacebuilding and Violent Extremism.* London/Washington, D.C.: Peace Direct, 2017. Online: https://www.peacedirect.org/us/publications/full-report-peacebuilding-violent-extremism/.

Frazer, Owen and Christian Nünlist. "The Concept of Countering Violent Extremism." In *Center for Security Studies Analyses in Security Policy,* No. 183. Zurich: Center for Security Studies, December 2015.

Funk, Nathan C. and Abdul Aziz Said. "Localizing Peace: An Agenda for Sustainable Peacebuilding." *Peace and Conflict Studies,* 17/1 (2010) 101–143.

Galtung, Johan. "Violence, Peace and Peace Research." *Journal of Peace Research* 6/3 (1969) 167–191.

———. *Peace by Peaceful Means: Peace and Conflict, Development and Civili-zation.* Oslo: International Peace Research Institute, 1996.

Galtung, Johan, et al. *Searching for Peace: The Road to TRANSCEND.* London: Pluto, 2000.

Geertz, Clifford. *The Interpretation of Cultures: Selected Essays.* New York: Basic Books, 1973.

Giscard d'Estaing, Sophie. "Engaging Women in Countering Violent Extremism: Avoiding Instrumentalisation and Furthering Agency." *Gender & Development* 25 (2017) 103–18.

Gurr, Ted Robert. "Why Minorities Rebel: A Global Analysis of Communal Mobilization and Conflict Since 1945." *International Political Science Review/ Revue internationale de science politique* 14 (1993) 161–201.

Gur-Ze'ev, I. "Philosophy of Peace Education in a Postmodern Era." *Educational Theory* 51/3 (2001) 315–36.

Holmer, Georgia. "Countering Violent Extremism: A Peacebuilding Perspective." *United States Institute of Peace Special Report* 336. Washington, D.C.: USIP, September 2013. Online: https://www.usip.org/sites/default/files/SR336-Countering%20Violent%20Extremism-A%20Peacebuilding%20Perspective.pdf.

Hultquist, Philip. "Power Parity and Peace? The Role of Relative Power in Civil War Settlement." *Journal of Peace Research* 50/5 (2013) 623–34.

Jeong, Ho-Won. *Peace and Conflict Studies: An Introduction.* Aldershot: Ashgate, 2000.

———. *Peacebuilding in Postconflict Societies: Strategy and Process.* Boulder: Lynne Rienner, 2005.

———. "Structure." In *Conflict,* 2nd edition, edited by Sandra Cheldelin et al, 181–94. New York: Continuum, 2008.

Khan, Humera, and Adnan Ansari. "Countering Violent Extremism Framework." In *The Ecology of Violent Extremism*, edited by Lisa Schirch, 197-209. New York: Rowman & Littlefield, 2018.

King, Elisabeth, and Robert O. Matthews. "A New Agenda for Peace: 20 Years Later." *International Journal* 67 (2012) 275–93.

King, Martin Luther, Jr. "Letter from Birmingham Jail." 1963. Online: https://web.cn.edu/kwheeler/documents/Letter_Birmingham_Jail.pdf.

Kroeker, Wendy. *Multidimensional Peacebuilding: Local Actors in the Philippine Context*. Lanham, Maryland: Lexington, 2020.

Lederach, John Paul. *Building Peace: Sustainable Reconciliation in Divided Societies*. Washington, DC: United States Institute of Peace Press, 1997.

———. *The Moral Imagination: The Art and Soul of Building Peace*. Oxford: Oxford University Press, 2005.

Lederach, John Paul. "Addressing Terrorism: A Theory of Change Approach" In *The Ecology of Violent Extremism*, edited by Lisa Schirch, 241–54. New York: Rowman & Littlefield, 2018.

Mac Ginty, Roger. *No War, No Peace: The Rejuvenation of Stalled Peace Processes and Peace Accords*. New York: Palgrave Macmillan, 2006.

McCandless, Erin, et al. "Vertical Integration: A Dynamic Practice Promoting Transformative Peacebuilding." *Journal of Peacebuilding & Development* 10 (2015) 1–9.

Myers, Emily, and Elizabeth Hume, eds. *Peacebuilding Approaches to Preventing and Countering Violent Extremism*. Washington, D.C.: Alliance for Peacebuilding, 2018. Online: https://www.allianceforpeacebuilding.org/afp-publications/peacebuilding-approaches-to-4-2018?rq=peacebuilding%20approaches%20to%20preventing%20and%20countering

Paffenholz, Thania, ed. *Civil Society and Peacebuilding: A Critical Assessment*. Boulder: Rienner, 2010.

Richmond, Oliver P. "The Globalization of Responses to Conflict and the Peacebuilding Consensus." *Cooperation and Conflict* 39/2 (2004) 129–50.

Richmond, Oliver P. and Jason Franks. *Liberal Peace Transitions: Between Statebuilding and Peacebuilding*. Edinburgh: Edinburgh University Press, 2009.

Richmond, Oliver P. *The Transformation of Peace*. New York: Palgrave Macmillan, 2005.

Santos, Soliman M., Jr., and Paz Verdades M. Santos. *Primed and Purposeful: Armed Groups and Human Security Efforts in the Philippines*. Joint Publication: Quezon City, Philippines: South-South Network for Non-State Armed Group Engagement; and Geneva: Small Arms Survey, 2010. Online: http://www.smallarmssurvey.org/fileadmin/docs/D-Book-series/book-12-Philippines/SAS-Armed-Groups-Human-Security-Efforts-Philippines.pdf.

Schellenberg, J. A. *Conflict Resolution: Conflict, Theory and Practice*. Albany: State University of New York Press, 1996.

Schirch, Lisa. *The Little Book of Strategic Peacebuilding*. Intercourse, PA: Good Books, 2005.

Schirch, Lisa. "Strategic Peacebuilding—State of the Field." Peace Prints. *South Asian Journal of Peacebuilding* 1/1 (2008) 1-17. Online: http://wiscomp.org/peaceprints/peaceprints.php?pid=1.

Schirch, Lisa, ed. *The Ecology of Violent Extremism: Perspectives on Peacebuilding and Human Security*. Lanham, MD: Rowman & Littlefield, 2018.

Schmid, Alex P. "Violent and Non-Violent Extremism: Two Sides of the Same Coin?" International Centre for Counter-Terrorism Research Paper. The Hague: ICCT, May 2014. Online: https://www.icct.nl/download/file/ICCT-Schmid-Violent-Non-Violent-Extremism-May-2014.pdf.

Schomburg, William. "Countering Violent Extremism: Gimmick or Solution?" Humanity in Action USA, October 2016. No Pages. Online: https://www.humanityinaction.org/knowledge_detail/countering-violent-extremism-gimmick-or-solution/.

Slachmuijlder, L. *Transforming Violent Extremism: A Peacebuilder's Guide.* Washington, D.C.: Search for Common Ground, 2017. Online: https://www.sfcg.org/transforming-violent-extremism-peacebuilders-guide/.

Smith, Dan. "Towards a Strategic Framework for Peacebuilding: Getting Their Act Together." Overview report of the Joint Utstein Study of Peacebuilding. Oslo: PRIO —International Peace Research Institute, 2004. Online: https://www.regjeringen.no/globalassets/upload/.../210673-rapp104.pdf.

Smith, Dan. *Trends and Causes of Armed Conflict.* Edited Version. Berlin: Berghof Research Center for Constructive Conflict Management, 2004.

Stewart, Frances. *Horizontal Inequalities: A Neglected Dimension of Development.* Helsinki: United Nations University/World Institute for Development Economics Research, 2001. Online: https://www.wider.unu.edu/publication/horizontal-inequality

Tickner, J. Ann. "What Is Your Research Program? Some Feminist Answers to International Relations Methodological Questions." *International Studies Quarterly* 49/1 (2005) 1–21.

Toft, Monica Duffy. "Getting Religion?: The Puzzling Case of Islam and Civil War." *International Security* 31/4 (2007) 97–131.

Trifonas, Peter Pericles and Bryan Wright. "Introduction." In *Critical Issues in Peace and Education*, edited by Peter Pericles Trifonas and Bryan Wright, 1–7. New York: Routledge, 2011.

UNDP. *Preventing Violent Extremism through Promoting Inclusive Development, Tolerance and Respect for Diversity.* New York: UNDP, 2016.

UNESCO. *Teacher's Guide on the Prevention of Violent Extremism.* Paris: UNESCO, 2016.

UNESCO. *Preventing Violent Extremism through Education: A Guide for Policy-Makers.* Paris: UNESCO, 2017.

Volkan, Vamik. *The Need to Have Enemies and Allies: From Clinical Practice to International Relationships.* New York: Jason Aronson, 1988.

Zelizer, Craig, and Robert A. Rubenstein. "Introduction." In *Building Peace: Practical Reflections from the Field*, edited by Craig Zelizer and Robert A. Rubenstein, 1–15. Sterling, VA: Kumarian, 2009.

Zembylas, Michalinos and Zvi Bekerman. "Peace Education in the Present: Dismantling and Reconstructing Some Fundamental Theoretical Premises." *Journal of Peace Education* 10/2 (2013) 197–214.

11

Threshold Concepts in Teaching Islam

An Exploration of Pedagogical Content Knowledge for Jihad and War

—MUALLA SELÇUK

T hreshold concepts often address troublesome knowledge with lack of organizing principles, and they cannot easily be accommodated within one's existing meaning frame. Although they are difficult to understand, when taught properly, threshold concepts can be gateways to new ways of viewing things and interpreting subjects. In this chapter the subjects of jihad and war are considered as threshold concepts in Islamic education. The chapter aims to propose a framework for pedagogical content knowledge within which teachers may advance their own reflective practice and empower their students to make meaningful connections between the message of the Qur'an and life situations. Broadly, these fall into three parts.

The first part sets out some educational and methodological considerations on understanding the Qur'an as the primary source in Islamic religious education. It consists of the conceptions, the preconceptions, and the patterns of religious commitments that students of different backgrounds bring with them to learning. What is the prevailing understanding of the Qur'an? And how does the Qur'an define itself? Such a consideration will give insight into the key role of the Qur'an in the formation of religious thought for Muslims, historically and today.

The second part offers a critical analysis of the verses of the Qur'an related to jihad and war, focusing on the relationship among the knowledge of its first addressee, life situations, time period, historical and cultural settings, and the revealed text. The question of what is textual and what is contextual—inspired by recent developments in academic theological discussions amongst Muslim scholars—will be at the center of the analysis. The discussion here is to show the profound effect on the verses of the Qur'an made by the context.

The third part examines the key components of the role of the teacher in framing pedagogical content to overcome the barriers in their students' understanding. To achieve this aim, it is important to make clear whether learning activities and method of assessments are actually in line with the most important outcomes advocated by public schools in teaching religion. Such sensitivity by a teacher would be one of the crucial aspects of teaching threshold concepts in religious education. Therefore, a teaching and learning model coined Conceptual Clarity Model (CCM), developed by the author, will be presented to assist teachers of Islam in bringing content and pedagogy together for personal growth and promoting community cohesion in a climate where extremism is an ever-present threat.

Introduction

My aim in this chapter is twofold. First, I wish to suggest teaching jihad and war as the "threshold concepts," as Meyer and Land have termed.[1] The core question of the chapter would then be how can we teach jihad and war to our students in a way that prevents narrow and sometimes violent extremism and helps them maintain loyalty to their faith while being open and respectful to others? As a result, my second suggestion is that the question of how best to teach these concepts is intimately related to the question of how best to develop with the students an understanding of the nature of the Qur'an. The contribution which religious education might make to peace education cannot be discussed without entering into the hermeneutical circle of scripture and violence, since the sacred text can be seen as offering justification for violence. The idea of "scriptural violence" considers violence that is based upon sacred books of a religious tradition and examines the ways in which those texts can be seen as offering a mandate for violence and conflict.[2] The task that emerges here for education requires an inner renewal of understanding the text that enables people to exercise their faith responsibly. The link between religious texts and violence can only be broken by a considerable examination of the self-understanding of the text and its meaning for believers. In establishing this twofold aim, I turn first to a theoretical consideration of the role of threshold concepts in teaching Islam, in particular to the role of the

1. See Meyer and Land, eds., *Overcoming Barriers*.
2. See, for example, Selengut, *Sacred Fury*.

representation of the Qur'an in education. Second, I focus on conceptual clarity, a model that teachers of religion might use to enable students to master such concepts in a learning context and have a better understanding of the message of the Qur'an. It should be pointed out here that one of the elements I will present is the importance of conceptual clarity that requires the teacher to be invested in the exploration of the content to assist students in crossing the threshold of jihad and war. Specifically, I delineate two pedagogical stages in the student's achievement of threshold concept mastery—reflection on the current situation and reflection on the relationship between the text and the context. In the service of facilitating both, I prefer the use of questions as a source of education. In conclusion, I highlight what might be termed an educational consideration of using the idea of the universal message of the Qur'an which, if ignored, could inhibit students' learning. Encountering the universal message of the text within its historical context works as one of the key components for the teachers to provide students with a pedagogical content knowledge so that students can respond creatively to the challenges of violent extremism.

The Role of Threshold Concept in Teaching Jihad and War

A threshold concept is defined as a transformative gateway, possessing certain properties that lead to a new understanding. It represents a transformed way of understanding or interpreting or viewing something without which the learner cannot progress. As a consequence of comprehending, a threshold concept may thus be a transformed internal view of subject matter, subject landscape, or even worldview.[3] The theory of threshold concepts points out that students encounter various threshold transitions related to particularly difficult concepts in their learning process that must be moved through in order to grasp more fully a particular discipline of knowledge.[4] The role of threshold concept in teaching jihad and war shares key features with the body of this educational research theory. Mayer and Land put the characteristics of threshold concepts to be:

> a. *Transformative* in nature, creating a new understanding, view and way of describing the subject. In that, once understood, its potential effect on student learning and behavior is to occasion a significant shift in the perception.

3. Meyer and Land, eds., *Overcoming Barriers*, 3.
4. Meyer and Land, eds., *Overcoming Barriers*, 4.

b. Probably *irreversible*, causing a fundamental change that cannot be unlearnt. In that the change of perspective occasioned by acquisition of a threshold concept is unlikely to be forgotten or will be unlearned only by considerable effort.

c. *Integrative* in nature, that is, it exposes the previously hidden interrelatedness of something, creates a conceptual change that opens the way to new connections and relationships to be perceived.

d. Possibly often *bounded*, in that any conceptual space will have terminal frontiers, bordering with thresholds into new conceptual areas, helping define scope of the subject or the discipline.

e. Potentially *troublesome*, embodying knowledge that is problematic to grasp or difficult to integrate into current understanding.[5]

In this chapter, three characteristics of threshold theory will be highlighted to provide an effective way of viewing the concept of jihad and war. These are namely: being transformative, integrative and potentially troublesome. The notion of threshold concept, with its three functions, can provide a fresh insight for teaching and learning Islam especially in religious education where there is generally a monolithic approach and students usually "get stuck" in absolute truth or literal meaning without seeming to grasp the underlying meaning of the Divine Message. By stressing the transformative, integrative and yet troublesome features in the concepts, teachers will be empowered to move from teaching about the concepts to exploring their own pedagogical content knowledge. The result can be transformative for religious educators of Islam to help students through their own journeys so that education can become a portal for understanding other theological concepts.

Although the idea is very new, the notion of threshold concept seems to extend an invitation to the teachers to examine again their practices and to make meaningful connections between theory and practice.[6] The contribution of threshold theory to the field of religious education could open new fields of understanding and raise other questions that form the basis of further inquiry.[7]

5. Meyer and Land, eds., *Overcoming Barriers*, 7.
6. See Land, et al., *Threshold Concepts in Practice*.
7. Rymarz, "A Response: Threshold Concepts," 165.

Troublesome, Transformative and Integrative: What Do These Three Premises Entail?

Troublesome knowledge is the knowledge that comes from perspectives that conflict with our own. Perkins analyzes the nature of troublesome knowledge and suggests that knowledge might be troublesome for different reasons. Such knowledge, according to Perkins, can involve difficult, specialized language, be counter-intuitive, alien or be incoherent with no organizing principle. The troublesome knowledge appears in different forms, such as ritual knowledge in the sense of its routine character, inert knowledge, conceptually difficult knowledge, foreign or alien knowledge. I will draw particular attention to the form of foreign or alien knowledge related to jihad and war. The relationship of jihad and war with Islam, which means peace in its name and its message, seems to create a daunting task in understanding. Those who are familiar with teaching Islam in interreligious contexts are probably aware of the hardship. The troublesome knowledge is reflected in the difficulty that students have in answering a question along the following lines: Islam means peace, why then war? Perhaps the first question that comes to mind is how could a religion of peace become an ideology of violence? Religion is often held up as a vessel of peace, both theological and social. How, then, to understand its violent currents? On theological grounds we believe that extremism must be rejected. However, throughout the world extremist movements are flourishing in all religions and faiths: what are their causes?[8]

Jihad and war are seen as a "troublesome learning space" that emerges, especially, when forms of interreligious learning are used that engage students in exploring their own worldview as they explore those of others. Education needs to unpack these concepts. A short glance at how relationship is addressed or not addressed in religious education curriculum will clarify the point. The curriculum, usually, tends to avoid the subject of religion and violence. Though jihad is an important topic, this is implicit rather than explicit and recently the concept has been withdrawn from curricula in public school, at elementary and secondary levels, in Turkey.[9] Thus, education does not mention how religious teaching should face the issues of extremism and violence. In order to overcome fear and build mutual understanding between different faith traditions, we need to address

8. Meyer and Land, "Threshold Concepts and Troublesome Knowledge," 11; Perkins, "Constructivism and Troublesome Knowledge," 39.

9. "Öğretim Programlarını İzleme ve Değerlendirme Sistemi," T.C. Milli Eğitim Bakanlığı, http://mufredat.meb.gov.tr/ProgramDetay.aspx?PID=318
http://mufredat.meb.gov.tr/ProgramDetay.aspx?PID=319.

the link between violence and religion responsibly. Conflict between peace and war brings considerable frustration to the table both conceptually and theologically. The barrier to their learning appears to lie at a deeper level. It is important for linkages to ways of thinking within the theology of Islam, mainly in how the Qur'an considers the issue.

There is a growing consensus that Islamic theology is currently being misused by extremists to advance their own agenda. But that theology could actually have a vital role to play in countering violent extremist ideology. For the future of religion, in this aim, and in order to overcome fears and insecurity and build trust, it is crucial to try to point out the potential of religion as a source for world peace. Yet, at the same time, we must not lose sight of the potential of religions for violence in order to counteract internal theological tendencies that could be misused to support violence.[10] Hull illustrates this well when he says: "Only theology itself can speak to this situation, for theology deals with the nature of faith from inside. Nothing can judge faith but faith itself. Only faith can relativize faith."[11]

Students, when encountering such troublesome knowledge experience uncertainty and anxiety, but this can also be a place of transformation and a scope for pedagogical shift.[12] Potential barriers can be possible moments of theological and pedagogical success. There lies an opportunity for receptiveness and growth. Uncovering a threshold experience can be a mastery place that transforms how students see their discipline.[13]

Transformative learning is concerned with altering frames of reference through critical reflection of both habits of mind and points of view. For example, critically reflecting on the idea of the sacredness of life in religions and respecting the dignity of the other can have an impact of improving our relationships with people who are not like us. Through critical reflection of biases and assumptions, we can relocate understandings, change worldviews, and create transformative learning experiences.[14] Our frames of reference help us to understand our experiences in this world and to revise old assumptions. The transformative nature of theology as a threshold disposition implies a perspective shift that changes the learner's worldview.[15] I argue that transformation is dependent on the disposition of the theology

---

10. Lähnemann, "The Contribution of Interreligious," 2.

11. Hull, "Religion, Violence and Religious Education," 597.

12. Massignon and Mathieu, "Meeting Gods and Religions in School," 86.

13. See Salmona, Dan, and Wood, "The Importance of Liminal Space for Doctoral Success," 153–64.

14. Mezirow, *Transformative Dimensions of Adult Learning*, 89.

15. See Valk and Selçuk, "Journeying into a Peaceful Islam," 243–63.

presented to the young throughout education and in our attempts at principles of transformation that transcend, and thereby unify, our specific contextual concerns. In order to move to a new level of understanding a new disposition of learning needs to be achieved.

Another aspect of the transformative nature of threshold concepts is closely linked to the nature of the discipline. Developing a learning disposition may itself be a threshold in a culture of religious education where there is an absolute claim of religion. Transformative education in Islam calls for a liberation from ready-made answers toward reflecting on the problem solutions, and not only solutions, but on the problems that Muslims face these days. Bringing the notion of threshold concepts can be a means to break down the barrier between the knowledge embedded in the culture and academic knowledge. Here religious faith is not a matter of being confined in what students implicitly know, but of being moved to new ways of knowing in order to bridge faith and life. Even at a post graduate level in higher education, I observe, it can be hard for students who come from a religious background with authoritative, unified readings of the text, and for those who believe the text has a monolithic interpretation to open up themselves to multiple perspectives and interpretations.

Integrative: the meaning of jihad is illustrated by the variety of its uses. Seemingly disconnected ideas such as duty, obligation, and central component, are in students' vocabulary. Each usage integrates many different ideas and uncovers previously hidden, interrelated meaning in the concepts that students learn.

One can present jihad as "the first obligation for Muslims that comes after Iman Billâh (Belief in God)." Another may translate it as "Holy War" and claim that "the call to holy war is central to Islamic doctrine." Another explanation is that "jihad is the striving for good and the struggling with evil." Still, someone states that "jihad is the name of every attempt to purify one's soul."

Each of these usages has been supported by collections of verses from theology and, doubtless to say, connected to the divine message. What response then should education make to those different perceptions and definitions? How might religious education assist the learners to gain understanding in such concepts with no organizing principles? What does it mean to address these concepts in the Qur'anic context? How does the text try to position us? Which points are addressed, in jihad and war, through history and which aspects are missing?

In the field of religious education, good teaching will depend, first of all, on a clear idea of religion.[16] Such dissimilar and, at times, outright contradicting discourses are typical in the students' surroundings. Such examples show that, at least where the educators have to decide issues in this area during the teaching process, they call for ground principles on which their decisions should be based to achieve a desired outcome of the education.

What is gained from this analysis that is useful for teaching Islam? Threshold concepts seem to present important reference points across Islamic religious education. Threshold theory gives us a lens and insight to observe and reflect on our teaching experiences. Looking through the characteristic of threshold concepts theory can be a transformative gateway that leads to a new understanding and opens many further dimensions for a better education. Furthermore, a threshold concept approach suggests several perspectives in which each of these challenges might be met and helps students and the teachers feel more confident in coping with them. Threshold concept theory, with accompanying teaching models, will help teachers progress beyond troublesome knowledge to gain a language and theological ideas for building a possibility for new knowledge to support the educational process. An exploration of the intersections between threshold concept theory and teaching models also proves a productive area to create pedagogical content knowledge for religious education.

Conceptual Clarity Model (CCM) in Crossing Thresholds

If educators wish to engage with the notion of threshold concepts, they may need to come to a new way of thinking or view about their own teaching. The Conceptual Clarity Model is a helpful analytical model in inquiry into threshold concepts in teacher training of Islam.[17] As illustrated below, the model is composed of five stages that move from a broad overview of the problematic nature of the concept being taught to reflective learning from the text in order to affirm possible theological dialogue with social science, and how they all relate to effective pedagogies. It posits reflective questions in each stage in order to reach conceptual clarity so that the tradition can be regarded as an open offer of meaning to integrate faith to life.

16. See Nichols, "Roots in Religious Education," 113.
17. Selçuk, "Interreligiouse Bildung," 201–12.

	Stages	Example Questions
Stage 1	Reflections on the current situation	What do learners have in stock?
Stage 2	Exploring of text and context relationship	What did the text mean for the first addressee? Whether the theological principle fits with the universal message of the text.
Stage 3	Reflections on personal development	What does it all mean to me as a person and as a Muslim today?
Stage 4	Reflections for common good	As people of faith how can we contribute to the wellbeing of society?
Stage 5	Integration of content with effective pedagogy	What is the best way to integrate the subject with life?

Table 11.1: Conceptual Clarity Model (CCM)

With the increase in the use of reflective learning in almost every subject of the curriculum, teachers are being asked to be involved with this kind of learning. Teachers who may not consider themselves to be reflective are being asked to encourage their students to reflect! In this chapter the usage of reflective thinking also implies developing the ability of reflective thinking for teachers as well as for their students.

Here we need to remind ourselves that reflection is not only an intellectual act. The Qur'an values reflective thinking and presents it as a psychological process and also as an action-oriented and a historically embedded act that illuminates the relationship between social or cultural behaviors and personal choices. Some examples are:

"And all things we have created by pairs that haply, you may reflect."

(al-Dhāriyāt 51:49)

"Do they not reflect on the Qur'an? Or are there locks open their hearts?"

(Muḥammad 47:24)

"Man should reflect on what he/she was created from."

(al-Ṭāriq 86:5)

"Will you not then reflect?"

(al-Ṣaffāt 37:155)

"And verily you know the first creation. Why, then, you do not reflect?"

(al-Wāqiʿah 56:62)

While reflective thinking is no longer a rare or unknown approach in Islamic tradition, religious education, almost at every level, continues to treat teaching as a transmission. The motto "stand and deliver" or what I call, "you sit still and I instill"[18] describes well both the practices and the general attitude of teaching and learning. We have not made considerable progress in bringing the many forms of scholarly ways of teaching into religious education. Teachers tend to rely on a variety of materials such as textbooks and workbooks as sources for their activities, but they rarely rely on the Qur'anic text. I argue, it is only by self-critical investigation that we can secure historical order and harmony in learners' minds. Because fundamentalists believe that there is only one truth that has been revealed to them, it is the task of religious education, in this respect, to maintain an understanding that God is the ground of all reality and no one has a monopoly on the truth.

The model considers Islamic religious education as a relational activity which maintains *musālama* (peaceful relationship) between God, human being, and the whole creation. As it is shown in the chart above, its five key stages are: (1) reflections on the current situation; (2) exploring text and context relation; (3) reflections on personal development; (4) reflections for common good; and (5) integration of the content with an effective pedagogy. Each of five stages is important in its own right. The teachers may use one stage or a combination of several, or use it as a whole, depending on the aims and objectives in which they intend to develop students' skills, knowledge, and attitudes regarding the issue.

The model is both practical and theoretical. Some teachers may be interested in the actual situation, and, by means of questions, collect examples or inspirations from existing successes to provide food for thought and push students to move from their comfort zone. Thus, they disclose what their students have in stock. Some might want to start with findings from social sciences to help reflect on what it means to be a Muslim in history and today, developing students' appreciation of and commitment to socially just ways of living. Some may be interested in exploring text and context relationships and highlight the importance of the context through historical-critical analysis, uncover the spirit of the text, and develop the ability of discerning messages that are directed to the original hearers of a specific time and place

18. Selçuk, "Opening the Eye of the Heart," 255–61.

and those that are intended for general audiences of every time and place. Some may want to pick from the relevant educational theories to assist their students and provide further activities that may be used in different aspects of life to facilitate different forms of learning. Presentism, for example, is common among students. Students tend to view past events through present knowledge and values. But recognizing situations in history in relation to contemporary society needs multiple, serious, and well-elaborated perspectives: that is what deserves understanding.[19]

The model relates to reflective learning by means of existential, cultural, and historical questions and empowers teachers of Islam to develop thinking skills, clarify presumptions, and seek faith with understanding. To demonstrate ways of implementation, in this chapter I will expressly use the two stages of the model: (1) reflections on the current situation and (2) exploring text and context relationship.

In the first stage, I will present the prevailing understanding among Muslims regarding the Qur'an as the "word of God." In the next stage of exploring text and context relationship I will show how teachers can encounter the text with in its historical context in regard to jihad and war.

Stage 1: Reflecting on the Current Situation: Uncovering Threshold Barriers and Dispositions about the Common Understanding Regarding the Qur'anic Text

This stage aims to reflect on the habits, beliefs, practices, perceptions, and the experiences around the concepts being taught. The deep reason why jihad and war are hard to introduce to students is that, in order to understand a body of theological knowledge, students often must re-evaluate or distort parts of their understanding about the Qur'an.

The question that follows, then, is "what does the Qur'an say about itself?" Indeed, the question of the nature of the Qur'an almost seems to have disappeared from discussions about Islam. Teaching Islam, be it in the form of schooling or vocational training for the mosque or learning through life, is by its very nature a process of engagement with the Qur'anic text. However, other educational activities have often replaced raising this inner question. Such ways often appear to be in the quality of reading the text. For example, many Qur'anic courses engage with the text in a very effective process that still ignores this fundamental question. In these courses,

---

19. Perkins, "Constructivism and Troublesome Knowledge," 39.

students read the Arabic text under the guidance of a trained teacher and great emphasis is placed on reciting it and also on memorizing the text as an affirmation of religious piety. The default is that reciting the text is seen as a technical skill. More emphasis on reading as recitation avoids the issue of the texts' meanings and functions in the life of the believers. What is missing is reading for understanding and self-reflection on the text. Yet, the two relations with the Qur'anic text are two educational practices that should be conceived of as reciprocal rather than either or. In other words, what we do in religious education as a matter of fact when we read or understand is intimately bound up with our students' full development.

Although relatively little research has been completed on the usage of the Qur'anic text in classrooms, the research by Julian Stern can present a picture. Stern says: "Muslim pupils may memorize the Qur'an, but teachers should avoid using people who memorize the Qur'an as a novelty. Rather, teachers could develop a knowledge of how and when this example may appropriately be incorporated into a lesson: It should be a voluntary activity."[20] Depending on the teacher's view, Stern introduces three points commonly raised by religious education teachers on how to approach the Qur'an in classroom settings: (1) What are the best ways that schools can use the sacred text of Islam? (2) What potential for good learning in religious education in general is there in the development of good uses of the Qur'an in schools? and (3) How can teachers be helped to do better work with the Qur'anic text in teaching religion with various age groups?[21] Stern also reports that those discussing the use of the Qur'an in religious education often report a fear of making mistakes when using the Qur'an in any way.[22]

I believe that the only way to regain reflective ground in teaching Islam is by raising the question of how does the Qur'an describe itself—openly and explicitly as a core question, a question of realizing the aims of the message, and as a research area in religious education. The question of the self-understanding of the Qur'an is not the question of religious education (my scholarly field) but of those fields in which the theology of Islam is rooted: Tafsir, Hadith, Fiqh, and Kalam. Religious education in its current form does not work well to offer the student a holistic understanding of the Divine Message. Therefore, it is up to us as religious educators entering into interdisciplinary studies for a creative engagement toward a philosophy of education that is more supportive of our students' development for a deeper understanding of Islam.

20. Stern, *Teaching Religious Education*, 13.

21. Stern, *Teaching Religious Education*, 14.

22. Stern, *Teaching Religious Education*, 15.

272 TEACHING IN A WORLD OF VIOLENT EXTREMISM

In the book project entitled *Kur'an ve Birey* (The Qur'an and the Individual),[23] scholars of Tafsir, history of Islam, and religious education entered into conversation with the Qur'an from interdisciplinary views and worked on the history and context of the text for education that answers the challenges of reading for self-understanding. The book project begins with analyzing the names of the Qur'an. Behind the aim of analyzing the names lies the assumption that the real meaning of the Qur'an is to be found in the text itself to correct the misconception and the perceptions that students bring with them to learning settings.

In the Qur'an there exists almost fifty-five names that define the Qur'an.[24] To mention some of them: *al-Kitāb* (Book), *al-Mubīn* (the Luminous), *al-Karīm* (the Noble), *al-Nūr* (the Sacred Light), *al-Rahmān* (the Mercy), *al-Mubārak* (the Blessed), *al-Hādī* (the Guide), *al-Munādī* (the Inviter to Faith), *al-Nadhīr* (the Warner), *al- 'Azīz* (the Mighty), *al- 'Ilm* (the Ultimate knowledge), *al-Tadhkira* (the Reminder), *al-Ḥakīm* (the Full of wisdom), *al-Musaddiq* (the Confirming Scripture), *Kalām* (Words of Allah). Among these, three basic names will be explained briefly to make the names intelligible.

al-Kitāb

In the Qur'an, the word *al-Kitāb* (the Book) is generally used for the sum of the revelations that are delivered to all the prophets. While naming previous revelations as *al-Kitāb*, the Qur'an also names itself as al-Kitāb (Yūsuf 12:1; al-Shu'arā' 26:2; al-Qaṣaṣ 28:2; al-Naml 27:1).

The Qur'an is a clear and glorious book. There is no doubt that the Qur'an emerges from the Divine. None of a false component can reach it (Fuṣṣilat 41:42). The Qur'an should be understood, should be learned and should be thought (Āl 'Imrān 3:79). It should be explained (Āl 'Imrān 3/187). Beyond everything, it is the word of God. Furthermore, in a sense, the Qur'an considers both the human and the universe as books, too. The Qur'an is a book that should be read with the book of the universe and the book of the human being. Neither the universe nor the human being can be comprehended as they ought to be without the Qur'an, nor can we understand the Qur'an without information of the human being and the universe.

---

23. Selçuk et al., *Kur'an ve Birey*, 2.
24. Selçuk et al., *Kur'an ve Birey*, 2.

al-Furqān

The root meaning of *furqān* is to differentiate. The Qur'an puts things that are together or mixed in existence in their own places and categorizes them. In this sense it is named as *al-Furqān*.

The first verse of al-Furqān Surah says: "Blessed is He who sent down the Criterion to His servant, that it may be an admonition to all creatures."

If so, one of the characteristics of the Qur'an is to clarify. As is well known by the Muslims, the Qur'an, with its character of differentiation, has contents which distinguish between good and bad, beautiful and ugly, righteous and dishonest, truth and falsehood, order and chaos, permissible and forbidden, sin and good deed, right and wrong, darkness and brightness.

We see the differentiating character of the Qur'an in the relations of human beings with Allah and the universe repeatedly in the text. Since the Qur'an aims to grow mature individuals, it helps them clarify their positions toward life situations, people, and all creation. The Qur'an contributes to making right preferences for people in complex situations. There are sound scales in the hands of those who are trying to understand the Qur'an with the book of the universe together. Allah has already said in the twenty-ninth verse of the Surah al-Anfāl that He would give humans the skill and power to distinguish good and bad if they behaved stably and were in a careful, delicate and alert state of mind toward the revelation of God. Then, the Qur'an dissolves the confusion in the mind, heart, and soul of humans who are in complex relations so they can gain clear understanding and comprehension.

al-Kalām

Al-Kalām has been attributed to Allah and used as *Kalāmullah* (Words of Allah) in some parts of the Qur'an (al-Baqarah 2:75; al-Tawbah 9:6; al-Fatḥ 48:15). This name is the usage of language which is the symbolic way of entering into connection with the addressee. Muslims believe that the last verbal contact of Allah with mankind appeared in the seventh century by means of the Qur'an. Words have effect on the addressee and leave impressions on their mental and spiritual worlds. Especially if words have been used in their correct usages, the effect on addressee is greater. While the Qur'an was being delivered, that was the case. Verses were delivered according to the requirements of the conditions. As a matter of fact, many of the verses have been delivered for specific reasons. These are called *asbāb al-nuzūl* (the Occasions of the Revelation).

When we analyze the names of the Qur'an, we can see that the text presents itself neither as an encyclopedia nor as a book of constitution or laws. The Qur'an is mercy and a gift of Allah for humanity and Muslims. Knowing how to benefit from this Divine Source is related to deep understanding and sound interpretation. The primary goal of the Qur'an is to raise spiritual and humanitarian individuals who love their Lord and all creation, and are peaceful, and sensitive in their relationship. We can deduce this message from many of the verses of the Qur'an:

> "Nay, —whoever submits His whole self to Allah and is a doer of good,—He will get his reward with his Lord; on such shall be no fear, nor shall they grieve." (al-Baqarah 2:112)

> "Indeed, those who have said, 'Our Lord is Allah' and then remained on a right course–the angels will descend upon them, and say, 'Do not fear and do not grieve but receive good tidings of Paradise, which you were promised.'" (Fuṣṣilat 41:30)

> "Whoever does righteousness, whether male or female, while he is a believer–We will surely cause him to live a good life, and We will surely give them their reward according to the best of what they used to do . . ." (al-Naḥl 16:97)

> "O mankind, indeed, We have created you from male and female and made you peoples and tribes that you may know one another. Indeed, the most noble of you in the sight of Allah is the most righteous of you. Indeed, Allah is Knowing and Acquainted." (al-Ḥujurāt 49:13)

> "Bestow a favor, And perform your works well; indeed, Allah loves the doers of good and loves those who perform their works well." (al-Baqarah 2:195)

> "Nay, —Those that keep their plighted faith and act aright,— verily Allah loves those who act aright." (Āl 'Imrān 3:76)

> "And those saved from the covetousness of their own souls,— they are the ones that achieve prosperity." (al-Ḥashr 59:9)

At the beginning of revelation in Mecca, the Qur'an focused on the belief of *Tawḥīd* (Oneness of God) and the belief of the hereafter. And then mindfulness of God and worship, as they contribute to personal development and growth, was ordered. Meanwhile the importance of good deeds was also being expressed. We do not see jihad and war at this period of Qur'anic revelation. However, when it came to the period of Medina, then war and jihad come into play in a defensive purpose.

Stage 2: Exploring Text and Context Relationship: Encountering the World of the Text within its Historical Context

Exploring the text and context relationship has pedagogical and theological value. By unpacking the context, we come to understand the deep meaning behind the verses revealed as well as the perspective required to pass the thresholds. This is a missing part for Islam in education, so far.

My suggestion in Islamic religious education is that, if the message of the Qur'an is to speak with education, it must have its own standing ground from which to speak. We must not let the literal meaning set the ground rules. Islamic religious education as a subject has the task of being abreast of its times with a broad perspective to reach people living in a modern, democratic, and pluralistic society. This is one of the keyways to reduce absolutism. As research on fundamentalism reminds us, absolutism is an important component to the fundamentalist outlook. For the fundamentalists of any faith, the holy text of their respective religions has divine origins and are consequently inerrant and beyond questioning.

The book project, *Kur'an ve Birey* (The Qur'an and the Individual) as mentioned above, offers a hermeneutical approach for teaching and learning Islam that helps learners grasp the differences in understanding the message due to time and space. The book states, unless the context of the verses is identified, we do not understand their meaning fully. In other words, context decides how we interpret and perceive the meaning of God's message. Pursuing the same line of analysis, we can say that the ability to elaborate the verses from the perspective of text and context relationship is a theological basis for transformative education that will help to detect and reduce the risk of extremism. A marked feature of text and context relationship is its concern with the changing nature of life. When we speak about context today, we mean something entirely different from what the life was for the first addressee. As such, we are not only concerned with the meaning of the verses but also with the role of political, cultural, social and historical factors. Encountering God's message in culture and history raises an awareness to differentiate between time bound aspects and universal human experiences such as birth, death, love, friendship, success and failure, health and sickness, peace and war. Such shared experiences give us the opportunity on how to approach teaching the message. You focus on the common or on the particular within a culture, or both. Your position determines the outcome of your teachings. The distinction between historical context and universal human experiences is essential to the process of understanding the message of the Qur'an.

A central component of teaching is to develop contextual thinking in a discursive tradition which has produced historically contingent categorizations of doctrines and practices such as Islam. Contextual thinking takes place around the questions of what happened before and during the time of the Prophet? What did the Qur'an bring to the fore? What developed in history? What are the essentials for today? The objectives in terms of developing teachers' contextual thinking skills are:

- Experiencing that the context is the background and the horizon at the same time.

- Gaining a broader perspective on the ethos of the knowledge in the Qur'an as well as its moral and intellectual grounding.

- Being aware of the link between past, present, and future while communicating with the text.

Understanding Jihad and War within the Textual and Historical Context of the Qur'an

"Jihad" denotes an extraordinary human endeavor, one taken to the limits in an effort for the sake of God and promotes the welfare of one's fellows. In the widest meaning, it connotes making an effort and struggling in a way that pushes the whole limits of human beings. Jihad covers all types of moral self-sacrifice and effort for human beings' goodness for the sake of God. It is said in the Qur'an that none of the efforts of human beings will be in vain (al-ʿAnkabūt 29:69). There is an intimate relationship between jihad and the meaning of human existence of in the world.[25] For the purpose of their creation, it is necessary for human beings to do their best in using all their capabilities and skills properly. The purpose of human creation is to know Allah, to recognize Him, to believe in Him and work for Him. During the realization of this purpose people must expend effort for their intentions to gain moral qualities.

The word jihad comes from the Arabic root *j-h-d* and its derivations in the Qur'an are attested in thirty-six verses. This root means "to strive" and is the root for other verbs emphasizing effort and struggle to achieve perfection in difficult tasks. Jihad certainly represents a sense of totalizing effort. In the Qur'an there are many examples in which such efforts are mentioned

25. Selçuk, "Die Definition von 'Jihad' und die Bedeutung," 51–52.

in psychological, sociological or in similar context (see al-Baqarah 2:218, al-Nisāʾ 4:95, al-Ḥajj 22:78, al-Furqān 25:53).

The root of the term "jihad" is also reflected in a term used in Islamic jurisprudence: *ijtihād*. The latter describes an intellectual effort to interpret and understand faith and life.[26] The human individual must make every imaginable effort to make fitting use of his or her God-given opportunities and capabilities, particularly their intellectual capacity. Along this journey to truth and virtue that brings the individual closer to God, one encounters many inward and outward obstructions that must be grappled with. This fact is also made clear by the statement of the Prophet following a battle, according to which, now that the *lesser* jihad had come to an end, it was time to turn to the *greater* jihad, i.e., to the elimination of inward obstructions.[27] Jihad encompasses every ethically legitimate defense against threats and attacks directed against human dignity, religion, one's own family, and one's own country.

Jihad is often incorrectly translated as "holy war": This meaning symbolizes Islam as a religion of violence. This kind of translation also creates an obstacle in the critical task, namely that of building bridges of mutual understanding between religions. At a purely linguistic level, we should recognize that holy war in Arabic would sound like *al-ḥarb al-muqaddasah* rather than jihad. Neither in the Qurʾan nor in the Hadith can we find such an expression.

We can better understand the meaning of jihad and its relation to war by reading the verses according to their revelation period either in Mecca or in Medina. My own studies on the Meccan verses allow me to say that these verses provide the theological framework for the religious education of Islam as a religion of conscience based on the individual's choice and responsibility. While the priority of the Mecca period is the individual, in the Medina period the priority has shifted to society. As that message was rejected in practice, and the prophets and his followers were persecuted and forced to migrate to Medina, some aspect of the message changed in response to the socioeconomic and political realities of the time. Migration to Medina (*hijrah*) was not merely a tactical step but also signified a shift in the content of the message itself. The difference is clearly shown in close examination and comparison of the Qurʾanic texts and Sunnah dating from the Mecca stage and those following the migration to Medina.[28] When we look at the verses revealed in Medina, we find expressions dealing

26. See Erdem, "Cihad."
27. Erdem, "Cihad," 122.
28. See Taha, *The Second Message of Islam.*

with social order and politics. These verses handle concrete social topics and they need to be interpreted according to their historical and timely context. Therefore, I consider the verses revealed in Mecca as the very core of Islam and as subject knowledge in education.

At the heart of this distinction is a shift in perception without which understanding cannot be reached easily and students will not be able to cross the threshold. When education of Islam is approached from this point of view, some of the threshold concepts—not only jihad and war but also others such as the view toward other religions and faiths and the status of women—may be seen as conditioned by different understandings of basic human needs from that time.

I want to highlight the significance of historical context of the Qur'anic verses in providing pathways to aid both teachers and learners in relation to overcoming thresholds. Considering the chronological and theological thinking relationship provides a concern for both contextual and human needs. This historical perspective will help the educators find guiding principles, explore forms of teaching, and acknowledge the importance of the context(s) of the verses. At this point we can discuss the historical settings of war in the Qur'an. We learn from Gözeler's book that Muslims were given permission to make war for the first time in surah al-Ḥajj verses 39–40.[29] It reads:

> "To those against whom war is made, permission is given to right, because they are wronged; and verily God is Most Powerful for their aid." (al-Ḥajj 22:39)

> "They are those who have been expelled from their homes in defiance of right, for no cause except that they say, "Our Lord is God." If God did not check one set of people by means of another, there would surely have been pulled down monasteries, churches, synagogues, and mosques, in which the name of God is commemorated in abundant measure . . ." (al-Ḥajj 22:40)

In verse 39, the technical term is *yuqātilūna* ("those against whom war is made"), which, using passive voice, means war can be waged only if a community is attacked. War in the Qur'an is told through the words derived from the q-t-l root and it has its own frame to be determined. War related subjects in the Qur'an are defined through words with a different root from j-h-d, meaning that jihad is not directly related to war. The Qur'an forbids cruelty, unfairness, and killing human beings. It defines killing someone without a

---

29. Gözeler, *Kur'an Ayetlerinin Tarihlendirilmesi*, 217–19.

reason as killing all human beings. War is contingent and temporary, and peace is actual and stable. Peace is put in front of Muslims as an aim.

Surah al-Ḥajj was sent down in the Medinan period. If noticed, permission in a general means was given to Muslims who were exposed to torture, oppression, and injustice in Mecca. This permission is not for them to go to war mandatorily, but is a license for the believers, who have countered all attacks with patience and tolerance from the very beginning, stating that they can defend themselves against the attackers to save their lives. According to reports narrated by al-Ṭabarī (d. 310/923), this permission is for those among Muslims setting out for migration from Mecca to Medina, who faced barriers.[30] It is obvious that here, permission is based on self-defense.

We already have stated that the jihad concept has a larger meaning in terms of semantics. The Qur'an speaks on war particularly with words that derive from *q-t-l* root. The fact that subjects in the Qur'an related to war are expressed with words deriving from a different root, shows clearly that jihad does not directly mean war.

Before *hijrah*, the Muslims were not told to fight with polytheists; they were ordered to live in peace. In this period, the Prophet Muhammad was announcing the verses to the public. Meanwhile both he and his companions were being exposed to torture and pressure. The Muslims were told to be patient and to forgive. In the period where pressures got more violent, Muslims first migrated to Abyssinia and took shelter there. They never chose the way of war. After all, as a messenger of God, the Prophet Muhammad was told that he was just the bearer of warning and good tidings. It was told that he was not a tyrant over people. In the 125–128 verses of the Surah al-Naḥl, a Meccan Surah, we read:

> "Invite (all) to the Way of thy Lord with wisdom and beautiful preaching; and argue with them in ways that are best and most gracious: for thy Lord knoweth best, who have strayed from His Path, and who receive guidance."

> "And if ye punish, let your punishment be proportional to the wrong that has been done to you: but if ye show patience, that is indeed the best (course) for those who are patient. And do thou be patient, for thy patience is but from Allah; nor grieve over them: and distress not thyself because of their plots. For Allah is with those who restrain themselves, and those who do good."

In these verses, it is mentioned that, while the Muslims can counter with harshness, it is a more preferable way for them to be patient.

---

30. See al-Ṭabarī, *Cāmi' al-Bayān 'an Ta' wīl Āy al-Qur' ān*, 16: 573–77.

Following the chronological order, the 190th verse of the Surah al-Baqarah says: "Fight in the cause of Allah those who fight you, but do not transgress limits; for Allah loveth not transgressors." In this verse, it is clearly understood that a defense aimed war is mentioned. The expression of *"do not transgress limits; for Allah loveth not transgressors"* forbids unjust attacks, disobeying the rules of the war, unnecessary bloodshed, and harming the environment. According to the exegete al-Zamakhsharī (d. 538/1144), this verse not only forbids starting a war, but also forbids the killing of women, children, elders, attacking a union with whom there is a treaty, and preparing surprise attacks.[31] In fact, this verse shows that war also has morality and rules. Thus, murdering civilians is against the rules of the war and exceeds the bounds of justification.

The killing of innocent people, people who have not actually participated in war, with suicide bombs, does not have any relationship with Islam. According to the Quor'an, death sentences can only be given as a result of a verdict based on the constitution of a state. There are no verses on which the mentality of seeing terror and violence as permissible, can be grounded in the Qur'an.

Rather, the Qur'an states that diversity is a richness. The thirteenth verse of the Surah al-Ḥujurāt says: "O mankind! We created you from a single (pair) of a male and a female, and made you into nations and tribes, that ye may know each other (not that ye may despise each other). Verily the most honored of you in the sight of Allah is (he who is) the most righteous of you. And Allah has full knowledge and is well acquainted (with all things)."

Reasons for War in the Text

And slay them wherever ye catch them, and turn them out from where they have turned you out; for persecution and oppression are worse than slaughter; but fight them not at the Sacred Mosque, unless they (first) fight you there; but if they fight you, slay them. Such is the reward of those who suppress faith. (Surah al-Baqarah 2:191).

This verse mentions two main reasons for war. The first one is persecution. In the verse, it is told that persecution is worse than killing. Hence, facing a society of persecution is a reason for war. Persecution means conditions that will shake the society from its foundations and gradually cause the

31. al-Zamakhsharī, *al-Kashshāf*, 1:396.

loss of social and political union. War is seen as a tool that will end chaos and enable a society to rise on its own values. The second reason is the aggressive attitude of the enemy. If noticed, both reasons are part of social and political realities, not theological ones.

Surah al-Nisāʾ verse 90 says:

> Except those who join a group between whom and you there is a treaty (of peace), or those who approach you with hearts restraining them from fighting you or fighting their own people. If Allah had pleased, He could have given them power over you, and they would have fought you: Therefore if they withdraw from you but fight you not, and (instead) send you (guarantees of) peace, then Allah Hath opened no way for you (to war against them).

This verse indicates that the enemy who has asked for shelter to a society that has a treaty with Muslims, shall not be touched and when offered peace, war should not be declared. As understood from here, Muslims must not wage war on societies that do not attack them directly.

Surah al-Tawbah verses 12–14 reads:

> But if they violate their oaths after their covenant, and attack you for your Faith,–fight ye the chiefs of Unfaith: for their oaths are nothing to them: that thus they may be restrained. Will ye not fight people who violated their oaths, plotted to expel the Messenger, and attacked you first? Do ye fear them? Nay, it is Allah Whom ye should more justly fear, if ye believe! Fight them, and Allah will punish them by your hands, and disgrace them, help you (to victory) over them, heal the breasts of Believers.

In these verses, the text orders war to be waged on those who have abolished the treaties with Muslims and declare war on them. Orders and encouragements for war in the Qurʾan always take place as a precaution of defense against the attempts of enemies. In this occasion, war is ordered to Muslims as a way to keep their existence.

War Being the Work of Professionals

The 20th verse of Surah al-Muzzammil mentions that a group will go for expedition in the way of God. Another group is ordered to read the Qurʾan, pray, and render the arms levy. It supports the idea that not everyone shall go to war. Instead of everyone going to war, one group should stay where they are in order to study their faith well and relay it to those who return from war. The 122nd verse of Surah al-Tawbah reads:

> "It is not for the Believers to go forth (all) together: if a contingent from every expedition go forth to devote themselves to studies in religion, and admonish the people when they return to them,- that thus they (may learn) to guard themselves (against evil)."

That is to say, partially, a professional group for war existed at that time. Certainly, in the time when the Qur'an was sent down, wars were not waged with regular armies as they are now. Hence, individuals who could fight in their own conditions, joined war. Here it is possible to say that not every person is intended to join war in the way of God. Especially in our time, war must be the work of professionals, completely. It is not acceptable that young people, whose profession is not soldiery, are persuaded and sent to fight. Many youngsters, who will give precious support to their societies in their future, are wasted in these fights.

From the examination of some of the verses related to war, one can see the Qur'an orders fighting conditionally within specific situations. As mentioned above, in the Medinan period the Qur'an was responding to the actual needs of human society of the time in a specific occasion.

War is casual and temporary, but peace is actual and permanent. However, wars can happen due to political, military, and economic reasons. Such wars were waged during the period in which the Qur'an was sent down. Thus, verses relating to war are in the Qur'an. We should keep in mind that the universal aim that is put in front of Muslims is peace. On the other hand, decision for war has political, military and administrational sides. This is the work of the political power and the state.

Recent scholarship in Turkish academia is developing new ways of doing theology that consider the importance of context, learning from the roots of traditions, from the occasions of the revelation, and reflecting on the text and context relationship. A diversity of approaches in the contemporary academy emerge which consider contextual perspectives to a certain extent. Even if contextual perspectives might not be fully valued, they explore the place of contextuality in Islam and identify key issues facing theologies which make explicit the place of human context in history and today. They call for reflective and responsive education which articulates clearly the contextual factors that shape the meaning.[32] However, in religious education the challenge continues because the threshold often relates to

---

32. See Öztürk, "Cihad Ayetleri."

personal convictions and common codes of society; in this regard the new is not always welcomed.

Text and context relationship offer a way to see if claims have been made on behalf of faith are valid or aligned with what the text says in the Meccan period. The realization of the distinctions between two periods is also important for the reader to understand what views are relativized or excluded through the history of Islam. Reflecting on the text and context relationship, therefore, is an important scholarly skill in order to grasp the text at a deeper level and reach to its universality, whether the theological principle is applicable in real life situations or whether it is a specific case, only. Learning to read the Qur'anic text as part of a process of becoming conscious of one's experience as a historically constructed person within shared human experiences provides systematic use of the text in the classroom. It may serve as a basis to make the learners see both the universal features and see how historical and universal aspects differ.

Concluding Thoughts and Further Research: From Concepts to Pedagogical Content Knowledge

This chapter was an attempt to capture and qualify the transitional process and developmental insights offered by threshold concept theory and explore its potential through a Conceptual Clarity Model which allows us to establish a relevant pedagogical knowledge on our teaching practices of Islam. The point of departure for this chapter was: What would be the best way of teaching Islam when students confront troublesome issues such as jihad and war? However, the present study invites us to be reflective on a more principled level in Islamic education and proposes thinking skills as a complement to threshold concepts.

In Islamic religious education literature, there has been an emphasis on conceptual understanding to represent a high quality of teaching and learning Islam.[33] But this had to be broadened to cover additional skills and ways of thinking to facilitate scholarly religious thought as an aim of religious education. Different interpretations of religious concepts need specification and the logical relations between these must be established as to avoid the risk of monolithic understanding.[34] Crossing this threshold is difficult for those trained in a monolithic way, but once crossed, it alters their vision and practice of education entirely. Ways of reflective thinking support learners in moving through thresholds to the discipline.

33. See Arslan, "A Holistic Approach in Education."
34. Attfield, "Conceptual Research in Religious Education," 82–83.

The chapter offers, at the very beginning of learning, the need to know how the Qur'an presents itself. A self-investigation of the text is as important as knowing about the identity of the Qur'an as a holy book and a way of life. Teachers should be aware of any concept that can be difficult to some of the learners. Therefore, teachers should ask students to reflect on their learning process. Islamic religious education needs to do more about the problem of communicating the Qur'anic message to the people of our time. This is in line with what is generally accepted in religious education.[35] The teacher is not the giver of the content and the students are not the receivers of knowledge anymore.

There is further need to investigate the role of skills that act as threshold: How do students best learn these skills? How can we improve reflective thinking in teaching Islam? How do we balance threshold concepts and skills? We should develop our understanding of the challenge of violent extremism and of what works in tackling it: prevention by means of reflective communication with the text. We must not only be conscious and aware of the manipulators' tricks but also reach conceptual clarity in order to effectively resist them. Religious education must have a preventive role and reduce the risk of extremism as an engaged intervention in our attempts at fostering mutual understanding among people of different faiths.

Bibliography

Arslan, Seyma. "A Holistic Approach in Education from The Perspective of the Islamic Understanding of Human Being." In *Teaching Religion, Teaching Truth: Theoretical and Empirical Perspectives. Religion, Education and Values 1*, edited by Jeff Astley, Leslie J. Francis, Mandy Robbins, Mualla Selçuk, 119–33. London: Lang, 2012.

Aslan, Ednan, and Marcia Hermansen, eds. *Religion and Violence: Muslim and Christian Theological and Pedagogical Reflections*. Wiesbaden: Springer, 2017.

Attfield, David. "Conceptual Research in Religious Education." In *New Directions in Religious Education*, edited by John M. Hull, 77–74. Lewes, UK: Falmer, 1982.

Erdem, Engin. "Cihad," *İslamiyet-Hıristiyanlık Kavramları Sözlüğü*, Eugen-Biser-Vakfı İşbirliği ile edited by Mualla Selçuk, Halis Albayrak, Peter Antes, Richard Heinzmann, Martin Thurner, 1: Ankara: Ankara Üniversitesi Yayınevi, 2013.

Gözeler, Esra. *Kur'an Ayetlerinin Tarihlendirilmesi*. İstanbul: Kuramer, 2016.

T.C. Milli Eğitim Bakanlığı. "Öğretim Programlarını İzleme ve Değerlendirme Sistemi." http://mufredat.meb.gov.tr/ProgramDetay.aspx?PID=318 http://mufredat.meb.gov.tr/ProgramDetay.aspx?PID=319.

Hull, John M. "Religion, Violence and Religious Education." In *International Handbook of the Religious, Moral and Spiritual Dimensions in Education*, edited by Marian de Souza et al., 591–605. Dordrecht: Springer, 2009.

---

35. Ucan and Wright, "Improving the Pedagogy of Islamic Religious Education," 203.

Lähnemann, Johannes. "The Contribution of Interreligious Initiatives to Human Rights Education" In *Human Rights and Religion in Educational Contexts*, edited by Jeff Astley, Leslie J. Francis and David W. Lankshear, 323–34. Cham, Switzerland: Springer, 2016.

Meyer, Jan H. F., and Michael T. Flanagan, and Ray Land, eds. *Threshold Concepts in Practice*. Rotterdam: Sense, 2016.

Taha, Mahmoud Mohamed. *The Second Message of Islam*. Translated by Abdullahi Ahmed an-Na'im. Contemporary Issues in the Middle East. Syracuse: Syracuse University Press, 1987.

Massignon, Bérengère and Séverine Mathieu. "Meeting Gods and Religions in School Classroom Interaction in France." In *Dialogue and Conflict on Religion: Studies of Classroom Interaction in European Countries*, edited by Ina ter Avest, Dan-Paul Jozsa, Thorsen Knauth, Javier Rosón and Geir Skeie, 84-96. Münster: Waxmann, 2009.

Meyer Jan H. F., and Ray Land, eds. *Overcoming Barriers to Student Understanding: Threshold Concepts and Troublesome Knowledge*. London: Routledge, 2006.

———. "Threshold Concepts and Troublesome Knowledge: An Introduction." In *Overcoming Barriers to Student Understanding: Threshold Concepts and Troublesome Knowledge*, edited by Jan H. F. Meyer and Ray Land. London: Routledge, 2006.

Mezirow, Jack. *Transformative Dimensions of Adult Learning*. Jossey-Bass Higher and Adult Education Series. San Francisco: Jossey-Bass, 1991.

Nichols, Kevin. "Roots in Religious Education." In *Priorities in Religious Education: A Model for the 1990s and Beyond*, edited by Brenda Watson, 113–24. London: Falmer, 1992.

Öztürk, Mustafa. "Cihad Ayetleri: Tefsir Birikimine, İslam Geleneğine ve Günümüze Yansımaları." In *İslam Kaynaklarında, Geleneğinde ve Günümüzde Cihad*, edited by Ahmet Ertürk, 99–163. İstanbul: Kuramer, 2016.

Perkins, David. "Constructivism and Troublesome Knowledge." In *Overcoming Barriers to Student Understanding: Threshold Concepts and Troublesome Knowledge*, edited by Jan H. F. Meyer and Ray Land, 33–47. London: Routledge, 2006.

Rymarz, Richard. "A Response: Threshold Concepts in Religious Education and Theology." *Journal of Adult Theological Education* 13.2 (2016) 163–70.

Salmona, Michelle, Dan Kaczynski, and Leigh N. Wood, "The Importance of Liminal Space for Doctoral Success: Exploring Methodological Threshold Concepts." In *Threshold Concepts in Practice*, edited by Ray Land, Jan H. F. Meyer, and Michael T. Flanagan, 153-64. Rotterdam: Sense, 2016.

Selçuk, Mualla. "Die Definition von 'Jihad' und die Bedeutung für die religiöse Erziehung in einer Welt des religiösen Pluralismus." In *Islam, Frauen und Europe, Islamicher Feminismus und Gender Jihad-neue Wege für Musliminnen in Europa?*, edited by Ina Wunn and Mualla Selçuk, 45–58. Stuttgart: Kohlhammer, 2013.

———. "Interreligiouse Bildung: Sich Selbst und den anderen (er)kennen: Theologische Fakültat der Universitat Ankara Beispiele aus dem Lehrplan der Weltreligionen." In *Islam und Europa*, 154–66. Ankara: Deutsche Botschaft, 2015.

———. "Opening the Eye of the Heart: Parents and Teachers as Storytellers." *Religious Education: The Official Journal of the Religious Education Association* 110 (2015) 255–61.

————. "Teaching Beyond Normativity: What Opportunities Does Religious Education Have to Create Brave Spaces and Overcome Cultural Biases?" *REA Annual Meeting 2018 Proceedings: Creating Brave Spaces* (2018) 201–12.

Selçuk, Mualla, Halis Albayrak, and Nahide Bozkurt. *Kur'an ve Birey*. Ankara: Turhan Kitabevi, 2010.

Selengut, Charles. *Sacred Fury: Understanding Religious Violence*. Lanham, MD: Rowman & Littlefield, 2017.

Stern, Julian. *Teaching Religious Education: Researchers in the Classroom*. London: Bloomsbury, 2006.

al-Ṭabarī, Ibn Jarīr. *Cāmiʿ al-Bayān ʿan Taʾwīl Āy al-Qurʾān*. Edited by ʿAbdullah b. ʿAbdulmuḥsin al-Turkī. Cairo: Dār Hajr, 2001.

Ucan, Ayse D. and Andrew Wright. "Improving the Pedagogy of Islamic Religious Education through an Application of Critical Religious Education, Variation Theory and The Learning Study Model." *British Journal of Religious Education* 41 (2019) 201–17.

Valk, John, and Mualla Selçuk. "Journeying into a Peaceful Islam: A Worldview Framework Approach." In *Religion and Violence: Muslim and Christian Theological and Pedagogical Reflections*, edited by Ednan Aslan and Marcia Hermansen, 243–63. Wiesbaden: Springer, 2017.

al-Zamakhsharī, Maḥmūd b. ʿUmar. *al-Kashshāf ʿan Ḥaqāʾiq al-Tanzīl waʿUyūn al-Aqāwīl fī Wujūh al-Taʾwīl*. Edited by ʿAdil Aḥmad ʿAbdulmawjūd et al. Riyadh: Maktaba al-ʿUbaykan, 1998.

12

Christian Theology in an Age of Violent Religious Fundamentalisms

From Intrareligious Dialogue to Interreligious Engagement

—SATHIANATHAN CLARKE

"The Tree of Knowledge again and again tempts one at the cost of neglecting the more important tree, the Tree of Life." (Raimon Panikkar)

"[Our] journeys into the dense magnolia jungles of wounded memory [and violated body] would illuminate . . . a new way of writing theology." (Charles Marsh)

Introduction

The world is constantly undergoing change. Some changes are random and unexpected. COVID-19 arrived in 2020 almost like an invasion. The virus took the uncommon pathway of an interspecies mutation as it made its visitation upon our global human family. As I complete this reflection, the United States of America (my home for twenty-five years and where I have been a naturalized citizen for the last seven), has become the worldwide epicenter of this pandemic. Ironically, my wannabe "great" nation, which purposefully spent much of its precious time, energy, and resources on trying to keep human bodies and foreign goods out of its borders, appears embarrassingly unprepared to deal effectively with the onslaught of this deadly virus. Referred to as Trump's Border Wall, this symbolic barricade has "become the most expensive wall of its kind any-where in the world."[1] Not surprisingly, the much-touted 11 billion dollar wall did not deter the wily virus.

Other changes though have been more calculating and deliberate. The virus of fear and hate that drives violence against the other did not need the help of other species. Such violence has a long history of targeting those that did not conform to the normative make-up of human selves. The combination of unresolved phobia and determined rage has kept a watchful societal eye on various expressions of "the other" that are a threat to the religious, racial, and sexual ideal of the self. This essay focuses on violation and violence against the religious other. More specifically, it endeavors to pave pathways to understand the theological/ideological justifications for the violation of the rights of religious others and confront the violence that is discharged from the workings of religiously inspired systems.

The expansion of violent religious fundamentalisms of various sorts, closely aligned with the ascendency of strong nation states, are carefully plotted and stealthily rolled out in our age. Against the twenty-first century backdrop of clashes between diverse world religions, this paper reflects on understanding this phenomenon and inquiring into the theological response to this destructive movement. Even though I will briefly point to the fact that "competing fundamentalisms" is a multi-religious phenomenon,[2] for the most part, I will confine our discussion to Christianity in the United States of America.

The Growing Menace of Violent Religious Fundamentalisms

To start with, I must offer a justification for why I utilize the term religious fundamentalism. After all, there is a host of terms to name the hydra-headed beast. Combative religion, muscular religion, jihadi religion, strong religion, and violent religious nationalism are some of the generic expressions in vogue. Others are more religion specific, such as "Militant Buddhism,"[3] "Islamic Jihadism,"[4] "Vicious Hindutva,"[5] and "Christian

1. Burnett, "$11 Billion and Counting."
2. For a detailed argument of the recent history and characteristics of "competing fundamentalisms" in three of the most populous world religions, see Clarke, *Competing Fundamentalisms.*
3. Lehr, *Militant Buddhism.*
4. Pektas and Leman, eds., *Militant Jihadism.*
5. Ananthamurthy, *Hindutva or Hind Swaraj.*

Right."[6] Cognizant of the plethora of options, why retain religious fundamentalism to name such a violent movement embedded within and energized by a constructed theology?

The origin of the expression "fundamentalism" lies in early twentieth-century American Protestant Christianity.[7] Then it was originally used to describe a particular view of biblical authority that emphasized literalism and the inerrancy of Scripture, partly in reaction to the wave of modern science, rational philosophy, and antireligious secularism escalating in the nation during that century. "The Fundamentalism Project" coordinated by Martin E. Marty and R. Scott Appleby, which produced five large volumes between 1989 and 1995, freed the term from its confinement to Christianity. It spearheaded several multi-religious studies on this development around the world and delineated several characteristics of fundamentalism. The prominent features of religious fundamentalism included the following: shrewd *selectivity* of key events and texts (both within the religious tradition, and in relation to the aspects of modern society that it opposed); embracement of a *dualistic worldview*; subscription to an *absolutist and inerrant* view of scripture; reinforcement of the *sense of an elect, chosen membership* separated by sharp boundaries from outsiders; and uncritical acceptance of *organizational authoritarianism*. Contemporary fundamentalism, it must be noted, represented by various world religions, takes to extreme the quest for certitude within its own ranks by violently demolishing the convictions of other religious and secular worldviews. Thus, religious fundamentalisms aggressively assert that there is only one valid way and seek to publicly exclude those who do not think and behave in a like manner. The nation-state, which governs how people act based on how they think, becomes an important vehicle in transforming a parochial religious worldview into becoming a national one. While the "world renouncing" form of fundamentalism retreats quietly into its own alternate domain, the "world conquering"[8] form of religion is especially prone to violent actions against those they consider to be non-believers.

Christian fundamentalism has had its ebbs and flows in the United States over the last one hundred years. Even as it has spread well-funded tentacles into world evangelization, Christian fundamentalism, along with

6. Williams, *God's Own Party*; and Stewart, *The Power Worshippers*.

7. Martin E. Marty attests that the term fundamentalism, which originated in the United States, "cannot be found in dictionaries before the 1920s." Marty, *When Faiths Collide*, 57. For a comprehensive account of the origins and development of fundamentalism in the United States, see Clarke, *Competing Fundamentalisms*, 35–62.

8. These terms are explored in Almond, et al, "Examining the Cases," in *Fundamentalisms Comprehended*, 445–82.

its sometimes-in and sometimes-out white evangelicals, has always set its sight on making Christian America great. In a contrived logic, somewhat at odds with the plain sense of the teachings of the historical Jesus, becoming great and being Christian were conflated in order to pursue Christian fundamentalism's national calling (chosen nation) to bring to fruition the wellbeing of the world (redeemer nation).[9] Christian fundamentalism has seen a national resurgence in the last decades, playing a particularly active national role in the emergence of Donald Trump's election to the presidency in 2016. So, apart from many of the characteristics that energize and consolidate Christian fundamentalism mentioned by Marty and Appleby, the desire to capture the nation-state, with an eye to conquering the world, has become a dream partially realized in actuality. The "willingness to take a stand and fight" against all forces that threaten the preeminence of religion[10] has more overtly led to Christian fundamentalism taking a driver's seat in what is heralded to be a Christian America.

There are numerous scholars analyzing the pact between Christian fundamentalism and strong nationalism over the last four years.[11] For the purposes of this essay, let me simply point to the confidence expressed by sixty-three percent of white evangelicals about the success with which Christian beliefs have transformed American national policies. "Heading into the 2020 election season, a Pew Research Center survey . . . finds that white evangelicals largely see Trump as fighting for their beliefs and advancing their interests, and they feel their side generally has been winning recently on political matters important to them."[12] Retaining the word fundamentalism for this essay acknowledges the close historical connection between Christianity and nationalism in the United States. After all, fundamentalism arose as a mostly self-acclaimed and substantially respectable label to describe a collective Christian identity in the United States of America during the first part of the twentieth century. So, allowing the term religious fundamentalism to refer to what is taking place in the United States at this time speaks to its historical continuity with the century-long Christian movement that is deeply vested in political outcomes.

9. For a comprehensive study on the way in which these "myths" (chosen nation, innocent nation, and millennial nation) are woven together in Christian America, see Hughes, *Christian America and the Kingdom of God*.

10. Marsden, *Understanding Fundamentalism and Evangelicalism*, 1.

11. See these recent works: Seidel, *The Founding Myth*; Kruse, *One Nation Under God*; and Whitehead and Perry, *Taking America Back for God*.

12. https://www.pewforum.org/2020/03/12/white-evangelicals-see-trump-as-fighting-for-their-beliefs-though-many-have-mixed-feelings-about-his-personal-conduct/.

Christianity in the United States joins other world religions in playing a weighty role in effecting the make-up of the nation-state. Thus, over the last couple of decades in this century, along with Buddhism in Sri Lanka and Myanmar; Islam in Iran and Saudi Arabia; and Hinduism in India; Christian fundamentalism in the United States is alive, well, and even thriving. In all these fundamentalist expressions, there is an indispensable symbiosis between a convicted *communal mind-set* that is unwaveringly committed to an *absolutist world-view* rooted in revealed scripture and a collective *ethical modality* that claims to be the embodiment of supposedly closed and seemingly *straightforward world-ways*. No wonder, then, that capture of the nation-state becomes crucial for strong religions: one needs a legitimate public platform to translate hallowed belief into mundane practices. Upholding and cultivating unwavering belief in a comprehensive and complete divinely revealed worldview is only part of the theological ingredient that goes into the configuration of violent religious fundamentalisms. Cognitive assent within headstrong believers must be accompanied by strong mechanisms to affect life in the real world. This is why the nation-state is sorely needed for religious fundamentalists. On the one hand, the nation-state craftily employs religious mantras and rituals to publicly endorse and reinforce common belief. On the other hand, the nation-state effectively oversees the process wherein divinely manifest macro-beliefs are enforced as everyday micro-practices of all persons, often by the use of violation and violence meted out against other religious and secular communities.

Safe Sanctuaries of Intrareligious Dialogue within the Hearts of Soft Coreligionists and the Heads of Strong Believers

A strong-headed Christian nation is using its muscle to authorize violation against the religious and secular other and enact violence against those who are a threat to its proscribed Judeo-Christian ethical practices. The sophisticated machinery of the nation-state veils much of the violation and violence perpetuated against religious and secular others perceived as a threat to the reinforcement and expansion of the Christian worldview and it accompanying world-ways in the United Sates. The venomous rhetoric of President Trump against Muslims is well documented. In a 2019 Washington Post essay titled "A short history of President Trump's anti-Muslim bigotry," Brian Klass states, "Trump is an Islamophobic bigot. As president his words matter. He is using them to spread hatred. And deranged, unwell or evil people have allegedly been inspired by those words to target the very people that

Trump targets in his speeches and his tweets."[13] Much more dangerous is that this hateful word-spew is methodically translated into policy decisions that sow violations against foreign Muslim-majority countries and U.S. citizens who are Muslims. Christian fundamentalists, in legitimizing and valorizing such violations, may not be implicated in raw acts of gruesome targeted beheadings or grotesque mass executions. However, Christian fundamentalism's complicity with the expanding reach of a regime disciplining and punishing particular collectives, with a special eye toward "Islam as Antichrist," cannot be minimized just because the spectacle of violation and violence is concealed behind a strong nation-state.

There is a strong correlation between the Christian fundamentalist worldview and the "just" violence perpetuated against Muslims within the United States and abroad. Chrissy Stroop writes in *Foreign Policy* (March 26, 2019): "the first time I remember hearing Islam equated with terrorism from the pulpit, 'A good Muslim,' our head pastor, Marcus Warner, intoned that Sunday morning, '*should* want to kill Christians and Jews.' Today, in the wake of the shootings in Christchurch, New Zealand, it should be considered every bit as offensive as the worst anti-Semitic tropes."[14] A theology that dubs religious enemies as terrorists is tied to a national strategy that targets them as possible lethal threats. Daniel Hill makes a useful "distinction between a hot-blooded and a cold-blooded violence." I believe much of Christian fundamentalism in the twenty-first century is so well versed in carrying out "cold-blooded violence" that they often like to point a finger at hot-blooded violence as being the only form of religion-based aggression that exists. While this builds up the idea that only other religions are violent and hurtful in the world, it also helps to hide violence perpetuated with stunning success by the collusion of Christian fundamentalists with the U.S. nation-state.[15]

In this overflow of religious fundamentalism onto the public square, intrareligious dialogue that matters cannot merely take place either within the soft hearts of coreligionists or inside the weighty heads of religious believers. I am using the term "intrareligious dialogue" as suggested by Raimon Panikkar. On the one hand, it includes "an inner dialogue . . . in the depth of my personal religiousness, having met another religious experience on that very intimate level." On the other hand, intrareligious dialogue includes a profound heart-through-head in-house dialogical

13. https://www.washingtonpost.com/opinions/2019/03/15/short-history-president-trumps-anti-muslim-bigotry/.

14. https://ChrissyStroopforeignpolicy.com/2019/03/26/americas-islamophobia-is-forged-in-the-pulpit/.

15. Hill, "Fundamentalists Faith States," in *The Fundamentalist Mindset*, 87.

exchange between multi-religious practitioners. Intrareligious dialogue leads to blessed mutual transformation when the meditation of intimate hearts is conjoined with the deliberation of mediating heads.[16] I submit that these comfortable intrareligious bubbles need to be burst for the sake of serving the life of world of religious and secular communities. The so-loved world of God, rather than just the company of co-religionist faithful, is in need of the gospel of peace in our violent world. The flow of blood has spilled over from religious garrisons to affect the world violently; this is not the time to dialogue about peace between believing hearts "strangely warmed" by the One Divine Parent or among enlightened heads giddy with divinely inspired thoughts.

Let me start with the sacred caverns of the heart that is celebrated as the meeting place of religious dialogue partners. Dialogue, thought of as living Word piercing through the core of human beings, is taken to be most authentic when it takes place deep "within the cave of the heart."[17] While one can find instances of such a dialogue from the history of western Christianity, Sara Grant, working out of a Hindu-Christian context, puts the argument for rediscovering the potency of interiority well. She makes a case, at a time in which liberation theology was surging in India, that inwardness must be reclaimed "when a tidal wave of activism threatens to engulf the world." Dialogue between religions can only take place, she maintains, within "the 'cave of the heart' as the Upanishads call it, where God dwells, not as in a tabernacle, within and yet separated from man [sic], but as the living Source of his being, of his very 'I.'"[18] Such a focus on the heart as the residence of the divine and as the *sanctum sanctorum* of discourse about sacred things is at the center of most religions. Fundamental Christianity in the United States, along with its close cousin (Evangelical Christianity), have always come non-dialogically after the heart of people from other religions and no-religion through its crusades both at home and abroad. Interestingly, such a focus on capturing hearts for the Gospel is often propagated by those whose hearts are steeped in seizing control over worldly things such as land, wealth, and human beings. Gathering bleeding hearts may even be a cover to hide the overreach of religion into worldly power. Confining the working of the Gospel within the cavern of human heart, even in heart-to-heart dialogue between multi-religious representatives, cannot lead to transformation of

16. Panikkar, *The Intrareligious Dialogue*, 73–74.

17. I am taking this phrase from the title of Swami Abhishiktanada's book *Hindu–Christian Meeting Point: Within the Cave of the Heart*. In the translator's foreword, Sara Grant lays out the crux of this meeting in the *guha* (Sanskrit term translated as cave or secret place) succinctly.

18. Grant, "Introduction," *Hindu-Christian Meeting Point*, vii.

the whole world for the purposes of God's kingdom. Transforming these exterior elements, which are ticking powerfully in the real world, is needed for true conversion for all God's children to live into the dreams of God's heart, which is the kingdom of God.[19]

In a similar celebration of interiority, but moving from the heart to the head, another form of intrareligious dialogue brings illuminated minds together in a common exploration of themes that could be extrapolated from sacred scriptures, treasured as God's revelation by different religious communities. The Archbishop of Canterbury initiated one significant ongoing project that brings weighty thinkers from Christianity and Islam into dialogue within secure hallways of the academy in 2002. Travelling around the world, "the Building Bridges Seminar is an annual international gathering of scholar-practitioners of Islam and Christianity for the purpose of deep dialogical study of texts— scriptural and otherwise— selected to provoke complex discussion of a carefully framed theme, such as revelation, prophethood, prayer, science and religion, or human destiny."[20] As Lucinda Mosher states, commenting on the 2017 seminar in Washington D. C., the project is a "gathering together of Christian and Muslim scholars and texts, with sufficient time for high-quality interaction with both." "Wonderful things happen," she concludes, "when people come together to speak of, and with, the Divine—because God joins them."[21] Bound together as "peoples of the book," Christian heads get together in "deep dialogue" with Muslim heads in the hope of discovering common themes in their respective sacred books. Usually confined to religious sanctuaries or halls of academies, "talking heads" exchanged profound insights on scripture and theology that illuminated Christian and Muslim minds.

Releasing Intrareligious Dialogue from the Seclusion of Sanctuaries to Undertake Interreligious Engagement on the Stage of the Nation

Interior sanctuaries of heart and head still serve as the dominant domains for religious dialogue. These separated-from-the-world spaces of dialogue

19. I am using an idea from D. R. Nagaraj, who highlights the Dalit leader B. R. Ambedkar's criticism of M. K. Gandhi's appeal to the internal conversion of Caste Hindus in India. Ambedkar distrusted conversion of Caste Hindus, especially their hearts. He advocated instead for political and legal solutions to aid the liberation of his people during the freedom struggle (Nagaraj, *The Flaming Feet and Other Essays*).

20. Mosher and Marshal, "Introduction," in *Power Divine and Human*, 1.

21. Mosher, "Conversations on Power," in *Power Divine and Human*, 169.

focus on subtle theological matters concerning the imagined and actual God, the false and true self, the virtual and real world, and the absent and present kingdom of God. Such modes of intrareligious dialogue are conceived of as an exchange of meditative silence or deliberative words regarding the sacred conducted by select representatives from each religious community. I am not disputing the fact that such dialogue may indeed enlighten heads through the illumining Word and set hearts aflame through the enkindling Spirit. My concern is that such encounters of dialogue pay scarce attention to the fact that embodied religious agents are also engaged in violent exchanges in social and material spaces. Religious communication between religions within the interiority of human beings, be it in hearts or heads, may enable deep exchange of spiritual riches stored in the safety vaults of human experience. However, in the context of religious fundamentalisms' brutal consequences in the real world, what is needed is interreligious exchange that can also protect bodies from being rent asunder by violence.

The need of the hour is to accept the responsibility of dialogue that keeps abreast with the movements of religious fundamentalism whereby religiosity flows from head and heart onto the world to shape it violently in the name of God. Such a consciousness to include the world outside, even while not neglecting the inner life of the religious adherents, was already affirmed in the late 1970s and early 1980s. The World Council of Churches in 1977 recognized that even though "[i]t is easy to discuss religions and even ideologies as though they existed in some realm of calm quite separate from the sharp divisions, conflicts and sufferings of humankind," dialogue must be directed to the domain "which includes major Christian involvement in political and economic stresses and social problems."[22] The 1984 document of the Pontifical Council for Interreligious Dialogue further opened up the public square when talking about the interior and exterior spheres: "the dialogue of theological exchange" and "the dialogue of religious experience" represent one side of the coin, while "the dialogue of life" and "the dialogue of action" represents the other.[23] Mediating between inside the heart and head must thus face the action-packed world of life outside. In a 2019 essay, Wesley Ariarajah ends his historical survey of the global interfaith dialogue movement by pointing the way forward. On the one hand, "It is now clear,"

22. Guidelines on Dialogue with People of Living Faiths and Ideologies, WCC 1979 https://www.oikoumene.org/en/resources/documents/wcc-programmes/interreligious-dialogue-and-cooperation/interreligious-trust-and-respect/guidelines-on-dialogue-with-people-of-living-faiths-and-ideologies.

23. The 1984 the document of the Pontifical Council for Interreligious Dialogue http://www.vatican.va/roman_curia/pontifical_councils/interelg/documents/rc_pc_interelg_doc_19051991_dialogue-and-proclamatio_en.html.

he says, "that interfaith dialogue has to deal with questions of "religion and state," "religious freedom," "religious extremism," and "the rights of minority religious communities" in nations that have a dominant religion and culture." On other hand, such questions lead to determining "who the partners of dialogue should be, and about the nature, purpose, and goals of interfaith dialogue."[24] The agenda of dialogue is set from outside of the gathered hearts and head of the religious faithful. "Partners" for dialogue might involve different "goals," which deal with freedom, violent "extremism," and minority "rights," all of which primarily have to do with the public square. It is time, I submit, to adopt a change in nomenclature from intrafaith or interfaith dialogue to interfaith engagement.

In embracing the term interfaith engagement, I am following Douglass Pratt. While pushing for dialogue between religions to be profoundly "self-reflective" in its impact "upon theological thinking," he also imagines the promise of the term "interfaith engagement," especially in its outward reach to become entangled with matter in the real world. "The contemporary challenge of interfaith engagement," says Pratt, "is to address pressing critical concerns of peace, justice, human rights, the environment, and inter-communal co-existence—to name but a few. To do this successfully, dialogue needs to be more than a mere talkfest: it needs to engage deeply."[25] So, the present obligation for Christians in our contemporary global context of violence emanating from competing religious violence is to journey from soft spaces of dialogue to hot spots of engagement. Such a deliberate relocation of interreligious engagement from soft spaces with meek conversation partners to hots spots with strange religious or political actors with real power to wound sentiments and harm bodies brings much risk and requires some imagination. If one seeks to contain the wild beast, one has to draw closer to the fiery creature. It is imperative that contemporary interreligious exchange deal with the violation and violence, which have a basis in absolutist scripture, stringent ethical practices, and divine mandates to capture nation states.

24. Ariarajah, "Interfaith Dialogue," 627.

25. Pratt, *Christianity and Other Faiths*, 15. Also, see Hedges, "Interreligious Engagement and Identity Theory." Also see Torres, "The Presence and Absence of Faith."

Theology for Interreligious Engagement against the Backdrop of Violation-spawning and Violence-prone Christian Fundamentalism in The United States

Thus far, I have put forward a case for relocating the art of dialogue to embrace the practice of interreligious engagement in our historical context where muscular religion spawns violation and legitimizes violence by taking hold of the nation state. But what about the theological task of such interreligious engagement as it reaches out to the outermost circle in the hope of sowing seeds of life rather than death? To answer this question within my own context, let me return to the issue of the expanding influence of Christian fundamentalism in the United State in our time.

Christian fundamentalists in the United States have managed to have their cake and eat it too! They are passionate about leveraging constitutional rights for the objective of protecting churches so that they might flourish without any state interference,[26] even while they work zealously to influence the Christian make-up of political representation in the great American nation. Strong Christian political leadership not only professes to make it easy for adherents to live out the ethical implications of the divinely revealed worldview in all its fullness, it also undertakes measures to alter the United States so that the Christian lifestyle flourishes as the norm. This normative Christian way of living is promoted to counter the dangerous lifestyles of religious others (the Muslims, in particular) and the ungodly life choices of non-religious secularists (the Atheists, in particular). In contemporary United States, overwhelmed by a giddying diversity of lifestyles and a confusing surplus of ethical choices, Christian fundamentalism carves out a

---

26. Interestingly as Christian fundamentalism has gained in strength in the United States, there is a move dismissing the constitutional basis for the separation of Church and State. In an in-depth essay titled "Constitutional Myth #4: The Constitution Doesn't Separate Church and State" aimed at keeping the Christian Right from fusing the states and the church, Garrett Epps' concludes thus:

> The words "separation of church and state" are not in the text; the idea of separation is. Article VI provides that all state and federal officials "shall be bound by oath or affirmation, to support this Constitution; but no religious test shall ever be required as a qualification to any office or public trust under the United States." The First Amendment's Establishment Clause . . . provides that "Congress shall make no law respecting an establishment of religion"— meaning that not only no church but no "religion" could be made the official faith of the United States. Finally, the Free Exercise Clause provides that Congress shall not make laws "prohibiting the free exercise" of religion.

https://www.theatlantic.com/national/archive/2011/06/constitutional -myth-4-the-constitution-doesnt-separate-church-and-state/240481.

cocksure pathway to live the moral life and promises justice for those elect ones suffering a variety of discriminations for living out God-ordained practices in a God-forsaking world. The nation is a platform on which President Trump promises to make Christianity and America great again. In this political-yet-religious project, Trump offers to treat, even if in the mode of a "bully," Christian fundamentalists, along with a bandwagon crowded with evangelicals, "as an interest group in need of protection and preferences."[27] These Christian interest groups make an offer in return (*quid pro quo!*): the, overwhelmingly white, strident Christians and strong nationalists will put their blessed weight behind this "least traditionally religious President in living memory."[28] Michael Gerson, himself an evangelical, points to this alliance between Christian extremism and political opportunism to access and exert power in present-day United States:

> A prominent company of evangelical leaders—including Dobson, Falwell, Graham, Jeffress, Metaxas, Perkins, and Ralph Reed—has embraced this self-conception. Their justification is often bluntly utilitarian: All of Trump's flaws are worth his conservative judicial appointments and more-favorable treatment of Christians by the government. But they have gone much further than grudging, prudential calculation. They have basked in access to power and provided character references in the midst of scandal.[29]

It is against this backdrop in which Christian fundamentalism makes use of the nation-state to spawn violation and legitimize violence against religious and non-religious others that I wish to reconceive the theological task of interreligious engagement. The two theological trajectories that I propose for interreligious engagement are grounded on Christian presuppositions that must be made explicit. First, as I have already made abundantly clear in the previous section, Christian theology must be public. In a context where strong religion engenders violation and violence in the real world, theology summons Christianity to embrace the wellbeing of all communities. Theology must be critical reflection on Divine Word(s) saturating all flesh. Second, without discounting orthodoxy (righteous/correct opinion) Christian theology needs to emphasize orthopraxis (righteous/correct action). The former weaves a theological web of meaning while the latter sieves a flow of ethical practices. Both live and grow out of each other. "Sure there is a body of belief" in religion, admits Kwame Anthony Appiah, "But there's also what you

27. Gerson, "The Last temptation."
28. Gerson, "The Last Temptation."
29. Gerson, "The Last Temptation."

do—call that practice."[30] Finally, while Christian theology is therapeutic to the Church and the world, it has a special vocation to serve the meek, weak, and the crushed one. Appiah does point to a third dimension of religion, which follows from belief and practice: "And then there's who you do it with—call that community or fellowship."[31] While accepting "community" as a third mark of religion, I affirm, along with a company of liberation theologians, that "who you fellowship with" becomes a crucial test of the gospel of Jesus Christ. The rugged cross (the crushed ones by the rulers of Great nation) or the gold crown (the exalted ones carving out a Christian nation) characterizes two different configurations of fellowship.

The first theological components that needs to be inserted into inter-religious engagement is contrary to the central security that faith traditions offer to fundamentalists in general: the unwavering confidence in the supremacy of their own religion and the immense desire to promote its truth in the world. Situating this discussion within the context of the United States, a nation under the sway of violation-spawning and violence-prone Christian fundamentalism, I suggest that *public confession rather than absolute assertion be incorporated in all forms of witness to the Gospel in interreligious engagement* both with folks from other religions and those of no-religion. Jennifer McBride, drawing from the work of Dietrich Bonhoeffer, suggests such a reconfiguration in being Christian "for the world."[32] She confronts two tendencies identified with Christian fundamentalism. On the one hand, interreligious relations with other religious and secular communities has stemmed from the confidence of possessing "right knowledge" through revelation contained in the sacred Bible. This theological stance leads to thinking that Christian public witness grows out of the special status of being in possession of right saving knowledge given through the divinely gifted Bible. On the other hand, interreligious relations with other religious and secular communities has arisen from the confidence of being divinely (s)elected to be the ideal moral community for the others to imitate. This theological assertion projects the Christian community as the chosen moral exemplar, something like a community of light showing forth the divinely acceptable way of life in the midst of other communities swayed by darkness. Both of these forms of witness are fueled by a divine mandate to influence the nation state to hold fast to orthodoxy and live out orthopraxis for the sake of the reign of God over all human beings.[33]

30. Appiah, *The Lies that Bind*, 36.
31. Appiah, *The Lies that Bind*, 36.
32. McBride, *The Church for the World*.
33. McBride, *The Church for the World*, 23–54.

Instead of Christian witness as triumphalist assertions of "right knowledge" or "right morality," in relation to other religious and secular communities, I believe, in concurrence with McBride, that it is much more appropriate to conceive of interreligious witness along the lines of public confession signifying repentance.[34] To start with, a preparatory step for interreligious engagement would involve public confession: an honest acknowledgement of Christianity's complicity in violating the God-given dignity inherent in the belief and practices of religious and non-religious others. Not only does this turn Christian-initiated interreligious engagement away from the grandstanding characteristics of fundamentalist religion but it also invites all communities to the possibility of mutual transformation through public confession and overt redirection. Such a public confession also de-escalates the consolidation of violent religious power by the majority in the United States (Christianity) and injects vulnerability into the majority religious community to the truth witnessed to by religious minorities (Muslims, Sikhs, Hindus, Buddhist etc.). The rationale however for such a model of interfaith engagement is not just pragmatic. Christian witness as public confession is at its core imitative of the Jesus way. "We tend to think that as the sinless one, Jesus distinguished himself from sinners," says Jennifer McBride. Instead of "setting himself up as a model of ethical perfection," she continues, "Jesus was in solidarity with sinners"[35] and suffering ones. After all, Jesus' mode of engagement reveals that while he judged the world, he simultaneously identified fully with sinners and victims and took on their condemnation. Jesus' identification with such sinful and suffering ones was so steeped in love that he willingly takes on such judgement of the world onto himself. The cross, which is the crux of the gospel, symbolizes such a public confession in full view of the world.[36]

34. I am drawing from McBride's idea of "public confession" toward repentance, which is what she suggests is being a witnessing Church in the world.

35. McBride, "The Witness of Sinners."

36. I am drawing from McBride's excellent work. Summarizing her argument in *The Church for the World*, she states in the following in an interview: "First, as God incarnate, he assumed sinful flesh, as Paul says in Romans 8:3. He took on human nature's damaged state and through his body became intimately acquainted with the complexity and messiness of fallen existence. Second, he begins his public ministry by being baptized with sinners in response to John the Baptist's call to repent and in this way, "numbers himself with the transgressors" (to use Isaiah's language about the suffering servant). Third, and finally, refusing to be called good (Mark 10:18), he instead accepts responsibility for sin as a convicted criminal on the cross. Throughout his ministry Jesus denies any claim about his own moral righteousness and instead actively accepts responsibility for the world's sin and suffering on the cross out of love for fellow human beings." McBride, "The Witness of Sinners."

For all Christians, including fundamentalists in the contemporary United States, this would mean thinking of public witness as confession slouched toward repentance within the ethos of interreligious engagement. It embraces the open, vulnerable, and sacrificial stance of Christianity's public witness as a continued practice in relationship with other religious and secular communities. The Christian community in imitation of Jesus offers to become the ongoing presence of Christ in the world. The marks of the Christian community that are on display in interreligious engagement are the marks of Jesus lifted high on the cross. These marks are manifest in at least three acts:

- the act of public confession that Christians are entwined with the sinfulness of the world;

- the act of repentance that forges solidarity with suffering and sinful ones; and

- the act of joining the process of living out the work of Christ by drawing close to the sinned-against ones for transforming the life of the world.

Rather than triumphant shouts that Christians possess the truth or moralistic claims that they are the yardstick for ethical living, the community accepts its solidarity with sinners and those who suffer in the world even as it repents for not furthering the life of others in the world. If this is the core theme guiding interfaith engagement for Christians, it offers a counter model to the pronouncement and posture of Christian fundamentalism in the United States. Such a confessional mode of interreligious engagement model lifts up another way of being in the world, which might lead to self-(Christian) and mutual-transformation (other religions and secular traditions) toward a communal disposition of self-giving and other-serving.

A second theological trajectory follows the first motif for Christian interreligious engagement in the world of competing violent fundamentalisms: public confession as a community posture slouched toward repentance implies a realignment of fellowship. Christian interreligious engagement in a context where religion is complicit in violation and violence in the world involves moving away from aligning with the exalted ones of a strong nation and moving toward solidarity with those crushed by the great America. There is a cost to repentance. In keeping with its root meaning in Greek, *metanoia* ("change of heart") conjoins a turning away from all the strong allies of the heart-of-stone and a turning toward the wounded allies of heart-of-flesh. Such a reconfiguring of fellowship in the context of Christian fundamentalism's reach over the nation-state, however, is more than just a repentant posture. A ready stance also entails a new vocation. In this situation, it means turning away from promoting the "common good" of great United States and turning toward the drudgery of "uncommon work" among those crushed by the will to such greatness. By "uncommon work," I mean toil that is more demanding and thus less appealing for most "common good" ventures in our world of religion-instigated violence. Christian-initiated interreligious engagement focuses on and draws close to those crushed by violence, especially connected with destructive patterns of Christian fundamentalists, and its White Evangelical collaborators, in so-called Christian America. There is much praiseworthy interreligious conversation on sifting the common Word (Scriptures) to find common ground to journey together to the common good. I believe, however, that the men, women, and children who have been crushed by the violence of fundamentalism cry out for religions to band together for the uncommon work of drawing close to the sites of violence in order to counter such bloody religion with the balm of peace. Let me elaborate on this point.

There is already much global thinking around the interreligious responsibility to find resources for building peace in the "Common Word" represented by the Qur'an and the Bible. Take, for example, the influential October 13, 2007 fifteen-page letter entitled "A Common Word Between Us and You" (ACW). Addressed to Christian communities across the world, this letter was signed by 138 Muslim scholars and leaders representing every branch of Islam. The interreligious communiqué set in motion an impressive process of dialogue both in academic and religious communities to find "common ground" within "the common Word" for journeying toward peace in our age of global conflict. This endeavor to pave pathways of harmony and peace among religions was acutely needed in the context of spreading violence, especially between Christianity and Islam. ACW makes this point unambiguously in the last paragraph that ends the letter, which states: "So let our differences not cause hatred and strife between us. Let us vie with each other only in righteousness and good works."[37]

ACW had immediate impact on Christian constituencies in The United States of America. The Yale-initiated Christian response entitled "'A Common Word': Christian Response" (2007) was swift and affirming. It affirmed that such "common ground" of love of God and neighbor is not "something marginal . . . [or] merely important to each . . . [but] something absolutely central to both" Islamic and Christian Scriptures.[38] Let me quote the response more fully:

37. http://www.acommonword.com/the-acw-document/.
38. http://faith.yale.edu/common-word/common-word-christian-response.

That so much common ground exists—common ground in some of the fundamentals of faith—gives hope that undeniable differences and even the very real external pressures that bear down upon us cannot overshadow the common ground upon which we stand together. That this common ground consists in love of God and of neighbor gives hope that deep cooperation between us can be a hallmark of the relations between our two communities.[39]

Continuing the positive progression of such interreligious dialogue, the then Archbishop of Canterbury Rowan Williams did a remarkable job of linking the common ground of love of God and neighbor, which is anchored in the common Word, with the more expansive and inclusive goal of renouncing violence, which undercuts collective wellbeing, and embracing the common good of all humanity. The mission of religious communities, as Williams' sees it, is twofold. First, interfaith dialogue and cooperation is a vehicle "to break the current cycles of violence, to show the world that faith and faith alone can truly ground a commitment to peace."[40] Second, interfaith dialogue and cooperation also invites religious communities "to find ways of being far more effective in influencing our societies to follow the way of God in promoting that which leads to human flourishing."[41] Interreligious engagement thus enables communities "to follow the way of God" that leads to the common good of "human flourishing." The progression from common Word to common ground and then onto common good is rootedness in God's word, God's love for the world, and God's desire for the wellbeing of all creation.

While fully convinced that such a journey from discovering interreligious common ground of love in common Word must accompany communities toward common good, I also feel the need to ponder another direction for interfaith engagement through a process of action and reflection. This entails interreligious convergence around uncommon work among those crushed by violence, especially connected with destructive patterns of violent fundamentalisms. The multi-religious coming together in the twenty-first century calls for uncommon work for protecting and promoting common worth, starting from the spilled blood of the victims of violence that often have some connection to conflicts legitimized, if not fueled, by religions. We have become painfully aware of the vulnerability of collectives of women, children and, religious or ethnic minorities suffering violation and violence

39. http://faith.yale.edu/common-word/common-word-christian-response.
40. Williams, *A Common Word for the Common Good*, 13.
41. Williams, *A Common Word for the Common Good*, 13.

because of the reach of Christian fundamentalism into the workings of the nation-state in the U.S. Christianity. Rather than the wisdom of elite men and some women setting the agenda, strategies, and goals of common good, this bottom-up dynamic of interreligious engagement will tap into the hope and tactics of those most targeted by religious fundamentalism. Interreligious engagement that is Christian forms a community by fellowship with the suffering ones to resist violation of human worth/dignity and violence against other forms of belief and ways of living in our diverse nation. Such a reconceptualization of common ground will thus be founded upon the "blood that cries out from the earth"[42] even as it pounds at the doors of common Word contained in Scriptures to protect those crushed by violence and harness human flourishing for all.

More important though is the theological warrant for the promise of such a common ground for the uncommon work of protecting and promoting common worth. Let me draw on Christian idiom. The "Word-made-flesh" that is continuously revealed in the crucified ones of this world provides a theological basis for the uncommon work of protecting worth among the crushed ones and promoting life among all God's human family. Human struggle against the forces of violence is imitative of "the way of God" revealed in Jesus Christ. Christ's solidarity with the victims of violence is represented by the cross and echoed in Jesus cry of forsakenness from this symbol of violence: "My God, my God, Why have you forsaken me" (Mark 15:34). This chilling cry outside the gates of the city of Shalom/peace (Jerusalem) by the violated body of the crucified One becomes the basis for public interreligious theology that echoes eternally and universally. It is this eternal cry of the One stripped of worth that draws Christians alongside those who suffer violation and violence at the hands of the exalted ones of the great nation. This, for Christians, is what makes God the God of love, not only for all of humanity but especially for those in danger of losing their human worth and unable to live life gifted to them by the Creator. Moltmann urges us to refocus the agenda of our interfaith efforts: "We do not so much need interfaith dialogue, interesting though they are," he says. Instead, what we need from interreligious collaboration "is a common struggle for life . . . life that is human and natural in short, life that is worth living in the fruitful living space of the earth."[43]

We might even take Moltmann's suggestion as a call to invert the sequence of interreligious relations. Our contemporary context in the United

---

42. I take this from the title from a book: James Jones, *Blood that Cries Out from the Earth: The Psychology of Religious Terrorism.*

43. Moltmann, *Sun of Righteousness Arise!*, 77.

States first invites interreligious engagement to commit to uncommon work by drawing close to communities of suffering ones in their struggle to overcome violation and violence against them. Dialogue then becomes a second step, which correlates what has been learned from the wisdom of crushed ones with what we have inherited as revealed wisdom from hearts set aflame by the Divine One or from heads enlightened by the sacred Word. Wisdom from the community of the suffering ones, living between the categories of "the poor in spirit" (Mt 5: 3) and "the reviled and persecuted" (Mt 5:11), is whispered, chanted, drummed, and wailed. Victims of the great nation-state and the elite national church usually murmur such soul-body knowledge. The bonds of affliction knit these stories together. Those who tell these tales of pain and joy, despair and hope, fracture and faith bear the marks of systemic violence and systematic violation. Yet they are the blessed in the community of Jesus. In the words of Bonhoeffer, "The fellowship of the beatitudes is the fellowship of the Crucified."[44] God as revealed in flesh, for Christians, draws close to those who are crushed by the violence of religious and political systems in order to promote the struggle for life starting from among those whom death threatens to deny God's gift of life. Perhaps, this common ground of blood that screams from below is much more vested in *eu-topia*—the place of the good—rather than common good without a *topia* (place) on earth.[45] In a context of violence emanating from religions, I think of the *uncommon work* for religious communities as being in step with those crushed by violence. This is the interreligious space of encounter and it is from here that we receive the mandate and objectives of uncommon work. Not only is this a component of the Christian vocation manifest by the life of God in Jesus Christ, but it is also a way for all religious communities to be engaged as collaborators in God's mission of protecting the human worth of every member of God's one human family and promoting the wellbeing of the whole of creation.

Conclusion

In concluding this essay, let me offer a synopsis of my argument. I started by setting up the backdrop for understanding violent fundamentalism as a global movement rooted in religious sources but routinized through strong nation-states. While pointing to such a worldwide trend, I mainly kept an

44. Bonhoeffer, *The Cost of Discipleship*, 114.

45. For a much more in-depth discussion on the differences between *eu-topia* ('the place of the good') and *ou-topia* ('a non-existent place'), see Sobrino, *No Salvation Outside the Poor*, 81.

eagle's eye on the spawning of violation and legitimizing of violence from Christian fundamentalism in the contemporary United States. Building on the public aspiration and operations of religious fundamentalism, I then went on to make a case for the urgent need to move away from the safety of intrareligious dialogue. Rather Christians need to embrace the risky business of interreligious engagement. It is ripe time for intrareligious relations to escape their confinement within the enclave of kindred hearts or agreeable heads and instead answer the call to be engaged with the effects of religious violence on the world stage.

The last constructive part of the essay explores two theological avenues for Christian theology in the midst of the absolutist, aggressive, and expansionist vision and mission of religious fundamentalism. Notably, there is a pressing need to undercut fundamentalism's unwavering confidence in the supremacy of its own religion and immense desire to promote its own version of *The* truth to encompass the entire world. Situating this discussion within the context of the United States, where Christian fundamentalism is an influential force in social and political life, I argued why *public confession rather than absolutist assertion* characterize all forms of witness to the Gospel in interreligious engagement.[46] But religion is not only about belief; it is as much defined by behaving in the world. A second theological component inviting collective action, thus, needed to be injected into interfaith engagement. In the present context of violent fundamentalisms, I proposed a move from deep discourse on matters of *common good* to reimagine strategies of banding together for *uncommon work*. By this, I mean work that is more demanding and thus less appealing for most "common good" ventures in our world of religion-instigated violence. Such uncommon work for protecting the common worth/dignity of every person is symbolized by the crucified, who represents the suffering ones at the hands of the exalted ones propping up a great nation. Uncommon work for common worth of all human beings costs something for the celebrators of God's gracious benevolence. Christian-initiated interreligious cooperative engagement that is rooted in the cross of Christ will need to focus on and draw close to those crushed by violence on the world stage, especially as they challenge the destructive patterns of violent fundamentalisms.

46. I write this reflection in the North American context in 2020. I am well aware that in locations where Christianity is a minority religion, like in my own country of origin (India), there will be quite a different emphasis: a call for *public advancement of religious difference*. In contexts where Christianity is a marginal religion (for example, Christianity is less than three percent of the population of India), interreligious engagement needs to secure the unique presence and strengthen the distinctive testimony of such a community that is pushed to the margins.

Bibliography

Abhishiktananda, Swami. *Hindu-Christian Meeting Point: Within the Cave of the Heart.* Delhi: ISPCK, 1983.

Almond, Gabriel A., Emmanuel Sivan, and R. Scott Appleby. *Fundamentalisms Comprehended.* Chicago, University of Chicago Press, 1995.

Ananthamurthy, u. r. *Hindutva or Hind Swaraj.* Harper Perennial: Noida: 2018.

Appiah, Kwame Anthony. *The Lies that Bind: Rethinking Identity.* New York: Liveright, 2018.

Ariarajah, S. Wesley. "Interfaith Dialogue: Milestones of the Past and Prospects for the Future." *Ecumenical Review* 71 (2019) 614–627.

Bonhoeffer, Dietrich. *The Cost of Discipleship.* New York: Simon & Schuster, 1995.

Burnett, John. "$11 Billion and Counting: Trump's Border Wall Would Be the World's Most Costly." *NPR.* https://www.npr.org/2020/01/19/797319968/-11-billion-and-counting-trumps-border-wall-would-be-the-world-s-most-costly.

Clarke, Sathianathan. *Competing Fundamentalisms: Violent Extremism in Christianity, Islam, and Hinduism.* Louisville, KY: WJK, 2017.

Epps, Garrett. "Constitutional Myth #4: The Constitution Doesn't Separate Church and State." *The Atlantic.* https://www.theatlantic.com/national/archive/2011/06/constitutional-myth-4-the-constitution-doesnt-separate-church-and-state/240481/.

Gerson, Michael. "The Last Temptation: How Evangelicals, Once Culturally Confident, Became an Anxious Minority Seeking Political Protection from the Least Traditionally Religious President in Living Memory." *The Atlantic.* https://www.theatlantic.com/magazine/archive/2018/04/the-last-temptation/554066/.

Hedges, Paul, "Interreligious Engagement and Identity Theory: Assessing the Theology of Religions Typology as a Model for Dialogue and Encounter." *Journal for the Academic Study of Religion* 27, Issue 2 (2014) 198–221.

Hill, Daniel. "Fundamentalist Faith States: Regulation Theory as a Framework for the Psychology of Religious Fundamentalism." In *The Fundamentalist Mindset,* edited by Charles B. Strozier, David M. Terman & James W. Jones, 80–88. New York: Oxford University Press, 2010.

Hughes, Richard T. *Christian America and the Kingdom of God.* Chicago: University of Illinois Press, 2009.

Jones, James. *Blood that Cries Out from the Earth: The Psychology of Religious Terrorism.* New York: Oxford University Press, 2008.

Kruse, Kevin. *One Nation Under God: How Corporate America Reinvented Christian America.* New York: Basic Books, 2015.

Lehr, Peter. *Militant Buddhism: The Rise of Religious Violence in Sri Lanka, Myanmar and Thailand.* Cham: Springer, 2019.

Marsden, George M. *Understanding Fundamentalism and Evangelicalism.* Grand Rapids: Eerdmans, 1991.

Marty, Martin E. *When Faiths Collide.* Malden, MA: Blackwell, 2005.

McBride, Jennifer M. *The Church for the World: A Theology of Public Witness.* New York: Oxford University Press, 2012

———. "The Witness of Sinners: Interview by David Heim." *Christian Century,* 2013. https://www.christiancentury.org/article/2013-11/witness-sinners.

Moltmann, Jürgen. *Sun of Righteousness Arise! God's Future for Humanity and the Earth.* Minneapolis: Fortress, 2010.

Mosher, Lucinda, and David Marshal, eds. *Power Divine and Human: Christian and Muslim Perspectives.* Washington, DC: Georgetown University Press, 2019.

Nagaraj, D. R. *The Flaming Feet and Other Essays: The Dalit Movement in India.* New Delhi: Seagull, 2011.

Panikkar, Raimon. *The Intrareligious Dialogue.* Rev. ed. Mahwah, NJ: Paulist 1999.

Pratt, Douglas. "Christianity and Other Faiths: Exploring Interfaith Engagement." *Studies in Interreligious Dialogue* 26 (2016) 5–19.

Seidel, Andrew L. *The Founding Myth: Why Christian Nationalism Is Un-American.* New York: Sterling, 2019.

Sobrino, Jon. *No Salvation Outside the Poor: Prophetic-Utopian Essays.* Maryknoll, NY: Orbis, 2008.

Stewart, Katherine. *The Power Worshippers: Inside the Dangerous Rise of Religious Nationalism.* New York: Bloomsbury, 2020.

Torres, José Francisco Morales. "The Presence and Absence of Faith: Being Faithful to Christian Particularity and Committed to Interreligious Engagement." *Insights* 134 (2019) 16–22.

Whitehead, Andrew L. and Samuel L. Perry. *Taking America Back for God: Christian Nationalism in the United States.* New York: Oxford University Press, 2020.

Williams, Daniel K. *God's Own Party: The Making of The Christian Right.* New York: Oxford University Press, 2012.

Williams, Rowan. *A Common Word for the Common Good* (14 July 2008). https://s3.amazonaws.com/berkley-center/080714WilliamsCommonWordCommonGood.pdf.